NORTH KOREA AND THE BOMB

NORTH KOREA AND
THE BOMB

A Case Study in Nonproliferation

Michael J. Mazarr

St. Martin's Press

ISBN 0-312-12443-0

Library of Congress Cataloging-in-Publication Data

Mazarr, Michael J., 1965-
    North Korea and the bomb : A case study in nonproliferation /
Michael J. Mazarr.
        p. cm.
    Includes index.
    ISBN 0-312-12443-0
    1. Nuclear weapons—Korea (North)   2. Korea (North)—Politics and
government.   3. United States—Military policy.   4. Nuclear
nonproliferation. I. Title.
UA853.K6M39 1995
327.1'74—dc20   94-34868
                                                                  CIP

Interior design by Digital Type & Design

First Edition: May 1995
10 9 8 7 6 5 4 3 2 1

FOR WILLIAM J. TAYLOR, JR.

A fine soldier and scholar, an unparalleled mentor, a superb friend, and a tireless and selfless laborer for a peaceful and unified Korea.

CONTENTS

PREFACE

Nonproliferation has now become a central focus of U.S. foreign and defense policy. As of this writing, both the U.S. Department of Defense's Bottom Up Review of military forces and the Joint Chiefs of Staff's National Military Strategy have identified the spread of weapons of mass destruction as the chief threat to the United States and its interests abroad. Substantively and bureaucratically, nonproliferation is getting more attention than ever.

Yet even now, few analysts have conducted in-depth case studies of nonproliferation efforts. Most foreign policy officials and experts in the United States were used to viewing nonproliferation as a subset of larger U.S. Cold War policies, rather than as self-contained diplomatic endeavors. Few books or articles have examined the idea of nonproliferation itself as it is applied in a particular case.

This work seeks to begin filling that gap in the literature. It offers a detailed, move-by-move account of the international effort, led by the United States, to dissuade North Korea from acquiring nuclear weapons. Chapters 9 and 10 draw some early lessons from the experience with North Korea and attempt to lay out a coherent, comprehensive strategy for nonproliferation, something that, despite all the new attention, the U.S. government has yet to enunciate.

I completed most of the research for this study while a Senior Fellow in International Security Studies at the Center for Strategic and International Studies in Washington, D.C. My research there was supported in part by a generous grant from the Korea Foundation.

In the most fundamental and important ways, however, my research and thinking about Korea was informed and supported by Dr. William Taylor, Jr., currently senior vice president at CSIS and my supervisor during my tenure there. Bill has established a standard for academic honesty and support for younger scholars unmatched anywhere in Washington. His counsel, assistance, generous encouragement of my work, and friendship were as indispensable to this effort as they were to my broader career. This book is therefore dedicated to him.

After I left CSIS, my work in finishing this book was conducted during spare hours outside my regular job as legislative assistant and chief writer in the office of former Congressman Dave McCurdy. Dave is an immensely warm, intelligent, and supportive boss, but he may not agree with all of my conclusions, and should in no way be associated with them. This book represents solely my own views.

Finally, I must acknowledge those kind individuals who lent me hours of their time and years of their experience in interviews. To preserve their anonymity, the footnotes will not identify them by name.

In Japan, I benefited from discussions with Foreign Ministry and Japan Defense Agency officials, Diet members and staff, and academics during a Foreign Ministry–sponsored trip in October of 1991; with officials of the Asian Affairs and American Affairs bureaus and the Nuclear Energy Division of the Foreign Ministry during an October 1992 visit; and with Foreign Ministry and JDA officials at the East-West Center/Pacific Forum CSIS Asia-Pacific Senior Seminar in December 1993.

Many current and former U.S. officials shared generously of their time. These included Eugene Price, Robert Kanede, and Mark Fitzpatrick of the U.S. Embassy in Tokyo in October 1992; numerous officials in the U.S. Embassy in Seoul from 1989 through 1993, most recently and especially Mark Minton and William McKinney in October of 1993; Admiral William Pendley of the U.S. Defense Department; State Department Korea experts including Robert Carlin, John Merrill, and C. Kenneth Quinones; former U.S. ambassador to Korea, and tireless supporter of Korea scholarship, the Honorable Donald Gregg; and the following officials of the Bush and Reagan administrations: Paul Chamberlin, William Clark, Arnold Kanter, James Kelley, James Lilley, Robert Manning, Douglas Paal, and Brent Scowcroft.

To verify facts on developments in the Clinton administration, I had the benefit of additional conversations with Steve Fetter, then of the Department of Defense, Joel Wit, Linda Gallini, Gary Samore, and Ambassador Robert Gallucci at the Department of State; and former Secretary of Defense Les Aspin. Stephen Linton of Columbia University shared generously of his vast knowledge of Korean culture and the perspectives of the government in Pyongyang.

I also relied on the counsel of many South Korean Defense and Foreign Ministry officials and academics whom I met in the course of five CSIS conferences in Seoul from 1989 through 1993. Of special assistance were Major General (Retired) Joon Boo Ahn, former Blue House policy adviser Dr. Hak Joon Kim, Ho Jin Lee and other members of the American Affairs Bureau of the Foreign Ministry, the scholars of the Foreign Ministry's Institute on Foreign Affairs and National Security (IFANS), and my good friends at the

Korea Institute for Defense Analyses: Young Koo Cha, Gyoo Yeol Lee, Taeho Kim, and Taewoo Kim.

I had the benefit of three sets of conversations with North Korean academics and diplomats—at CSIS in 1989, at a United Nations conference in Beijing in 1992, and at a Cargegie Council seminar in New York in 1993. Finally, in Beijing, Washington, and elsewhere, I obtained the perspective of a handful of Chinese and Russian scholars and officials; Mr. Vladimir Rakhmanin of the Russian Embassy was especially helpful.

I owe a special debt of gratitude to those individuals who read and commented on various portions of the book. Peter Zimmerman of CSIS shared some of his knowledge on nuclear physics, or at least what of it my distinctly non-scientific mind was able to grasp. Bob Carlin, Paul Chamberlin, Don Gregg, John Merrill, James Pierce of the U.S. Embassy in Seoul, and Ken Quinones commented on a number of the historical and analytical chapters. Mitchell Reiss and Taeho Kim gave exhaustive comments on substantial portions of the book, and their careful eyes and demanding scholarship helped produce a far better work. I extend my warmest thanks to each of them, and note that any errors of fact or judgment that remain are entirely my own responsibility.

To all of these individuals, I extend my heartfelt thanks and appreciation.

I should offer a brief note about the use of Korean names. I have standardized the usage throughout the text to the form used commonly for high-ranking officials: family name first, followed by the first and middle names, each word separate and initially capitalized—as in President Kim Young Sam or Kim Il Sung. Thus in all cases, family names come first.

MICHAEL J. MAZARR
February 1995

NORTH KOREA AND THE BOMB

■ 1 ■

TEST CASE FOR A NEW ERA

In early June 1994, Selig Harrison embarked on his fourth trip into the closed and secretive society of North Korea.[1] He had first been there in 1972 in a previous career as a journalist; he was then Northeast Asian bureau chief of *The Washington Post*. Later he enrolled in the ballooning ranks of foreign policy experts working out of Washington think tanks, joining one of the most prestigious—the Carnegie Endowment for International Peace. It was as a Carnegie scholar that Harrison had returned to Pyongyang in 1987 and again in 1992.

By the spring of 1994 the risk of war was in the air. As will be described in detail in chapters 7 and 8, North Korea scoffed at world pressure and removed the spent fuel from its main nuclear reactor—fuel which contained enough plutonium for several nuclear weapons. Defueling the reactor was yet another North Korean step toward a nuclear arsenal, and the United States warned that this action would lead inevitably and rapidly to economic sanctions. North Korea replied that sanctions meant war; South Korea began calling up its reserves for a temporary drill, and some in the U.S. Congress urged a rapid reinforcement of U.S. troops in the South.

Harrison's views on North Korea were well known in Washington circles. He had come to anchor the liberal wing of North Korea watchers. For years Harrison had complained that the United States gave insufficient attention to North Korea's security concerns and too often belittled the North and its leadership. There were hawks and doves in Pyongyang, Harrison contended, just as there were in Washington and Seoul; a tough line only played into the hands of the hawks. Harrison gradually made one argument the centerpiece of his view of U.S. policy toward North Korea: the United States, he complained, was not being explicit enough in the package of incentives it was offering the North in exchange for cooperation on the nuclear issue. His case had been strengthened in November 1993, when a major North Korean statement called for exactly the sort of big "package deal" Harrison had been proposing for some time.

Now Selig Harrison was to have another audience with North Korea's Great Leader, Kim Il Sung. They met at one of Kim's residences outside Pyongyang, a summer retreat in the coastal foothills outside the capital. Accompanied by a handful of North Korean officials and translators, they talked for two hours and had lunch.

As he had several times previously, Kim Il Sung complained to Harrison that, despite the accusations of the world community, "we don't have any nuclear weapons or any intention of making them." Kim added: "It gives me a headache when people demand to see something we don't have. It's like dogs barking at the moon." As the United States had more than 10,000 nuclear weapons, Kim said, "What would be the point of our making one or two nuclear weapons? We would be a laughingstock."

Kim Il Sung used the opportunity of the visit to confirm a major new diplomatic initiative—a sign of how isolated North Korea had truly become, having to rely on visiting scholars for diplomatic purposes. In the days before Harrison met with Kim, other North Korean officials had outlined to the visiting American the basic elements of a proposed deal. If the United States would guarantee credits to allow the North to purchase a new type of nuclear reactor, the North Korean officials suggested, they would freeze their nuclear program until the new reactors arrived. Once those reactors were delivered, the North would completely dismantle its plutonium reprocessing facility and its as-yet incomplete two hundred–megawatt reactor—the focus of the world's concern about its nuclear intentions.

When he met with Kim Il Sung, Selig Harrison brought up this proposal. "Yes; that's a very good proposal; we could do that," Kim replied. Then he turned to his chief nuclear negotiator, Kang Sok Ju, and asked for clarification. Their brief discussion in Korean was not translated, though Harrison noted the apparent nature of the relationship between the Great Leader and his subordinate—one of mutual respect, not sycophancy.

Kim turned back and spoke even more forcefully. "Yes, my colleague has made a good proposal. I support it. We will do that."

Selig Harrison announced the offer when he returned from Pyongyang. The very same proposal, given to former President Jimmy Carter when he conducted his own trip to the North a few days after Harrison's, would have dramatic implications for the U.S.–North Korean crisis then unfolding in Asia. For Harrison, the import of Kim's offer was obvious; for others with a less sympathetic view of the North, it was not so clear. But on one point there could be no argument: as a result of the Harrison and Carter visits, the drift toward sanctions, for good or ill, had been arrested. The drive to control North Korea's nuclear ambitions would now return to the diplomacy that had been underway for more than two years. Within four months, U.S. and North Korean negotiators would strike a bargain that looked very much like the one Harrison and Kim Il Sung discussed casually over lunch.

As his meeting with Kim Il Sung was ending, Harrison asked about U.S. demands for inspections of the North. Kim had been surprisingly upbeat during the conversation; he had said few critical things of the United States and had even insisted that U.S.–North Korean relations were improving. Now Kim, a chain-smoker, shook his cigarette at Harrison and threw down his matches for emphasis. Talking of North Korea and the United States, Kim said, "The point is, we must be on good terms with each other, and then we will both know everything about each other. And we mustn't put [forth] preconditions. How can you expect [us] to let a country with which we are still at war know everything about our country?"

A TEST CASE OF NONPROLIFERATION

What was the true status of North Korea's nuclear program, and what were the goals of its nuclear research? How did South Korea, the United States, and Japan succeed in coercing the North into allowing international inspections of its nuclear facilities in the first place? How did the final agreement of October 1994 come about?

This work attempts to answer these questions, and others surrounding North Korea's mysterious nuclear weapons program, as fully as possible. It examines what is known of the history and status of North Korea's nuclear ambitions and of U.S. and international efforts to halt them. Taking up the story of U.S. and allied diplomacy in detail in 1989, and relying on the open media as well as dozens of interviews with U.S., South Korea, Japanese, Chinese, and North Korean officials, the book traces that diplomacy through October 1994—when Washington and Pyongyang reached a dramatic, unprecedented agreement ostensibly to end the North's nuclear ambitions.

The result is not so much a study of international relations theory or a historical treatise as it is a story, an account of nations and their leaders reacting to a security dilemma. So far, it is a story with a reasonably happy ending; but the final chapter has yet to be written, and careful efforts will be required to resolve the issue. As they continue their dialogue with Pyongyang, policymakers in Seoul, Washington, Tokyo, and elsewhere might benefit from a comprehensive history of the diplomatic campaign they have waged to date, and this book attempts to lay out that history.

My primary purpose, however, is to go one step further than a mere recounting of events. Having examined the North Korean nuclear program and the worldwide effort to slow or halt it, I will turn to the fundamental question of this study: what lessons does the Korean case hold for other nonproliferation efforts? Chapters 9 and 10 address this question. As they will make clear, the lessons transferable from one case of nonproliferation to another are in fact more modest than might be assumed. But the Korean example nonetheless offers important—and, this volume will contend, unexpectedly controversial—guidance to those involved in the tricky business of nonproliferation.

THE NEW PROMINENCE OF NONPROLIFERATION

Such a study is especially timely because halting the spread of weapons of mass destruction has become something of a cottage industry. Always an important consideration for the United States, since the late 1980s it has achieved top billing on almost all lists of foreign policy and defense priorities. Books are written, bureaucratic careers are made, and defense programs are justified on the basis of the threat to the United States and its allies posed by the proliferation of nuclear, chemical, and biological weapons.

"Proliferation of weapons of mass destruction and advanced delivery systems," Sidney Graybeal and Patricia McFate write in one typical assessment, "is clearly emerging as *the dominant threat to national and international security.*"[2] Similar sentiments emerged in the results of a summer 1993 *Times-Mirror* poll of about 650 "opinion leaders." Of the ten groups polled—opinion leaders in such fields as news media, business and finance, cultural affairs, foreign affairs, and religion—*nine* ranked "preventing the spread of nuclear weapons" first among all U.S. foreign policy goals. The other group, the "general public," ranked it second, behind the more prosaic aim of "protecting jobs of American workers."[3]

It is little wonder then, that in the U.S. Department of Defense's long-awaited 1993 Bottom Up Review, proliferation consistently receives top billing on lists of U.S. foreign and defense policy challenges for the 1990s and beyond. Proliferation beat out such issues as regional conflict and the risk of a new Russian threat.[4] And the U.S. Joint Chiefs of Staff's 1994 "National Military Strategy" identifies the spread of weapons of mass destruction as the top military threat facing the United States.[5] During late 1993 and early 1994, U.S. President Bill Clinton, National Security Adviser Anthony Lake, and then-Secretary of Defense Les Aspin all gave major speeches highlighting the importance of the issue.

In part this newfound emphasis on nonproliferation stems from the end of the Cold War. When the Soviet Union was brandishing 30,000 or more nuclear weapons at the United States, the threat of a handful of Pakistani or Indian bombs (or even North Korean ones) did not seem so consequential to Washington. It was certainly an important issue, but not a dominant one. Proliferation was a second-tier concern.

Now the Soviet Union has disappeared, and no other nation has taken its place as America's global rival. It is very possible that no other country possesses the combination of economic, political, and military strength to assume such a role, even if it desired to. In such an environment, threats that once were secondary are now of primary importance. Those responsible for U.S. defense policy have reached to the back of their shelves, brought out a varied collection of once-ancillary issues and concerns, dusted them off, and placed them at the centerpiece of U.S. foreign and defense policy. Proliferation, along with such eclectic dangers as drug smuggling, migration, and the expansionist designs of regional bullies such as Iraq, is such an issue.

But proliferation has quickly become the dominant member of this club of second-tier interests. One sees the profound role played by proliferation in U.S. relationships with those countries where it remains an issue. As the following chapters will make clear, from about 1989 until late 1994, virtually all broader analysis of U.S. policy toward Korea gave way to a single-minded focus on stopping the North's embryonic nuclear program. U.S. relations with Pakistan continue to be held hostage by the Pressler Amendment, imposed as a sanction for Pakistan's nuclear work. Critics of the U.S. approach to Ukraine argue that U.S. officials have neglected that country's immense strategic importance amid an overwhelming desire to obtain its agreement to nuclear disarmament.

In part, proliferation became the post–Cold War threat of choice because it neatly marries concerns of conservatives and liberals, arms-buildup hawks and arms-control doves. Both groups view with alarm the spread of weapons of mass destruction, and most liberal and conservative foreign policy analysts are largely on the same page on the issue of nonproliferation. Thus, in December 1993 one found arms controllers like Wisconsin Arms Control Project Director Gary Milholland and hawks like columnist Charles Krauthammer joining forces to urge economic sanctions, and if necessary military strikes, to deal with the North Korean nuclear challenge. Those foreign policy observers whose opinions diverge from the consensus form an equally diverse group: it was not only the liberals afraid of a new war in Korea who advocated a more moderate U.S. stance toward North Korea during the crises of 1993, but also a handful of Reagan and Bush administration officials—such as Bush administration Assistant Secretary of State for East Asia and the Pacific William Clark, Bush's Ambassador to South Korea Donald Gregg, and Reagan National Security Adviser Richard Allen—who believed that, to a certain extent, the best approach when dealing with an anachronistic renegade like North Korea was to use one of three alternatives: engage it; mollify it; or simply forget about it.

The emphasis on nonproliferation is also a measure of the essential threatlessness of the current moment.[6] For despite all the talk about the issue, the actual danger posed to the United States and its interests from nuclear proliferation remains quite small. The United States has no strategic interests in South Asia that would require us to confront the Pakistani or Indian arsenals; if those two nations chose to annihilate each other in a nuclear war, it would be one of the greatest tragedies in history but no great threat to the well-being of most Americans. Israel's bomb is of little concern except insofar as it incites such hostile states as Iraq, Iran, and Libya to respond in kind. North Korea has few reasons to attack the United States with whatever primitive nuclear arsenal it manages to cobble together.

The threat posed by proliferation is also mitigated by the lack of delivery means for weapons of mass destruction. No proliferant possesses an intercontinental-range missile, and most estimates suggest that none will for at least another decade. The threat is further undermined by the fact of deterrence: if the United States could keep the Soviet Union and China from using the bomb against it for more than forty years with the threat of retaliation, would not the same basic strategy work against Iraq or North Korea?

And yet proliferation, while not comparable to the threat posed by the Soviet Union during the Cold War, does hold dangers. And the United States has good reason to restrain the spread of weapons of mass destruction. In the first instance, this is true because the spread of such weapons would reduce the U.S. freedom of action in the world. It would immensely complicate the U.S. task in regional conflicts. Imagine, for example, confronting an Iraq that had just seized Kuwait *and* that possessed a small arsenal of nuclear weapons. It would be harder to gain public approval for a U.S. response to a nuclear-armed aggressor and harder to conduct such a response even if the public agreed.

There are other reasons why the United States has reason to fear, and, where possible, to slow the proliferation of weapons of mass destruction. Deterrence by threat of retaliation, which served so ably during the Cold War, might not work in the new circumstances. Washington has yet to see what a nation in possession of nuclear weapons and on the brink of total defeat might do, because that situation never arose during the Cold War. In a new Korean war, for example, deterrence could easily fail: on the verge of being conquered, with nothing to lose, the North might choose to lash out with nuclear weapons. Eventually, too, proliferants hostile to U.S. interests will find a way to deliver their bombs to the United States—with submarines or tramp steamers today, with long-range missiles a decade from now. And the spread of nuclear, chemical, and biological know-how increases the risk of mass-destruction terrorism.

Nonproliferation is therefore clearly in the U.S. national interest, and its status as a top foreign policy priority is understandable. But it is important to recognize, both in general terms and in the context of the North Korean case, that nonproliferation is a relative interest, not an absolute one.[7] It does not, in all cases and at all times, pose an immediate threat to vital U.S. national interests. The United States has learned to live with many nuclear arsenals or quasi arsenals around the world, and may be able to live with more. Furthermore, in a given case—with Ukraine or Israel, for example—the strategic importance of good relations with a given state may outweigh the U.S. interest in addressing that country's nuclear ambitions.

These facts have two consequences. First, they establish boundaries on the scope of U.S. nonproliferation efforts. The United States did not go to war to halt the Chinese or Indian nuclear weapons programs; it would not have fought to stop a Brazilian or Argentine bomb; and it is not likely to start a war with North Korea to halt its nuclear research unless the North brazenly pursues an all-out nuclear weapons program. In some cases, notably Israel, U.S. national interests have prevented Washington from even sanctioning the proliferant or mentioning publicly the existence of its arsenal. As the following chapters will make clear, the result, at least in the Korean case, has been an emphasis on an agreement that does not represent exactly what Washington would have wanted, but rather the best deal that could be achieved short of military action.

Second, the relative, as opposed to absolute, threat posed by the spread of weapons of mass destruction creates one relentless question in each case of nonproliferation: what is the definition of success? In the long term, that definition can usually be expressed by some vague statement about a complete and total end to all nuclear, chemical, and biological weapons research in worrisome countries. In the short term, however, such radical solutions will seldom be possible. Few nations will be ready to follow South Africa and simply come clean about their entire nuclear program.

We are left, then, to discover some less complete and more realistic short-term goals for nonproliferation. These goals must respect and flow from a close analysis of U.S. national interests. In each case of proliferation, the U.S.

desire to stop or slow the nuclear (or chemical or biological) program will be weighed against other interests. Those interests might have to do with direct bilateral relations with the proliferant, as in the cases of Israel or India; they might relate to third-party considerations, as with China's role in the North Korean nuclear issue; or they might involve economic interests, as with the U.S. desire for trade with China even as it feels a need to punish Beijing for its arms transfers. In each case, therefore, the U.S. definition of success in non-proliferation, the near-term goals at which Washington aims and the methods used to achieve them must respect other U.S. interests. And finally, the U.S. strategy for nonproliferation must be connected to a broader vision of the future of nuclear weapons in world politics. Again, such less-than-absolute definitions were on display in Korea, where the agreement of October 1994 reflected a gradual and flexible, rather than immediate and absolute, conception of success.

NORTH KOREA AS A TEST CASE

These facts vastly complicate the practice of nonproliferation, something that has become readily apparent in Washington's dealings with North Korea. In many ways, the U.S.-led effort to halt North Korea's nuclear program was, along with the civil war in Bosnia-Herzegovina, one of the first examples of extended, multilateral, post–Cold War diplomacy. This role imbues the diplomatic campaign over the North's research, and the U.S. component of that diplomacy, with a special importance.

Some might argue that the Persian Gulf War of 1990 to 1991 was the first major post–Cold War political-military challenge for the United States and the so-called New World Order. And indeed it was, but it was also, in a sense, an easy challenge to meet. Iraq's aggression was obvious and unjustified; no major, or even minor, power had an interest in backing Saddam Hussein against the American response; the remedy for Iraq's invasion was relatively obvious; and the war turned out to be short and surprisingly painless. Indeed, the whole episode was quite brief, spanning, in a diplomatic sense, the seven months from August 1990 to February 1991, and in military terms less than six weeks, from January 17 to February 28.

In contrast, the international diplomacy aimed at North Korea's nuclear program has now dragged on for almost a decade, if we date its outset at the December 1985 meetings in Moscow when, under pressure from Soviet officials (acting at the request of the United States), North Korea signed the Nonproliferation Treaty (NPT). Worldwide efforts to gain access to the North's nuclear facilities accelerated after the spring of 1989, when new and disturbing evidence of North Korean weapons research began to emerge. The diplomacy entered a stage of intense negotiation in roughly mid-1991. Over time, this extended diplomatic campaign has had to reconcile divergent interests: South Korea and Japan have generally opposed a confrontational approach, but both also want badly a verifiable end to the nuclear program; China rejected sanctions against the North; and the U.S. aim has been to pursue its global nonproliferation imperatives.

Like the Bosnian case, the Korean nuclear issue in some ways represented a better test of post–Cold War U.S. foreign policy than did the Gulf War. Korea provided a more valid challenge, a vexing series of dilemmas rather than a single and obvious case of aggression. As the following chapters will make clear, the United States has met that test unevenly. That same phrase would constitute a charitable verdict on the U.S. actions in Bosnia.

The approach of the Nonproliferation Treaty Review Conference in 1995 lent the nonproliferation effort in Korea even greater precedent-setting significance. At that conference, the members of the Treaty will decide its future— whether it is to be continued, modified, or abandoned. In the context of long-standing charges by nonmembers such as India that the NPT institutionalizes an unfair division between nuclear haves and have-nots, the worldwide treatment of North Korea carried important implications for the future of the nonproliferation project writ large. A very tough stance might have alienated some developing countries already uncomfortable with the NPT's inherent inequity; an ineffectual response might have ruined the NPT's credibility.

THE COMPLEXITY OF NONPROLIFERATION

The effort to halt the North's nuclear research also assumes great importance because it is not, in the final analysis, merely a nuclear issue.[8] It holds explosive implications for the evolution of the Korean Peninsula and the architecture of regional security. This interconnection of issues and interests (which will be present in any case of proliferation to a greater or lesser extent) imbues the Korean case with a mind-boggling complexity. And it demonstrates what happens when the apparently simple goal of nonproliferation collides with the real world—and, specifically, when the blunt U.S. desire for nonproliferation bumps up against other U.S. interests and the interests of other states.

This complexity stemmed from a number of sources. In the most basic sense, for the United States and all other actors, nonproliferation came into conflict with their broader policy toward North Korea. For a variety of reasons—to reduce tensions on the peninsula, for example, and to prepare the way for and reduce the eventual cost of unification—South Korea had, by the late

1980s, acquired a distinct interest in engaging the North in a growing web of economic and political contacts. This basic realization was expressed in South Korean President Roh Tae Woo's 1988 policy of *Nordpolitik,* which called for a simultaneous engagement of the North and its communist allies. Japan also saw the benefits of engagement, and during the 1980s began a dialogue with Pyongyang raising the possibility of formal diplomatic relations, business investment, and reparations payments for damage to Korea during Japan's colonial era. Though some officials in Washington encouraged this trend, it was halted by concerns about the North's nuclear research, so that by 1992 the policy toward North Korea adopted by many major regional actors had been taken hostage by nonproliferation imperatives.

Within South Korea, therefore, the nuclear crisis engaged a host of deep-seated nationalistic emotions. It was intimately related to the problem of uni-fication, delaying South-North dialogue on the issue and preventing South Korean businesses from building an economic infrastructure, a unification safety net, in the North. Nationalistic objections to this policy of linkage could be heard more and more often in Seoul during the early 1990s; many South Koreans especially objected to the Roh government's promise not to develop nuclear reprocessing facilities, a decision taken at the request of the United States.

At times, these disagreements manifested themselves in bureaucratic dis-putes within the South Korean government. By the fall of 1993, for example, there was much talk in Seoul of a prominent fissure within the Kim Young Sam administration over policy toward the North: the Ministry of Foreign Affairs and the National Unification Board were said to favor a softer-line approach based on engagement and carrots, while the Agency for National Security Planning (South Korea's intelligence organization, the former KCIA) and the Blue House National Security Adviser allegedly wanted a turn toward a tougher approach emphasizing sticks such as economic sanctions. This debate reflected South Korea's basic split personality on the nuclear issue: Seoul wanted engagement, but it also wanted an end to the North Korean nuclear program.

Throughout the course of diplomacy, then, it was not always accurate to speak of a "South Korean" position as opposed to a Japanese or Chinese or Russian or American one. The reality was more complex, involving various constituencies within each specific government, and sometimes within indi-vidual departments or even specific offices within those departments.

In North Korea, too, although we cannot be sure about the domestic con-tours of the issue, nuclear politics had clearly become intertwined with fun-damental questions of regime survival. By the early 1990s, the North's nuclear program had been explicitly tied both to the North's urgent drive to acquire outside investment, diplomatic relations, and economic aid, and to the gradual process of succession of power from Kim Il Sung to his son, Kim Jong Il. North Korea's multiple, overlapping—and, it is important to stress, probably evolving—motives for nuclear research injected further complexity into the issue. And as in the South, one can assume that some degree of policy debate went on in Pyongyang as well, although the scope and seriousness of that debate—and what the United States might have done to help the so-called doves—were not at all clear.

China's stance added complications into the mix. For its own reasons, Beijing had no interest in a confrontational policy toward the North. Its officials repeatedly emphasized that China would veto sanctions introduced in the United Nations Security Council, and constantly and publicly warned the United States against a tough approach. Given these views, and given the fact that China's location and capabilities meant that it could undermine any international effort to isolate the North, Beijing's position established strict boundaries for U.S. nuclear diplomacy.

In sum, the need for a multilateral solution substantially complicated the nuclear diplomacy toward the North. A unilateral U.S. approach was never a serious option. South Korea and Japan obviously had to be consulted, and U.S. policy had to respect the views of the Chinese. This multi-sided diplomacy was effective when coordinated, perhaps more effective than a unilateral policy could ever have been, but that coordination was a vexing challenge. If a ubiquitous and unprecedentedly rigid multilateralism is indeed a central feature of the post–Cold War era, then the diplomacy of that era will also be unprecedentedly challenging.

The North Korean case therefore suggests that nonproliferation will be a highly complex, differentiated, and multi-sided enterprise, both because of the varied and evolving motives of the proliferants and because of the complex and frequently divergent interests of the major players involved. This conclusion has two specific implications.

First, the intricacies of particular situations mean that a single-minded U.S. insistence on nonproliferation can cause as many problems as it solves. In the Korean case, U.S. nonproliferation imperatives had to be balanced against the intersecting interests and realities mentioned earlier. Again, this points to the fact that nonproliferation is not an absolute interest, but an interest to be balanced against others. It also indicates that generic nonproliferation strategies will seldom be appropriate, a point that will be taken up in chapter 10.

The conclusion, however, drawn by both U.S. observers and nationalist South Koreans, that the United States and South Korea had *conflicting* interests in their nuclear diplomacy is not a fully accurate one. As noted earlier (and explored in chapters 4 through 6), Seoul's desire for engagement of the North was certainly stronger than that of the United States. But South Korea also urgently wanted an end to the North Korean nuclear program and was not willing simply to forget about the North Korean drive for the bomb. Japan similarly insisted on an end to the North's program. At base, then, Washington, Seoul, and Tokyo—and, to a lesser and more qualified degree, Beijing and Moscow, neither of which had (or have) any interest in a nuclear-armed North Korea—shared a strong commitment to the same objective.

The question, of course, was one of means. And this was where the global imperatives of U.S. nonproliferation policy might have caused problems, urging a resort to sanctions and threats before the South was ready for them. As it turned out, however, U.S. officials of both the Bush and Clinton administrations managed to avoid (thus far) a confrontational approach. But the risk of a true U.S.–South Korean split did become evident in 1994: in the fall of that year, the two flipped positions—South Korean officials, angered at the North's failure to respond to repeated U.S. and South Korean offers, became more insistent on a tough approach to the North than their U.S. counterparts. President Kim Young Sam made unprecedented public attacks on the U.S. stance in talks with the North, and commentators in Seoul stressed the need for a more independent South Korean position.

The danger therefore remains that, in other cases, a strict U.S. adherence to a theological view of nonproliferation will spark antagonism with other states, including friends and allies, and subvert the goal of nonproliferation itself. If nonproliferation comes to be viewed as a goal that overrides other U.S. and multilateral interests, it will both undermine those interests and often fail on its own terms. That result is still very possible in the Korean case if Washington decides to override allied concerns and pursue the route of economic sanctions and military threats in some future crisis.

Avoiding such an outcome requires placing nonproliferation in its proper context. But it also requires something else: agreement between the United States and its allies on a realistic and coherent definition of success in the nonproliferation effort. Again, the issue is a balancing of national interests, a weighing of political-military risks and costs. U.S. policymakers must ask themselves, What would it cost us to achieve X or Y definition of success in nonproliferation? And are we prepared to pay that cost? In some cases—say, the acquisition of nuclear weapons by a radical regime that has promised to use them, or is generally expected to use them as rapidly as possible against the United States—the threat to U.S. national interests will be sufficiently clear as to justify a more absolute definition of success. In most cases, however, the issue will be more murky.

Asking such questions in advance will be indispensable in preventing damage to U.S. credibility. For if the United States assumes its interest in nonproliferation to be too absolute and pushes a given case to a crisis, it may discover only at the last moment that the American people and Congress do not have the will to press the standoff to a conclusion. Should the United States make a number of threats and promises, get to the very brink of a conflict, and then back off, the credibility of its overall nonproliferation policies will have been shattered. This risk was clearly evident in the North Korean case, and in fact some commentators worried that President Clinton's retreat from his bold 1993 assertion that North Korean possession of a bomb was unacceptable had fatally undermined U.S. credibility and the viability of the Nonproliferation Treaty.[9]

The second broad implication of the intricacies of nonproliferation complicates the task further: because of the numerous issues and interests involved, *even after* the original motives for the proliferation have faded, it may not be in the proliferant's interests to resolve the nuclear issue. In the Korean case, for example, even supposing that officials in Pyongyang recognized the hollowness of the U.S. nuclear threat by 1993, their nuclear program had become intertwined with so many other considerations, from unification to succession in the North, that they had little interest in simply removing the nuclear question from the table. In other words, the complex phenomenon of proliferation is not like a geopolitical flu, whose symptoms will disappear when its underlying causes are addressed. It is more like a cancer whose causes are impossible to pin down and that can, at best, be controlled and limited with the hope of an eventual cure.

THE RESEARCH AGENDA

Given the growing importance of the practice of nonproliferation and the precedental nature of the North Korean case, a close examination of the North's alleged nuclear program and the international campaign to stop it seems warranted. I have endeavored in the following chapters to relate the events surrounding that diplomatic campaign as accurately and completely as possible. For the most part, I leave it to subsequent analysts to draw the complete lessons of the case.

This book seeks to answer four fundamental questions, and it is the answers that provide the basis for the discussion in the two concluding chapters. Those questions are:

1. *What Are North Korea's Motives?* Why does it appear to desire a nuclear arsenal, and what does that tell us about the proper scope of nonproliferation?[10]

2. *What Is the Role of Multilateralism?* Multilateral approaches have been heralded as everything from the panacea of the post–Cold War era to a useless and dangerous substitute for the proper pursuit of individual national interests. But, as chapter 8 will argue, multilateral approaches, whether ad hoc or institutionalized, will almost always be necessary in nonproliferation. The Korean case may give some insight into the relative usefulness and nature of multilateralism.

3. *What Is the Best Nonproliferation Strategy?* This question will depend in part on the answer to the first question. The answer may also be different from one case to the next.

4. Finally and most fundamentally, *what is the definition of success in nonproliferation?* The importance and relevance of this question were outlined earlier.

Chapters 2 through 8 aim to answer these questions; chapters 9 and 10 draw lessons and conclusions from them. What follows is not merely an account of a series of events, or a political science textbook. It is, as with most things that involve the showy North Korean regime, a drama of many episodes. Hopefully, there is still time to learn something from it, to build upon the October 1994 accord and find a way to achieve both nonproliferation goals and broader U.S. and allied interests on the Korean Peninsula. This book aims to help with that process of learning.

For the Agreed Framework has not resolved the nuclear issue on the Korean peninsula; it has merely committed the parties to resolve the issue over the course of the next several years. Much can still go wrong. The framework agreement itself could fall apart, a possibility described in the epilogue. Now more than ever, the United States and its allies need an intelligent and energetic policy toward North Korea—a policy grounded in the lessons of the last five years. In defining and discussing those lessons, this book offers the building blocks for a sound future policy.

■ 2 ■

THE ORIGINS, 1945–1980

Korea has long been the scene of nuclear tensions for the United States. Indeed, it was because of Korea that Washington, more than at any other moment since 1945, directly threatened the use of nuclear weapons to compel action by another nation. The target was China; the purpose was to bring a halt to the seemingly endless Korean War.

The U.S. nuclear bluster over Korea actually began rather early in the war. After sending ten nuclear-configured B-29s across the Pacific in July 1950,[1] President Harry Truman promised in November of that year that the United States would take "whatever steps are necessary" to stop the Chinese intervention, claiming that the use of nuclear weapons had always been under "active consideration."[2] Earlier, on April 11 of 1950, Truman, fearing Soviet intervention, had said that China and the Soviet Union would be responsible for whatever might happen if they widened the war. The administration also sent envoy Charles Burton Marshall to Hong Kong with a warning for China that made reference to U.S. nuclear weapons.[3]

Dwight Eisenhower was elected in 1952 in part on a promise to end the Korean War. By that time, after a seesaw first year, the war had settled into a prolonged stalemate in which United Nations forces were exchanging substantial casualties for little measurable progress on the ground. China and North Korea, perhaps hoping to wait the Americans out, were stalling at the peace talks at Panmunjom. Eisenhower's administration was looking for something to break the deadlock, and it soon settled on nuclear weapons. In February 1953, Eisenhower began to drop "discreet" hints of a willingness to use nuclear force,[4] and at the May 15, 1953, National Security Council meeting he argued that nuclear bluff and bluster would be a cheaper solution to the stalemate in Korea than conventional war. That month the United States made a number of direct references to the possibility that a continued war might invite the U.S. use of nuclear weapons.

The most famous threat was delivered by Secretary of State John Foster Dulles. In conversation with India's leader, Jawaharal Nehru—known to have close ties to China—Dulles remarked that the United States would use "stronger rather than lesser" military means if the Panmunjom talks collapsed.[5] This ambiguous code, the Americans hoped, would be read in China for what it was—a threat of nuclear war.

Just two months later, in July 1953, the United States, China, and North Korea concluded an armistice ending the Korean War. Dulles and Eisenhower both claimed afterward that the threat of nuclear weapons played a major role in bringing about the truce agreement that ended the war.

NORTH KOREA: MOTIVES FOR A BOMB

The United States thus exposed North Korea, during its infancy as a nation, to the fearsome power and enormous political value of nuclear weapons. The lesson was apparently not lost on North Korea's leaders, and early U.S. nuclear threats are one important thread in the tapestry of the North's motives for a nuclear program.

Any analysis of a proliferation case study must begin with a consideration of the basic question: motive. Despite the pressures of a near-anarchic world system, states do not pursue the development of nuclear weapons without a reason. The associated costs, both financial and political, establish a presumption against acquiring nuclear arsenals. It is only when a state's perceived vulnerability or desire for attention or prestige overcomes that presumption that proliferation will take place.

This conclusion flatly denies the validity of the "technical school" of proliferation analysis, which holds that the availability of nuclear weapons in itself constitutes sufficient motive for pursuing them. If states can acquire the bomb, this line of thinking goes, they will. The Korean case does not support that notion; rather, it suggests that the "motivational school" of proliferation is correct—the idea that a state requires very specific and powerful motives to seek a nuclear arsenal, motives intimately connected with that state's view of its own security. Nonproliferation therefore becomes more than the mere denial of technology (although that can play a role); it demands a more broad-ranging and subtle process of diplomacy to address the proliferant's motives.

at the beginning of the chapter, during the Korean War the United
e a series of implied and direct nuclear threats in efforts to dis-
rth Korean and Chinese aggression. This thinking reflected the pol-
uld come to dominate Eisenhower's defense planning: the "New
which the deterrent value of nuclear weapons served as an inex-
bstitute for conventional parity with the Soviet Union and China.
Eisenhower would adopt the overall nuclear strategy of massive
, which argued that the U.S. response to any significant Communist
n, even a limited one, would be an all-out nuclear retaliation. The
ine explicitly reserved the right to use nuclear weapons first if U.S.
orces were losing in a regional war. During this period the United
s fully prepared to use theater nuclear weapons to resolve regional
Taken together, these policies must certainly have intensified the
ean concern with the U.S. nuclear threat.[18]

Korea was not the only nation to react to U.S. nuclear threats in this
China responded to the U.S. bluster during the Korean War by under-
own nuclear program after the end of the war,[19] and U.S. nuclear
ship with India during the early 1970s may have marginally con-
New Delhi's desire for a bomb.[20] In a similar manner, the North
who had depended solely on China and the Soviet Union for nuclear
before the war, may well have decided that only the possession of
nuclear force would guarantee their security.

after the Korean War, the United States continued to give Pyongyang
o seek the bomb. In January 1955, the Chairman of the U.S. Joint
Staff, Admiral Arthur W. Radford, made the U.S. nuclear pledge to
rea explicit on his visit to Seoul.[21] Even though the armistice that
e war had banned the introduction of new weapons, the Neutral
Supervisory Commission, the monitoring agency for this agreement,
d at the beginning of 1958.[22] The United States wasted no time: at the
nuary 1958, the U.S.–led United Nations Command announced that,
ponse to numerous Communist violations of the armistice, it was
ing nuclear-capable weapons systems into South Korea.[23] It con-
he presence of nuclear 280-mm artillery shells and nuclear-tipped
n the South.[24]

the next several years, according to accounts that emerged later, the
States deployed additional nuclear systems to South Korea. In 1959,
orce brought Matador cruise missiles, with a range of 1,100 kilometers,
ninsula; in 1961 they were followed by the Mace, an 1,800-kilometer
issile. Later, in the 1960s, U.S. forces in Korea would acquire Atomic
ion Munitions, essentially nuclear land mines designed to slow a

It becomes an exercise in addressing the demand side—the motives that give
rise to proliferation—as well as the supply side of the equation.

This being the case, a discussion of motives is critical for any study of strategies for nonproliferation. To be successful, any nonproliferation strategy must
answer all, or nearly all, of a proliferant's motives. It can do this in several
ways: with threats designed to outweigh the allure of a nuclear arsenal with
the risk of military or economic sanctions; with promises or diplomatic initiatives aimed at relieving the proliferant's fears and reducing its need for
nuclear weapons; or with a combination of both. But whatever strategy is
adopted must be tailored to the proliferant's particular reasons for seeking
nuclear weapons in the first place. In this sense, an understanding of North
Korea's possible motives for pursuing the bomb will provide a foundation on
which the rest of this work will rest. In particular, the Korean case suggests
that the motives for proliferation are often enormously complex and inter-
woven with other national interests, and that they evolve over time.[6]

BASIC RATIONALES

North Korea's interest in acquiring nuclear weapons appears to date from the
mid-1950s. The North's nuclear policy appears initially to have been a reac-
tionary response to U.S. nuclear threats rather than an offensive gesture.
There is evidence that officials in Pyongyang considered their lack of nuclear
capabilities to be a potentially fatal weakness in the face of the U.S. nuclear
umbrella that protects the South. United States nuclear threats have pervaded
North Korean strategic thoughts and actions since the Korean War, and may
have played a decisive role in stimulating North Korean leaders to embark
upon their own nuclear weapons program.[7]

North Korea's drive for military self-defense and independence probably
consisted of a number of specific lines of thought or emphasis. All were
aimed at one fundamental goal—regime preservation. In each case, the difficulty of finding an easy answer to Pyongyang's security concerns illustrates
the vexing challenge posed by nonproliferation.

First and most fundamentally, the North wanted a nuclear arsenal to deter
U.S. nuclear use and to counterbalance the U.S. nuclear umbrella. This became
especially necessary in the wake of Moscow's establishment of diplomatic
relations with the South and with the aborted August 1991 Soviet coup, after
which the North began to doubt the reliability of its traditional military ally
and source of nuclear protection.[8] This first motive could have either an offensive or a defensive cast, depending on whether the North wanted to deter a
U.S. nuclear response to its own military action or protect itself against a

U.S.–sponsored South Korean offensive thrust north. In either case, as a result of the U.S. nuclear umbrella over the South, North Korea has had reason to fear U.S. nuclear first use—and thus, at one time, was described as the "sole nuclear aspirant in the developing world today that faces an overt nuclear threat from a superpower."[9] For a time, the North also feared an emerging South Korean nuclear weapons program as well.[10]

In addressing this issue, U.S. and South Korean officials confronted the question of just how elaborate the North's security aims were. While the North's nuclear arsenal initially provided a response to U.S. nuclear threats, it may eventually have provided, for officials in Pyongyang, a lever to force the entire U.S. military presence out of the South. Thus, at times, North Korean officials, including Kim Il Sung, have mentioned the complete withdrawal of all U.S. troops from the South as a precondition for resolving the nuclear issue. In a slightly less ambitious vein, Pyongyang has often referred to the general U.S. nuclear umbrella as a roadblock to dialogue and has insisted on a withdrawal of U.S. nuclear pledges to the South. Yet North Korea has not pressed either of these issues, and in private conversations North Korean officials admit that neither objection is serious.[11] Nonetheless, these statements illustrate the difficulty of drawing a firm line beyond which no security compromises will be made.

Second, North Korea may also have viewed a small nuclear arsenal as insurance against an eventual South Korean conventional superiority.[12] In this sense nuclear weapons might represent a North Korean version of the 1950s U.S. nuclear-reliant strategy of the "New Look," achieving deterrence on the cheap. South Korean military analyst Song Young Sun estimates the total cost of the North Korean nuclear program at more than $200 million, a trifling amount compared to the South's reported $5 billion total defense budget.[13]

Third, North Korean leaders probably viewed nuclear weapons as a means of obtaining diplomatic leverage, forcing the world to take notice of their concerns, and promoting direct, bilateral talks with the United States. Pyongyang had been seeking greater attention, particularly in Washington, for decades, especially since the mid-1980s. North Korean officials may have viewed a nascent nuclear capability as the key to doors long barred to them. And they were right: the North received more attention in international government and media circles during 1991 and 1992 than it had in the previous decade.[14]

The problem for U.S. and South Korean officials was to determine in advance at what point the North would be willing to surrender this leverage. Steps taken to convince the North to abandon its nuclear program (or, at least, to allow international inspections) could easily have fed this motive. The more initiatives Seoul and Washington made, the more North Korea might see

the value of prolonging debate over the issue additional dilemma called for a finely tuned enough to make it think it had made adequate u while foreclosing the possibility of further co

Fourth, some leaders in Pyongyang may ha gram would help promote scientific achieveme and thus bolster the regime's legitimacy prior Kim Il Sung to his son, Kim Jong Il. Many in th gram, reportedly under the control of the your tant to him for this reason. His role in the prog his position in the government, and the po weapons may have been attractive to a leader the first time. The only means of undermining vince Kim Jong Il and his supporters that their p doned the nuclear program through both the pro contacts if they did so and threats of sanctions

Fifth and finally, the possession of nuclear we North to reduce its dependence on China and R dom of independent action.[16] This was an especi fall of 1991, by which time the Soviet Union ha tions with the South for a year and, through the c coup, been placed in the hands of more radica Moscow's former military alliance with Pyongy again assumed the character of a security issue; t in the absence of its former ally and in the face the South. Addressing the North's general securi the best means of reducing the North's need for drive for independence.[17]

Together these five reasons provide a tapestry North Korea to desire nuclear weapons. None of are the products of history. This chapter reviews th Korean nuclear weapons program in order to u scope and nature of these motives.

U.S. NUCLEAR THREATS

The first, and potentially most significant, influenc thinking came from U.S. threats to use nuclear South. United States foreign and defense policies i nuclear weapons during the 1950s and 1960s, and

North Korean advance, and nuclear-tipped Nike Hercules antiaircraft missiles. Like U.S. forces throughout the world, U.S. units in South Korea became thoroughly nuclearized.[25]

United States nuclear weapons remained a focus of North Korean concerns. Kim Il Sung, like Mao Zedong and other leaders of states without nuclear arsenals, attempted to put forward a brave face. In 1963 he declared that "We have to fortify our entire country. By doing so, we can defeat those who have atomic weapons even though we do not possess them ourselves."[26] And the North Korean military prepared for nuclear attack by burrowing deep into the ground.[27] Nonetheless, North Korean leaders must have recognized—as did the Chinese—that these were at best halfway measures. As long as the United States enjoyed a nuclear monopoly on the Korean Peninsula, North Korea would operate at a fatal disadvantage in war. North Korean statements reiterated these concerns through the mid-1970s.[28]

The cumulative result of these U.S. policies was to confront North Korea with a real and growing nuclear threat. This would have been especially troublesome to the North if its strategy were offensive: the closer they came to success in their efforts to provoke a revolution in the South, officials in Pyongyang may have believed, the more real was the danger that the United States might be tempted to use nuclear weapons to stave off defeat. This prospect must have energized North Korea's search for the ultimate deterrent—not, probably, to use preemptively against the South, but to forestall U.S. nuclear use in the event of a revolutionary or conventional war.

THE NORTH AND ITS ALLIES

During this same period, tensions between North Korea and its principal allies, China and the Soviet Union, could well have provided the North Korean government with another powerful reason to seek nuclear weapons. Although North Korea is sometimes portrayed as confidently and adroitly playing Moscow and Beijing off each other, in fact the Sino-Soviet split and recurrent mistrust in each part of the triangular relationship has often left Pyongyang in a vulnerable position. By the 1960s the Soviet Union and China may have seemed to Pyongyang to be too far apart to be properly "balanced" and too surly to be reliable partners. As two RAND Corporation analysts have noted, North Korea "is in a fundamentally weak and disadvantageous position vis-à-vis its powerful neighbors. It needs much from them, but has little to offer in return. . . . Far from a North Korean tail wagging the Russian or Chinese dog, therefore, North Korea has constantly had to scramble to adjust to policies of the USSR or the PRC which are often adopted for reasons having nothing to do with Pyongyang but which have an important effect upon it."[29] Over time, the uncertainty and dependence inherent in this position may have sparked a search for the supreme independent deterrent—a nuclear arsenal.[30]

From the very beginning, Kim Il Sung is said to have recognized that he could not trust his revolution in the hands of any outside power, and he insisted on a significant degree of autonomy. Before the Korean War, Kim reportedly argued to Stalin that the United States would not respond to a Soviet-backed North Korean thrust south; when Kim was proved wrong, he lost much credibility in Moscow.[31] In December 1955, Kim formally introduced the concept of *juche,* or self-reliance, which would become the guiding principle of his government—and he did so, according to a number of North Korea watchers, because the growing vilification of Stalin and pro-détente sentiment in Moscow threatened the partnership between North Korea and the Soviet Union. Kim's biographer Suh Dae Sook refers to the whole concept of *juche* as Kim's "effort to find Korean identity as a counterweight to Soviet influence."[32] *Juche* has a military component—*jawi,* the principle of military self-defense. According to Suh, *jawi* "demands that every state build military forces on its own and not depend on the military forces of other countries."[33]

Kim Il Sung tasted the capriciousness of Soviet and Chinese policy shortly thereafter. At the Third Party Congress of the Korean Workers' Party (KWP) in April 1956, Soviet and to a lesser extent Chinese officials backed Kim's opponents in disputes over the proper shape of North Korean economic modernization. Representing the Khrushchev government that had just weeks before denounced Stalin's repression and personality cult, Soviet delegates— led by future leader Leonid Brezhnev—promoted Kim's rivals and called for a "collective" leadership in the North. When Kim left the country that summer, the pro-Soviet and pro-Chinese factions in his government openly challenged him. On his return he purged most of his opponents from the government, relying on the support of political allies from his guerrilla days in Manchuria; but in an extraordinary step, Soviet and Chinese officials allegedly traveled to Pyongyang and forced him to reinstate the rebels.[34] Eventually Kim managed to force them out and consolidate his rule, but he had learned an important lesson about the uneven reliability of his patrons.

After a period of consolidation and calm in the later 1950s, North Korean perceptions of threat may have grown again beginning in 1962. Through 1961, Pyongyang had tried to remain neutral in the simmering Sino-Soviet dispute, hoping to retain the favor of both.[35] In July 1961, Kim signed mutual defense treaties with China and the Soviet Union respectively. By 1962, however, having apparently decided that Moscow was fundamentally untrustworthy, Kim tilted toward China. His reasons were probably varied: continued anger at Moscow's forceful intervention in North Korean domestic politics, fear that the Soviet Union might suddenly abandon him as it did China in 1960, and disappointment at Moscow's apparent unwillingness to confront U.S. military power in the Taiwan Straits and in Cuba.[36] Believing that the Soviet Union had capitulated to the United States during the recent Cuban missile crisis, officials in Pyongyang apparently worried that they would face the same fate as Fidel Castro—abandonment—if they confronted the United States again.[37] In 1962, Kim backed China in its war against Soviet-sponsored India, and the North Korean press stepped up its criticisms of Soviet policies. Through 1963 and 1964, Moscow and Pyongyang traded harsh rhetoric, and Khrushchev canceled virtually all aid to North Korea.[38]

China had withdrawn its troops from North Korea in 1958, and Kim's army relied heavily on the Soviet Union for military equipment and supplies. Meanwhile, with U.S. help, South Korea had moved rapidly ahead in developing a modern army, and arguably achieved military superiority on the peninsula by the early 1970s. Concerns in Pyongyang about the South's burgeoning military power must have been exacerbated by the Park Chung Hee coup in South Korea on May 16, 1961: North Korea had little idea what to expect from a South whose peaceful, reform-oriented government had been overthrown and whose military leaders had seized power. A South Korean strike north was not out of the question, and part of Kim's response was to sign mutual defense pacts with China and the Soviet Union within two months of Park's coup.

The situation clearly demanded a North Korean response, and in December 1962 Pyongyang announced that it would henceforth place "equal emphasis" on military preparedness and economic development. The North began to spend roughly one-third of its budget on its military and instituted a vast program of militarization that fortified the whole country, required up to five years of mandatory military service without leave, and formed a huge militia that drew in virtually the entire able-bodied population. New arms factories were built and hidden in huge underground dugouts. This immense effort strained the North Korean economy to the breaking point, but Kim and his aides were apparently convinced that drastic measures were required.[39] Significantly, Kim asserted the importance of *juche* in the military field, suggesting that the North needed a capability to produce locally the basic elements of defense.

This buildup continued through the 1980s, and may have gradually placed the North somewhat more at ease about its position. And in 1965, Pyongyang and Moscow managed to patch up their frayed relationship: in February of that year, new Soviet Premier Alexei Kosygin led a high-level delegation to Pyongyang, and eventually Soviet aid returned. The relationship was not always rosy. In the late 1960s, Kim's regime lashed out at U.S. intelligence systems, taking hostage the USS *Pueblo* and its crew and shooting down a U.S. EC-121 reconnaissance plane; both moves outraged Soviet leaders, then engaged in the first stages of their planned détente with the United States. North Korea responded with blasts at Moscow in the party newspaper *Nodong Sinmun,* and Moscow retaliated by reducing its economic aid. The Soviet policy of peaceful coexistence was to Kim "unthinkable heresy" when applied to the Korean Peninsula. Nonetheless, until the mid-1970s, Soviet–North Korean relations remained on a reasonably even keel.[40]

The same was not true of Pyongyang's ties to China, which entered their first period of crisis during the Chinese Cultural Revolution of the late 1960s. Chinese and North Korean publications dueled over various ideological questions, and military units from the two nations actually exchanged fire several times between 1967 and 1969 over a disputed border area. By April 1970, Zhou Enlai was in Pyongyang in an effort to repair the friendship, but the late 1960s were another period of security crisis for North Korea. In 1969, China and the Soviet Union clashed at the Amur River, while Soviet–North Korean disputes over Moscow's policy of détente reached perhaps their most troublesome level since 1965. And some North Korean officials worried that same year about Japan, which they felt might join or supplant the United States as sponsor of the South and become a major new threat.[41] In sum, the tangled history of North Korea's relations with its sponsors kept Pyongyang constantly on edge about its security—and on the lookout for a reliable security guarantee.

AN EMBRYONIC NUCLEAR PROGRAM

Various reports suggest that while the U.S. nuclear threat to North Korea grew and the North's position in Sino-Soviet machinations remained fluid, the North's embryonic nuclear program slowly took shape. From the end of the Korean War to 1970, the program's history can be traced in light of the external threat to Kim's regime and its perceived need for additional security guarantees. This process appears to have accelerated during the early 1960s, when the North experienced a major security crisis. Kim Chong Min, a North Korean defector and reportedly former high-level official in the North Korean Ministry of Public Security, contends that Pyongyang's serious interest in nuclear weapons began in the first half of the 1960s—just after Kim's December 1962 call for nationwide military preparedness.[42]

Even before the Korean War, Soviet scientists were reportedly scouring North Korea for uranium-bearing Mozanite sand. Very quickly after the war, the North initiated its work on what was ostensibly a civilian nuclear power program. In June 1955, North Korean scientists participated in an East European Scientific Conference on the peaceful uses of nuclear energy. In 1956, the North concluded two agreements with Moscow that provided Soviet support for Pyongyang's nuclear research. Those agreements were expanded and matched by similar accords with China in 1959. During this period, the Soviet Union trained North Korean technicians at its Dubna Nuclear Research Institute in Moscow.[43] Working together at North Korea's Academy of Sciences, North Korean and Soviet scholars established a nuclear research facility at Yongbyon, about sixty miles north of Pyongyang, in 1964.[44] That same year, the North began a major uranium mining survey and discovered vast indigenous sources of the raw material for nuclear reactions. Kim Il Sung's nuclear infrastructure was ready for a major expansion.

The year 1965 may have been the first watershed in the history of the North Korean nuclear program. In the wake of the February Kosygin visit, Soviet assistance to the North resumed, and by June the North had received a small, two- to four-megawatt Soviet research reactor. The design was an early one, using 10 to 20 percent enriched uranium and a distilled water cooling and speed moderating system. This was quickly installed at Yongbyon, along with a 0.1 megawatt nuclear research lab called a "critical facility," and formed the core of the North's nuclear program for two decades. The reactor began operations, it is believed, in 1967. Ten years later, in July 1977, in a move that was not widely reported, North Korean officials signed an International Atomic Energy Agency (IAEA) "Type 66" safeguards accord and opened the small research plant for inspection. Most recently, IAEA officials examined the plant in May 1988 and again in June 1989, and as a result of this relationship, IAEA officials were actually assisting the North with uranium mining at Pyongsan even as the world fretted about the risk of a North Korean bomb.[45]

As far as is known outside North Korea, during the remainder of the 1960s North Korean scientists labored away at the small power plant at Yongbyon. The area was cordoned off, barred to entry by foreigners and even North Koreans not working directly on the program. Gradually the North managed to boost the power of its first, small nuclear reactor. But it eventually came under IAEA inspection, and, for a time at least, caused little concern in Washington or Seoul.[46]

THE THREAT OF A SOUTH KOREAN BOMB

In the late 1960s, North Korea was in the midst of what it might have believed to be a major challenge to its security. Its relations with China had hit rock bottom, and though ties with Moscow were amicable on the surface, serious tensions persisted over the Soviet pursuit of détente and the policy of peaceful coexistence. Meanwhile, U.S. nuclear weapons and the Park Chung Hee regime stood menacingly to the south, and Pyongyang entertained new worries about the role of Japan. Once again, circumstances provided North Korean leaders with the motive to take dramatic measures to augment their security.

One element of this response was to take a softer line toward Seoul, engaging the South in bilateral discussions during the early 1970s. Contacts between North and South Korean Red Cross societies led to political talks and a joint communiqué on peaceful reunification dated July 4, 1972. Further meetings were less successful, however, and North Korea suspended the dialogue indefinitely in August 1973 and rejected President Park's proposal for dual membership in the United Nations.[47] Nonetheless, the talks succeeded in reducing tensions, and, significantly, the North had chosen to avoid provocations for a period of several years, remaining on the strategic defensive while its security position was clarified.

By this time, however, a new threat had appeared: strong indications emerged that South Korea might build a nuclear arsenal of its own. Ironically, the late 1960s and early 1970s were a period of security crisis for Seoul as well as Pyongyang. The U.S. withdrawal from Vietnam appeared to signal a U.S. departure from direct involvement in Asian affairs. President Richard Nixon entered into negotiations with Seoul on reducing the level of U.S. forces in South Korea, and a total of 24,000 U.S. troops were withdrawn by 1973.[48] Under the Nixon or Guam Doctrine of 1968, Washington instructed U.S. allies to take primary responsibility for their own defense, while the United States offered arms transfers, naval and air support, and a nuclear backstop. To South Koreans, troop withdrawal symbolized the reduction of the U.S. commitment and a deteriorating regional security environment.[49] U.S. overtures to China further worried the South Korean military about the U.S. dedication to providing a nuclear umbrella.

In response, Seoul not only undertook active lobbying in Washington for continued support—a process that would end in the "Koreagate" scandal of the late 1970s—but also increased efforts at military self-reliance. One South Korean general told an American analyst that President Park Chung Hee "decided upon a secret 'Master Plan' for producing nuclear weapons in 1970 following President Nixon's announcement of possible U.S. force withdrawals from Korea under the 'Guam Doctrine.'"[50] In 1971, President Park reportedly ordered his Weapons Exploitation Committee to explore the possibility of producing an indigenous nuclear arsenal.[51] Park also initiated an ambitious $5 billion Force Improvement Plan (FIP), which increased the percentage of South

Korea's gross national product devoted to defense from 5 percent to 7.5 percent per year and included plans for modern fighter aircraft, upgraded tank forces, acquisition of high technology U.S. antitank missiles, and domestic production of small arms.[52]

South Korea, therefore, had the motive to acquire nuclear weapons to replace the fading U.S. security commitment. It also possessed the means: a modern and growing nuclear power industry.[53] A former high-ranking Korean government official told a U.S. House subcommittee in February 1978 that the Weapons Exploitation Committee

> voted unanimously to proceed with the development of nuclear weapons. Subsequently, the Korean Government discussed purchase of a nuclear fuel reprocessing facility from France and a mixed-oxide fuel reprocessing lab from Belgium. The explosion of an Indian nuclear device in April 1974 using fissionable material produced with the assistance of a Canadian NRX research reactor led to greater caution by nuclear technology suppliers, however, and the Belgians and the Canadians withdrew offers for certain technology. Negotiations between the ROK and France continued for some time over a reprocessing facility.[54]

Like North Korea, South Korea took a variety of steps to reassure the world community that it only meant to use nuclear technology for peaceful purposes.[55]

By 1976, South Korea's scientists seemed to have the theoretical knowledge and technical expertise to build nuclear devices. One South Korean lawmaker would later claim that President Park had once told him the work "was making 95 percent progress."[56] Without an ability to check their work through test explosions, however, they were limited to simple designs; the risk of being caught ruled tests out as a practical measure.[57] Difficulties in manufacturing nuclear weapons, however, may have been less of a concern if the South's intention was not actually to build them, but merely to wring concessions out of the United States and to halt a perceived U.S. disengagement from the peninsula. Like other latent nuclear states, South Korea certainly was able to gain leverage over the United States, and as a result, access to a wide range of advanced technologies as the United States tried to discourage nuclear development.[58]

The United States learned of the South Korean nuclear weapons effort shortly after India's 1974 nuclear test, and Washington quickly focused on the task of convincing Seoul to end its nascent program.[59] On June 12, 1974, the *Washington Post* reported President Park Chung Hee's remarks that South Korea could produce nuclear weapons, but would refrain so long as the U.S. nuclear umbrella remained over Korea.[60] A year later, U.S. Defense Secretary

James Schlesinger tried to end further discussion of South Korea's nuclear option by stating that the U.S. nuclear umbrella covered Korea. United States Secretary of State Henry Kissinger reportedly halted a French–South Korean reprocessing deal and the weapons program that same year by threatening to cancel the U.S. security commitment to South Korea. South Korea finally gave in late that year after the United States threatened to withhold financial credits for the South Korean nuclear power industry.[61] The Korean government official who gave information to the U.S. Congress testified that "by some time in 1975, any ROK nuclear weapons program had been canceled and the negotiations for purchase of a fuel reprocessing facility also ended."[62]

Strong U.S. support for the South continued, after an initial signal in the opposite direction, during the Carter administration.[63] Even so, hints circulated that while South Korea abided by the nonproliferation agreement, it was still contemplating nuclear weapons acquisition. On June 12, 1975, less than a month after ratifying the Nonproliferation Treaty (NPT), President Park Chung Hee declared that "if the U.S. nuclear umbrella were to be removed, we [would] have to start developing our nuclear capability."[64] South Koreans used the threat to deter any other U.S. plans to reduce its forces in Korea. In these events we find confirmation of one widely cited motive for pursuing nuclear weapons: they provide leverage against countries that oppose their acquisition. North Korean leaders would learn the same lesson in the early 1990s.

THE NORTH REACTS

North Korea appears to have responded to the threat of a South Korean bomb in four distinct but complementary ways. It moved to reaffirm ties with and obtain new security pledges from traditional allies. It once again publicly denounced the importance of nuclear weapons and claimed an ability to defend itself comfortably without them. It expanded its formal commitment to nonproliferation, hoping to encourage—or force—the South to do the same. And the North continued work on its own nuclear weapons program, beginning work on the large reactor at Yongbyon that would cause so much concern in the 1980s and 1990s.

North Korea turned first to its oldest and arguably most reliable ally, China. During his April 1975 trip to Beijing,[65] Kim Il Sung reportedly requested Zhou Enlai's support in establishing a North Korean nuclear weapons program and discouraging U.S. nuclear threats against North Korea by placing it under the People's Republic of China's (PRC) "nuclear umbrella." Available evidence suggests that although China's reaction was somewhat unenthusiastic, it did provide significant assistance, including an expansion of training for North

Korean nuclear scientists and technicians. The extent of the nuclear weapons related technology transfer, however, is unknown.[66] Later, Kim Il Sung sent KWP Secretary Kang Song San to visit China's Lop Nur nuclear test and research facility in March of 1977. During his visit, Kang attended a reception hosted by the Seventh Ministry of Machine Building, the ministry responsible for PRC ballistic missile development.[67]

A second line of response, particularly when the North was again the target of explicit U.S. nuclear threats (as in 1975), was to deny the importance of nuclear weapons. Kim Il Sung played down the nuclear threat: "Even if war burst forth in Korea," he argued, the United States "would not be able to use nuclear weapons. How can they use nuclear weapons here in Korea when friend and foe will grapple [with] each other? Should the enemy use nuclear weapons he will also get killed."[68] Ironically, Soviet Foreign Minister Eduard Shevardnadze used these same arguments with North Korean officials in 1990 when threatened with the North's intention to complete work on nuclear weapons.

Officials in Pyongyang also apparently hoped that a more open commitment to international nonproliferation agreements would be useful in building world pressure against the South. These steps were necessary to provide cover for the North's ally, the Soviet Union, which as a party to the NPT was prohibited from supplying nuclear materials that might be used for weapons production. North Korea joined the IAEA in September 1974, a move probably calculated to create an image of compliance among members of the international community and magnify world pressure on South Korea to abandon its own nuclear program.[69] North Korea's reactions to individual South Korean moves are instructive: when in July 1977, for example, the South Korean National Assembly endorsed the development of a more explicit capability to produce nuclear weapons,[70] the North responded by signing the "Type 66" agreement with the IAEA that provides for inspection of its small reactor.[71] Once again, Pyongyang may have hoped to convince the South and the world that it was complying with nonproliferation norms and to paint the South as the nation intent on bringing nuclear weapons to the peninsula.

During this period, work on the North Korean nuclear program continued, work that would eventually produce a second, much larger reactor at Yongbyon and growing world concerns about North Korean proliferation. In the mid-1970s, North Korea reportedly negotiated with the Soviet Union over the purchase of additional nuclear reactors, and North Korean scientists continued training at Moscow's Dubna Nuclear Research Institute.[72] Eventually, Pyongyang would convince Moscow to supply a larger graphite reactor, which would be installed at Yongbyon in the early 1980s and would become the focus of the world's concern.

Perhaps because of its relatively primitive level of technological sophistication, however, North Korea was seldom cited during this period as a notable
proliferation risk. Given the clear levels of Soviet and Chinese support and the
North's expanding nuclear infrastructure, this omission seems, in retrospect,
difficult to understand. Whatever the reason, North Korea continued its nuclear
research—whether directed to weapons development or not—far from the prying eyes of Western inspection or intelligence agencies.

THE COMING TRANSFER OF POWER

Another growing concern for North Korea during the 1970s was the planned
succession of power from Kim Il Sung to his son, Kim Jong Il. That succession, organized during the 1970s and fully in view by the Sixth Congress
of the Korean Workers' Party in October 1980,[73] was well underway by the
mid-1980s. North Korean leaders might have believed that, for a number of
reasons, the fate of the succession was intimately tied up with their evolving nuclear program. And with the death of Kim Il Sung in July 1994 (an
event discussed in chapter 8) their concerns on this score took on very immediate relevance.

North Korea's succession carries special importance because it seems to be,
in the eyes of Pyongyang's elite, the ultimate expression of *juche*. It would
insulate the North from the pressures of the superpowers, even those from former allies such as China and the Soviet Union. "The Kim succession," a
North Korean academic told Arizona State professor Jo Yung Hwan in 1979,
"would not only save [North Korea] from a post-Stalin or post-Mao type of
crisis, but would also prevent remnants of the pro-Soviet or pro-Chinese factions from requesting intervention or assistance from either Moscow or
Beijing." The Kim Jong Il succession, underway now at the time of this writing, may represent "the core of North Korea's 'survival politics.'"[74]

As much as two decades before Kim Il Sung's death, leaders in North
Korea must therefore have seen anything that would promote the succession
as a top priority. And the North Korean nuclear program almost certainly came
to be viewed in just such a context.

To begin with, the primary challenge facing a Kim Jong Il regime would be
legitimacy. The younger Kim is rumored to be an odd sort, mistrustful, arbitrary, brutal, obsessed with movies, addicted to late-night partying.[75] He is
widely believed to enjoy little loyalty among Pyongyang's elite (although there
is hardly any evidence to substantiate this claim) and many observers—
including prominent North Korea watchers in Beijing and Seoul—have long
predicted that his rule would be short-lived. Indeed, as will be noted in chap-

ter 8, his actual ascension to power in 1994 was greeted with skepticism and persistent rumors that he would not take the helm in the North.

Well before July 1994, Kim Jong Il and his allies may certainly have considered nuclear weapons as an important adjunct to his legitimacy. A nuclear-armed North Korea would enjoy much greater importance and leverage in the international community, and such power might be seen by some in Pyongyang to offset what they believe to be the younger Kim's shortcomings: lack of political legitimacy, poor governing skills, and the absence of a military background.

Of course, nuclear weapons themselves would not justify one regime over another, for even if the younger Kim were toppled the North would still have its nuclear arsenal. In order to benefit Kim Jong Il's standing, therefore, the drive for the bomb would have to be combined with adroit international bargaining, ostensibly under the younger Kim's control, to make that nuclear arsenal work to the North's benefit. Kim Jong Il would thus be seen as the leader who could use the threat of a nuclear arsenal to preserve the North Korean regime. North Korea's stubborn back-and-forth diplomacy of 1993, with its demands for ever-greater concessions and its threats of war, has all the hallmarks of such an approach, and occurred just at a time when the formal transfer of power between the Kims was nearly at hand.[76]

In using the nuclear card to obtain concessions, Kim Jong Il would probably be after the two things of most importance to his regime: a reduction of the U.S. presence on the peninsula and increased economic interaction with the outside world. The issue of the U.S. nuclear and conventional presence in South Korea was examined earlier. If Kim Jong Il could strike a deal that would further reduce the U.S. threat to the North, he would gain added legitimacy.

But perhaps of most immediate importance was the state of the North's economy. By the early 1990s, with the collapse of the Soviet Union and a reduction in Chinese aid, North Korea's economic performance had slowed to a crawl. In 1992, by a number of reports, it contracted nearly 8 percent, and in late 1993 North Korean officials made unprecedented statements confirming the economic crisis they faced. If the younger Kim could play the nuclear card to gain outside investments in the North's planned special economic zones, Japanese reparations payments, and the surge of South Korean investment many observers have expected for several years, he would put the North Korean regime's future on a much sounder footing. And inasmuch as "reformist technocrats" are often viewed as Kim's primary challengers after the succession,[77] improving the North's economic performance would also do much to preserve Kim Jong Il's political fortunes.

The coming succession crisis in North Korea, and the attendant importance of such factors as regime pride and legitimacy and economic progress, may therefore have endowed the North Korean nuclear program with added significance beginning in the 1970s.

JUSTIFICATIONS FOR THE BOMB

By 1980, then, North Korea perceived itself to be standing alone, trapped between the Sino-Soviet conflict to the north, the Sino-American alignment to the west and Japan to the east, and over half a million hostile soldiers to the south. A North Korean spokesperson told an Italian delegation in February, "If we do not make the correct moves, we run the risk of being crushed or sold."[78]

To conclude that North Korea's nuclear program was solely a response to U.S. nuclear threats may be too simple a statement. There are hints of North Korea trying, through nuclear arms, to obtain a diplomatic leverage, to reduce dependence on China and Russia, to gain an edge over South Korea's coming conventional superiority, made nearly inevitable by the South's rapidly growing economy, and to set the stage for the first hereditary transfer of power in history by a Communist regime.[79] These factors, however, can be classified broadly as a reaction to a looming danger. United States nuclear threats, in light of the instability of North Korea's alliance with China and the Soviet Union, and the superiority of the combined South Korean and U.S. conventional forces, may well have convinced the North that a nuclear program was a strategic necessity.

More broadly, we are left with the five potential motives for pursuing the bomb—and the occasionally intractable dilemmas in responding to those motives—noted at the outset of this chapter. North Korea may have been interested in nuclear weapons, among other reasons, to counterbalance U.S. nuclear forces, provide a hedge against South Korean conventional superiority, acquire leverage in the world community, give muscle and legitimacy to its regime (especially just before, during, and for some time after a succession of power), and gain a measure of independence from its Soviet and Chinese sponsors. Any nonproliferation strategy aimed at the Korean Peninsula would have to come to grips with each of these issues, reassuring the North in some cases and threatening it in others. It was, to be sure, a vexing task.

Vexing, but not impossible—for what the North needed, in particular, from the international community was trade and some degree of political acceptance. And this fact gave other countries substantial counterleverage over the North just at the moment when such influence was badly needed. The North had long represented perfectly Korea's traditional nickname of the "Hermit Kingdom," but officials in Pyongyang may by the mid-1980s have decided that only through expanded contacts with the outside world could their reclusive, stagnant society (and, by extension, their political system) survive. The North needed the outside world as badly as the world needed the North to abandon its nuclear program, and this mutual dependence created the possibility of a successful nonproliferation strategy.

Pyongyang thus hoped to guarantee its military security on the one hand while promoting economic advancement on the other. Both were necessary for regime survival; neither alone would be sufficient. North Korea's decision, increasingly evident over the next decade, was apparently to try to finesse the issue by doing both—acquiring nuclear weapons *and* improving its relations with the outside world. One South Korean observer described the result in late 1993.

> The truth may be that Pyongyang is seeking obviously contradictory policy goals at once. On the one hand, it develops nuclear bombs for no more complicated purpose than to defend its increasingly rickety regime with it. On the other, it desperately needs to improve its relations with its neighbors, . . . to escape international isolation and lessen its economic hardship. More importantly, it appears that despite the repeated, unambiguous admonition to the contrary from Seoul and the United States, Pyongyang has believed it possible to achieve both policy goals at the same time. In other words, Pyongyang has so far believed that it could cheat.[80]

The next five chapters essentially offer the story of the outside world's efforts to grapple with these two policy goals.

In this two-track policy, North Korean leaders may actually have been able to convince themselves that they were not "cheating" per se. Many aspects of nuclear research and technologies related to a nuclear program are fully acceptable under the NPT. For example, the production and stockpiling of plutonium is not prohibited; that plutonium must merely be declared to the IAEA. Japan is a member in good standing of the treaty, and yet no one doubts that in the future it will possess large amounts of plutonium and be able to assemble a nuclear arsenal in short order if it chooses to do so. Over time, a few people may even begin to wonder how far Japan has moved along that road. But as long as Japan adheres to the terms of the treaty and honestly declines to construct any operable nuclear weapons, it will face no sanctions. As one observer has concluded, the NPT "legally allows signatories to do everything but the very last step of putting fissile material into a bomb shell."[81]

North Korea may have hoped to toe this same line, remaining faithful to the letter of the NPT while assassinating its spirit by developing a capability to have a nuclear arsenal. But for all Pyongyang's hopes to finesse the issue of NPT membership, the tensions and contradictions of its approach slowly became apparent over the next thirteen years. North Korea wanted the world to know that it had a latent nuclear capability, for deterrent and prestige purposes, but also hoped that the world community would never acquire conclusive evidence of such a capability. With one hand it welcomed and applauded international inspectors, while with the other it worked to hide its nuclear facilities and delay the inspection process. The basic dilemmas inherent in this approach would emerge in 1993, when the two faces of North Korea's nuclear policy collided head-on.

■ 3 ■

THE MEANS, 1980–1990

In the spring of 1989, a U.S. intelligence team traveled to South Korea to brief officials on North Korea's progress in nuclear weapons.[1] Although concern about the North's nuclear research had been growing since the mid-1980s, it was only recently that U.S. intelligence had noticed disturbing signs that the North was more serious about the bomb than Seoul or Washington had thought. U.S. intelligence experts and government officials were coming to share what they knew and begin the process of coordinating a more energetic response with Seoul.

The briefing was intended for a small number of top-ranking South Korean leaders. Unable to contain the explosive topic to principals, however, and faced with each ministry and agency's demand to be included, the South Korean side eventually staged the event in front of a large audience. The U.S. intelligence experts were shocked; they had come to discuss some of their most sensitive secrets, highly classified information gathered from U.S. spy satellites, and had no desire to do so with such a large number of people.

In the end, the American side made the decision to go ahead with the briefing in a sanitized form. And it was in that fashion that it appeared in most major South Korean daily newspapers the next day, having been leaked almost immediately.

The basic facts offered in the briefing were stunning and frightening. North Korea was building a plutonium reprocessing facility, the U.S. experts said, one of the telltale signs of a nuclear weapons program. North Korea's nuclear power program appeared, after all, to be the basis of a nuclear arsenal. And it was now left to Seoul and Washington to find a way to stop it.

MAKING A BOMB

Washington's growing interest in the North Korean nuclear program stemmed from the rapidly accelerating nuclear research in the North. During the 1970s and 1980s, North Korea continued to work on its growing nuclear program. The early 1980s were a considerably ambitious time for Pyongyang: during this period, the North constructed a large second nuclear reactor at Yongbyon to complement the small research reactor it had obtained from the Soviet Union in 1965. Once discovered, this second reactor immediately began to raise concerns in the West. It was much larger than an average research plant, yet was not attached to any power grid that would allow it to serve as an energy producer. It was also of a design nuclear engineers considered most suitable for one deadly task—making plutonium, a by-product of a nuclear reactor that is a favorite material of bomb builders.

During this same period, more disturbing evidence emerged of a growing North Korean interest in nuclear weapons. Other elements of a nuclear weapons program—an explosive detonation site to test nuclear warhead designs, various secret military facilities, and eventually a plutonium reprocessing plant—began appearing on satellite photos. And North Korean defectors talked of covert plans to produce nuclear weapons, based at Yongbyon and elsewhere. Taken together, these revelations led directly to an international campaign aimed at ending the North's nuclear ambitions.

As the outside world began to take notice of North Korea's nuclear work, Pyongyang's own thinking about the justifications for its nuclear program may have been changing. As the U.S. nuclear threat receded, both as a product of the end of the Cold War and because of such concessions as the withdrawal of U.S. tactical nuclear weapons from the South, nuclear motives related to the North's economic gain and the cementing of its father-son succession appeared to gain added prominence. These motives added new layers of complexity to the nuclear program and created new barriers to a successful U.S. nonproliferation policy.

As concern over North Korea's nuclear research grew in the West, speculation centered on how the North might be trying to build a bomb, and how close it might be to producing nuclear weapons. Even as this book is being written, nearly a decade after the United States first pressured the Soviet Union to gain North Korea's agreement to the NPT, there are no firm answers to these questions. A broad analysis of the rudiments of nuclear proliferation does, however, provide a few clues.

In essence, a nuclear explosion is a complex—and very noticeable—way of converting mass into energy.[2] In a nuclear reaction, atoms, prompted by bombarding neutrons, split into two or more parts. This splitting, or "fission-ing," creates both energy and neutrons that shoot off and split more atoms. The result is a chain reaction five million times more explosive than chemically based explosives like TNT. When exploded through fission, a softball-sized piece of plutonium can level a city. To date only two substances have proved generally practical for use as the fissioning material: Uranium 235 (U-235) and Plutonium 239 (Pu-239). Both substances must be manufactured: U-235 does not exist in nature in the concentration necessary to produce a nuclear explo-sion; Pu-239 does not exist in nature at all. Producing either or both of these substances thus becomes the first task of any proliferant.

Of the two, U-235 is generally thought to be more challenging to make. On average, about seven-tenths of one percent of natural uranium ore is U-235. Separating out most of the ore's other components is not too difficult, but one other uranium particle poses a special challenge: U-238, which differs from U-235 by only a tiny amount of mass. The material U-238 is deadly to nuclear bomb designers, because it absorbs neutrons and slows down, rather than speeds up, the nuclear reaction. Because the two cannot be distinguished chemically, they must be pulled apart with incredibly sensitive systems that rely on the tiny difference in mass.

In the Manhattan Project, U.S. scientists used, among others, a method known as gaseous diffusion to achieve this goal. Uranium, in the form of a gas (UF_6), was forced through a porous barrier; because the rate of seepage, or dif-fusion, depends on mass, the U-235 seeps through just a little faster than its cousin, U-238. The trick was that, each time this was done, the uranium was only enriched—made more purely into U-235—by a tiny amount. It took some four thousand separate diffusions in order to turn natural uranium into weapons-grade material with a purity of more than 90 percent U-235. This process was hugely expensive and required thousands of megawatts of power to operate. It was also immensely challenging: the UF_6 gas was highly cor-rosive, and the porous barriers proved extremely time-consuming to perfect.

The difficulty of this and other uranium enrichment techniques has led one observer to conclude that "a country with limited scientific and technical resources is very unlikely to be able to design and build a workable [uranium] enrichment facility because of the tremendous complexity not only of the chemical and industrial processes involved but also the extraordinary materi-als science required."[3] This conclusion needs to be qualified in light of Iraq's eventual success in centrifuge technologies. Nonetheless, uranium enrich-ment remains an expensive, difficult, painstaking process that demands a con-siderable degree of scientific and industrial sophistication. Iraq had broad access to Western technology; most proliferants without such access have chosen the plutonium route. The question of a possible North Korean uranium bomb will be considered in more detail later.

Recognizing the daunting challenge involved in uranium enrichment, scientists working in the original Manhattan Project turned to Pu-239 as an alternative. This material does not exist at all in nature, and is only produced as the by-product of a nuclear reaction including uranium. During World War II, Manhattan Project scientists had to build primitive nuclear reactors especially for this purpose. Today, however, the world is covered with nuclear power plants that churn out plutonium at very high rates; any nation with a budding nuclear industry could attempt to build a nuclear arsenal to go along with it. This, of course, is the rationale for IAEA inspections—to make sure that civilian power plants are not being covertly used for military purposes.

For two reasons, plutonium reprocessing has commonly been seen as more attractive to proliferants than the manufacture of a uranium bomb. First, plutonium reprocessing may be somewhat easier than uranium enrichment; it does not demand quite the technical complexity, cost, or energy requirements of gaseous diffusion or other uranium enrichment methods. The Indian reprocessing facility was reported to cost $30 million, and others estimate the reprocessing cost of one bomb's worth of plutonium at as little as $1 million to $3 million.[4] Second, even imperfectly reprocessed plutonium will explode. The bang will not be as big as with a pure Pu-239 core, but a sizeable nuclear explosion will result nonetheless. Theoretically, plutonium directly out of a reactor core could simply be fashioned into a weapon and exploded.

The greater attractiveness of the plutonium route may be waning, however, in part because designing a plutonium bomb poses a number of challenges that a uranium bomb avoids. Plutonium is much more difficult to handle, for example. But the primary drawback of the plutonium route relates to the design of the explosive trigger. Uranium is less radioactive than plutonium, and to get a nuclear reaction, one only needs to take two pieces of U-235, neither of which alone would produce a chain reaction, and slam them together very suddenly. Just how suddenly is the key: U-235 reacts slowly enough that a simple "gun" design could be used, in which a piece of conventional high explosive would shoot one piece of U-235 into the other. For Pu-239, however, radiating neutrons at an incredible rate, that system would not work; the two pieces would begin interacting before they hit, producing, at best, a small explosion. What is required is an implosion technique in which the simultaneous detonations of high explosive around the surface of a sphere of Pu-239 are used to compress the sphere to the point where the chain reaction will begin. This task—molding and setting off a high-explosive shell to create a near-perfect spherical shock wave—is extremely demanding. Advanced nations use "krytrons," electrical switches that deliver high-voltage pulses in a fraction of a second, to achieve the simultaneity required. To this day, fifty years after the Manhattan Project, very few nations can master this challenge; most have attempted to steal krytrons rather than produce them indigenously.[5]

This is not an absolute advantage of uranium bombs, however, because many modern-day proliferants prefer to use implosion designs even with uranium cores—although South Africa's nuclear weapons program, for one, used gun-type designs. Iraq's bomb, for example, would have used implosion triggers. The advantage is one of degree: an implosion weapon is far more efficient and deadly, needing only about half as much fissile material to produce the same explosion as a gun design bomb—not an unimportant consideration for an aspiring proliferant struggling mightily to acquire each gram of weapons-grade uranium.

Suppose, then, that a country wanted to produce the raw material for a nuclear arsenal. What route would it take? Unless it possessed advanced technology or the money to buy it—neither of which North Korea has—it might well choose the plutonium route, perhaps inspired by the success of the Indian and Israeli plutonium-based nuclear arsenals and tempted by the related economic benefits of a system of nuclear power plants. It would choose a reactor design that maximized plutonium output and minimized foreign involvement in its nuclear infrastructure, thus reducing its dependence on foreign sources of supply. And, eventually, it would build a plutonium reprocessing facility and a high-explosive test site to develop the Pu-239 and the implosion trigger needed for a plutonium bomb. Then, with time, diligence, and a little luck, the proliferant could count on a steadily growing nuclear arsenal.

North Korea appears to have followed exactly this plan. Its second nuclear reactor at Yongbyon was an indigenously designed, gas-graphite, air-cooled reactor using natural uranium as fuel.[6] The design apparently was drawn from two older European models: the 1958 French G-1 nuclear reactor and the British Calder Hall design of the same period. As proliferation expert Leonard Spector has written, this type of reactor is "well suited to the production of plutonium and has been cited as the logical choice for would-be nuclear states with limited industrial capabilities." The design is especially attractive because it avoids "the need for enriched uranium or heavy water—two commodities that are extremely difficult to produce and which North Korea would have had to import."[7] Both Israel and India used very similar reactors as generators of plutonium for their nuclear programs.[8]

Especially worrisome was the fact that none of North Korea's nuclear reactors appeared to be hooked into any power grids. If not so connected, the reactors could not be used in the traditional role as power plants supplying electricity to surrounding cities and towns. They could only be used for "research," presumably to prepare the way for a set of true, power-generating reactors to come. But the large Yongbyon reactor was much more powerful than the average research reactor, and North Korea already possessed such a research facility in the Soviet-supplied reactor in operation at Yongbyon. The power-grid issue would therefore play an important part in debates about North Korea's nuclear intentions.

By September 1982, recent reports from South Korea suggest, construction was underway on the second reactor's nuclear core and the nuclear control building. By December 1984, the reactor's telltale cylindrical smokestack had taken shape, and other buildings were nearing completion. Finally, on February 5, 1987, it was reported that Western intelligence services had verified that steam was being vented from the reactor's cooling tower, thus confirming that a nuclear reaction was underway and the facility was operational.[9]

DISCOVERY AND PRESSURE TO JOIN THE NPT

Some time in the mid-1980s—it is not known exactly when, but is often reported to have occurred during 1984—a U.S. intelligence satellite, believed to be the super-modern KH-11, made what might have been a routine pass over Yongbyon. The information it brought back must have startled U.S. analysts: clear evidence of the construction of a second reactor at Yongbyon, one big enough, when operating at full power, to produce one bomb's worth of plutonium every year.[10]

There was little that the United States could do on its own about this discovery. What it could do, however, was to use global organizations and international legal standards to force the North to allow outside inspections of the facility. This was the purpose of the International Atomic Energy Agency (IAEA), whose inspectors enforced the terms of the NPT. Once under IAEA inspection, any nuclear facility would be much less dangerous; all available evidence suggests that no nation has been able to smuggle the fissile materials for a bomb project out of a reactor under IAEA safeguards. If the North would allow IAEA inspections, then the worries of U.S., South Korean, and Japanese officials would be considerably eased.

Getting the North to allow inspections would eventually take more than eight years. At first, the difficulty was that North Korea was not a member of the NPT. Like China and other independently minded developing nations, the North argued that the treaty favored developed-world nuclear "haves" over developing-world nuclear "have-nots." So while the North had agreed to IAEA inspections of its small, 1960s-vintage Soviet-supplied reactor, it did so outside the bounds of the NPT itself. And it was not immediately clear what leverage the United States had over the North.

So the United States turned to an ironic source: the Soviet Union. U.S. officials reminded Moscow of its obligations under the Nonproliferation Treaty (the Soviet Union *was* a member) not to transfer nuclear weapons-related technology to third countries, and questioned the use to which North Korea was putting Soviet assistance. Anxious to maintain the Soviet Union's image as a dedicated foe of proliferation, and probably just as keen as their U.S. counterparts on avoiding a North Korean bomb, the Soviets complied. When, therefore, North Korean KWP Secretary Kang Song San visited Moscow in search of trade agreements in December 1985, he reportedly got something more: an insistent Soviet request that the North sign the NPT. To encourage the North to do so, Soviet officials offered to transfer four new 440 megawatt nuclear reactors and help the North set them up.[11] Later, however, Moscow would insist on hard currency payment for the reactors—a demand North Korea was in no position to meet.

On December 12, 1985, Kang signed the NPT in Moscow on behalf of North Korea. Immediately the process became mired in technical disputes. Pyongyang had a grace period of eighteen months to conclude an IAEA safeguards agreement and submit a list of nuclear facilities for inspection. The IAEA, however, appears to have mistakenly sent the wrong kind of agreement at first, one designed for individual sites (a Type 66 agreement) rather than one providing for general inspections (a Type 153).[12] The IAEA provided a correct draft safeguards agreement in June 1987, but again the deadline for North Korean response—December 1988—passed without action.

During the 1980s, the North raised the nuclear issue in a number of public statements. At the Sixth KWP Congress in October 1980, Kim Il Sung repeated the long-standing North Korean demand for a nuclear-free peninsula. By 1986, Pyongyang had extended this request to include tripartite talks (with the South and the United States) on nuclear weapons in Korea. In July 1988, May 1990, and July 1991, North Korea called for the withdrawal of U.S. nuclear forces in the South and for a general agreement to a nuclear-free zone in Korea.[13] Through these statements, North Korea established, at least in principle, its readiness to forgo the nuclear option if certain conditions were met. But its seriousness would not be tested until 1992, when it finally agreed to IAEA inspections.

AN ALTERNATE ROUTE: A URANIUM BOMB?

Inspecting the North's nuclear reactors would provide no guarantee against a North Korean nuclear arsenal if the North took a different approach: fashioning a nuclear force based on uranium. North Korea has vast natural reserves of natural uranium—millions of tons, according to some estimates. If it had a means of purifying the rough natural substance into weapons-grade material, with a purity of 90 percent or more U-235, the North could produce nuclear devices without using a single gram of plutonium from its nuclear reactors.

Some reports have indeed suggested that the North was pursuing this second route. Military analyst Joseph Bermudez warned in September 1991 that the South Korean estimate of a North Korean bomb by the mid-1980s was "based upon the belief that North Korea needs to first process plutonium to produce a nuclear weapon. If, instead, North Korea is pursuing its nuclear weapons programme in the same multiple path fashion as the Iraqis did, and wanted to achieve a nuclear weapons capability sooner, it apparently possesses the scientific, technological and industrial capacity to currently produce a small, crude, enriched uranium bomb."[14] A number of North Korean defectors with access to information on their nuclear program have also claimed to have heard that Pyongyang's engineers were attempting to process uranium into weapons material.[15] One South Korean analyst contends that "every nation seeking nuclear weapons has pursued both paths," and that "it is hardly conceivable that North Korea would rule out the uranium path."[16] After its Osirak nuclear reactor was bombed in 1981, depriving it of its intended source of plutonium, Iraq turned to uranium as the basis of its nuclear program—and came frighteningly close to success.

When one considers each of the possible techniques for uranium enrichment, however, the potential for North Korean work along these lines seems to lessen.[17] Two means of enrichment—centrifuge (as pursued by Iraq) and laser separation—require advanced technologies that North Korea would have had to import. Such shipments probably would not have escaped the notice of Western security agencies, and there are few reports of uranium enrichment-related equipment being shipped to the North. The centrifuge portion of the Iraqi program, for example, depended on "a large foreign procurement network to obtain subcomponents, manufacturing equipment, and classified and unclassified design information."[18] The high-tech carbon fiber rotors that spin inside centrifuges proved especially troublesome to Iraqi engineers. A few nations have used a third technique of uranium reprocessing, "nozzle separation," but this again requires high levels of technical sophistication.[19]

A more likely route might be gaseous diffusion, which requires less technological sophistication than the other means. As previously noted, the Manhattan Project engineers used this technique to produce highly enriched uranium. But gaseous diffusion is very expensive and requires large, conspicuous buildings. And only technologically advanced nations could be expected to master the demanding task of producing workable filters through which the corrosive UF_6 gas must pass.

Finally, North Korea could have employed another technique, also used in the Manhattan Project and later adopted by Iraq: electronmagnetic isotope separation (EMIS). Iraq was able to pursue this route without large amounts of imported technology, and the West might not have found out about it at all had it not been for defecting Iraqi engineers.[20] Machines used for this method are called calutrons. Using huge magnets, calutrons bend a beam of uranium ions; because the lighter U-235 atoms respond more to the magnetic push than U-238, they can be separated and collected. Details of the U.S. calutron efforts during World War II have long been declassified.[21] The drawback of the calutron method is that the magnets soak up vast amounts of electrical power—as much, U.S. officials in the Bush administration were told, as the entire output of the Tennessee Valley Authority.[22] Still, their simplicity of design makes them a tempting route for proliferants, especially ones with a deficient industrial base.

Information we do have about the North's nuclear program, and about comparative ones, indeed suggests that, at least from the perspective of energy requirements, a calutron enrichment process might be within Pyongyang's grasp. One North Korean defector has claimed that the North located some of its nuclear facilities at Yongbyon in part because of the planned Taechon Hydroelectric Plant, which is located near Yongbyon and began construction in October 1986. The defector, Kim Chong Min, contends that one of this plant's major purposes has been to supply electricity to Yongbyon; and, although Kim does not mention this, Taechon could also serve the Pakchon area, just to the southwest of Yongbyon.[23] Iraq's calutron complex in the area of Tuwaitha used some nine electrical generator complexes, each rated at more than thirty megawatts, to supply a reprocessing system capable of producing several hundred grams of weapons-grade uranium annually.[24] North Korea's Taechon hydroelectric plant is reported to produce 760 megawatts of power,[25] more than enough for a simple reprocessing system.[26]

But the North would need far more than just energy to fashion a bomb from uranium. As noted above, uranium enrichment is generally believed to be the more difficult technique for producing weapons-grade materials, especially for a nation as technologically weak as North Korea. And no substantial evidence has emerged that the North has attempted to acquire the necessary technology.

In short, the possibility cannot be ruled out that North Korea could be using a domestically produced gaseous diffusion or electromagnetic separation system (or even imported centrifuges), supported by the North's extensive hydroelectric power network, to enrich uranium and build bombs. The uranium route would be attractive because uranium bombs are amenable to the most rudimentary form of bomb design. Nonetheless, there is no clear evidence, nor even substantial circumstantial indications of any kind, to support such a claim, at least in the unclassified literature.[27] And there are strong reasons to believe that the technical challenges of uranium enrichment may be beyond the capabilities of indigenous North Korean science and industry. International pressure on the North has therefore concentrated on getting access to the North's supply of plutonium, the main reactor at Yongbyon, and on measuring and tracking down the plutonium that the reactor may have produced to date.

THE EVIDENCE MOUNTS

During the late 1980s, a number of other strands of evidence combined to establish a portrait of North Korea as a nation at work on a nuclear arsenal.

China, with close ties to North Korea's civilian nuclear industry, may have noticed this evidence first. A South Korean government official claimed that Chinese representatives had said as much during Seoul-Beijing talks in 1992. The Chinese officials reportedly indicated that, as early as 1987, Beijing was suspicious of North Korea turning its nuclear power research to work on a bomb. China responded, according to these reports, by withdrawing all its nuclear technicians from the North and halting new transfers of nuclear technology.[28]

Whether or not that was true, by the spring of 1989 clear evidence of a North Korean nuclear program was emerging in the West. To some, the most stunning development was evidence that Pyongyang was indeed assembling a plutonium reprocessing plant capable of fashioning the waste from its nuclear reactors into weapons-grade material. In May 1989, the Seoul paper *Joong-ang Ilbo* reported that the U.S. Central Intelligence Agency (CIA) possessed evidence proving that North Korea had built such a reprocessing facility at Yongbyon.[29] Given the North's abundant supply of natural uranium, it had no need for reprocessed fuel; the only logical purpose for a reprocessing facility was to produce nuclear weapons.

More details of the facility gradually emerged.[30] It was huge—some 180 meters in length and 20 meters wide, by sheer size the second largest plutonium reprocessing facility in the world (second only to the U.S. PUREX plant, and significantly larger than Japan's Dokaimura facility). Its size and other features led experts to conclude that it was capable of handling well over 200 tons of spent plutonium per year, far more than could ever be produced at Yongbyon and enough to encompass a large, multi-reactor nuclear system. Although the North for some time denied any interest in reprocessing, when

IAEA Director General Hans Blix visited the building in May 1992 and pronounced it "undoubtedly" a reprocessing facility, the North admitted its work
in the area. For the time being, U.S. officials could be relatively certain that
the facility was not open for business; operational plutonium reprocessing
facilities give off telltale amounts of the radioactive isotope Krypton 85,
which helped the United States track Soviet production of plutonium in the
1950s.[31] Nonetheless, the plant seemed a clear indication of North Korea's sinister motives, and it was this evidence that led U.S. officials to Seoul in the
spring of 1989 to brief the South Korean government, as described at the
beginning of this chapter.

Other evidence raised one more disturbing possibility: the North might
have constructed other, smaller reprocessing facilities. Because the Yongbyon
reprocessing facility was so massive and apparently complex, many observers
assumed that some type of test or pilot facility would have been constructed
first.[32] An IAEA report prepared after Director General Hans Blix's visit in
May 1992 suggested that a quick jump from a radiochemical laboratory to a
massive reprocessing facility on the scale of the Yongbyon building was
"hard to understand for anyone whose thinking is formed by international
experience." "The timetable of operations and the industrial logic," the report
concluded, "seemed to suggest that a small pilot plant should have preceded"
the big Yongbyon facility.[33] Such a pilot facility would not have to have been
very large. Given the North Korean skill at digging, such a facility could easily have been hidden entirely underground, concealed from the prying eyes of
Western intelligence satellites.

Later in the summer of 1989, more troubling news emerged with the discovery of another key element of a nuclear weapons program. In July, the
Korea Times reported the existence of a high-explosive test site at Yongbyon
used to develop the sophisticated explosive casings for nuclear weapons.[34]
By 1992, U.S. and South Korean officials had suggested that the North
had conducted more than seventy explosive tests there.[35] The North's test site
was, to some in the U.S. government, even more disturbing than the reprocessing plant. While reprocessing can be part of a legitimate civilian nuclear
power program, explosive tests are a veritable smoking gun of a nuclear
weapons program.[36]

Finally, that same year, Western intelligence services discovered North
Korean work on a third, even larger nuclear reactor at Yongbyon. This plant was
believed to have been under construction since 1985, and was expected to have
an output of fifty to two hundred megawatts. Like the main Yongbyon reactor it would use natural uranium as fuel, thus eliminating the need for foreign
fuel supplies—and foreign control.[37] If rated at the higher end of the estimated

power levels, this plant would have produced enough plutonium each year for several bombs. And because it, like the second reactor, did not appear to be connected to a power grid, international observers feared that its purpose, too, was the production of material for a nuclear arsenal.

AN OPTIMISTIC THOUGHT: NORTH KOREAN INCOMPETENCE

A few optimistic observers have read the North Korean nuclear program's tea leaves differently. Despite the North's best efforts, they contend, Pyongyang simply could not master the arcana of nuclear weapons design. We have already seen how uranium enrichment might be beyond their grasp. Desperately short of hard currency, receiving little technical support from China and even less from the former Soviet Union, and having only a mediocre corps of scientists and engineers at its disposal, it is possible that by 1990 Pyongyang had never got very close to developing a nuclear bomb at all. But it nonetheless used its secretly futile nuclear program as a bargaining chip to wrest concessions from an unwilling but fearful West.

Some evidence to support this conclusion emerged during the May-June 1992 IAEA visits to Pyongyang. On closer inspection, the vaunted reprocessing facility was less than half complete, even after at least three years of work; whether this stemmed from North Korean limitations or a deliberate campaign of deception is unknown. North Korea claims that the main Yongbyon reactor, which most Western analysts had assumed to be rated at about thirty megawatts, has at its peak achieved only about half that power. If true, this would point to possible North Korean difficulties even in basic civilian nuclear engineering. Of course, the claim could also be an outright lie, designed to deflect IAEA attention from North Korean plutonium stocks.

Russian officials have also reportedly confirmed parts of this hypothesis. Stanford professor John Lewis said in 1992 that officials in Moscow pointed to difficulties in the North's nuclear weapons program that arose in the mid- to late-1980s. The Russians supposedly said that these difficulties essentially ended progress toward the bomb and that it was after this time that Pyongyang decided to obtain what concessions it could in exchange for suddenly meaningless IAEA inspections.[38] As of late 1993, Russian officials were saying that, based on what they knew of the technical abilities of the North Koreans they had trained, it was highly possible that the North was simply incapable of assembling a workable bomb—and they further claimed that Chinese officials made this same argument to Moscow.[39] Mikhail Ryzkhov, chairman of the Committee for International Relations of the Ministry of Atomic Energy in Moscow, said in September of 1993 that, based on the opinions of Russian scientists who had worked in the North, "Our view is that North Korea does not have the capability of developing nuclear warheads within a few years. . . . [Instead] North Korea, having no capability of producing nuclear weapons, pretends to the outside world that the North Korean development of nuclear weapons is impending. The Russian nuclear specialists are of the general opinion that North Korea is trying to use this as a bargaining chip for negotiations with the United States."[40]

Officials from other former Communist bloc countries have said the same thing. One former East German ambassador to North Korea reports having had some German scientists over to the Embassy for a drink in 1989. The scientists were in the North offering technical assistance. At one point the ambassador, his curiosity piqued, asked simply, "So, do they have the bomb?" His question sparked long and sustained laughter; "no," the scientists said, the North could not build a bomb.[41]

If this thesis is true, then the North's subsequent agreement to IAEA inspections makes sense. Having recognized that they could not, at least for some time, make a bomb, North Korean officials would have taken the obvious route of bargaining away their nonexistent nuclear program for as many Western concessions as they could get. When IAEA inspections occurred, presumably, the North would get a passing grade, because its nuclear weapons program had not reached fruition. As Australian scholar Andrew Mack has pointed out, however, there is one troubling flaw in this argument: if the North's program had indeed stalled, why was Pyongyang so stubborn about the type and number of inspections it was willing to allow?[42] There may have been some reasons—the North would not want outsiders prowling around its military bases under any circumstances—but, through 1992 at least, North Korea continued to behave suspiciously enough to warrant concern.

The suggestion of North Korean incompetence fits neatly with a related notion: the idea that Pyongyang *purposefully* revealed evidence of its nuclear program. As noted in the previous chapter, most of the North's motives for developing nuclear weapons, such as deterring the United States and acquiring leverage, required that the outside world have some notion of the existence of a North Korean bomb. Otherwise, deterrence would not work, and regional powers would see no need to offer concessions to the North. North Korea would therefore have a perverse motive for *allowing* itself to be caught in nuclear weapons research—up to a point. Yi Chang Kon of Seoul's Atomic Energy Research Institute wonders why explosive tests, for example, would be conducted in such close proximity to the Yongbyon research site, when they could be much better concealed if conducted in some distant mountain pass and when their detonation at Yongbyon threatened to disturb the delicate machinery operating there. "One cannot help but reach the conclusion," Yi argues provocatively, "that high-explosive tests that would leave such traces were conducted deliberately so that they could be seen."[43]

If this was the North Korean intent, they conducted their bait-and-switch game clumsily. The North drew attention to the one site, Yongbyon, where it had left conclusive evidence of its violations of the NPT, evidence that would emerge during IAEA inspections of late 1992. The problem, of course, was that the North could not discount the risk of revealing evidence of past wrong-doing, even if its nuclear weapons work had been largely suspended for the time being. By the early 1990s, then, the contradictory elements of the North's nuclear policy—wanting the world to know about its nuclear program, but try-ing to avoid blame for its nuclear ambitions and hoping to expand its economic contacts with other countries—were becoming untenable.

In large measure the two elements were untenable because North Korea, if it indeed wanted to drop hints about its nuclear capabilities, did too good a job. For although the theory of Pyongyang's nuclear incompetence enjoyed some popularity, the more common interpretation as of 1990 was that the North was indeed close to completing a bomb. The sum of information on the North Korean program, most observers concluded, indicated that the world had less than five years to stop the North before it acquired a nuclear arsenal. Perhaps the closest thing to a specific official timetable for the North's nuclear program emerged in July 1989. In an article published that month, So Yong Ha, an expert at South Korea's National Defense Intelligence Headquarters, sur-veyed the available evidence and came to a simple—and worrisome—con-clusion. From the perspective of South Korea, he wrote, "our estimate is that the time frame for potential North Korean production of a nuclear weapon will be the mid-1990s. This seems reasonable since we believe that North Korea at present has the ability to develop nuclear weapons, but it will take three years to produce 20 kg of plutonium from the second nuclear reactor com-pleted in 1987, one to two years to process it, and then one year to build a nuclear bomb for testing."[44] This, then, was the challenge: South Korea, the United States, and other interested parties had roughly until 1994 to convince the North to abandon a nuclear weapons program that may have been planned for nearly four decades. To do so, Seoul and Washington would employ every diplomatic tool at their disposal.

THE STAKES

As they tried to convince the North to abandon their nuclear program, U.S., South Korean, and Japanese officials slowly began to appreciate the true importance of the North Korean nuclear issue. At stake was not only the location of a few errant grams of plutonium, but the entire security situation in East Asia. If the North Korean nuclear crisis were mishandled, the consequences would be both far-reaching and severe.

North–South Korean dialogue had been expanding since 1988 and was poised to enter a promising new phase. The election of Kim Young Sam in the South brought to power an innovative, reformist government dedicated to improved North-South relations and cooperation on a host of fronts. A new nuclear standoff held the risk of destroying this progress and, as the North approached an operational nuclear capability, raising the specter of a new war.

The nuclear crisis also risked undermining the hope for a stable and peaceful unification in Korea. Officials in Seoul were (and are) wringing their hands at the potential cost of reunification; the bill could run to $1 trillion and be accompanied by mass flows of refugees to the South and civil strife. South Korean leaders look to investment in North Korea as a form of safety net that would mitigate these effects. But the freeze on economic contacts and risk of new sanctions sparked by the North's belligerence could have pushed the North closer to collapse, making a "soft landing" less likely. And any open conflict between North and South would have destroyed that goal forever.

To a certain degree, South Korea's transition to a civilian democracy was also at risk in the crisis. Kim Young Sam is the first true civilian and democratic leader in South Korea since the Korean War. The South's move from dictatorship to democracy began in earnest only in 1987, and remains tentative. Kim is only now moving aggressively to root out many aspects of societal and policy control exercised by the South Korean military and its allies. A new war scare might have allowed the military to reassert its dominant role in South Korean politics and would have made further progress in civil rights unlikely. That in turn could have destabilized the South Korean political scene, driving hundreds of thousands of students into the streets and creating an atmosphere of civil unrest. On the other hand, Kim Young Sam's precarious political situation would also lead him to play to the right wing in Seoul, attacking North Korea and criticizing perceived U.S. concessions in talks with Pyongyang— a stance that will be especially evident in chapter 8.

North Korea's threat also called into question the growing trend toward multilateral approaches to security in Northeast Asia. Many countries, including the once-reluctant United States, have joined in pushing for such multilateral efforts. Constructive discussions would be unlikely, however, in an atmosphere of tension, especially when Russia and China held different opinions from the United States on dealing with North Korea. Crises, whether sparked by proliferation threats or other causes, bring divergent national perspectives to the fore and make the compromises necessary for multilateralism less likely.

A permanent state of crisis surrounding North Korea would also have immensely complicated Japan's search for a stable and yet meaningful security role in Asia. Japan remains a key regional wild card, watched closely by its neighbors, its future defense and foreign policies largely undecided. New tensions in Korea, an accelerated North Korean nuclear program combined with missiles capable of reaching the Japanese islands, and the prospect of a messy and violent Korean unification would create new concerns in Tokyo and perhaps begin the widely feared process of Japanese "remilitarization."

Washington's goal of promoting reform in, and good relations with, China would also have suffered at the hands of a prolonged confrontation with North Korea. As noted, Beijing retains considerable differences with the United States on policy toward North Korea. If the situation had worsened, the United States and China could easily have found themselves on opposite sides of the issue. Eventually, worsening relations between the two could have led to U.S. sanctions against China itself, which would have impaired economic—and thus, perhaps, political—reform in China. President Clinton's recent Executive Order on China policy indirectly reaffirms the importance U.S. officials place on growing Sino–U.S. trade; had the crisis continued—and, it is still necessary to say, if the crisis continues—the United States may have been (and may be) compelled to act against its interests in China in attempting to discipline North Korea.

Finally, a mishandling of this crisis might have undermined the renewal of the Nonproliferation Treaty. With the NPT renewal conference approaching in 1995, many developing nations and potential proliferants were undoubtedly watching the world reaction to North Korea with great interest. Had it been too harsh, some countries in the developing world might have taken it as another sign of the "nuclear imperialism" that some believe is characteristic of the stance taken by nuclear powers. NPT renewal is already complicated by a number of complaints by the nuclear have-nots, especially regarding nuclear testing and strategic arms control, and an overly confrontational approach to North Korea would have added another bone of contention. Yet if the U.S. and world answer to the North's provocation was too accommodating, those on the threshold of nuclear weapons status might have taken heart and decided that the best way to obtain concession was to misbehave. Preserving the spirit of the NPT therefore required a delicate balancing act; that challenge for U.S. and South Korean officials was clear.

THE U.S.–SOUTH KOREAN DIALOGUE CONTINUES

After the spring 1989 U.S. intelligence briefing to South Korean officials, and with the stakes of a North Korean nuclear program firmly in mind, Washington and Seoul began to work out the details of a nonproliferation campaign directed at the North. This campaign began to be implemented seriously in mid-1991. But before that time, from late 1989 through mid-1990, U.S. and South Korean officials began to gather the building blocks of a diplomatic effort to halt the North Korean nuclear program.

To conduct a thorough review of the North Korean motives for the bomb and some outline of a strategy for responding to it, the Bush administration convened an interagency group to review the issue in early 1990.[45] The goal was to step back, take stock of the overall situation, and piece together a strategy aimed at gaining the North's compliance with nuclear inspection demands. Chaired by Assistant Secretary of State Richard Solomon, the group was at first vast and unwieldy, involving representatives from every conceivable agency and directorate. Eventually a smaller group emerged, composed of people from the key organizations: State, Defense, the National Security Council, the Arms Control and Disarmament Agency, and the Joint Chiefs of Staff. Over time, the group worked through policy papers, memos, and proposals from its members to develop a coherent policy toward the North.

The interagency group decided on a number of specific elements of a nonproliferation strategy toward North Korea. Its strategy would rely on the now-famous combination of "carrots and sticks," although most U.S. officials prefer other names for their approach. One called it "putting the North in a vise—smiling all the while—and offering it a way out," thus combining pressure with the prospect of benefits if the North agreed to inspections. The vise was to be supplied largely by existing conditions—by the North's continued global isolation and economic decline—combined with increased diplomatic pressure and strong reaffirmations of the U.S. security commitment to South Korea. The way out would be offered by the promise of political and economic benefits, eventually including diplomatic relations with the United States and Japan as well as economic investment and aid.

Eventually, the group recognized that little progress would be made without addressing the U.S. tactical nuclear presence in the South—or, in official parlance, the U.S. policy of "neither confirming nor denying" such a presence. After bypassing the issue several times, the group kept returning to it. Eventually it issued a report with three primary findings: the United States should resolve the tactical nuclear issue in the South; Washington should not enter into a protracted negotiation—it should make its initial offer and then end concessions to the North; and U.S. officials should assemble a coalition to encourage North Korea to accept the offer, with China, Russia, and Japan identified as especially important partners besides South Korea.

During the course of 1991, as a result of the security review, this basic approach would be supplemented by specific initiatives designed to break the deadlock and provide the North with a reason—or an excuse—for agreeing to inspections. Not all of the moves were spelled out by the review; besides the tactical nuclear withdrawal, the others evolved gradually, over time.

Once this process was put into effect, it constituted perhaps the first major example of a reasonably clearly defined nonproliferation effort in post–Cold War U.S. diplomacy. And, for a time, it seemed to be working well. As chapter 4 explains, North Korea did indeed agree to IAEA inspections in early 1992. Yet if the North accepted the initial round of IAEA probes on the assumption that it could hide its nuclear weapons program, as Iraq had done, then in fact the U.S. diplomacy may not have convinced the North to make any fundamental decisions at all. North Korea may have merely been continuing its two-track strategy: pursuing its nuclear weapons program and bargaining it away at the same time. And again, the two elements of this contradictory policy would collide in 1993, bringing the progress in nuclear diplomacy to a sudden and complete halt.

One question that plagued U.S. and South Korean officials in the course of their diplomacy was how explicitly they would lay out these various incentives. Clearly, the North was to be offered advantages for cooperating on IAEA inspections even as it was shown the dangers of refusing to cooperate. But what specific advantages would be laid on the table? And on what terms?

The next three chapters will contend, in part, that it was because the U.S. and South Korean governments hesitated to answer these questions that their nuclear diplomacy largely failed through the first half of 1993. As things developed, neither Washington nor Seoul ever laid out a clear road map to North Korea, a specific schedule of concessions to be offered in exchange for particular North Korean moves. U.S. and South Korean officials also displayed an extreme aversion to offering the initial concession, and so debates about which side was responsible for the next move slowed nuclear negotiations to a crawl for months at a time. This maddening refusal to take decisive action was most tellingly evident in November 1993, when, after a U.S.–ROK presidential summit in Washington and with the need for sanctions growing closer every day—surely the right moment to decide on a bold course of action—U.S. and South Korean leaders danced around the issue of a "package deal" and, in the end, offered nothing new in their approach to the North.

Even in direct U.S.–DPRK discussions, U.S. representatives at first refused to offer anything more than general assurances that North Korea could expect better economic and political treatment if it addressed the nuclear issue. Such bland promises proved insufficient to persuade the North Koreans that they had something to gain by allowing full inspections. And even after the North did respond to U.S. overtures in 1992, Washington and Seoul failed to follow up their success with evidence that nuclear cooperation carried benefits. When the North moved to abandon the NPT in March 1993, it did so at least in part because it had nothing to lose.

AN EVOLVING CHALLENGE

During this period, a number of important elements of the North Korean non-proliferation challenge had begun to make themselves clear. For one thing, even in the mid-1980s, the multilateral nature of the issue was readily apparent. The United States needed Moscow's help in encouraging the North to join the NPT; and looking to the future, no U.S. policy could hope to succeed without the active participation of South Korea and at least the tacit agreement of Japan and China.

Second, the West possessed little hard evidence about North Korea's actual nuclear capabilities. This paucity of clear facts, particularly as to the true progress of the North Korean bomb project, would plague the nonproliferation effort for years to come. The lack of concrete evidence meant that the United States would never know exactly where to draw the line or to give further concessions.

Third, there appears to have been no significant debate at the outset of the U.S. nonproliferation campaign in Korea about its eventual goals. U.S. officials seem to have taken for granted a relatively absolutist definition of success: persuasive and verifiable evidence that every element of the North Korean nuclear program had ceased. There was apparently no discussion, and certainly no public dialogue, of whether anything less would satisfy U.S. interests.

Fourth and finally, North Korea's motives for a weapons program appear to have broadened and become more firmly entrenched in Pyongyang's thinking during the late 1980s. A program that may once have been viewed largely as an ultimate security guarantee began to demonstrate its value as a source of various forms of political and economic leverage. This development complicated the nonproliferation task for the United States and served to make North Korea less willing to see the nuclear issue resolved quickly.

Taken together, these four developments did not portend an easy task for the United States. Working through sometimes unwieldy multilateral channels on the basis of incomplete evidence, Washington began its diplomatic campaign with a definition of success that did not meet North Korea's basic security

interests, at least in the short term, and that was unachievable except through the sort of confrontational means that no other regional powers desired. This essential mismatch between the U.S. goals in the nonproliferation effort and the realities of the proliferation case itself would become more and more evident in the following years.

▪ 4 ▪

THE WORLD RESPONDS, 1990–1992

D uring the late 1980s, Soviet policy toward the Korean Peninsula took an abrupt turn. Mikhail Gorbachev's program of perestroika and his de-emphasis of the military confrontation with the West put the two Koreas in a new light for Moscow. Gradually, the trade and investment opportunities offered by the South began to attract far more Soviet attention than the colorless Communist solidarity and frightening military paranoia of the North. South Korea encouraged the attention through its campaign of *Nordpolitik,* aimed at expanding trade and diplomatic relations with North Korea's communist allies.

By 1990, Moscow's thinking had evolved to the point where it was ready to open formal diplomatic relations with South Korea for the first time in Soviet history. In September of that year, Soviet Foreign Minister Eduard Shevardnadze traveled to Pyongyang to deliver the bad news.[1] Shevardnadze was not a happy messenger: not too long before, he had promised North Korean leaders that the Soviet Union would never take such a step. Now he was going to the North, not only to deliver a profound blow to Kim Il Sung's regime, but to break his own word.

But even Shevardnadze may not have been prepared for the reaction he faced. Furious North Korean officials accused Moscow of breaking faith with an old ally. They pleaded, cajoled, and accused the Russians in a stormy session that lasted for some time.

Eventually, it became clear that the Soviet position was inflexible. So the North Koreans played their last card. They bluntly threatened to obtain nuclear weapons if the Soviet Union went ahead and established relations with Seoul. If Moscow is no longer our ally, they said, then we must take new steps to provide for our own defense.

Shevardnadze was not impressed. What would the North do with nuclear weapons, he asked, when using them would cover the North in radioactivity as well? What good is an ultimate deterrent if it will destroy the very thing you are trying to protect?

The Koreans rebuffed Shevardnadze's questions and continued to assert that the Soviet action would produce a North Korean nuclear arsenal. Moscow ignored the threats and established formal diplomatic ties with South Korea on September 30, 1990.

GROWING CONCERNS ABOUT THE NORTH

As noted in chapter 3, by 1990 officials in Seoul and Washington had become extremely concerned about the progress of the North's research into nuclear weapons. North Korea dismissed such allegations and demanded that any consideration of nuclear weapons in Korea begin by examining the reported presence of U.S. tactical nuclear bombs in the South. North Korean diplomats claimed at an IAEA Board of Governors meeting in February 1990 that they had signed the NPT on the assumption that the U.S. nuclear threat, as embodied by U.S. tactical nuclear weapons in, and an explicit U.S. nuclear umbrella over, South Korea, would be removed. Until it was, they said, they could not fulfil their NPT commitments.[2] Still, there was a silver lining in the statement: based on its rationale, if the United States did withdraw its tactical nuclear weapons from the South, North Korea would lose its major excuse for delaying IAEA inspections.

Unknown to U.S. or South Korean officials, Soviet intelligence was at this time receiving disturbing, though cloudy, signals about the status of the North Korean project. On February 22, 1990, a top secret KGB document, revealed in March 1992, suggested that the North had actually *completed* a bomb. "The KGB has received information from a reliable source," the brief report, signed by then-KGB chief Vladimir Kryuchkov, read,

> that scientific and experimental design work to create a nuclear weapon is continuing in the DPRK. . . . According to information received, development of the first atomic explosive device has been completed at the DPRK Center for Nuclear Research, located in the city of Yongbong in Pyongan-pukto Province. At present there are no plans to test it, in the interests of concealing from world opinion and from the controlling international organizations the actual fact

of the production of nuclear weapons in the DPRK. The KGB is taking additional measures to verify the above report.[3]

Still, most official estimates put the date of a North Korean bomb some years
off—and indeed, many Russian and Chinese officials remained privately convinced that the North was incapable of assembling a bomb. There still
appeared to be time to slow the program and obtain IAEA inspections before
the North completed work on a bomb.

In 1991, therefore, South Korea and the United States began to implement
the various elements of an integrated political, economic, and military campaign designed to persuade Pyongyang that allowing inspections—and eventually, abandoning its nuclear ambitions—would be in its best interests. This
strategy took shape in Washington during the second half of 1990 and the first
half of 1991, partly as a result of the interagency review mentioned in the previous chapter. U.S. officials did not lay out all the elements of this policy in
advance; much of it was ad-hoc, developing over time in response to the
pressure of circumstances. The policy rested on the foundation of the tactical
nuclear withdrawal and the shoring up of the U.S. deterrent posture in South
Korea; other elements were added as the process moved forward. Nonetheless,
the broad outlines of the strategy were clear enough, and the additional incentives that would be added later fit into that strategy.

As it evolved in 1991, the U.S. strategy consisted of four primary elements, each of which is described in detail here. At the centerpiece of the effort
would be the unequivocal statement that no U.S. nuclear weapons were based
in South Korea (or, as some interpreted it, the withdrawal of the U.S. tactical
nuclear weapons that had been based there since the 1950s). The United
States also reaffirmed U.S.–South Korean security ties to convince the North
it would gain nothing by delay. Third, Washington and Seoul suspended the
annual Team Spirit military exercise, long condemned by the North as
provocative, for one year. Fourth and finally, high-ranking U.S. government
officials agreed to a long-standing North Korean request for direct U.S.–DPRK
talks—but only for a single session, with more to follow if the North cooperated and allowed nuclear inspections. All four were high on North Korea's
agenda, and U.S. and South Korean officials calculated that none would pose
a threat to the security of the South.

As this diplomacy evolved, it became clear that there was frequently no
such thing as a "U.S." or a "South Korean" position on any given issue—any
more than, given the complicated motives outlined in chapter 2, there could
be said to be a monolithic North Korean position. Within each government,
bureaucratic debates went on between various departments. In general, as

might be expected, the U.S. Department of State and Korean Ministry of Foreign Affairs frequently held to the position that North Korea possessed legitimate security concerns that needed to be addressed, and that engaging in a dialogue with the North and offering certain concessions was the best way to go about that process. The ministries of defense in both countries, reflecting their primary mission of military preparedness and deterrence, generally adhered to a tougher line. The national security advisers in Washington and Seoul, Brent Scowcroft (and his top Asia hand, Douglas Paal) and Kim Chong Whi, fell somewhere in between, trying to assemble a coherent strategy toward the North that would take into account the concerns of both sides.

Given the critical role in policy of information on North Korea and its nuclear program, the intelligence communities in both Washington and Seoul naturally played a major role as well. The State Department's Bureau of Intelligence and Research, as one former U.S. official put it, "anchored the left wing" of the debate, arguing for a policy aimed at redressing North Korea's security concerns as well as pressuring it. Both the Central Intelligence Agency and the Defense Intelligence Agency adhered to a much tougher line, in part—as will always be the case—because of the personal views of the specific analysts involved.[4]

The bureaucratic debate, however, was not a simple two-sided affair. Officials in the defense departments of both countries were not averse to positive diplomacy. Some in the U.S. Department of Defense, for example, argued for removing the uncertainty about alleged U.S. tactical nuclear weapons in the South, and others favored moving Team Spirit to a biennial schedule for budgetary reasons having nothing to do with North Korea's nuclear program. Even within a specific organization, differences were apparent; Scowcroft, for example, had a reputation as being extremely tough on Korea, while many involved in the bureaucratic process saw Paal as a moderating force. Other agencies made themselves heard: the National Unification Board in Korea (and its head, the vice prime minister) argued for dialogue with and engagement of the North; in Washington, the rise of bureaus and offices dedicated to nonproliferation added a voice for toughness on the nuclear issue.

In short, then, the nuclear issue was as complex within South Korea and the United States as it was within the North. Any story of how U.S. and South Korean nuclear diplomacy evolved must take account of the varying ideas and perceptions within the two governments.

A review of this nonproliferation strategy reveals a number of things. First and most important, the strategy was not merely punitive. It combined incentives—initiatives designed to address the North's threat perceptions (or, some would say, excuses) and promises of better relations and economic aid—with the threat of continued isolation from the world community.

Second, however, the concessions made as part of the strategy were, in a sense, not concessions at all. Rather, Washington and Seoul had been leaning toward such moves as a nuclear withdrawal and a biennial Team Spirit exercise for some time, and the fact that they supported the nonproliferation strategy allowed U.S. and South Korean officials to make a virtue of necessity. This suggested that the United States might not in the future pursue a similar strategy if similar initiatives needed to be manufactured. And this, in fact, was exactly what happened after the second half of 1992, when U.S. diplomacy produced almost nothing of substance to offer North Korea.

Third and finally, during the process of convincing the North to allow inspections, the United States and South Korea manifested somewhat different views of the nuclear issue and the most promising tactics for dealing with it. While the differences were in most cases only of degree, the Korean case nevertheless demonstrates how the United States and its allies can have divergent perspectives on ways of dealing with proliferation issues.

STEP ONE: A U.S. NUCLEAR WITHDRAWAL

The first major component of U.S. diplomacy was a military initiative aimed at convincing Pyongyang that it did not need nuclear weapons to guarantee its security. In May 1991, U.S. officials hinted that Washington would be willing to confirm that there were no nuclear weapons in Korea.[5] There were various reasons for this change of heart over what had been, as chapter 2 suggested, a central element in the U.S. and South Korean deterrent posture since the late 1950s. U.S., and to a lesser extent South Korean, officials had come to believe that such weapons no longer contributed to deterrence and would over time increasingly become a political liability. Moreover, the U.S. experience in the Persian Gulf War suggested that high-technology conventional weapons alone were sufficient for deterrence and war fighting in the modern era.[6] Nuclear weapons stationed on the territories of U.S. allies, weapons whose presence in Korea the United States never truly confirmed or denied, had in many cases become an anachronism.

In the context of the North Korean nuclear issue, the advantages of a U.S. nuclear withdrawal in Korea—or rather a nuclear clarification, since the presence of the nuclear weapons was not officially admitted—quickly became apparent. To those in the U.S. and South Korean governments concerned with addressing North Korea's security concerns, a withdrawal of U.S. tactical nuclear weapons from the South was the sine qua non of any serious nonproliferation effort. This had emerged as the consensus of the Bush administration interagency group. Even those skeptical of the North's motives saw value in making a number of concessions to see how serious the North was about bargaining away its nuclear program. Such steps would have the added advantage of demonstrating to the international community, and especially those nations (like China and Japan) opposed to a confrontational attitude toward the North, that the United States was giving diplomacy a serious try.[7]

In early June 1991, the U.S. offer to denuclearize Korea became more explicit. The *Los Angeles Times* reported that the Bush administration was "considering removing U.S. nuclear warheads from South Korea as part of a concerted effort to get North Korea to halt" its nuclear program. "In a series of interviews," the *Times* noted, "Bush administration officials acknowledged that proposals for some sort of reduction or phase-out of U.S. warheads are being studied."[8]

North Korea appeared to be in the midst of a reevaluation of its own. It had already modified its position on UN membership, having proposed a shared UN seat earlier in the year, after decades of insisting on a single, separate seat for both Koreas. Then on May 28, it agreed to join the United Nations jointly with the South—although only after being told by China that Beijing would no longer veto such a move in the Security Council. North Korean officials did not waste any time connecting this move to corresponding flexibility on the nuclear issue: within days, Pyongyang's ambassador in Vienna, Jeon In Chu, said the North was ready to reopen discussions on signing the safeguards agreement.[9] Just over a week later, North Korea's special envoy announced in Vienna that a full North Korean team would arrive in July to work out the details of signing IAEA safeguards.[10] During July, the first tangible sign of progress was reached: in the middle of the month, DPRK officials initialed an IAEA full-scope safeguards agreement, pledging to sign it in September.

Later in the year, the United States gradually moved to implement its tentative decision to withdraw nuclear weapons from Korea. In September, U.S. Undersecretary of Defense for Policy Paul Wolfowitz reportedly met with Kim Chong Whi, Blue House (the South Korean presidential residence) national security adviser, to discuss the nuclear initiative.[11] On September 27, President Bush made a major televised speech announcing dramatic nuclear weapons reductions, including the withdrawal of all U.S. ground- and sea-based tactical nuclear weapons throughout the world. The following day, the North Korean Foreign Ministry praised the action.[12]

In fact, the Bush administration had originally intended to include its tactical nuclear initiative in the president's August 2, 1990 foreign policy address at the Aspen Institute. Those responsible for Korean policy were already mulling over strategy toward the North by that time, and the U.S. nuclear initiative in Korea might have occurred earlier had the speech gone ahead as intended. However, just hours before the Aspen speech, Iraq invaded Kuwait. Suddenly faced with the need for regional deterrence, top Bush administration officials decided that the nuclear initiative would provide Iraq with too much comfort. They hurriedly deleted reference to the initiative at the last moment, and Iraq's gambit in the Middle East indirectly served to delay this important arms control initiative by more than a year.[13]

Once the initiative was announced, worries arose in Seoul and Washington as North Korea appeared to be attaching new conditions to allowing inspections. At the North-South prime ministerial talks, North Korean Premier Yon Hyong Muk demanded that South Korea renounce any form of U.S. nuclear umbrella and bar any overflights or port calls by nuclear-armed U.S. aircraft or ships.[14] This was an important and disturbing demand, because it was almost certainly further than the United States would be willing to go. If the North continued to insist on a complete renunciation of the U.S. nuclear umbrella, progress toward IAEA inspections might end.

By October 1991, North and South Korea were discussing the issue face-to-face in their prime ministers' talks, which had begun in September of 1990. At its fourth session on October 22-25, 1991, North Korean officials called once again for a nuclear-free zone in Korea and demanded a U.S. nuclear withdrawal as a precondition for IAEA inspections. And again, the North Korean proposal contained elements aimed directly at the U.S. nuclear umbrella, such as a ban on visits to Korea by nuclear-capable aircraft or ships as well as a prohibition on any alliance that included a nuclear umbrella. South Korean Prime Minister Chung Won Shik rejected these conditions and called on the North to allow inspections and abandon its nuclear program. The stalemate continued.[15]

Nonetheless, South Korea moved quickly to take advantage of President Bush's tactical nuclear initiative. On November 8, South Korean President Roh Tae Woo announced a far-reaching initiative calling for a nonnuclear Korean Peninsula.[16] Roh declared that the South would not "manufacture, possess, store or use nuclear weapons" and called for a ban on all nuclear reprocessing on the peninsula.[17] At the same time, a top Blue House official declared that all U.S. nuclear weapons in the South would be removed at the earliest possible date;[18] and indeed the following day, *Chosun Ilbo* reported that a high-ranking ROK government source had disclosed a U.S.–ROK agreement to "start withdrawing tactical nuclear weapons . . . before the end of the year."[19] The United States and South Korea had moved firmly to remove the North's fundamental excuse for rejecting inspections: its claim that it was threatened by nuclear attack from U.S. tactical nuclear weapons in the South and the U.S. policy of refusing to "confirm or deny" the presence of those weapons.

WORRIES GROW

Despite this apparent progress, in the fall of 1991, disturbing signs emerged that the North might be going all-out for a bomb. These facts had to do with North Korean discussions with its traditional allies, the Soviet Union and China. In September 1990, as Moscow prepared to establish diplomatic relations with South Korea for the first time, official North Korean statements warned that, if Moscow took such a step, a triangular alliance would be in place against it and Pyongyang would have no choice but to provide for itself "some weapons for which we have so far relied on the alliance."[20] As noted at the beginning of this chapter, North Korean officials made these same threats directly to Soviet Foreign Minister Eduard Shevardnadze, but Moscow ignored them and established relations with Seoul.

A year later, the failed August 1991 coup against Soviet President Mikhail Gorbachev and the subsequent emergence of even more radical reformers in Moscow shook North Korea's government to the core. Pyongyang turned to its last, but unenthusiastic, ally, China. Kim Il Sung had reportedly sought Chinese approval for a nuclear weapons program for decades, but by late 1991 that message may have turned from request to statement. In September 1991 reports emerged that, in August 1991 meetings, North Korean officials notified their Chinese counterparts of Pyongyang's intention to acquire a nuclear arsenal and asked once again for approval. The Soviet coup, the North Koreans were reported to have said, had removed any doubts about their need for the bomb. And growing U.S. and South Korean anxiety about the North's weapons program only egged them on: "the more the hostile forces are afraid of nuclear weapons," the report quoted one North Korean official as crowing, "the more we should arm ourselves with them."[21]

Moreover, a comparison with the Iraqi program, which was reportedly only a few months away from a bomb at the time of the Gulf War, was to many experts chilling. The maps of Iraq's nuclear facilities published after the UN inspection teams scoured the country looked very much like the rough sketches that portrayed North Korea's program. Iraq had, and North Korea was then believed to operate, high explosive test facilities, nuclear power plants, and uranium acquisition programs; the North had plutonium reprocessing facilities as well. Iraq was known to have developed, and some civilian analysts have claimed that North Korea has sought, enrichment technologies such as centrifuges and calutrons (although, as we have seen, this latter claim has little evidence to support it and has never been made by the U.S. government). Each program had its own area of advantage: Iraq's project, financed with billions in oil wealth, proceeded along many avenues with redundant equipment and was rich in Western technology; North Korea's program was poorer but had its own natural source of uranium, a crucial commodity Iraq lacked.

The Iraqi example also suggested that, even if Kim allowed inspections, the risk of a nuclear Potemkin Village would be great. Pyongyang was expert at hiding its military facilities underground, and would probably not put all of its key nuclear weapons facilities where the IAEA could find them—at Yongbyon. When the North agreed to inspections, it may have believed that the agency would continue its ineffectual pattern established in Iraq. The North may also have hoped that revelations of past nuclear work could be downplayed in the context of a warming relationship with the United States. But North Korea would confront a very different IAEA, and this fact would later produce a crisis on the peninsula.

STEP TWO: REAFFIRMING U.S.–ROK SECURITY TIES

The most confrontational rhetoric from the United States and South Korea emerged at the 23rd annual U.S.–ROK Security Consultative Meeting (SCM), held in Seoul on November 20-21, 1991. Prior to the SCM, Seoul had been trying to downplay the notion that it was interested in aggressive responses to the North's nuclear ambitions. On November 15, South Korean Defense Minister Lee Jong Koo denied that his government was considering a preemptive attack. Military action would not even be considered if the North Korean program continued, Lee claimed. "If the United Nations Security Council or other international institutions decide on military sanctions against North Korea," Lee said, "and if it means war on the Korean Peninsula, the government will oppose it."[22]

Yet the SCM was a calculated part of the nonproliferation strategy, designed to add an element of toughness and pressure into the collection of incentives aimed at the North. Just two days after Lee's statement, the Korean press quoted a South Korean official to the effect that Washington and Seoul planned to go to the United Nations and "present a resolution on the forcible nuclear inspection of North Korea" if diplomatic methods failed. The official said ominously that "the ROK and the United States preclude any immediate military action, *at least for now*" (my emphasis).[23]

At the SCM itself, South Korean officials opposed any suggestions of military action,[24] but agreed to consider economic sanctions or blockade and possibly intrusive spy flights over North Korean territory. U.S. officials, including Secretary of Defense Richard Cheney, suggested a postponement of a planned reduction in U.S. troops stationed in South Korea and South Korean leaders agreed.[25] U.S. and South Korean officials also agreed to step up their annual military exercise, Team Spirit, and include in it F-117 "Stealth" fighters, Airborne Warning and Control System (AWACS) aircraft, Patriot air defense missiles, and other examples of U.S. high-technology prowess. "If they missed Desert Storm," one high-ranking American official said of North Korea, this would be "a chance to catch a re-run."[26]

Some conciliatory messages did emerge from the SCM, if Pyongyang was attuned to them. For one thing, U.S. press reports for the first time indicated that the United States would be willing to consider international inspections of its own military bases in the South, which the North had demanded for some time. During the meeting, a South Korean government source also declared that President Roh was likely to declare South Korea fully nuclear-free during President Bush's upcoming January visit.[27]

By the fall of 1991, the combination of pressure and incentives seemed to be having an effect in Pyongyang. Even as the SCM concluded in Seoul, Choe U Chin, deputy director of the Institute of Disarmament and Peace, in Washington for an academic conference, strongly implied that the North would sign IAEA accords in February of the following year.[28] And on November 22, a South Korean official also predicted that Pyongyang would sign the IAEA accord in February, because it "does not want its nuclear issue to move to the United Nations." The official reported that "We received information from the United States and China that North Korea has already decided internally to sign the Nuclear Safeguards Accord."[29]

On November 25, 1991, Pyongyang announced a new and important offer. An official Foreign Ministry statement promised to sign IAEA inspections accords when the U.S. process of nuclear withdrawal was announced to have *begun,* not when it *ended* as the North had previously said.[30] The statement endorsed simultaneous nuclear inspection, and also called for U.S.–North Korean and North-South talks aimed at providing inspections.[31]

As if in response to the North Korean statement, three days later, on November 28, South Korean news sources reported that the United States had indeed begun withdrawing tactical nuclear weapons from the South and that it would inform the North of this process.[32] On December 11, South Korean Prime Minister Chung Won Shik announced that there were no U.S. atomic weapons in the South and offered to open U.S. military bases to inspection in exchange for inspections of North Korean nuclear facilities. Chung proposed "pilot" inspections of Yongbyon and the base at Kunsan.[33] "This is as close as anyone can come to calling the North's bluff," said a U.S. official at the time. One news report suggested that the initiative was designed "to give the government of President Kim Il Sung a face-saving means of backing away from its nuclear arms development program."[34]

The extent of those conciliatory gestures to the North soon became an issue between the United States and South Korea. Even by late 1991, not all the players in Seoul were fully on board with the U.S. policy of linking economic and political contacts to a resolution of the nuclear issue. Thus the process of North-South ministerial negotiations had continued despite the recurring tensions over the nuclear issue. On November 30, South Korea's Foreign Minister Lee Sang Ok explained their rejection of calls to link North-South dialogue to the nuclear issue: "We must simultaneously pursue effective progress in inter-Korean dialogue and deterrence of North Korea's nuclear arms development," he insisted. "Forestalling dialogue over nuclear controversy is not an effective method."[35] Korean-language media stirred up this supposed disagreement for months, turning routine U.S. official visits into brow-beating sessions in which the South was supposedly prevented from engaging the North in economic and political contacts as it desired. Even high-ranking South Korean officials had the impression, as one later said, that "the U.S. government opposed a rapid improvement in North-South relations."[36] During the January 1992 U.S.–ROK summit in Seoul, President Bush added his voice to those U.S. officials urging President Roh to move slowly on North-South relations.

Another issue that would eventually produce some discord in the U.S.–ROK relationship was that of nuclear reprocessing. In the wake of the Gulf War—and the attendant discoveries of a vast, undetected Iraqi nuclear weapons program—U.S. officials were not sanguine about the IAEA's ability to inspect the North. They saw a bilateral, North-South inspection regime, with broader and more intrusive inspection rights than the IAEA, as a way of stiffening the monitoring system, and urged South Korea to propose such a program.[37] For its own reasons, Seoul had been thinking along similar lines. The result was North-South talks over what would become a major agreement to abandon nuclear weapons and nuclear reprocessing, which would be signed at the end of 1991.

As part of this accord, South Korea agreed to surrender the right to reprocess spent nuclear fuel in order to obtain a similar North Korean pledge. But Seoul did not apparently come to this decision—which some in the South, accurately or not, viewed as economically costly—without pressure: Washington had to make a "strong pitch" to the South to give it up, including a meeting in Hawaii between Undersecretary of Defense Paul Wolfowitz and Assistant Secretary of Defense for Asian-Pacific Affairs Carl Ford, and South Korean National Security Adviser Kim Chong Whi. In large part because Japan was not being asked to make the same sacrifice, South Korean officials were not at all happy with this U.S. request, but they nonetheless complied.[38] Since that time, many South Korean defense analysts and most of the Korean-language press have been critical of the decision.

Nonetheless, amid these reports of U.S.–ROK squabbling, North-South prime ministerial talks and other contacts persisted even when progress on the nuclear issues appeared to be stalled. These talks bore important fruit in October 1991 with the writing of the rough draft of a wide-ranging agreement: the historic North-South "Agreement on Reconciliation, Nonaggression, and Exchanges and Cooperation between the South and the North," also known as the North-South "Basic Agreement," was signed in December. The document created few new concrete confidence-building measures or inspection mechanisms, but was symbolically profound. In it, North and South Korea pledged to "recognize and respect" each other and to cease interference in each other's internal affairs, and made a pledge of nonaggression, a measure that had been under negotiation for years. The agreement did establish some mechanisms of tension reduction, including a North-South Liaison Office, a Joint Military Committee, a military-to-military hotline, and other steps.[39]

During this same period, later reports in the South Korean media suggested that businessmen from the South, with the approval of their government, met with top North Korean officials in an effort to promote economic contacts. Between December 8 and 10 in Beijing, according to these reports, North Korean Deputy Premier (and reputed chief of external economic relations) Kim Tal Hyon held secret meetings in Beijing with representatives from South Korea's Samsung and Lucky Goldstar groups. At the meetings, Kim allegedly asked the two Southern economic conglomerates to participate in the North's next seven-year economic development plan. He reportedly promised further economic openings and a cooperative attitude toward South Korean companies. Whether or not those meetings took place, on December 11, Kim was appointed head of North Korea's State Planning Committee, which oversees the seven-year plan.[40]

At the fifth ministerial talks on December 10 to 13, 1991, the Basic Agreement was finalized amid great hope for an accelerated process of North-South discussion and tension reduction. Despite the U.S.–South Korean disagreement about the nature of linkage, to many in Washington as well as Seoul, this constructive North-South dialogue played a critical role in the overall U.S.–ROK-Japan nonproliferation strategy. Combined with references to the potential for North-South trade,[41] these talks made clear to Pyongyang some of the advantages of choosing moderation: better relations with the South (and thus the outside world), progress toward unification, and an infusion of South Korean capital and business expertise. United States officials hoped that these opportunities would constitute a powerful political and economic incentive to resolve the nuclear issue.

STEP THREE: TEAM SPIRIT

The third step in the evolving U.S. strategy toward North Korea involved the U.S.–ROK Team Spirit military exercises. Seoul began to let it be known that it was ready to reconsider the 1992 version of Team Spirit if progress were made on the nuclear issue.[42] On December 16, 1991, South Korean Vice Prime Minister Choe Ho Chung said South Korea's decision on whether to continue Team Spirit would depend on developments in the inter-Korean talks on nuclear issues. "The government has not yet made a decision to stop or scale down the drill," Choe said. "Such a decision could be made if the [inter-Korean] contacts relating to nuclear issues progress."[43]

Like the nuclear withdrawal, however, U.S. and South Korean military and civilian officials had been discussing changes in Team Spirit for some time.[44] Substantial differences of opinion existed within both governments about the usefulness of the drill. The huge exercise costs roughly $150 million[45] and disrupts the lives of tens of thousands of people in the South, and there had been talk for some time of making it a biennial event. As North-South relations improved and the military threat from the North abated somewhat (as a product, if nothing else, of worsening North Korean relations with Russia), the time appeared ripe for such a change. It was in part a fortunate coincidence that U.S. and South Korean thinking on Team Spirit had changed in time for it to become the second major carrot offered to the North. Within the U.S. government, the Department of State led the charge to have Team Spirit suspended or cancelled, and by 1991 it made headway in interagency debates. Like the nuclear initiative, however, the one-year suspension of Team Spirit was also taken to address North Korean security concerns in the nuclear context.

Throughout the discussions on Team Spirit, from 1991 through 1993, Seoul generally had the final say on the status of the exercise.[46] U.S. officials had ideas about the exercise and made suggestions, but as a sign of their commitment to the alliance, did not want to force South Korean leaders to take initiatives with which they were not comfortable. By 1991, those in Seoul who saw the exercise as a useful bargaining chip, and who believed that the North needed to be rewarded for progress to date, had gained ascendance. Thus the exercise would be suspended in 1992, and later, during consideration of both the 1993 and 1994 exercises, South Korean officials made it abundantly clear that they were willing to cancel it in exchange for additional North Korean concessions.

On December 18, South Korean President Roh Tae Woo gave a Blue House speech in which he reiterated his November 8 pledge not to manufacture, possess, store, deploy, or use nuclear weapons. He went one important step further, however, and declared "emphatically and unequivocally" that "there do not exist any nuclear weapons whatsoever, anywhere in the Republic of Korea." Roh called on the North to match its words with deeds and allow inspections of its nuclear facilities.[47] Significantly, the United States concurred with Roh's statement: asked at a December 18 press briefing whether the United States had "any dispute with any portion" of Roh's announcement, U.S. Department of State spokesman Richard Boucher said, "No. . . . U.S. policy is consistent with that enunciated by President Roh and with President Bush's nuclear initiative."[48]

North Korea moved quickly in response. On December 22, an official North Korean statement indicated that Pyongyang would sign IAEA accords when the United States formally confirmed Roh's claim about the withdrawal of U.S. tactical nuclear weapons, and agreed that mutual inspections should take place between the DPRK and United States. "We declare that," the statement said, "on the assumption that the United States will announce its clear position, we will sign the nuclear safeguards accord as stipulated in" the NPT.[49] A day later, however, Seoul rejected these new conditions and called for continued work through the North-South talks and the IAEA;[50] nevertheless an important channel appeared to be opening.

The next major sign of progress emerged from the North-South talks. On December 26, at an ad hoc meeting on the nuclear issue, North Korean negotiators reportedly stated that they would sign the IAEA accords presently and that they believed Roh's nonnuclear pledges. And talks on the distinct North-South nuclear agreement made important progress: the North proposed draft agreements for a denuclearized Korean Peninsula, rather than its more common nuclear-free zone ideas.[51] At this meeting, South Korean representatives restated their intention to cancel the 1992 Team Spirit exercise if the North signed IAEA accords.[52] Yet while major progress was made on the 26th, no final nonnuclear agreement was reached. The two sides were not far apart—South Korean chief negotiator Lee Dong Bok said the North's proposal was "very close if not identical to ours"—but had not quite resolved their differences.[53]

On the 28th, there were more talks, but still no agreement. Lee Dong Bok said he was "cautiously optimistic" that the meeting set for the 31st would prove decisive. A main sticking point continued to be the North Korean side's unwillingness to specify a date for signing the IAEA accord. The North also called for inspections of military facilities only in the South, not admitting that its own military bases might have to be inspected as well.[54]

Finally, at Panmunjom on December 31, North and South Korea signed a historic Joint Declaration for the Denuclearization of the Korean Peninsula.[55] Each side pledged not to store, manufacture, possess, or otherwise obtain nuclear weapons; and importantly, they promised also to eschew any nuclear reprocessing capability—a provision that would require the North to dismantle the alleged plutonium reprocessor at Yongbyon. The accord was to be verified by Korean inspection teams distinct from IAEA groups, and it signaled improving relations between the two sides and offered an additional opportunity for inspections of North Korea's ominous facilities. Yet outside analysts noted the general pact's lack of a robust inspection agreement[56] and important differences remaining in the draft regulations governing inspections proposed by the two sides.[57] Although few realized it at the time, this North-South agreement would become the centerpiece of the nuclear debate—and a stubborn obstacle to resolution of the issue—within a year.

At the time, however, the North-South agreement provided a convenient justification to fulfil the promise made by Seoul to suspend Team Spirit for a year. This policy would be codified in early 1992, before the March kickoff date for the annual exercise. The 1992 exercise would indeed be suspended, with some apparently positive results in North-South dialogue; but with this initiative, the fate of Team Spirit had become irrevocably linked to the status of North-South relations. U.S. and South Korean military leaders would thus have to endure a constant on-again, off-again routine for the next several years, as political leaders in Seoul and Washington first pledged to suspend Team Spirit because of progress in nuclear talks, then threatened to hold it to punish North Korean intransigence.

STEP FOUR: U.S.–DPRK TALKS

The results of a year of political, economic, and diplomatic persuasion became apparent early in 1992, when North Korea agreed to inspections. The stage was set for final progress on January 5 and 6 when President Bush visited Seoul. He and President Roh formally offered to cancel Team Spirit as soon as the North signed the IAEA accords. Yet Bush also expressed skepticism about the North and generally took the opportunity to reiterate the need for watchfulness and to stress the strength of U.S. commitments. Meanwhile, President Roh reminded the North of the economic price it was paying for delay.[58]

A final component of the political diplomacy campaign was an increasingly explicit U.S. offer to Pyongyang of improved diplomatic relations if progress were made on the nuclear issue. This involved behind-the-scenes assurances that formal U.S.–North Korean diplomatic ties would be strengthened once inspections occurred. Additional meetings took place during 1991 and early 1992. The result was the third major incentive to be offered the North: direct, high-level talks between officials of the two governments.

The first hints emerged that U.S.–North Korean nuclear talks were in the works during the January Bush-Roh summit. Apparently a tentative agreement to hold such an unprecedented meeting had been reached at the regular U.S.–North Korean sessions in Beijing during 1991. President Bush had wanted to announce the talks during his visit to Seoul, but North Korea, perhaps not wanting the announcement to take place in Seoul or unable to resolve political infighting in Pyongyang, hesitated. United States officials mistakenly took this to mean that the U.S. had been rebuffed; actually it was only a temporary delay.[59] On January 8, Scowcroft announced that the United States and North Korea would indeed hold an unprecedented "nuclear weapons conference" later in January.[60]

Those talks occurred on January 22. At the offices of the U.S. Mission to the United Nations in New York, two groups of about ten officials from the United States and North Korea, headed by Arnold L. Kanter, U.S. undersecretary of state for political affairs, and Kim Young Sun, North Korea's Korean Workers' Party (KWP) secretary for international relations, met in the highest-level contact between the two governments since 1953.[61] Each side began with a set of guarded talking points, but the meeting gradually moved into a careful, but wide-ranging, dialogue. After a full-morning meeting, the two sides continued their discussions over lunch.

Kanter's prepared message assured the North Koreans that the United States wished to pose no threat to them. But Kanter also argued that the fate of the North Korean regime was in their own hands. An economic miracle was underway in East Asia, all around the North, which every day left them further behind. Their choice was simple and fundamental: to cooperate on nuclear inspections and other issues of concern to the outside world and join the international community, or to see their nation descend further into poverty.

The U.S. side laid out a specific list of steps Washington expected of the North. These simply represented the implementation of two accords the North had already signed: the IAEA inspections agreement and the North-South nuclear accord, which included such things as regular IAEA inspections and a North-South inspection regime. In exchange, the United States was prepared to offer a continuing series of high-level discussions with the aim of discussing subjects of mutual interest—such as outside investment in the North, diplomatic recognition, and the like. But the benefits for cooperation were sketched out only in the vaguest of terms.

Kanter stressed that all U.S. nuclear weapons had been withdrawn from the South. And he reminded the North Korean delegates that the North-South nuclear agreement, if implemented, would allow North Korea to inspect U.S. military bases in the South to verify that claim.

Kim Young Sun responded with a prepared message of his own. It was somewhat more strident, demanding that the United States stop threatening the North, withdraw its nuclear weapons and troops from the South, and leave the nuclear issue to be resolved by Koreans. During the meeting, Kim accused Japan of being the primary threat in Asia, and proposed U.S.–North Korea–South Korea cooperation to address the Japanese threat. (The U.S. side promptly and angrily rejected this notion.) Kim also repeatedly attempted to get an agreement to a joint statement or a commitment for additional meetings, both of which Kanter rebuffed.

The meeting was an important step, but its meaning was diluted by the tone of the discussions that actually took place. Not all parts of the U.S. government were comfortable with direct U.S.–DPRK talks, in part because the North had sought such a dialogue for four decades precisely to drive a wedge between the United States and South Korea. Advocates of a U.S.–DPRK dialogue responded that circumstances had changed; the North had lost its major geopolitical sponsors, and was in a position of total weakness. North Korea was far along the path to an expanded relationship with the South, and would sign two important agreements in the fall of 1991. The United States risked little by talking to the North. Moreover, some officials pointed out that the United States had, in the 1970s, quietly made a proposal of mutual cross-recognition, under which China and the Soviet Union would grant full recognition to South Korea and the United States and Japan would do the same for the North.[62] Now that China and Russia had done just that, the United States and Japan—partly on the request of South Korea—were conveniently ignoring their earlier offer.

Nonetheless, in deference to those in the U.S. government concerned that U.S. contacts with the North not be seen as a sign of weakness, the mandate of the talks was changed from a dialogue to a lecture. The talks became a largely stiff, choreographed, set-piece enterprise. U.S. officials were not going to talk *with* the North Koreans as much as they were going to talk *at* them, to make clear the U.S. position.[63]

Any opportunity to develop the kind of personal relationships so crucial to business dealings with Koreans was sharply curtailed by such an approach. This failing was compounded by the U.S. refusal to have further sessions: at the end of the meeting, Kim Young Sun reportedly declared that he had established a personal relationship with Kanter that could lead to agreements,[64] but this admittedly risky potential was destroyed by the U.S. insistence on a single meeting.

But already by this time, on January 7 (the day after the Bush-Roh talks ended), a North Korean Foreign Ministry spokesman had announced the

North's intention to sign the IAEA safeguards agreement. He said, in part, that a U.S. nuclear withdrawal had been "the principled position to which we have consistently adhered in connection with nuclear inspection." South Korean leaders had "announced some time ago that there are no nuclear weapons in South Korea," and "the United States expressed through various channels its welcome of the South Korean authorities' declaration that there are no nuclear weapons in South Korea." As a result of this agreement, an IAEA spokesman said in early January that "At best we could be sending inspectors into Korea by late spring."[65] That same day, a South Korean spokesman formally announced the suspension of the 1992 Team Spirit exercises as agreed during Bush's visit; the following day, North Korea praised the Team Spirit cancellation in unusually positive language.[66]

The South Korean, U.S., and Japanese diplomatic campaign to end the North's nuclear program thus reached a critical milestone in January 1992. Just over a week after the U.S.–DPRK talks in New York, on January 30, Hong Kun Pyo, North Korean deputy minister of nuclear energy, and IAEA Director General Hans Blix initialed the IAEA safeguards accord in Vienna.[67] Worries abounded that many hurdles remained to be overcome before inspections would take place, and few observers trusted that the North would implement the agreement properly.[68] Nonetheless, Pyongyang was now officially committed to a process that would culminate in inspections of its nuclear facilities. This represented enormous progress over the North's position in February 1990, which had rejected inspections altogether on the grounds that the North still faced a U.S. nuclear threat.

On February 4, in the first clarification of the timetable for actual inspections, North Korean UN Ambassador Pak Gil Yon said North Korea would ratify the international safeguards agreement and allow inspections within six months.[69] The delay was a result of the need for Supreme People's Assembly (North Korea's nominal legislature) ratification; like any government, Pyongyang claimed, it needed its legislature's stamp of approval on a treaty. Skeptics argued that the North was merely stalling for time, hiding its nuclear program away before inspections could take place. In an attempt to speed the inspections process, in late February Seoul suggested that North-South inspections take place by mid-April and that the work of the Joint Nuclear Control Committee be accelerated.[70] The North rejected the proposal.

On February 25th, U.S. Director of Central Intelligence Robert M. Gates added new urgency to the negotiations with disturbing testimony to Congress. Gates testified that the North had a "deception plan" for hiding nuclear facilities, despite its December nonnuclear agreement with the South. Gates's argument, it was reported at the time, reflected a "growing consensus in the

Bush administration that North Korea's pledge" to eschew nuclear weapons "was not serious and that the country remains intent on continuing its nuclear weapons program."[71] Gates also suggested—in personal comments, not in his more formal prepared statement—that the North could be as close as a "few months" away from a bomb. This claim did not reflect the uniform opinion of the government; State Department experts, in particular, were upset by Gates's characterization of the North Korean nuclear program as an imminent threat. One State Department official was quoted as saying that a "more reasonable assessment" would put the North "several years" from a weaponized bomb.[72]

Perhaps in response to these growing concerns, Seoul, reports in Korean media suggested, was preparing to seek economic sanctions by the UN Security Council against the North if it continued to delay. Because the North's trade volume amounted to $4.6 billion in 1990 and $2.6 billion in 1991, further cuts would mean that the North "would not be able to sustain its economy any longer," an unnamed South Korean official said.[73]

THE ROLE OF JAPAN AND CHINA

As the U.S.–ROK diplomacy continued, the role of Japan and China became increasingly important. As North Korea's best hope for aid (in the form of colonial-era reparations) and investment, Japan played an important role in diplomacy toward the North. Tokyo's basic policy was to withhold any development assistance or investment until North Korea had resolved the nuclear issue to the satisfaction of the world community.[74]

Japan had reasons of its own to be concerned about North Korea's various military programs. Many Japanese officials dreaded the prospect of a North Korean nuclear arsenal at their doorstep; some dreaded it, in fact, more than even the far larger (but more stable) Chinese nuclear force, while others saw in the North Korean nuclear program a convenient rationale for theater missile defense or other programs that would counter the Chinese arsenal. Combined with North Korea's development of an intermediate-range missile capable of hitting much of Japan, Pyongyang's nuclear ambitions caused severe concern in Tokyo.[75] Some of North Korea's terrorist activities had also touched Japan, in the form of kidnappings of Japanese citizens and the use of Japanese passports for covert operations.

Nonetheless, for a time, competing interests in Tokyo threatened to undermine Japanese support for the isolation of North Korea. Lacking the U.S. responsibilities for deterrence in Northeast Asia and Korea, Japan has traditionally pursued a more independent policy toward North Korea, maintaining better relations with the North than either South Korea or the United States.[76]

The large population of Koreans in Japan, including many thousands with relatives in or sympathies toward North Korea, also complicated Tokyo's decisions. Many Japanese officials believed that if they assumed a confrontational attitude toward the North, they risked a violent response from the pro-North Korean organization in Japan, the Association of Korean Residents in Japan, or Chosen Soren (known in Korean as the Chongnyon). Some Japanese officials might have hoped that aid and investment in Korea before, during, and after unification would help mitigate anti-Japanese feeling on the peninsula and pave the way for amicable relations.

When North Korea in the mid-1980s began seeking closer ties with its neighbors, Japan was a major target—and because of Japanese political and economic interests in the North, Tokyo reciprocated the interest.[77] Already by 1983, up to 20 percent of North Korea's external trade was with Japan, and Japan also seemed North Korea's best hope for receiving full diplomatic recognition from a powerful capitalist state.[78] The process of diplomatic flirtation between Tokyo and Pyongyang culminated in the September 1990 visit to North Korea by Shin Kanemaru, a top leader of Japan's ruling Liberal Democratic Party, who promised massive reparations for Japan's colonial treatment of the North and the rapid achievement of full relations.

Those Japanese who pressed for closer ties to the North had a number of motives. Kanemaru himself was reportedly close to Japan Socialist Party head Makoto Tanabe, who mediated the Kanemaru–Kim Il Sung meeting in Pyongyang, and wished to be seen as someone who helped bring the socialist nations into the modern era. His personal ambitions therefore fueled his visit and other steps to promote closer Japanese–North Korean relations, steps that far outpaced the policies of Japan's Foreign Ministry. Politically, Japanese officials hoped that closer relations with the North would forestall any violent North Korean reaction to growing Japanese influence in the region. A few Japanese businesses were interested in investing in the North, which Japan had in fact colonized early in this century because of its abundance of raw materials and inexpensive labor. Expanding ties with the North would keep the Chongnyon Koreans in Japan happy. Finally, some observers have contended—but few Japanese will agree—that Tokyo hopes to shore up Kim Il Sung's regime and thereby put off the date of Korean unification, which some in Tokyo fear could create a new rival in Northeast Asia.[79]

Yet over time, the factors pushing Japan and North Korea closer together faded, while concerns surrounding the North's nuclear program became more intense. North Korea maintains a large debt to Japan, and until some servicing arrangement is worked out the Japanese government will not look favorably on the potential for trade. Japanese corporations gradually lost interest in the North when the risks and limitations of investments became more apparent; one Japanese official, when asked in late 1992 how much interest there was among Japanese businesses in investing in North Korea, replied simply, "None."[80] With Kanemaru's loss of influence in the fall of 1992 as a result of financial scandals, the main proponent of closer ties to the North had lost much of his power. In addition, the security issues surrounding the nuclear question appeared to most Japanese clearly to outweigh the potential benefits of closer ties to the North.

Japan, therefore, acceded easily to U.S. and South Korean requests that it put its plans for diplomatic recognition of and aid to the North on hold until the nuclear issue was resolved. Indeed, given the Japanese interests at stake, it is entirely possible that Tokyo would have pursued exactly the same policy even if the United States had not requested it.[81] The one crucial role the United States did play with regard to Japan was in the sharing of intelligence: U.S. and Japanese sources agree that the clear evidence of North Korean nuclear progress presented to Japanese officials by U.S. intelligence agencies was instrumental in firming up the consensus in Tokyo that supported the U.S.–South Korean policy toward the North.[82]

China took a more circumspect position. It consistently rebuffed U.S. efforts to strong-arm Pyongyang into inspections, arguing that the North Koreans would not respond favorably to demands. Throughout 1991, Chinese officials appeared sensitive to considerations of the North's fear of losing face and thought the United States was impatient in its dealings with the nuclear issue. There was little doubt, however, that Beijing had no desire to see a bomb in Pyongyang—not least because it might later be acquired by a unified Korea.

Yet U.S. officials were perhaps too quick to assume a complete Sino-American accord on the issue. For all the cooperation and occasional warmth in Sino-American relations, reducing the American presence and influence in Asia remained a major goal for many Chinese leaders. The longer the nuclear crisis could be dragged out short of a war, the more China stood to benefit: The United States would look weak and vacillating, while China's leverage— as the only major power left with influence over North Korea—would grow. So while China did not necessarily want North Korea to possess nuclear weapons, and while it certainly did not want to see the North implode, it did not share with the United States a clear vision of how, or when, those goals ought to be achieved.

Thus on November 14, 1991, China's Foreign Minister Qian Qichen declared at a news conference concluding an Asia-Pacific Economic Cooperation (APEC) meeting in Seoul that "dialogue," not pressure or sanctions, was the way to deal with the North Korean threat. A *New York Times* report described this as a "setback" for U.S. and South Korean "efforts to mount an international campaign to persuade North Korea to halt" its program. Qian said: "We do not want to see the existence of nuclear weapons on the Korean Peninsula. We hope to see the parties concerned engaged in effective consultation to find a solution to this problem, but we do not wish to see any international pressure."[83]

These comments and actions presaged China's position on the issue of sanctions during later crises over the North Korean nuclear program. In 1992 and 1993, U.S. desires to threaten sanctions against the North, particularly in the wake of the North's March 1993 claim that it would withdraw from the NPT, were restrained by China's opposition to any confrontational approach.

INSPECTIONS ARE APPROVED

On February 25—the same day as Robert Gates's gloomy testimony—news emerged from Vienna that growing concerns about North Korean delay would be answered. There IAEA representatives announced that they were close to agreement on "when and who" would be involved in nuclear inspections in the North.[84] North Korean roving ambassador O Chang Rim added that the Supreme People's Assembly would ratify the inspections in April, that they would not require Kim Il Sung's signature, and that the inspections would occur by June. This was the first reference to a specific Pyongyang-imposed timetable for inspections.[85]

As promised, on April 9, the North Korean Supreme People's Assembly ratified the government's agreement to allow international inspections. Minister of Atomic Energy Industry Choe promptly said that the North would "accept nuclear inspection without delay." This ratification started the clock on a ninety-day requirement to hold inspections; IAEA officials said they expected to receive the North's list of its nuclear facilities by the end of May.[86]

The agency revealed in April that North Korean officials expected to provide a formal list of facilities by mid-May, roughly two weeks ahead of the required deadline. If the list was sufficiently detailed, IAEA experts said, the agency could begin inspecting North Korean facilities before June 15—the date of an IAEA Board of Governors meeting that was expected to be highly critical of the North if progress had not been made.[87] By the end of April, almost everything was in place in preparation for the long-awaited international inspections of the alleged nuclear weapons factory at Yongbyon.

And the lesson of the negotiations seemed clear enough. Diplomacy had worked, at least up to a point. The gradual, nuanced strategy of pressure and incentives employed by Washington and Seoul had persuaded the North to take the step the world had awaited since 1985—allowing actual IAEA inspections of its nuclear facilities. But the U.S. and South Korean governments, soon distracted by presidential elections, would prove better at making the diplomatic breakthrough than following up on it. And within a year, another nuclear crisis would be looming on the Korean Peninsula.

The reason was not hard to find. During this period, the apparent U.S. victory in securing inspections obscured the possibility alluded to by Director of Central Intelligence Gates in his congressional testimony: that the North was not playing honestly. It is highly possible that during this period the North was trying to pursue two simultaneous, and somewhat contradictory, policies. By allowing inspections, Pyongyang hoped to gain added concessions from the outside world, especially economic aid and trade to revive its faltering economy. But at the same time, the North appeared determined to preserve some element of its nuclear program.

As suggested in chapter 2, North Korean leaders may have had good reasons to believe that the nature of the NPT would allow them to straddle this fence. But a tougher U.S. policy, a more energetic IAEA, and North Korea's own apparent uncertainty about how to proceed combined to ruin the hope in Pyongyang for a smooth resolution of the issue. North Korea's two approaches would finally collide in 1993.

■ 5 ■

THE IAEA MOVES IN, 1992–1993

In May 1992, Hans Blix, head of the International Atomic Energy Agency (IAEA), arrived in Yongbyon, North Korea, for a guided tour of the North's nuclear research facilities. Long the focus of international concern, the mysterious Yongbyon site was rumored to harbor a nuclear weapons program. As described in chapter 4, North Korea had agreed to IAEA inspections in February 1992 and notified the agency earlier in May of the facilities it would open for inspection. Now Blix had come, in advance of the formal IAEA inspection teams, to get an early reading on what the North was up to.

North Korea's relations with the South and the outside world, and ultimately peace on the Korean Peninsula, hung in the balance. A former South Korean defense minister had already called for military strikes on Yongbyon, and a growing number of policy analysts in the United States urged a confrontational approach. Late in February, U.S. CIA Director Robert Gates had warned that the North could be just a few months from a workable bomb. If the IAEA inspections did not go well, demands would escalate to isolate the North further and threaten military action.

In such a situation, North Korean officials had every reason to be as careful as possible, to limit Blix's exposure, to show him only the most innocuous things. Still, what the IAEA director saw was disturbing. The large building feared to be a plutonium reprocessing plant turned out to be exactly that. It was not quite finished and had less than half its equipment installed, but skeptical observers warned that the North could have stripped it in anticipation of the inspections. North Korean officials, who had consistently denied any interest in plutonium reprocessing, now admitted that they had actually been engaged in it, but had only acquired, they insisted, "tiny" amounts of bomb-grade material. The mountains around the nuclear plants were honey-combed with large bunkers buried deep underground—to protect against an attack, the North Koreans were quick to claim, although they would be equally useful in hiding more suspect elements of a bomb project.

Blix's visit did little to put to rest the fears of those convinced that North Korea was after an atomic bomb. He could not come back reassured, and even the first formal IAEA inspection in June was unable to give the North a clean bill of health. The tensions, mutual recriminations, and doubts that had surrounded North Korea's alleged nuclear weapons program would continue.

THE ROLE OF THE IAEA

Blix's unusual visit to the North was one important result of the international diplomacy sketched out in chapter 4. Once the campaign to get the International Atomic Energy Agency into North Korea had succeeded, it was time for the IAEA's scientists and officials to take over. Blix's brief tour, and the regular IAEA inspections that followed, were aimed at providing the guarantees sought by the outside world that North Korea's nuclear weapons program had been stopped.

Established in 1956 by the United Nations General Assembly, the International Atomic Energy Agency is an organization affiliated with the UN but independent from it. The IAEA's General Conference includes all its member nations, 114 countries as of May 1993. Its Board of Governors is made up of thirty-five specific members picked because of their knowledge of nuclear science or their strategic location. The board is served by a secretariat, headed by a director general. The United States remains the leading voice in the agency, if for no other reason than its substantial financial contributions.[1]

The IAEA's purpose is to monitor and help control the potentially danger-ous effects of the worldwide spread of civilian nuclear power. To the major powers, the primary risk is obvious enough—nuclear proliferation, in which developing nations use their civilian nuclear power plants as the building blocks of a nuclear arsenal. The IAEA combats this risk by conducting "ad hoc" and "regular" inspections at nuclear power sites, attempting to ensure that no potential nuclear-weapons material is being diverted from the fuel cycle.

In order to overcome the opposition of the nuclear have-nots, who have tra-ditionally opposed an international anti-nuclear police agency, the IAEA was in fact established with two somewhat contradictory purposes: to encourage and assist the development of nuclear power, in part by fostering the exchange of scientific and technical information; and to establish safeguards to ensure that the nuclear know-how was not put to military purposes. Perhaps because of this split personality, the agency had never been known for tough application of its safeguards. Its most famous failure came in Iraq, where the IAEA had found no evidence of wrongdoing before the 1991 Persian Gulf War—which uncovered a vast, multibillion dollar nuclear weapons complex spread across the entire country.

Yet the agency's reputation for lax enforcement was about to change. Washington and Seoul wanted a tough approach to the North, but the IAEA had its own reasons for taking a firm approach. After its disastrous performance in Iraq, the agency (and its leading members) was anxious to show that it had teeth. As the primary international proliferation watchdog group, the IAEA could not afford another major gaffe and still retain any semblance of credibility. Moreover, by late 1992, when clear evidence of North Korean cheating emerged, agency officials felt betrayed by the North. If it had appeared to be an easily confused dupe to the Iraqis, then, the IAEA would quickly become known to the North Koreans as a serious thorn in their side. Later, ironically, the very toughness U.S. officials so encouraged would create complications for the United States, when, in 1993, the IAEA's uncompromising stand on inspections actually may have hampered the U.S. desire to strike a deal with North Korea.

Well before it was allowed to inspect the large reactor and other facilities at Yongbyon, the IAEA had insisted on its right to do so. In September 1991, twenty-three member nations adopted a strong resolution calling for greater authority to be vested in the IAEA, allowing it to conduct "special" inspections—inspections on demand, as opposed to regularly scheduled ones—of suspected nuclear sites. The agency's charter allowed for such inspections, but they had never been demanded before. The resolution was aimed at, as much as any country, North Korea, whose continued refusal to allow IAEA inspections was causing real concern at IAEA headquarters in Vienna.[2] North Korea responded predictably, condemning the resolution as a hostile act and delaying efforts to cooperate with the agency.

In its traditionally cautious, nonconfrontational manner, the IAEA made a number of pointed comments about Korea in 1991. Dr. Jon Jennekens, IAEA deputy director-general, said he thought the North would agree to inspections soon. "I think it will not take too long," Jennekens said, "before Pyongyang signs the safeguard pact as North Korean leaders will surely come to realize that it is in the best interests of their people." North Korea "should inform us about the full status of their atomic energy research activity without further delay," Jennekens concluded.[3]

By December 1991, South Korea was attempting to use the IAEA to put pressure on the North. At the IAEA Board of Governors meeting that month, South Korean representatives reportedly asked the agency to cease its technical support for the North's nuclear power program, which was granted in connection with ongoing IAEA inspections of the small reactor at Yongbyon. As of December, the IAEA had plans to spend more than $300,000 in North Korea during 1992 on five major projects, helping North Korean scientists in areas ranging from uranium ore exploitation to finding industrial uses for radioactive isotopes.[4]

When North Korea officially agreed in principle to the denuclearization of the Korean Peninsula that same December,[5] progress was being made. Ho Jong, one of the North Korean representatives to the United Nations in New York, revealed on the 26th that officials from Pyongyang had begun negotiations with the IAEA on the nature and timing of inspections. The North's assumption, Ho indicated, was that ratification of the IAEA agreement was inevitable. Yet if the IAEA were to adopt more condemnatory resolutions, Ho warned, as it had at its September Board of Governors meeting, "this issue will be ruined."[6] Finally, as described in the previous chapter, North Korea reached agreement on inspections in February 1992, fully ratified the instruments of the IAEA full-scope safeguards agreement in April,[7] and hinted at the possibility of June inspections.

EARLY SIGNS: NORTH KOREA DESCRIBES ITS PROGRAM

The IAEA process upon which North Korea had embarked, which is roughly the same for all nations that submit to nuclear safeguards, contained four distinct phases.[8] The first requirement was North Korea's official report of its existing nuclear facilities. Second would come a series of "ad hoc" inspections to verify that list and gather some initial data about the nuclear program. Once the outlines of the inspection regime became clear, North Korea and the IAEA would sign various subsidiary agreements and attachments to the accord describing inspection procedures for specific facilities. Finally, the IAEA would begin the routine inspections designed to ensure that the nuclear facilities were not being used for military purposes.

In April and May 1992, the IAEA began receiving the first comprehensive information from North Korea about the size and status of its nuclear program. Pyongyang was required to submit a complete list of nuclear sites to the IAEA by the end of May. Apparently in a bid to demonstrate its good intentions, Pyongyang began providing information as early as mid-April[9] and indicated that its formal notification would come at the beginning of May. On

April 15, Kim Il Sung's eightieth birthday, North Korea took another unusual step: it broadcast a videotape showing its facilities at Yongbyon.[10]

During this same period, momentum was added to the process by a series of dramatic and secretive North-South discussions on a possible summit. Kim Il Sung reportedly sent a secret emissary to Seoul in April to propose a summit to South Korean President Roh Tae Woo; on April 15, Roh sent the director of the Agency for National Security Planning to Pyongyang to wish Kim a happy birthday and express a willingness to consider a summit.[11] The talks would later break down, but at the time they may have given North Korea even more incentive to cooperate.

Shortly thereafter, on May 4, North Korean officials in Vienna formally submitted their statement of nuclear infrastructure, a 150-page document revealing intimate details of their uranium mining sites, nuclear power plants, and other facilities, to the IAEA. IAEA spokesman David Kyd described the book as being "as thick as a small telephone directory."[12] As Pyongyang had promised, the report was early, delivered twenty-five days ahead of the IAEA deadline.[13] This represented, according to a North Korean spokesman, the "since.e efforts" of his government "for the denuclearization of the Korean Peninsula."[14]

While the IAEA did not release the North Korean document itself, an agency report laid out the facilities the North admitted to having. These included the small reactor and critical facility at Yongbyon, already under IAEA safeguards; a sub-critical research facility at Kim Il Sung University in Pyongyang; the larger operating reactor—listed as only five megawatts electric power—and another, even bigger reactor of fifty megawatts under construction at Yongbyon; a huge, two-hundred-megawatt plant being built at Taechon in North Pyongan Province; a nuclear fuel rod construction plant at Yongbyon; plus a radiochemical laboratory, two uranium mines, and two uranium concentrate plants.[15] It turned out that the North Korean list closely matched Western estimates of the scope of its nuclear program.

THE BLIX VISIT: MAY 1992

In early May, the North hosted IAEA Director General Hans Blix for the informal, six-day visit described at the beginning of this chapter.[16] Blix saw the facilities at Yongbyon, the two-hundred-megawatt power plant construction site at Taechon, uranium ore plants in Pakchon and Pyongsan, and research centers in Pyongyang. On his return he was tight-lipped, saying only, "I don't like very much to speculate."

Nonetheless, one clear lesson of the Blix visit was that North Korea was indeed engaged in plutonium reprocessing, contrary to its earlier claims. The massive primary reprocessing building at Yongbyon appeared to be about 80 percent complete and contained about 40 percent of the needed equipment. The rest, the North Koreans noted, was "on order but not yet delivered." North Korean scientists even admitted to having reprocessed some plutonium suitable for use in nuclear weapons. They claimed, however, that it was only a "tiny amount," and that they were interested in it for ultimate use in a breeder reactor. Later reports indicated that the North had admitted to reprocessing between fifty and one hundred grams, with one report specifying ninety grams, of plutonium.[17] The plutonium had been retrieved from a few rods of fuel in the large reactor that had been "damaged" and therefore removed. Although it was not known at the time, this issue—the "missing" plutonium from Yongbyon—would become the linchpin of the nuclear dispute in coming years.

On his return, Blix made special mention of the massive shelters and tunnels, which took several minutes to reach by escalator, that filled the mountains around Yongbyon. Obviously, North Korea had not wanted the world to see—or, perhaps, to be able to destroy—many of its key nuclear sites. And there was no way to know how many underground bunkers Blix was *not* allowed to inspect, or what they contained.

Blix was also flown by helicopter to the big, two-hundred-megawatt reactor at Taechon, begun in 1984 and due for completion in 1996. Blix said he saw poles capable of holding electrical lines near the plant, supporting the North Korean claims that its purpose was power generation. But the poles could easily have been a ruse, installed to support a misleading claim of innocence.

Some later reports claimed that, during the visit, North Korean officials made a proposal to Blix: the North would fully abandon any hope of reprocessing or other elements of a nuclear program—if the West would help it with additional technologies. Specifically, officials in Pyongyang, especially Premier Yon Hyong Muk, said they hoped to pursue a more advanced light-water reactor plant in the future to replace the outmoded, 1950s-style reactors then in operation. Light-water reactors, unlike the gas-graphite plant built at Yongbyon, are poorly suited to producing plutonium for nuclear weapons. In order to move toward a light-water system, however, the North would need outside assistance.[18] IAEA officials later denied offering a specific deal, but the light-water idea kept recurring in the nuclear dialogue—most pointedly during U.S.–DPRK talks in July 1993, when the United States reportedly agreed to facilitate the North's acquisition of light-water technology if concerns about the existing Yongbyon reactors were put to rest; in 1994, the light-water reactor idea reemerged at the center of a major U.S.–North Korean negotiating process.

After the visit, IAEA experts analyzed an extensive videotape shot by Blix's staff. IAEA spokesman David Kyd said in June 1992 that the video revealed an "extremely primitive" facility far from any capacity to produce plutonium for weapons.[19] The first reports out of Yongbyon, therefore, were generally favorable: although much remained to be learned, the North Koreans appeared to be cooperative, and there was no clear evidence that the North had been able to assemble a bomb.

The first formal IAEA inspections of the Yongbyon facility followed rapidly after Blix's visit. They began on May 25, 1992 and continued through June 7. They did not immediately uncover any evidence of North Korean dishonesty, but most outside observers believed that the whole truth had not yet emerged.

THE BILATERAL INSPECTION REGIME

By any measure, the world's diplomatic campaign aimed at North Korea's nuclear program had achieved dramatic results by June 1992. IAEA inspections were underway, North-South relations were somewhat improved, and talks between the two were underway on the scope of a Korean inspections regime. In July, North Korean Deputy Premier Kim Tal Hyon toured industrial plants in the South and talked of economic cooperation.

And yet this progress came to a halt in the second half of 1992, in part because the United States and South Korea slowed the implementation of their highly successful diplomacy of the previous two years. This hesitation arose most powerfully in Seoul; and it arose primarily because of the delays and frustrations in implementing the North-South Denuclearization Agreement. North Korean officials complained repeatedly that South Korea and the United States were not meeting the commitments they had made to the North. Specifically, North Korea wanted access to U.S. military bases in the South, to verify for itself (or so it claimed) that U.S. tactical nuclear weapons had actually been removed;[20] and it wanted a definitive end to the Team Spirit exercise.[21] North Korean officials insisted that they were meeting all the terms of the IAEA agreement and had seen none of the promised benefits.[22]

During the spring and summer of 1992, attention shifted from the IAEA inspections, which continued quietly, one round after another, at Yongbyon, to the negotiations between the two Koreas in the Joint Nuclear Control Committee (JNCC), the forum established to discuss and implement the North-South denuclearization agreement of the previous December. Through these talks, South Korea hoped to establish a rigorous system of inter-Korean nuclear inspection and to achieve what was not, at least up to that point, included in IAEA practice: the regular performance of "challenge inspections," or short-notice inspections-on-demand of North Korean nuclear facilities. Although South Korean and U.S. officials might not have recognized it at the time, their goal of challenge inspections was to prove a major stumbling block in talks with the North over the next year. Many South Korean officials also believed that, in the long run, solutions to the peninsula's problems would have to be worked out between Seoul and Pyongyang, and that an inter-Korean nuclear inspection arrangement was a promising—and critical—place to start.

In the JNCC meetings, however, it gradually became apparent that the North was unwilling to approve a plan for meaningful challenge inspections. At the JNCC talks, South Korea sought verification provisions that would enable them to inspect any North Korean military installation within forty-eight hours. Inspectors could not be limited to declared nuclear facilities, Seoul insisted, because North Korea could then simply move its alleged nuclear weapons research to military bases.

North Korean negotiators balked at such sweeping requests and demanded instead the right to visit U.S. and South Korean military bases, and in exchange were prepared only to offer inspections of Yongbyon and perhaps one other site. Perhaps because of concern that, if given broad access to military facilities, outsiders would learn how badly deteriorated North Korea's conventional military had become—or, of course, because it had simply been cheating on its NPT commitments—Pyongyang had made refusal of challenge inspections an article of faith by mid-1992. The North's policy was fully in evidence, for example, at the seventh JNCC meeting on July 21, 1992, when North Korean officials continued to reject demands that military facilities be included in the challenge inspections agreement.[23]

Throughout August 1992, the promising trend in inter-Korean relations began to show hints of a reversal.[24] Seoul rejected the notion of helping North Korea with light-water reactor technology until the North allowed challenge inspections.[25] The North canceled an accord it had proposed on mutual family visits by senior citizens; the South further slowed inter-Korean economic contacts. Reports emerged in Seoul that the South Korean policy might become more belligerent if no progress was made soon.[26] On August 31, even as the third IAEA team was arriving in North Korea for an inspection visit, another round of JNCC talks failed to make any progress.[27]

In early September, North Korea turned its attention toward U.S. military bases in the South. North Korean statements referred to claims by "officers"—presumably U.S. or South Korean, who had served at the Chinhae naval base in the South—that U.S. tactical nuclear weapons continued to be stored there. On September 14, North Korean Ambassador to Russia Son Song Pil urged that the base be dismantled;[28] the following day, an official

DPRK statement demanded inspections of U.S. bases in the South, again pointing to Chinhae as a nuclear weapons storage site.[29] On September 17, DPRK Ambassador-at-Large O Chang Rim said that the North would allow inter-Korean challenge inspections only when U.S. facilities in the South had been opened as well. "If and when South Korea agrees to inspections of U.S. military installations as we demand, a way will be found to resolve the question of mutual inter-Korean nuclear inspections," O said.[30]

In the second half of September, a number of signs of hope emerged that the two Koreas might be inching toward an agreement. The eighth session of North-South Prime Ministers' Talks took place on the 16th and 17th and produced three minor agreements, including one to implement the Reconciliation Agreement signed the previous December.[31] On the 17th, South Korean President Roh Tae Woo claimed that the risk from the North Korean nuclear program had declined substantially. The North's "determination to develop nuclear weapons," he said, "had become weaker." Roh speculated that outside pressure was having the desired effect.[32] The following day, IAEA Director General Hans Blix said at a news conference that the agency's work in North Korea had "proceeded well" and was on schedule.[33]

On September 19, another JNCC session discussed various draft proposals for an inspection regime and appeared to narrow the gap between the two sides.[34] That same day, South Korean Vice Economic Minister Han Kap Su said that Seoul planned to push inter-Korean trade before South-North nuclear inspections began—thus offering an important carrot to the North and appearing to violate the policy of linkage urged by the United States.[35] On the 29th, Chong Tae Ik, director of the South Korean Ministry of Foreign Affairs' North American Affairs Bureau and one of the leading architects of Seoul's northern policy, signaled flexibility on challenge inspections, noting that South Korea was willing to compromise on the frequency and allowed sites of the inspections if the North would agree to the principle of short-notice examinations.[36]

In the face of this hopeful progress and positive signals from the South, North Korea kept up its drumbeat of criticism. It had cooperated and allowed IAEA inspections, its officials argued, and was getting nothing in return. At first the North's complaints centered around an issue that had been a key North Korean demand: simultaneous inspection of U.S. military bases in the South. North Korean statements had established such mutual inspections as a clear precondition for IAEA visits, but, in an apparent concession, the North had agreed to the inspections even without this element. Now it returned to the issue. Pyongyang's Central News Agency replied to calls for inter-Korean inspections by repeating its demand for inspection of the U.S. bases.[37] In late September, a *Nodong Sinmun* article condemned the bases[38] on the same day that North Korean Foreign Minister Kim Yong Nam demanded inspections of U.S. facilities in a UN General Assembly speech.[39] To this core issue were added other objections: North Korea reacted harshly to a September 23 Roh Tae Woo speech to the UN urging the North to resolve the nuclear issue, calling it "dastardly";[40] that same day, the North Korean representative to the IAEA gave a presentation calling attention to Japan's nuclear research.[41]

A disturbing pattern had begun to emerge. North Korea appeared intent on delaying the North-South inspection regime and its threat of challenge inspections. And South Korea and the United States made this strategy possible, by refusing to rob North Korea of its excuses by allowing inspections of U.S. facilities in the South and taking other steps. In retrospect it is difficult to understand why Washington and Seoul did not move more energetically to defuse North Korean arguments about U.S. bases by simply opening them to outside inspection, as many U.S. military officers had long agreed that this would pose no threat to security. But no such initiative was forthcoming. And soon, other stumbling blocks would emerge.

Meanwhile, the South Koreans, who had once been resentful of the constraints imposed by the priority of nonproliferation, began to shift their position on linkage. As the months passed and the North remained intransigent, South Korean officials began to wonder if they could truly deal with the North in anything close to a businesslike fashion.[42] In the fall and winter of 1992, Seoul's view began to harden. The first signal of a tougher approach was South Korea's decision to go ahead with planning for Team Spirit 1993, a move that carried enormous risks for the process of negotiations. By 1993, as later chapters will explain, South Korea increasingly found itself in the position of stiffening what it now believed to be U.S. softness toward the North.

THE SPY RING CASE

It was at this tender juncture in the North-South dialogue, and this critical moment in the U.S. and allied nonproliferation campaign aimed at the North, that the South Korean government revealed—or chose to reveal—the existence of an alleged North Korean spy ring in the South. This revelation would have dramatic implications for relations between the two Koreas and for the mood in Seoul. Along with the South Korean decision to press ahead with Team Spirit, the spy ring incident served as one more nail in the coffin of the climate for a resolution of the nuclear issue.

The first hints about the existence of a North Korean spy ring surfaced in September 1992,[43] and by October 1 the South Korean Agency for National Security Planning (ANSP)—formerly the KCIA, Seoul's infamous main intelligence agency—announced that it would soon release information about the largest group of North Korean agents uncovered since 1948. The ANSP alleged that several dozen North Korean agents, including prominent South Korean labor leaders, in preparation for unification in 1995, had tried to establish political agitation groups and other organizations with the goal of disrupting South Korean politics.[44] Under the direction of Pyongyang's "spy master" Yi Son Sil, a seventy-year-old woman and high-ranking official in the North's KWP hierarchy, who came to the South under an alias in the early 1980s, more than four hundred people worked in the North's vast spy ring, ANSP spokesmen contended.[45] South Korean intelligence officials even hinted at possible connections with opposition lawmakers in the National Assembly.[46]

North Korea reacted angrily to the accusations, with the chief reunification organization in Pyongyang calling them a "preposterous falsity" and denying any involvement.[47] A more formal statement, issued on October 8, blamed the South for having "kicked up a vicious commotion to aggravate North-South relations and strengthen fascist suppression." The investigation, the statement went on, "proves that the South Korean authorities are not willing to implement the North-South agreement" signed the previous December.[48]

The new tensions over the spy ring case undermined the ongoing North-South dialogue. South Korea quickly canceled the scheduled visit to Pyongyang of a vice prime minister.[49] The South suggested that the visit could be held later, and proposed a meeting of officials to discuss the spy ring case; North Korea predictably rejected the request.[50]

The spy ring case may well have represented the honest result of a regular investigation. North Korea has repeatedly proved itself willing to engage in subversive activities aimed at the South. But the public nature and peculiar timing of the announcement by the ANSP—which is known to take a dim view of dialogue with North Korea—suggest that the truth about the spy ring case is somewhat more complex than it might first appear. One can detect a consistent pattern in South Korea in which Seoul publicized North Korean defectors or scandalous conspiracies by the North at critical junctures in the nuclear diplomacy, a pattern that entered high gear in 1994 as the United States and North Korea approached a deal. There were even rumors in Seoul that *North Korean* hard-liners, concerned that negotiations with the South were advancing too quickly, provided information about the spy ring to the ANSP in the hope that revealing it would stall future talks.[51] No evidence has emerged to support this belief, but it remains an intriguing possibility.

Whatever the origins of the spy ring case, however, its consequences were clear. It cast new suspicions and doubts on the process of North-South discussion and on the value of agreements with North Korea, since the

North-South reconciliation agreement of December 1991 had banned precisely those disruptive activities that allegedly were the purpose of the ring. The case poisoned the political climate for North-South relations in both Seoul and Pyongyang. Particularly in South Korea, in the words of one former South Korean official, the spy ring case was a "death blow" to moderates seeking an expanded dialogue with the North.[52]

TEAM SPIRIT 1993

During the summer and early fall of 1992, Washington and Seoul began reiterating that the suspension of Team Spirit in 1992 had indeed been a one-year decision, that this fact had been made clear to North Korea, and that planning was underway for the 1993 exercise. The first signs of this emerged in late 1992. In Seoul, officials claimed that the decision to hold the exercise in 1993 had already been made, when in fact all that had been decided was to begin planning for it.

Going ahead with the 1993 exercise would be a stunning move, an admission that U.S.–ROK nuclear diplomacy had achieved little of value since the previous year, and a resentful stab at the North for its perceived stubbornness. It would also be a step rife with dangers: Team Spirit had been one of North Korea's long-standing excuses for avoiding IAEA inspections in the first place, and conducting the exercise again would present Pyongyang with a gift-wrapped rationale to continue stalling on inter-Korean inspections. At the same time, U.S. and South Korean officials felt the need to signal the North that continued delay was unacceptable, even if the means of sending the signal carried the risk of exacerbating the delay.

North Korea made sure officials in the United States and South Korea appreciated those risks. On October 4, to set the tone for the annual U.S.–South Korean Security Consultative Meeting just a few days later, North Korea began adding Team Spirit to its list of concerns, alongside U.S. military bases. A North Korean broadcast that day claimed that the U.S. military presence in Korea continued to serve as a roadblock to a full nuclear agreement. After suspending Team Spirit in 1992, the statement proclaimed, the United States was "running amok with large-scale joint military exercises as a substitute for the Team Spirit exercise. . . . Announcing that it will resume the Team Spirit military exercise next year, the United States also staged the Focus Lens exercise some time ago . . . thus aggravating the military tension."[53]

Nonetheless, at the twenty-fourth U.S.–ROK Security Consultative Meeting in early October, 1992, South Korean and U.S. defense officials and military leaders made the decision to go ahead with planning for the exercise in 1993, deciding that the exercise itself would take place only if there was insufficient progress on the nuclear issue.[54] That decision was made for a number of reasons.[55] It was initially taken, in fact, in Seoul: the U.S. side was prepared not to include an announcement of Team Spirit in the 1992 SCM communiqué, but South Korean officials requested that planning for the exercise be undertaken. In part this was to give the bargaining chip greater value—Team Spirit could hardly be bargained away if it did not exist—and partly to send a signal to the North that it could not continue to stonewall in the JNCC talks and expect concessions. Interestingly, in Washington the Department of Defense made a largely unilateral decision to go ahead with the exercise; it was not subjected to interagency review, and some officials from other parts of the administration say they would have opposed it—if for no other reason, on the grounds that the choice ought to be left to the administration that would be in power when the exercise occurred, the incoming Clinton administration.[56]

Despite the statements of some U.S. military officers to the contrary, both Washington and Seoul undertook planning for the exercise with the expectation that they might well bargain it away, and remained prepared to do so until the very last minute. In fact, many U.S. officials disagreed with Seoul's judgment about the exercise and worried that holding it again would prove counterproductive. But Washington was not willing to overrule Seoul's decision. South Korea had begun to drift into a guarded and skeptical posture toward the North, a far cry from the confident and expansive rhetoric of *Nordpolitik*. Seoul would remain in a largely unbroken defensive crouch for the next two-plus years, and its growing toughness and conservatism on the nuclear issue would provoke a handful of fiery clashes with Washington.

South Korea's lead role in determining the fate of Team Spirit pointed to an important and growing connection between the exercise and the North-South challenge inspection regime. Although the cancellation of Team Spirit 1992 had served partly as one element of a broad nonproliferation strategy aimed at gaining general inspections in the North, by the end of 1992 the exercise had become linked to the very specific demands for short-notice challenge inspections that the South was making in the JNCC meetings. It was because of a lack of progress in those talks that the South decided to hold Team Spirit again.[57] Team Spirit had thus become firmly embedded in the process of North-South diplomacy, a dangerous, if inevitable, connection.

Once the decision had been taken to proceed with planning for Team Spirit, which was set to occur in March of the following year, politics conspired to prevent the later cancellation of the exercise. In both Seoul and Washington, new, reform-minded governments came to power in early 1993. Neither was in a position—particularly not Kim Young Sam's government in Seoul, which was being watched closely by the military and conservatives for any hint of an irresponsible stance on security issues—to cancel an exercise scheduled by its more conservative predecessors. Once the Roh and Bush governments started the process for Team Spirit 1993, the Kim and Clinton teams could do nothing but let it go forward.

While U.S. and South Korean officials certainly took into account the possibility that announcing the planning for Team Spirit could be counterproductive, the immediate effect of the decision played directly into Pyongyang's hands by providing North Korea with an excuse for continued delay. The early days of October 1992 therefore saw violent North Korean statements. On the 8th, various North Korean reports raised the long-dead issue of an indigenous South Korean nuclear program; these charges were repeated on the 13th.[58] On the 10th, a *Nodong Sinmun* article called the South Korean claim of a U.S. nuclear withdrawal a "sheer lie." By mid-October the North had focused on the issue of Team Spirit, calling its resumption "a criminal act" designed intentionally to disrupt implementation of the North-South accord, "put the brakes on North-South relations and drive the North-South dialogue to a crisis." Planning for the exercise, the Foreign Ministry statement continued, "is a reckless act casting dark shadows on the U.S.–DPRK relations which are showing signs of improvement."[59]

Predictably, the ninth meeting of the JNCC, held on October 22, achieved little. It reportedly lasted just two and a half hours, and Team Spirit was the only agenda item. The chief of the South Korean delegation said the two sides "did not even mention" the specifics of nuclear inspections. North Korea demanded that Team Spirit be canceled by the end of November if the talks were to continue, and threatened to abrogate the North-South reconciliation agreement.[60] That same day, Kim Chong U, North Korean head of the North-South Joint Economic Cooperation and Exchange Committee, issued a "press statement" indicating that North-South dialogue naturally could not proceed "while a large-scale thermonuclear war rehearsal is conducted with firing guns aimed at waging an attack on [us]."[61]

In the midst of this brewing controversy, the apparent U.S. confusion over its definition of success in the nonproliferation effort was in evidence in a statement by U.S. Arms Control and Disarmament Agency Director Ronald Lehman. On November 1, in a discussion with reporters, he essentially concurred with Roh Tae Woo's diagnosis of September 17: the risk posed by the North's nuclear program, Lehman claimed, had declined with the IAEA process. Inspections had "stopped" the North Korean weapons program, Lehman asserted, and "blocked the ability for [North Korea] to have a sizeable number of nuclear weapons over time."[62] This was a rough approximation of a definition of success proposed, and some said accepted, during the Clinton administration two years later: focus on stopping the North in its tracks—not, at least in the first instance, on answering all the questions about its past nuclear work.

But if Lehman was right (as chapter 9 will contend), and if his opinion was shared in other parts of the U.S. and South Korean governments (as Roh's statement suggested), why were U.S. and South Korean officials unwilling to reward North Korea for this major progress by canceling Team Spirit? If the danger inherent in the nuclear program had measurably declined, why risk everything with a tough insistence on immediate implementation of a challenge inspection regime? At issue was a definition of success in the nonproliferation effort. For most in Washington and Seoul, that definition did not merely include stopping the North Korean program, as Lehman implied had occurred; it included fully rolling it back and gaining near-absolute certainty about the status of all disputed plutonium and other elements of risk very rapidly. Guided by this definition—the broadly-accepted standard of success for nonproliferation efforts at the time, but one whose suitability to individual cases was seldom challenged—U.S. and South Korean officials pressed ahead. Although those officials could not have known it at the time, their tough approach would soon produce an international crisis of major proportions.

U.S. and, especially, South Korean officials were not unaware of the dangers inherent in North Korea's threats. They attempted to make the North understand that the exercise was still on the table, and would be suspended for the right price. Thus in November 1992, South Korean officials began showing flexibility on Team Spirit, promising to cancel the 1993 exercise if progress was made in the North-South nuclear talks by December.[63] In fact, as suggested earlier, the original decision to go ahead with planning for Team Spirit was taken in the hope that the threat of the exercise would produce North Korean cooperation and that Team Spirit would still be canceled. North Korea rejected these approaches, arguing that an end to Team Spirit had already been offered as an inducement for one North Korean concession—allowing IAEA inspections in the first place. Seoul and Washington, in Pyongyang's view, were trying to play the same bargaining chip twice.[64]

U.S. officials objected that this was a flat lie. North Korea had been fully informed, they said, that the 1992 Team Spirit cancellation was a one-year initiative. Nonetheless, the decision to proceed with planning for the exercise had given the North another excuse to avoid inspections for another year—and, as events would prove, to do much more than that.

By December 1992, a crisis appeared imminent. Already on November 3, Pyongyang had suspended all North-South contacts except the Joint Nuclear

Control Committee to protest Team Spirit. On November 27, the JNCC talks themselves collapsed over the issue, with the two sides departing and failing to set a date for the next meeting.[65] South Korean officials repeated their offer to cancel Team Spirit if the JNCC talks produced results, an increasingly unlikely prospect. And although a subsequent JNCC session was held in mid-December, no progress was made.[66]

THE IAEA'S DISCOVERY

At about this same time, a third area of dispute was coming to a head: the IAEA's first demand for special inspections. Earlier IAEA inspections in the North had turned up disturbing evidence of North Korean nuclear weapons research. By the end of 1992, the first hints began to emerge that the North had been caught in, at best, an inaccurate accounting of the true scope of its plutonium reprocessing. This information gave a new sense of urgency for the need for special inspections and put a dark cloud over all the progress that had been made in regular IAEA inspections to date.

This evidence began to emerge in late 1992. IAEA inspections produced technical indications that the North had reprocessed plutonium not once, as it claimed, but at least three times—in 1989, 1990, and 1991. Initially, IAEA scientists compared levels of isotopes in the plutonium samples provided by the North Koreans with levels in known North Korean plutonium waste; the two samples did not match.[67] Disturbed, the agency requested the right to collect additional samples, and did so by swabbing metal glove boxes and other compartments that held plutonium at the main Yongbyon reprocessing facility. Agency inspectors were using new, high-technology equipment that looked, among other elements, for Americium 241, a decay product of Plutonium 241. Americium 241 is a telltale sign of reprocessing; it decays over time and its spectrum provides information about the time reprocessing took place. By finding at least three different spectra of Americium, IAEA inspectors and scientists were able to date the North's reprocessing efforts accordingly.[68]

U.S. satellite photos eventually provided the IAEA with a good sense of where the North had hidden the plutonium waste from its reprocessing. Two sites near the Yongbyon compound drew U.S. attention. One was an outdoor facility with a particular layout of round and square holes, resembling closely a Soviet design of an outdoor site for solid and liquid nuclear waste. Iraq reportedly used very similar waste sites near its own nuclear facilities, and this new Korean facility was adjacent to a nuclear waste dump constructed in 1976. Just days before the arrival of an IAEA inspection team, North Korean workers could be seen on satellite photos covering the old site with earth and land-scaping it to hide it from IAEA inspectors and U.S. satellites.[69]

The second site was a large building, which the CIA reportedly called "Building 500," also alleged to be a receptacle for plutonium waste. During the winter of 1991, according to U.S. intelligence, North Korean workers had labored to dig trenches through frozen ground between the main reprocessing facility at Yongbyon and Building 500. These connections reportedly could be used to transfer plutonium waste without the knowledge of outside inspectors. Building 500 itself is something of a mystery: satellite photos allegedly reveal that the above-ground structure is set atop a massive concrete lower level, which was visible at first but then covered by huge mounds of earth pushed up against the sides of the structure. IAEA inspectors have been inside the building's upper level, but found no stairs or other evidence of a basement, and North Korean officials deny that a lower level exists.[70] Together, the outdoor waste facility and the mysterious building would soon become known as the two "suspect sites."

U.S. intelligence officials were at first reluctant to share this information. Showing the satellite imagery to the IAEA would require revealing some degree of the satellites' capability, and intelligence officials are schooled in the need to avoid divulging the "sources and methods" of their craft. Officials within the CIA at first vetoed proposals to brief the IAEA on their findings.[71]

Nonetheless, based on information gathered by its own inspectors, as early as November 30, the IAEA was sufficiently disturbed to call in North Korean Minister of Atomic Energy Industry Choe Hak Gun, Roving Ambassador O Chang Rim, and four others to relay its concerns. IAEA Director General Hans Blix discussed some of the information uncovered by the agency, told the North Koreans that they clearly had not declared all their relevant nuclear activities, and urged them to be more sincere. The following month, Blix reportedly made an informal request to send a special inspection team to Yongbyon after the fourth regular set of inspections, but was rebuffed by the North.[72]

Meanwhile, North-South talks were making little headway. The twelfth session of the JNCC, held on December 10, achieved no progress. Positions on both sides were hardening. The North continued to demand an immediate cancellation of Team Spirit and inspections of U.S. military bases in the South;[73] the South urged the conclusion of an inter-Korean inspection regime. Neither side seemed willing to move first.

The talks, one North Korean official mused after the meeting concluded, were "facing [a] danger of breakup."[74]

THE IAEA DEMANDS SPECIAL INSPECTIONS

In late January 1993, the IAEA began to discuss the possibility of a request for special inspections of the two suspect sites. The agency had never invoked special inspections before, and North Korea would provide the first test case of this newly-summoned power. Even before the IAEA made its final determination, North Korea rejected the idea out of hand, arguing that the sites were conventional military facilities not subject to IAEA purview—a total lie in the view of U.S. officials privy to secret intelligence.[75] This would become a common North Korean refrain in the months ahead: it could not allow the IAEA, or anyone else, free access to its conventional military bases. Such a step, Pyongyang claimed, would violate its sovereignty and undermine its military deterrent.

Illustrating the irony of the situation, this rebuke arrived from the North even as the sixth IAEA inspection team conducted its work at Yongbyon. No one could have known it at the time, but this would be the last IAEA team in North Korea for months. The IAEA group in the North made one last request to view the two alleged nuclear waste sites in the course of its normal examinations, and was again denied.[76]

North Korea had refused several informal requests for inspection of the two suspect sites, and the IAEA had run out of friendly options. On February 9, therefore, the IAEA took an unprecedented step in its history. It demanded a special inspection of nuclear sites not offered voluntarily by the target nation.[77]

Pyongyang's reaction was immediate and harsh. The IAEA move, fumed North Korea's official newspaper *Nodong Sinmun,* represented "a new plot to impair the prestige of the DPRK and isolate it" as well as "an unpardonable provocation aimed at infringing on and violating its sovereignty and dignity."[78] Apart from some slight indications of flexibility during the following months, North Korea remained adamant in its refusal to accede to IAEA special inspections. "If we accept the request to inspect ordinary military sites," exclaimed North Korea's Ambassador to the UN in Geneva Ri Chul, "at the end we will have to reveal all of our military facilities."[79]

At the same time, in a move that was, from the perspective of the IAEA process, terribly timed, Russian Deputy Foreign Minister Kunadze traveled to Pyongyang to deliver some bad news. That Kunadze stopped in Seoul first to notify the South Koreans of his intentions was disturbing enough to the North, but when he arrived in Pyongyang, he informed North Korean officials of a decision that a few years before would have been unthinkable: Moscow no longer intended to honor the military components of the 1961 Soviet-DPRK Treaty of Friendship and Cooperation. Pyongyang saw another of its dwindling number of umbilical cords cut.[80]

By mid-February 1993, the growing evidence of North Korean dishonesty on the nuclear issue, exacerbated by a combination of the spy ring case, Team Spirit, and the IAEA demands, had raised tensions in Korea to the boiling point. Lest anyone fail to appreciate the stakes, North Korean Ambassador to Russia Son Song Pil issued a clear threat in Moscow on February 15: if the IAEA persisted with its demand, Son indicated, North Korea might be forced to repudiate its IAEA status.[81]

From February 16 to 18, North Korean Atomic Energy Minister Choe traveled to Vienna, in the words of his government to "explain" the discrepancy over plutonium. It quickly became clear that the North had no intention of accepting the IAEA demand.[82] Choe reportedly claimed that the North had indeed reprocessed a tiny amount of plutonium on a second occasion, in 1975, using small, Soviet-supplied nuclear research "hot cells" located at Yongbyon. That work, Choe contended, accounted for the inconsistency; the IAEA did not accept the explanation.[83] Choe's visit accomplished nothing and, if anything, convinced the IAEA that the North had no acceptable explanation for the disturbing evidence of nuclear cheating.

On February 22, Choe issued a detailed statement, again making the North's case that it had cooperated with the IAEA and that all the fuss over missing plutonium was, in fact, nothing more than a misunderstanding.[84] On the same day, another North Korean official in Geneva, Chul Ri, raised a more serious issue, reiterating that the North was prepared to abandon the nuclear inspection regime. "If the IAEA continues to request a special inspection," Ri said pointedly, "then it forces [North Korea] not to implement her obligations under the [IAEA] agreement."[85]

But the agency was not about to be dissuaded because, also on February 22, at a closed Board of Governors meeting, the United States—for the first time, in some ways, since 1945—laid almost all its cards on the table. Since the previous winter, some U.S. officials had fought with those in the CIA who opposed releasing intelligence information on the two suspect sites. Eventually, those in the CIA opposed to the sharing were overruled—initially, in the Bush administration by CIA Director Robert M. Gates and Undersecretary of State Arnold Kanter, and later by the Clinton White House. (The Clinton team had to intercede to prevent the CIA from providing hopelessly fuzzy versions of the photographs, although even the ones eventually shown to the IAEA were distorted slightly by computers to keep from revealing the full capability of the U.S. satellites.) Top U.S. officials came to the conclusion that obtaining near-unanimous world support in pressuring North Korea warranted the risk of releasing sensitive information about the abilities of U.S. spy satellites. Thus it was that, with representatives from Libya, Syria, and Algeria on hand, U.S. officials shared the dramatic intelligence photographs of the nuclear waste sites that seemed to prove beyond a doubt that North Korea was lying about its nuclear program.[86]

The following day, the IAEA Board of Governors pushed the confrontation a notch higher. The board issued a resolution determining that access to the two disputed sites was "essential and urgent" and demanded North Korean acceptance of special inspections.[87] The resolution called on Director General Blix to report back on North Korean compliance within a month—essentially a deadline for North Korean agreement, after which many observers expected the agency to refer the matter to the UN Security Council for possible sanctions.[88] North Korea rejected the resolution, calling it "not just."[89]

Team Spirit was scheduled to begin on Tuesday, March 9. On March 8, North Korea published an order from Kim Jong Il as supreme commander of the Korean People's Army: "On declaring a state of war readiness for the whole country, all the people and the entire army." Team Spirit, the order contended, was "thoroughly aggressive in its content and purpose," a "nuclear war test aimed at a surprise, pre-emptive strike at the northern half of the country." As a result, Kim Jong Il ordered that "the whole country, all the people and the entire army shall, on March 9, 1993, switch to a state of readiness for war."[90]

Gradually, the collapse of the U.S. and South Korean nuclear diplomacy was becoming evident. After allowing six IAEA inspections, the North enjoyed virtually no benefits from the process—no economic aid or investment, no broader political contacts with Washington or Seoul or Tokyo, not even the ability to verify that U.S. nuclear weapons had been withdrawn from the South. Meanwhile, Pyongyang increasingly faced the demand—from both the South and the IAEA—to allow short-notice inspections of virtually any military site in the North. And by revealing a massive alleged North Korean spy ring and deciding to go ahead with planning for a 1993 Team Spirit exercise, South Korea had taken two actions almost calculated to force the North away from the negotiating table.

Apparently, the lessons of the previous year—that specific offers and incentives combined with a generally favorable negotiating climate had produced results—had faded from the memories of some South Korean and U.S. officials. Admittedly, evidence did emerge that the North was cheating, and North Korean officials showed little inclination to make major concessions in the North-South talks on denuclearization. At the same time, however, there may have been an opportunity to meet these setbacks with intensified diplomatic efforts and a slightly deepened embrace of the North, which would have represented a continuation of the previous year's successful diplomacy. As it was, U.S. and South Korean officials—particularly leaders in Seoul, feeling somewhat betrayed by the lack of progress in the JNCC talks—decided to reverse the diplomatic approach and revert to the old pattern of conveying messages through hard-line signals and threats.

The risks of the situation had in fact been emphasized earlier, on February 21, by a long editorial in the North Korean daily *Nodong Sinmun*. The IAEA, it warned, "is attempting to infringe on our republic's sovereignty." It called South Korea's support for the agency "an intolerable treachery and a nation-selling flunkeyist act intended to give rise to another war in our country." And North Korea's party publication issued a clear warning: "If any special inspections and sanctions are enforced on us, and if the sacred lands of our fatherland are trampled underfoot by big countries, this will be a dangerous fuse that will drive all lands, including the North and the South, into the crushing calamities of war."[91]

■ **6** ■

THE NPT WITHDRAWAL CRISIS, 1993

A s the pressures outlined in the previous chapter continued to build through 1992 and into early 1993, North Korean leaders were undoubtedly forced to reexamine the purposes and importance of their nuclear research. The remarkable testimony of a North Korean defector, published in the November 1993 issue of the South Korean magazine *Wolgan Chosun,* gives some hint as to the value of nuclear weapons for North Korea in the early 1990s.

Yim Yong Son, a former first lieutenant in the Korean People's Army, revealed that economic and social conditions in the North had become deplorable. For many people, food was scarce. Many industries hardly operated at all. And the armed forces went without adequate equipment, spare parts, fuel, and training.

One thing, however, rallied the spirits of military officers and men: the idea that Kim Il Sung's regime had built a bomb. "Officers and soldiers of the People's Army are proud of one thing," Yim wrote, "even under such terrible conditions: the development of nuclear and chemical weapons. Almost the entire People's Army believes that North Korea already possesses nuclear weapons. The People's Army is confident that North Korea will use them in an emergency."[1]

How the North might actually employ such weapons, Yim did not say. He offered no evidence for his claim that the North had a weapon, and his testimony must be taken in light of the fact that he was offering it with the support, and perhaps encouragement, of South Korean intelligence agencies. Nonetheless, his comments—the spirit of which was echoed by a number of other prominent North Korean defectors in 1993 and 1994—reflect one possible and intriguing way in which talk of a nuclear weapons program in North Korea could serve to the regime's advantage.

THE NORTH'S REJECTION OF THE NPT

In January 1993, the administration of the new U.S. president, Bill Clinton, inherited a brewing crisis in Korea. The lapse in diplomacy outlined in chapter 5 had alienated North Korea and set the stage for a confrontation. United States officials, however, both of the outgoing Bush administration and the incoming Clinton administration, continued to portray the issue in legalistic terms: the North had certain obligations under the NPT, and it must follow them. Any possibility of further rewards or benefits would be contingent on full North Korean compliance with IAEA demands and inspection requirements. This leitmotif—a narrow, legalistic interpretation of nonproliferation policy—continued to be evident in U.S. policy toward North Korea. Its consequences were predictable: stalemate, confrontation, and perpetual crisis on the peninsula.

An alternative did exist. From early on in the Clinton administration, elements in the Office of the Secretary of Defense—the civilian leadership of the Defense Department—argued for a bold option.[2] Defense officials, including Secretary of Defense Les Aspin, proposed a direct appeal to the top leaders in Pyongyang in the form of a high-level delegation. The problem could only be resolved by going directly to the source of North Korean policy, Defense officials reasoned; dealing with middle-level bureaucrats in New York or Geneva did not guarantee that the right messages were getting to Kim Il Sung. The Defense Department also envisioned a clear, compelling set of incentives to be offered the North once the high-level dialogue was underway. And some in Defense proposed a definition of success different from that of the IAEA and the nonproliferation specialists, one that focused on the North's future nuclear capability rather than whatever plutonium it may already have acquired.

It is important to stress that the Defense option was not perceived by its adherents, and does not appear in retrospect, as a concessionary proposal. The idea was to bring the issue to a head, to challenge North Korea with a direct appeal and a strong offer of a deal. If the North did not accept, at least some of the officials involved were prepared to push for sanctions and, if necessary, military action. Some proponents of the Defense view therefore saw their plan as the hard-line alternative, as opposed to the arguments of those who preferred to string the issue out over time. One U.S. official interviewed later described the Defense plan as a "sugar-coated ultimatum."

At first, the Clinton administration did not pursue this option. Defense was overruled in "principals meetings" among secretary-level officials by State, the Arms Control and Disarmament Agency, and the National Security Council. The other agencies argued that the Defense proposal was politically infeasible; conservative columnists and members of Congress were already having a field day attacking administration policy, the agencies argued, and a direct appeal to Pyongyang would be viewed as a sign of weakness. On substantive grounds, other agencies viewed the Defense idea as rewarding the North with high-level talks when it had not met its obligations under the NPT.

By itself, the Defense Department option did not represent any sort of silver bullet that would end the crisis in Korea. Nor was Defense alone in proposing ideas such as a high-level envoy or a package deal. And one response to the Defense proposal seems, in retrospect, to be quite valid: the North Korean nuclear issue had to be worked out gradually, over time, in tough negotiations; neither the complexities of the case nor the North Korean negotiating style were amenable to an ultimatum.

Nonetheless, the next three chapters will contend, in part, that U.S. policy gradually shifted in the direction of the Defense Department option—with two critical differences: the resulting offers to North Korea were made in the context of negotiations, not as a one-time, take-it-or-leave-it deal; and the U.S. government did not abandon the idea of including special inspections in the accord, as some at Defense were apparently willing to do. Despite these modifications, by October 1994 it could be fairly argued that the combination spelled out in the Defense proposal—a compelling package deal, a (somewhat unintentional) high-level visit to Pyongyang, the willingness to forgo special inspections at least for a time, and the threat of sanctions for noncompliance—had succeeded in bringing about a dramatic accord that, if implemented, would effectively resolve the North Korean nuclear issue.

In the short term, however, the Clinton administration was faced with a much more immediate barrier to a friendly engagement of North Korea. For, as a result of the disagreements outlined in chapter 5, North Korea announced in March 1993 its intention to abandon the Nonproliferation Treaty.

The North's move stunned the world. Many of the nations involved in the campaign to end Pyongyang's nuclear weapons program, most notably South Korea and the United States, were well aware of the continuing challenge the program would pose. Yet few had imagined that North Korean leaders would take the drastic step of renouncing the treaty altogether. No member of the NPT had ever repudiated the treaty, and U.S. and allied officials feared that Pyongyang's action could set a dangerous precedent.

Given the clear warnings that emanated from North Korea about its dissatisfaction with the status of nuclear diplomacy in the second half of 1992, it should hardly have come as a surprise when North Korea announced its withdrawal from the NPT. Both the nature and the seriousness of North Korea's concerns were well known, and at least two of its high-ranking diplomatic officials had as much as promised that Pyongyang would take that step or something like it. Nonetheless, North Korea's dramatic move caught the world off guard.

Pyongyang issued a long statement on March 12 which made two arguments. The continuing U.S.–South Korean Team Spirit military exercises, it claimed, violated the spirit of the North-South denuclearization agreement and posed a nuclear threat to North Korea. "The 'Team Spirit' joint military maneuvers run downright counter to the idea and purposes of the NPT," the announcement complained, "which calls for respect of territorial integrity and sovereignty and [a] stop to nuclear threat[s]." Indeed, the North reiterated its concern that U.S. nuclear weapons had not actually been removed from the South, as claimed by both Seoul and Washington, and argued that in any case Team Spirit was designed to reintroduce nuclear weapons to the peninsula. This "nuclear war rehearsal targeted against the DPRK" had raised tensions on the peninsula and "compelled our country to enter a semi-war state."[3]

Second, the North suggested that the IAEA had become a tool of American diplomacy. Its call for a special inspection of the two suspect sites meant that the IAEA had joined the United States "in its anti-DPRK machinations." If "we submissively accept an unjust inspection by the IAEA," the statement continued, "it would legitimize the espionage acts by the United States, a belligerent party vis-à-vis the DPRK, and set the beginning of the full exposure of all our military installations." Eventually, "our entire nation would be driven into confrontation and war and be made a victim of the big powers."[4]

"Under such [an] abnormal situation prevailing at present, we are no longer able to fulfil our obligations under the NPT," the declaration concluded. "The government of the Democratic People's Republic of Korea declares its intention to withdraw unavoidably from the nuclear nonproliferation treaty as a measure to defend its supreme interests." This did not, mean, however, that the North intended to pursue nuclear weapons; Pyongyang promised that it would "continue to make every effort to turn the Korean Peninsula into a nuclear weapon–free zone."[5]

North Korea's statement thus merely restated its complaints of the previous eight months. Pyongyang objected to Team Spirit, and it objected to the principle of unlimited IAEA (or South Korean) challenge inspections. U.S. and South Korean officials had known this for months but had not seriously investigated the possibility of some form of compromise, such as a gradual exchange of increasingly intrusive inspections for a series of incentives to the North. Nor had they worked to include in the inspection process things of value to the North, such as new South Korean investment. In March 1993 they paid the price for their lapse: North Korea was on the verge of becoming the first country ever to withdraw from the Nonproliferation Treaty, a disastrous precedent on the verge of the NPT extension conference in 1995.

In the wake of Pyongyang's statement, Washington and Seoul began assembling a worldwide campaign to keep North Korea in the NPT. The North's announcement would not become effective for ninety days (June 12) and this left U.S. and South Korean officials with three months in which to persuade, cajole, and threaten Pyongyang. In the end, they were partly successful: in June, the North suspended its NPT withdrawal and said that it was willing to undergo new inspections by the IAEA. But the legacy of the confrontation would be continuing tension over the IAEA's demand for special inspections and a persistent sense of urgency and crisis.

THE NORTH'S MOTIVES

Why did the North take this dramatic step? Possibly, North Korea's thinking on the status of the NPT in early 1993 reflected the evolution and expansion of its motivations for a nuclear weapons program. The concerns outlined here represent a level of thinking significantly advanced from the more narrow security focus of the 1960s and 1970s.

The easiest explanation is that the North was simply caught red-handed. Using technology North Korean scientists did not predict or understand, the IAEA had uncovered clear evidence of substantial plutonium reprocessing and, with the aid of U.S. surveillance systems, managed to pinpoint what amounted to a nuclear smoking gun—the two alleged plutonium waste sites at Yongbyon. Had the North permitted special inspections, this theory suggests, the United States would have confirmed its suspicions and the North would have been humiliated before the international community. Therefore it refused.

Note that this model does not assume that the North necessarily possesses an active nuclear weapons program, or that it had one at any time after 1991. All the theory requires is the assumption that the North had undertaken weapons-related nuclear research at one time, evidence of which would have been uncovered by the special inspections. The North may have feared the embarrassment of having old nuclear research uncovered as much as the risk of revealing an ongoing nuclear weapons project.

This model is one possible rationale for the North's abandonment of the NPT; there are others. All of them fall generally under the heading of regime preservation—undoubtedly Pyongyang's chief obsession in the 1990s. None of these other reasons is mutually exclusive with the first; indeed, it is very possible that the North initially feared being trapped in a lie, but once it considered its options also saw some potential benefits in the bold step of a threatened withdrawal from the NPT. Each of these rationales mirrors one or more of the overall motives for a nuclear weapons program discussed in chapter 2.

Perhaps the most common theory about the North's announcement is that it was prompted by succession politics in the North. With Kim Il Sung more than eighty years old, the North's snub to the international community could be viewed as a dramatic power play designed to rally the military and people behind his son, Kim Jong Il. A crisis would help prevent any dissident voices from raising objections to the younger Kim's rule and might distract people from the North's economic hardships. And North Korea's official language supported this theory, claiming as it did that Kim Jong Il had defended the North's dignity against attempts to impinge on its sovereignty. Kim Jong Il's announcements of military mobilization required pledges of loyalty to him personally, and all the key policy statements issued during the crisis emerged over the younger Kim's signature. South Korean Foreign Minister Han Sung Joo would say in the midst of the crisis that "This has all been Kim Jong Il's game. Everything has been in his name. And all the other indications are that he has been responsible for the decisions."[6]

In a more directly pragmatic vein, Pyongyang may have sought various concessions, including direct talks with the United States and economic aid, and conceived of nuclear horse-trading as a way to acquire them.[7] The diplomacy of 1991 and 1992 may have convinced the North that there were benefits to be gained from playing at the margins of the nuclear club. Nicholas Eberstadt has suggested that the North was employing a version of game-theory brinkmanship straight out of the pages of Thomas Schelling. Leaders in Pyongyang, Eberstadt argues, may believe that "the international community would feel more compelled to help prevent instability in the DPRK in the years to come if theirs were a nuclear state. Pyongyang might even hope that the prospect of nuclear instability in the DPRK could prompt the international community to help assure a successful transition of leadership from Father to Son, or to offer material assistance to forestall economic breakdown and its attendant uncertainties. Viewed from this perspective, nuclear weaponry may look like a promising instrument for helping to maintain the existing system [in North Korea]."[8] This theory is supported by 1991 rumors out of China, cited previously, that North Korean officials had asked Beijing for help in a final push for the bomb, crowing that "the more the hostile forces are afraid of nuclear weapons, the more we should arm ourselves with them."[9]

North Korea, and especially the Korean People's Army, also appeared determined to avoid setting a precedent of outside inspection-on-demand of their military installations. Such inspections could easily reveal information about the North's conventional military forces, and, more indirectly, could become a threat to regime stability by introducing outside information and influence into the country.[10] Official North Korean statements from 1992 onward are very explicit in rejecting the idea of unlimited outside inspections.

Finally, officials in Pyongyang may have viewed a threat of withdrawal from the NPT as a means of testing the new administrations in Washington and Seoul. A weak or conciliatory response from the governments of Bill Clinton or Kim Young Sam would have been a valuable lesson to Pyongyang.

Any or all of these motives may have been decisive. No matter which rationale was conclusive, however, one fact stands out: whatever its reasons to test the will of the international community, North Korea had nothing to lose except an ambiguous promise of a way out of its economic mess and self-imposed isolation. The United States and its allies had done little to invest the nuclear inspections process with significance for North Korea. Pyongyang saw itself getting the short end of the stick after having allowed the initial IAEA inspections, and may have seen little risk in challenging a process that had, in any case, brought it nothing of value.

A MUTED REACTION

Once the North announced its withdrawal, South Korea and the United States responded with moderate and nuanced diplomacy. Officials in both capitals avoided inflammatory statements that might have driven North Korea further into its isolation, and continued to emphasize carrots as well as sticks in their diplomatic campaign. This critical decision avoided a confrontation and set the stage for a resolution of the crisis that represented at least a partial success. Officials in both countries deserve praise for recognizing the North's signals that it actually hoped to be talked out of the NPT withdrawal, and thus preventing the crisis from escalating into a violent clash.

And indeed, the broad strategies of the Kim Young Sam and Clinton governments did rely on negotiations and dialogue rather than confrontation to solve the nuclear issue. Officials in both Seoul and Washington saw important reasons for holding to a moderate course. For Kim Young Sam, determined to reduce the influence of the South Korean military, perhaps the greatest threat to his administration would be a new crisis that would distract attention from his domestic priorities, stall his political and economic reforms, and perhaps, if the crisis became intense and protracted enough, bring the military back to the forefront of political life in Seoul. For the Clinton administration, the rapid and powerful recognition of the role of China and other regional powers suggested that any effort to reverse the North's decision would have to be fully multilateral. A tougher course toward Pyongyang might have fractured the global consensus on the issue.

Moderation was apparent even from South Korea's initial reaction to the North's announcement. Seoul proclaimed itself to be "extremely concerned" with the North Korean move, and "strongly urged" the North to reconsider its decision. But the statement made no threats, and merely noted that South Korea was "fully prepared to promptly and resolutely deal with any provocation by North Korea following its withdrawal from the NPT."[11] To reemphasize the seriousness of this warning, Seoul announced on March 13 that it was placing its military on alert as a "precautionary" step.[12] But other statements conveyed more disappointment than rage, and left the North a clear route to return to the NPT. Of course there could not be any North-South economic cooperation as long as the crisis lasted, Kim explained on March 15, but this was unfortunate for both sides. The world must cooperate to urge North Korea to reverse its decision, President Kim argued, but "we do not wish North Korea to receive pain or be further isolated in the international community." Kim even left the door open to an eventual North-South summit (which he still predicted would occur during his five-year term) and to the return to North Korea of Li In Mo, a Korean War–era journalist and Northern sympathizer imprisoned in the South for forty years.[13]

Other officials in Seoul reflected Kim's tone. New Foreign Minister Han Sung Joo, an internationally known and respected professor at the prestigious Seoul National University, told the South Korean National Assembly that "We must make all efforts to resolve this in a peaceful manner and not make the situation worse."[14] Han later said the issue should be resolved by the "involved parties" and wanted to avoid referring it to the United Nations; Seoul would work "so that the matter can be resolved without going as far as sanctions."[15] And on March 16, South Korean officials went ahead with a scheduled diplomatic meeting at Panmunjom with their North Korean counterparts and agreed to return Li In Mo to the North. Li traveled north three days later.[16]

Early U.S. reactions were similarly restrained. "We call upon North Korea to withdraw its statement immediately," State Department spokesman Richard Boucher said in the days after March 12, "and to take steps including full cooperation with the IAEA which will restore international confidence that North

Korea is fulfiling its international responsibilities in the nuclear area." When asked about the possibility of UN sanctions against the North, Boucher would not comment.[17]

South Korea also moved to cede responsibility for the issue to the IAEA. It was an IAEA agreement that the North had suspended, and Seoul argued that the agency was the logical avenue for coordinating the world response.[18] IAEA Director General Hans Blix was already moving the agency into action. Blix convened an emergency meeting of the IAEA Secretariat on March 12 and contacted IAEA Board of Governors member states about a gathering of the full board. Another IAEA official made reference to the agency's ultimate option if the North did not comply: to refer the matter to the UN Security Council for possible sanctions.[19]

Despite this generally soft handling, North Korea took a number of disturbing steps that suggested a growing bunker mentality. Reports emerged that Pyongyang had decided to expel all foreign diplomats, or at least deny them access to North Korean officials; had recalled delegations from abroad; had suspended many phone lines connecting Beijing to Pyongyang; and had begun jamming broadcasts of Radio Japan and the South Korean KBS radio station for the first time.[20] At the same time, North Korean officials tried to make it clear that outside sanctions would only escalate the crisis. Pyongyang's China Ambassador Chu Chang Jun said North Korea would adopt "a strong defensive countermeasure" if confronted with any threats or sanctions.[21] On March 15, Pyongyang's Foreign Ministry published an extensive refutation of IAEA claims against the North and defense of its rationale for departing the NPT.[22]

North Korea, it seemed, was digging in for a protracted standoff.

SEOUL AND WASHINGTON COORDINATE POLICY

North Korea's swipe at the NPT quickly took shape as the first major foreign policy crisis of two new administrations—the governments of Kim Young Sam in Seoul and Bill Clinton in Washington. Together they would have to find a way out of the crisis North Korea's withdrawal from the NPT had sparked.

Kim and Clinton had much in common. Both were young, reformist presidents elected in three-way races without a majority of the vote. Both represented the striving for change of a younger generation, and both promised to place primary emphasis on new programs for economic growth. Both had faced a challenge from an eclectic, populist businessman running against the political elite—Ross Perot in the United States, and Hyundai Chairman Chung Joo Yung in Korea. Both were held in suspicion by their respective militaries, and neither had a strong record on foreign policy or defense issues.

Kim Young Sam could hardly have been well-prepared for the crisis. His platform for inter-Korean relations, while not as ambitious as that of his left-wing rival Kim Dae Jung, nonetheless called for expanded economic and political contacts. Meanwhile Kim's administration prepared to conduct a housecleaning of the government, evicting former generals and other top officials who had participated in Seoul's military-run governments of the 1960s, 1970s, and early-to-mid 1980s. Kim's economic reform program, calling for an attack on what he viewed as corrupt practices in government and business, quickly became inseparable from his drive to oust military influence. Anything that strengthened the hand of the military would complicate his rule.

Clinton, inaugurated just two months before, had only the barest outline of a foreign policy team in place by March 1993. Secretary of State Warren Christopher and a handful of top aides were at the State Department, Secretary of Defense Les Aspin and few others were in the Pentagon, and a National Security Council staff, under adviser Tony Lake and his deputy Samuel Berger, was only beginning to take shape. Moreover, when the Clinton administration first took office, before the March 1993 crisis, North Korea was not even at the top of the list of foreign policy priorities; one administration official remembers it standing at about six or seven, behind more pressing crises in Haiti and Bosnia.[23] However, Clinton did have some well-regarded holdovers from the Bush administration in key positions, such as State Department spokesman Boucher and Assistant Secretary of State for East Asia and the Pacific William Clark.

Once the North announced its intended withdrawal from the NPT, there was no shortage of instant analysis calling for the rapid imposition of sanctions, economic as well as military, against the North,[24] and in other circumstances the temptation to engage in saber-rattling might have been severe. For the reasons noted earlier, however, neither Seoul nor Washington had any interest in exacerbating the crisis, and Kim's and Clinton's aides began the complicated process of coaxing, rather than blustering, North Korea back into the NPT.

For a time, therefore, North Korea confronted in the Kim and Clinton administrations officials dedicated to dialogue and opposed to the idea of provoking a crisis. Although it was not apparent at the time, however, the North also faced governments that felt themselves politically constrained from undertaking just the sort of bold engagement for which the North was calling. And over time, as crisis gave way to crisis, the North would come to realize that the Kim and Clinton administrations were determined to adhere to strict nonproliferation principles and burnish their images with the conservative wings in their countries.

Moreover, notable differences of opinion between the United States and South Korea began to emerge over time. In the early stages of the crisis, South Korea generally insisted upon a cautious approach, while U.S. officials were prepared to make more open reference to sanctions and other punishments the North would suffer if it did not change its policy. Thus the initial U.S. reaction was leavened with some tougher rhetoric. On March 13, for example, the *New York Times* reported that while the "exact details" of the U.S. response "remained to be worked out," at the heart of the U.S. policy would be a request for the UN Security Council "to issue an ultimatum threatening North Korea with economic sanctions." Secretary of State Warren Christopher was quoted to the effect that sanctions would be a leading option "if they [North Korea] continue on the path they are on."[25]

Nonetheless, most U.S. statements kept the moderate tone that characterized the general U.S. and South Korean response. On March 15, President Clinton made his first remarks about the North's action. Clinton avoided ultimatums and threats and emphasized the positive. "I am very disturbed by this turn of events, but I'm hoping it won't be a permanent thing," Clinton said. "There are several weeks ahead in which North Korea might reverse its decision and I hope that it will do so because we simply cannot back away from the determination to have IAEA inspections proceed there."[26] Clinton's remarks combined a tough adherence to the need for IAEA inspections with an unemotional and hopeful approach to the North.[27]

After a meeting with Secretary of State Christopher, South Korean Foreign Minister Han made a nuanced statement to the press in which he said that U.S. and South Korean officials had agreed on a graduated stick-and-carrot approach to persuading North Korea to reenter the NPT. "Pressure alone will not work," Han contended, arguing that they needed to offer North Korea concessions to reverse its policy. He suggested drawing up a list of possible benefits the North could obtain by agreeing to stay in the NPT. He listed among possible concessions allowing North Korean inspections of South Korean military bases, transforming Team Spirit into a much smaller exercise, offering guarantees to the North against attack, and expanding trade and diplomatic relations among North Korea and South Korea, Japan, and the United States.[28]

All of this was important, Han argued, because "we are dealing with a regime which is very dangerous, and which obviously takes its own conceptions of face and image very, very seriously."[29] Amazingly, the next full year would be taken up with sluggish U.S. and South Korean efforts to implement this simple notion. And ironically, as chapter 7 will explain, when the United States finally talked of offering the North such a package deal, South Korea balked.

Taken together, these early policies reflected a clear desire to avoid provocations or threats that would exacerbate North Korea's paranoia. As one news report summarized the reaction, "U.S. officials from President Bill Clinton down have been careful not to box the North Koreans in with explicit threats of international sanctions."[30] Washington's aim, in a sense, was to afford North Korea every opportunity to do the right thing.

COAXING THE NORTH BACK INTO THE NPT

By mid-March 1993, the U.S. and international effort to lead the North back into the NPT was underway in earnest. On the 17th, Assistant Secretary of State Robert Gallucci—soon to be the U.S. pointman on the nuclear issue—met in with Russian and British officials in Vienna to discuss strategy. The following day, the IAEA held its first full Board of Governors meeting since the North's announcement. The agency issued a resolution directing North Korea to honor its obligations under the NPT and reiterating the demand that the North allow inspection of the two suspect sites within one month.[31] The board set a date of March 31 for its next meeting, and this was widely interpreted as a deadline for North Korea to respond.

U.S. officials were meanwhile working out an agreed strategy among their allies. At a March 22 meeting at the U.S. Mission to the UN, representatives from the United States, South Korea, and Japan met and shared views on the crisis. Their concluding statement was an example of moderation, explicit promises, and veiled threats. It promised the North continued economic and diplomatic engagement if it returned to the NPT, expressed only "regret" at its intended departure, and called for continued international efforts to reverse the North's decision. One Japanese official phrased the results of the meeting as an agreement to persuade North Korea to reenter the NPT "while leaving open the possibility of improving relations with Pyongyang" if the nuclear issue were resolved.[32] A similar tone emerged from the late March meetings between U.S. Secretary of State Warren Christopher and South Korean Foreign Minister Han.

From its statements and actions, it was clear that Pyongyang was paying close attention to world reaction to its provocative move. The North's position seemed calculated to prompt concessions and discourage threats. On March 24, for example, perhaps encouraged by the restrained tone of U.S. and South Korean announcements and the conclusion of the 1993 Team Spirit exercise, the North announced that it was ending its state of "semi-war."[33] Disturbed by occasional U.S. references to sanctions, however, on the 29th Pyongyang warned of a "powerful self-defensive measure" if sanctions were applied—an ambiguous phrase that became ubiquitous in statements by North Korean officials in subsequent weeks. Once again drawing back from confrontation, however, on March 31 North Korean Ambassador Kim Kwang Sup said in Vienna that the North would accept "temporary inspections" of its declared nuclear facilities (not the two suspect nuclear waste sites) to allay outside concerns about its intentions.

Although such a limited visit would take place, this gesture did not satisfy the IAEA. On April 1, declaring North Korea to be in violation of its agreements with the agency and its commitments under the NPT, the agency's Board of Governors referred the matter to the UN Security Council. The IAEA had done all it could; North Korea had ignored its resolution of March 18, the agency declared, and further policy toward Pyongyang would have to originate in the Security Council.

The ultimate irony of the situation was that, after nearly a full additional year of back-and-forth diplomacy, this North Korean offer—a one-time inspection to preserve the continuity of inspections—would be accepted by the United States and the IAEA as an "important step" toward resolving the crisis. But in March 1993, the United States had not yet learned that it would be unwilling, and perhaps unable, to pursue a confrontational approach. It therefore continued to demand both regular and special inspections, and to threaten sanctions if the North did not comply. Referring the issue to the council was a step widely believed to represent a prelude to the imposition of sanctions; North Korea had promised to react violently to any punitive measures. A major confrontation seemed inevitable.

CHINA'S ROLE IN THE CRISIS

Almost from the moment that North Korea announced its intention to withdraw from the NPT, analysts and officials in Seoul, Washington, and Tokyo identified China as the key player in this new crisis. As North Korea's lone geopolitical sponsor of sorts (although even Beijing's "alliance" with the North now exists mostly on paper), China might be able to exercise some influence on Pyongyang's thinking. South Korea and the United States quickly set out to acquire China's assistance in the campaign to reverse Pyongyang's abandonment of the NPT.[34] And once the issue of sanctions was raised, it quickly became evident that China held the decisive cards in any world effort to isolate North Korea. Washington had little goodwill in Beijing on which to build: Sino-American relations from 1992 through early 1994 weathered angry disagreements over China's weapons exports (particularly M-11 missiles sold to Pakistan and possible chemical-weapons related supplies to the

Middle East) and its human rights practices (debated every year in Washington in high-profile confrontations over Most Favored Nation trading status). If China and the United States were to work together on Korea, their cooperation would have to be based on the merits of the case, not on the strength of a wider geopolitical partnership.

Very quickly, China defined itself as the advocate of a moderate diplomatic campaign toward the North. Beijing's motives in urging a diplomatic solution seemed clear enough. It had no desire to have North Korea come apart at the seams and pour millions of refugees into northeastern China, and economic sanctions might hasten just such a collapse. Moreover, concerned about the international community's close attention to Chinese weapons development and export practices, and touchy as always on the larger question of sovereignty, Beijing opposed the sort of robust nonproliferation standards that would allow global institutions like the IAEA to interfere in Chinese national policies. And although China had absolutely no interest in a nuclear-armed North Korea, Chinese officials—with nearly half a century of experience with Kim Il Sung and his regime under their belt—seemed confident that the matter could only be resolved through diplomacy rather than a confrontation. A new war on the peninsula might force China to pick sides, disrupt its economic modernization, and raise new questions in the power centers of Beijing about China's future course.

At the same time, U.S. officials recognized that no regime of sanctions could work without Chinese assistance. During the early U.S.–ROK discussions after March 12, a frequent topic was the likely role of China.[35] A South Korean official claimed that Han and Christopher had agreed that China would not veto a sanctions resolution and that, in any case, international sanctions would be effective "with or without Chinese participation."[36] This statement was quickly contradicted by another, unnamed U.S. official, who was quoted on March 30 as saying that "Sanctions require, absolutely require, that the Chinese participate,"[37] and this latter opinion became the consensus view as the crisis wore on.

China's refusal to be drawn into an international confrontation with the North established strict boundaries on U.S. and South Korean policy. China shares a substantial border with North Korea, and could simply ship supplies, or allow them to be shipped, in violation of any international embargo to which Beijing was not a party. China could also pressure other countries, including Russia and perhaps Japan, into opposing sanctions as well. Moreover, if it tried to enforce sanctions over Chinese opposition, the United States might have found itself in a confrontation with Beijing and in a position that would eventually lead to sanctions against China as well.

Beijing did not take long making its position clear. As early as March 23, Chinese Foreign Minister Qian Qichen unequivocally stated China's opposition to a provocative response to the North's abandonment of the NPT. "If the matter goes before the Security Council," Qian argued, "that will only complicate things." He stated flatly that Beijing was opposed to the use of sanctions.[38] From the beginning, China worked to tone down the initial UN resolution on the North, to avoid threatening language, and to pressure the United States to begin a dialogue with North Korea.[39]

Once the issue had been referred to the UN Security Council, China persisted in its campaign against the use of sanctions. On April 8, Chinese Foreign Ministry spokesman Wu Jianmin discussed Beijing's view in the wake of the IAEA briefing to the Security Council. Evidence that North Korea had nuclear weapons was "not convincing," Wu declared. "We have held all along that dialogue is more effective than pressure. To bring pressure to bear is not appropriate now." China was, however, "prepared to work in a concerted effort with the parties concerned to reach a solution," Wu said, but it must happen through "patient consultations."[40]

Yet any notion that China was somehow running interference for North Korea appeared to be dispelled in late April, when reports emerged of growing hostility between Beijing and Pyongyang. China was pursuing its "patient consultations" to no avail, and Chinese officials were becomingly increasingly frustrated with North Korea's intransigence.[41] For its part, Pyongyang may have resented pressure from its lone remaining sponsor. North Korea reportedly refused to accept Chinese delegations sent to discuss the issue and bolstered guard units at the Chinese border; China allegedly suspended civilian flights into Pyongyang.[42] According to some reports, North Korean troops even fired on their Chinese counterparts,[43] though North Korea quickly denied these claims.[44] Reports later emerged that in May, North Korean Deputy Foreign Minister Kim Yong Nam, stopping over in China on his way back to the North, departed without ever leaving the airport after being denied permission to enter Beijing.[45]

Throughout the crisis, China's position had a decisive impact on U.S. diplomacy.[46] Early discussions in the U.S. government of a hard-line response to the North after March 12 were discarded once the centrality of China's position was recognized. With the end of the Cold War, U.S. officials saw an opportunity to conduct the first truly international diplomatic campaign to promote nonproliferation. The U.S. response to North Korea's announced withdrawal from the NPT was therefore a product of multilateral diplomacy as much as of unilateral policymaking. Had China been an advocate rather than a staunch opponent of economic sanctions, the course of U.S. and international diplomacy after March 12 might have been entirely different.

AVOIDING A STANDOFF

In early April 1993, concerned about the referral of the nuclear issue to the
Security Council and the potential for a full-blown crisis, South Korea accelerated its own diplomacy in the hopes of finding a settlement before sanctions
had to be applied.[47] On April 6, Kim Young Sam again reiterated Seoul's
desire for a diplomatic solution. "We will act with moderation rather than
responding violently," he promised. "We do not want the North Korean regime
to be dismantled suddenly because this would threaten the security of the
whole peninsula."[48]

On April 5, North Korea made part of its agenda in the crisis clear, requesting direct talks with the United States. The nuclear crisis, the North's
announcement claimed, was "not a matter to be discussed in the UN arena but
a problem that should be resolved through negotiation between the DPRK and
the U.S."[49] Whether this was merely a ploy to delay sanctions, or whether the
North wanted to negotiate substantive issues, was not evident. What was
clear was that Pyongyang remained as determined as ever to talk directly to
Washington. North Korean officials may, in fact, have seen this as a major goal
of their nuclear brinkmanship of 1993.

At the same time, however, the North continued rattling its limited sabers.
On April 7, North Korean envoy to France Pak Dong Chun, in what he
claimed was a statement on behalf of his government, said the North was ready
for whatever might happen in the standoff. He reiterated the North's promise
to fight sanctions with "effective self-defensive countermeasures," and even
scorned the ultimate risk: "We do not want war," Pak boasted, "but we are not
afraid of it."[50]

That same day, the UN Security Council heard the IAEA's official report.
But restrained by Chinese reluctance to made demands or threats, the Security
Council could make only the most moderate statements. On April 8, based on
the IAEA briefing, the council merely declared itself to be "concerned at the
situation" and reaffirmed the importance of the NPT.

On April 22, the United States took another step in its process of moderate
diplomacy, agreeing to high-level talks with North Korea.[51] Both China and
South Korea supported such a dialogue, but Washington had opposed it on the
grounds that there was nothing to talk about. North Korea knew its obligations,
U.S. officials had contended, and could have a face-to-face dialogue when it
met them. But U.S. officials were increasingly concerned about isolating the
North, and their agreement to engage in new discussions represented, in part,
an admission that North Korea also had security concerns at stake in the crisis, and that the United States could not deal with the North alone—it needed

China. To demonstrate to Beijing that diplomacy was being given a fair chance, the United States was willing to meet with the North.

The first major sign of progress in the crisis was North Korea's agreement, noted earlier, to interim IAEA visits to reinspect those facilities the North had already opened to outside investigators. This visit took place during the first week of May. The IAEA team stayed in the North for more than a week, changing film in inspection cameras and checking other surveillance equipment.[52]

On May 5, U.S. and North Korean officials held a political meeting in Beijing, the thirty-second such meeting, in preparation for high-level talks at a later time.[53] The North requested the meeting, and together with the renewed IAEA inspections, the Beijing talks gave some in Washington hope that the North intended to resolve the crisis.[54]

Slowly, a UN Security Council resolution emerged with tougher language urging the North to reverse its decision. The resolution underwent extensive behind-the-scenes negotiation to answer Chinese concerns. The United States reportedly first presented a draft on April 23, and talks on changes proceeded for more than two weeks.[55] A draft was distributed in the second week of May, and the Security Council approved it on May 11. This draft was relatively mild, avoiding threats but going so far as to request that the North change its decision. Significantly, it also called on member states to exert their best efforts to resolve the crisis—which those involved recognized as code language for the U.S.–DPRK talks desired by China. Again, Washington was showing flexibility to convince Beijing that the diplomatic angle was being fully investigated. Predictably, the North denounced the resolution—while leaving the door open to a settlement of the crisis.[56]

China did not approve that mild edict, but did not veto it either, choosing to abstain. Even this decision reflected, in the eyes of the U.S. officials working with them, a significant change in the attitude of the Chinese, who might have rejected any Security Council statements several weeks before.[57] Multilateralism was thus working, slowly, for the United States, with U.S. respect for China's position—and North Korea's nettlesome intransigence—apparently winning approval in Beijing for a slight increase in pressure on the North.

Toward the end of May, more signs emerged of an impending three-way dialogue between Washington, Pyongyang, and Seoul aimed at resolving the crisis. By the 17th, both North Korean and U.S. officials were saying that a high-level U.S.–DPRK contact was imminent;[58] on May 25, it was announced that the meeting would occur on June 2 in New York.[59] On May 20, South Korea proposed a resumption of bilateral talks with the North, suspended the previous September, to discuss such issues as family unification.[60] The North reciprocated by suggesting the planning of meetings aimed at a North-South presidential summit,[61] and Seoul answered favorably.[62]

Despite these encouraging signs, concerns grew in Seoul and Washington that the crisis had entered a dangerous stage. Some nuclear experts publicly warned that North Korea might be preparing for a complete fuel replacement of the main Yongbyon reactor immediately after June 12, thus acquiring fifty tons of spent uranium fuel ripe with plutonium by-products. General Robert W. RisCassi, chief of the U.S.–ROK Combined Forces Command in the South, expressed concern that "the North could slide into an attack as an uncontrollable consequence of total desperation or internal instability."[63] On May 14, Seoul's Agency for National Security Planning reported to the National Assembly that the North could have two to three nuclear bombs in 1994 or 1995 if weapons development were not halted.[64]

The situation appeared to be deteriorating, and increasingly, it seemed there was very little the outside world could do about it. "Military solutions to the nuclear problem are too dangerous," a senior Japanese official said at the time. "And even if we can get them passed, economic sanctions probably won't do much good."

"The fact is," he concluded, "that all the options are bad."[65]

NATIONALISTS IN SEOUL

As debates over the nuclear issue evolved in South Korea, a new breed of nationalist South Korean legislators, writers, and academics began to make their voices heard. They argued that Seoul was too firmly in the grip of the United States, that South Korea needed its own nuclear policy. Many of the new nationalists pointed to South Korea's agreement to abandon nuclear reprocessing, a stance that placed limits on the South's civilian nuclear power industry, as an example of Seoul's willingness to subordinate its own interests to the overarching goal—pushed upon it by the United States—of nonproliferation. And some Koreans complained that the United States turned a blind eye to Japanese reprocessing and even stockpiling of plutonium while forcing the South to abandon both.[66]

As in most issues in South Korea's relations with the United States, the South's radical student groups held some of the most extreme opinions. The leader of one major student group told an interviewer in September 1993 that South Korea was being "pulled around by the United States" on the nuclear issue. The U.S. demand for challenge inspections, this student said, was an unfair burden on the North. He argued that the nuclear issue should be resolved in South-North negotiations, and that "the stumbling block to settlement to the nuclear issue on the Korean Peninsula is none but the United States." When asked if the "United States is always our enemy," this young South Korean replied, "That is right."[67]

Less extreme opinions, but ones still suspicious of the U.S. role in the nuclear issue, were held more broadly. An essay representative of this point of view appeared in the Seoul periodical *Wolgan Chosun* in April 1993. The writers argued that South Korea only gave up its reprocessing capability on the demand of the United States. They argued that, if left to U.S. leadership, the nuclear issue was likely to end in economic sanctions and talk of military strikes. The result was that "Korea is forced to simply support the position of the United States, a nuclear nation. As the dependency on the United States in the security and diplomacy arena deepens, Korea inevitably becomes increasingly vulnerable to the United States in other areas such as trade pressure or demands for increased defense burden sharing. As we defer to the wishes of our allies in nuclear policy, we retreat from independent national defense, and our dependence in the areas of diplomacy and economic intensifies as well." This "ironic, vicious circle," the *Wolgan Chosun* editors concluded, "is the burden that we bear."[68] As a corrective, the article recommended developing a vigorous civilian nuclear reprocessing industry in the South—with continued respect for nonproliferation, but also with the clear implication that, if South Korea's (or a unified Korea's) security someday demanded it, a nuclear arsenal could be developed.

One South Korean lawmaker even recommended a joint civilian energy project performed in cooperation with the North. National Assembly Foreign Affairs Committee Chairman Chung Jey Mun, known as a close ally of Kim Young Sam, pointed to the economic benefits of reprocessing and Japan's exploitation of the process. Chung argued that, "If Pyongyang's efforts are aimed at the peaceful use of nuclear energy, North Korea should ask for cooperation from us." He admitted, however, that the North's program seemed intent on producing a bomb.[69]

A few South Koreans went as far as to suggest an outright nuclear weapons program. Some proposed this course as a means of countering the North's program, others as preparation for Korean unification amid a hostile Northeast Asian security context. The pro-bomb factions were relatively small groups in the National Assembly,[70] and Kim Young Sam's Foreign Minister Han Sung Joo quickly squelched the campaign by announcing decisively that "Under no circumstances will we consider going nuclear ourselves," noting that to do so "would legitimize the North Korean nuclear program and thus perhaps provoke Japan to reconsider one of its own."[71]

Debates about South Korea's nuclear capabilities came to a head in October 1993, when South Korean Minister of Science and Technology

Kim Si Jung suggested publicly that the 1991 North-South denuclearization agreement be revised to allow reprocessing in the South. Kim said he had urged such a step on Kim Young Sam.[72] Other lawmakers and analysts joined the call: the influential daily *Chosun Ilbo* reported on October 10 that "the notion on [*sic*] 'nuclear sovereignty' is prevailing now not only among the parliamentary members, but also among the ordinary people . . . [it] has become a major critique against the government's nuclear policy."[73]

The government authoritatively rejected Kim Si Jung's ideas, and talk in Seoul of a renewed nuclear weapons program quickly ended. But the dialogue that continued over the need for the South to retain a reprocessing capability represented the same issue being treated in more diplomatic language. Thus the reconsideration of nuclear issues writ large in South Korea gave urgency to the standard nonproliferation argument that a bomb in Pyongyang would lead, rapidly and inevitably, to a bomb in Seoul as well—and from there, perhaps, to a bomb in Tokyo.

THE NORTH REVERSES COURSE

The U.S.–North Korean talks in New York on June 2 provided the most important signs yet that the crisis over North Korea's threatened withdrawal from the NPT was on the way to being resolved. Although convened at the eleventh hour, with Pyongyang's NPT withdrawal scheduled to become effective in just ten days, the talks nonetheless provided a forum for an exchange of views and, possibly, a face-saving concession that would allow the North to declare victory and rejoin the NPT. Upon arriving in New York, the senior North Korean delegate, First Vice Foreign Minister Kang Sok Ju, declared hopefully that "Our delegation will make every effort to bring good results to the talks," and asked that the United States do the same.[74]

According to press reports, the United States was adhering to a two-pronged strategy. On the one hand, top U.S. negotiator Robert Gallucci and his team insisted that the North remain in the NPT and allow IAEA inspection of the suspect sites at Yongbyon. But Gallucci also came armed with incentives, including a pledge of nuclear nonaggression against the North if it remained in the NPT and the possibility of additional talks on political and economic cooperation and an end to Team Spirit. Gallucci also reportedly suggested that U.S. and South Korean military bases be inspected simultaneously with the sites in the North, to address Pyongyang's complaint of unfair treatment.[75]

The negotiations were held in the offices of the U.S. Mission to the United Nations. The first day passed uneventfully, with neither side reporting any significant progress.[76] Still, the atmosphere remained positive; at the end of the day, Kang described the talks as "useful" and said they had occurred in a "frank and sincere atmosphere." The two sides agreed to meet again on June 4, and expectations were high that some compromise would be reached.[77]

These hopes were dashed after the 4th when no accord emerged.[78] In a third meeting on June 10, North Korea refused to remain in the NPT, but still held out hope for a last-minute reversal on Friday, June 11, when U.S. and North Korean officials would talk yet again. "The talks haven't failed yet," said North Korean delegation chief Kang. The issue would be "decided Friday afternoon," he said.[79] U.S. and South Korean officials alike talked of the need for sanctions if the June 12 deadline passed.

Finally, on Friday, June 11, 1993, North Korea announced that it was suspending its withdrawal from the NPT and would continue to abide by its commitments under the treaty. In the sparse joint statement that emerged from the U.S.–DPRK talks, North Korea made clear that it had decided only to "temporarily suspend the effectuation of the withdrawal from the Nuclear Nonproliferation Treaty as long as it considers necessary." For its part, the United States offered only the slimmest carrot: a pledge not to "use armed forces, including nuclear weapons, nor threaten" such use against the North (with the North promising the same). There was no mention of Team Spirit, simultaneous inspection of U.S. bases in the South, or economic incentives; nor did the North agree to IAEA inspection of the two suspect sites.[80]

In the wake of the talks, Gallucci called the North's announcement "a move in the right direction" and emphasized that the alternative would have been "extremely unfortunate."[81] South Korea, relieved that the prospect of sanctions could be put off, also welcomed the North's decision.[82]

As a number of critical analysts quickly pointed out, however, it was "too early for sighs of relief," because the "initial problem remain[ed]—Pyongyang [was] yet to agree to open key suspected nuclear facilities to international inspection."[83] U.S. officials argued that they were scheduled to engage in further talks with North Korea and intended to obtain the necessary IAEA inspections in those forums. There was no guarantee, however, or even promise by the North that this would happen, and indeed some North Korean officials continued to object to inspections of facilities they had long claimed were not related to their nuclear program.

Although U.S. and South Korean officials could not have known it at the time, this same series of events would repeat itself over the coming year. North Korea would agree to a small portion of the IAEA and U.S. demands, thus putting off sanctions and prolonging the nuclear dispute, while leaving the most important issues on the table. U.S. policy allowed this trend by remaining wedded to its own form of incrementalism and staunchly refusing to take decisive action of any sort, whether by offering the North a "package deal" or attempting to impose sanctions. This policy of gradualism held out little hope of a final resolution of the issue, which may have been exactly what North Korea desired.

On June 11, the IAEA Board of Governors met once again in Vienna. Its concern was more specific than Gallucci's. He had to keep the North in the NPT, but the IAEA was still focused on obtaining inspections of the two suspect sites—whether by special inspection or through a face-saving North Korean offer. The board adopted a summary of its proceedings that once again stressed the importance of full access to North Korea's nuclear facilities.[84]

U.S. and South Korean policy, aided by substantial behind-the-scenes pressure from Beijing, had succeeded in keeping North Korea within the NPT. In so doing, Washington and Seoul avoided a major international crisis and kept the door open to eventual North Korean compliance with IAEA demands, a door that would certainly have slammed shut once any sanctions were imposed. Yet in many ways the stage was merely set for a new crisis if the North refused to grant the IAEA access to the suspect sites. And that, as many predicted at the time, was exactly what the officials in Pyongyang would do—at least for a time.

■ 7 ■

ON THE ROAD TO RESOLUTION, 1993–1994

In late January 1994, the Reverend Billy Graham traveled to North Korea.[1] It was Graham's second trip. Reverend Graham had a long history of reaching out to the faithful in Communist and totalitarian societies, and in the early 1990s he decided to pursue similar work in Pyongyang.

Graham's first visit, in 1992, had gone well. North Korean authorities had allowed him to preach in a few small churches—in front, no doubt, of carefully hand-picked audiences. Graham met with Kim Il Sung, who proclaimed himself influenced by his Christian mother and insisted that his people enjoyed freedom of worship. And Graham carried a message from President Bush, a broad statement of goodwill and a promise of better relations if the nuclear issue was resolved. On his return, Graham's organization published a glossy pamphlet with photos and narrative from his journey.

In the time between his trips, the situation on the Korean Peninsula had gone through a roller-coaster ride of high tension, talk of war, and finally a relaxation as North Korea appeared to accept a U.S. proposal for continued inspections. But the deal was far from done, and the peninsula hung precariously on the brink of a major crisis once again.

Now Reverend Graham was back in Pyongyang, accompanied by his interpreter, Stephen Linton, and a small retinue of church officials. He had another meeting with Kim Il Sung. And he carried another message from an American president—this time, Bill Clinton. The thought, however, remained essentially the same: cooperate on the nuclear issue and the North would receive benefits.

Graham's advisers were concerned about the message. They feared that it was too blunt, too businesslike, stating U.S. policy as a lawyer would state it in court. It offered no warm greetings, no ritual. It hit directly at the problem rather than coming at it indirectly. Clinton had never met Kim before; he was forty years the Great Leader's junior; and the first message he would send was to be this gruff demand for cooperation. As one of Graham's Korea experts would say later, the statement was a form of "Godfather diplomacy": Play nice, Clinton was telling Kim, and I'll make it worth your while. Misbehave and I'll smash your knees.

Between tough-minded American lawyers or businesspeople, this message may have worked. But in Korean society, based as it is on personal relationships, considerations of face, and roundabout approaches to problem-solving, the Clinton message was inappropriate.

Graham and his staff worked for several hours trying to spin the message, to develop a context of remarks and statements so that, when the message was finally delivered, its rudeness would not be so apparent. But they remained anxious.

The two men met in a conference room behind a large hall in which Graham would speak. The room was divided from the larger space by sliding doors; Graham's staff later heard rumors that there were twenty or more North Koreans, each probably representing a different bureaucratic interest, with their ears glued to the crack between the doors. All wanted to know what the respected American religious leader would have to say, and how the Great Leader would respond.

Graham dutifully delivered Clinton's message, and then waited for Kim Il Sung's reaction. Kim became agitated, almost angry, and spoke loudly, shaking his fists. He argued that it was wrong for the United States to pressure the North, and that the North was the aggrieved party. The United States should be the one offering concessions, Kim said.

Reverend Graham tried to mollify the North Korean leader by explaining Clinton's situation. The news media, foreign policy analysts, and members of Congress were all demanding a tough policy toward the North, Graham said. Clinton is "doing the best he can, under the circumstances," to promote a peaceful end to the disagreement.

As Graham described the pressures on Clinton, Kim Il Sung nodded. He did not necessarily indicate agreement, but seemed willing to accept the American president's predicament—and to admit that Clinton might be sincere in his desire to resolve the issue peacefully. At the meetings, Graham never asked for any concessions, and the two sides reached no agreements. But the meetings provided an example of the sort of direct dialogue and nurturing of personal relationships that had been conspicuously absent from official U.S. diplomacy toward the North.

After their discussion, Graham and Kim retired to lunch. Over a meal of Korean delicacies, they discussed their childhoods and their experience of life. Kim again explained how his Christian mother had taught him the ways of the church. But he also admitted that he found fishing a more interesting diversion than religion. In interviews conducted several months later, Kim Il Sung would explain wistfully that he wished he could pursue his pastimes of hunting and fishing on a trip to the United States. He also hoped that, on the trip, he could "make some friends."

THE CONTINUING CRISIS

Much more diplomacy, however, would take place before Graham's trip. By early July 1993, the prospects for nonproliferation in Korea appeared to be looking up. North Korea's threat to abandon the Nonproliferation Treaty had been headed off at the eleventh hour by U.S. and South Korean diplomacy, and officials on all sides were talking optimistically about the future.

Few observers would therefore have predicted the nearly calamitous chain of events that marked the second half of 1993 and the first half of 1994. The U.S.–DPRK cooperation, such as it was, that led to the June 11 accord on the NPT collapsed into a new round of bellicose threats and name-calling. North Korea balked at further cooperation with the IAEA; U.S. officials began referring more explicitly to the likelihood of economic (and potentially military) sanctions; and the prospects for a peaceful solution to the crisis grew dimmer with each passing month. Fears of a new Korean war permeated Seoul and Washington—in November 1993, a top aide to South Korean President Kim Young Sam estimated the likelihood of conflict at 50 percent. This chapter describes and discusses these events and the attempt to resolve the nuclear crisis that followed them.

The U.S.–DPRK Dialogue Continues

With the agreement of June 11 in place, high-level U.S. officials continued their dialogue with their North Korean colleagues. The U.S. goal was to restore the continuity of IAEA inspections in the North and, somehow, obtain Pyongyang's agreement to the principle of special inspections. It quickly became apparent, however, that the optimism of early June was misplaced, and that fundamental U.S.–DPRK disagreements persisted.

One issue, largely ignored by the media in the wake of the June 11 accord but of great potential importance, was North Korea's stance regarding the

NPT. As far as the United States was concerned, having "suspended" its withdrawal from the treaty the North remained a full member, with all the obligations that membership connotes. Pyongyang read its policy a different way: the suspension represented, to North Korean leaders, a kind of deferral of their final decision. It therefore rejected the notion that its NPT status created legal requirements to allow inspections or to take other steps. This difference of opinion would be the basis for serious disagreements later in the year.

As 1993 progressed, the IAEA itself became another source of misunderstanding and delay. For its own reasons, outlined in previous chapters, the agency was determined to take a tough line with North Korea. In the wake of the NPT crisis, therefore, when a reevaluation of its agenda might have been in order, the IAEA continued to demand the full range of verification, up to and including immediate special inspections of the two disputed nuclear waste sites. To have worked so painfully throughout the spring of 1993 to avoid a North Korean rejection of the NPT only to have the IAEA return to the very demand that had sparked the crisis in the first place seemed hardly logical. The IAEA, however, is not tasked with making political judgments. Its purpose is merely to verify compliance with safeguards agreements. But this, of course, was the very paradox of the situation: the agency had entered a realm where political, not technical, decisions reigned supreme.

Finally, President Clinton, with no doubt the best of intentions in declaring U.S. fidelity to a valued ally, did little to create a warm climate for U.S.–DPRK talks when he declared, during a visit to South Korea, that North Korea would disappear if it employed nuclear weapons. His statements, and a series of open threats about economic sanctions from other U.S. officials, reflected the U.S. strategy of publicly both threatening North Korea and offering it a way out of isolation. These public threats and condescensions, calculated to provide the sticks and carrots of a two-track nonproliferation policy, at least on the surface produced nothing but North Korean bombast in return. And on a number of occasions, North Korea had proved itself fully capable of temporarily severing dialogue in response to a single idle remark.[2]

Nonetheless, as of early July 1993, some hope existed that the nuclear crisis was on its way toward resolution. U.S. and North Korean officials met in a second round of high-level talks. The two sides exchanged views, and the United States laid down two conditions for the continuation of dialogue: progress toward regular IAEA inspections, and a resumption of North-South political contacts.[3] Also at the talks, the United States dangled a new offer: it would assist the North in replacing its graphite-moderated nuclear reactors with light-water reactors, more modern and far less useful for acquiring bomb-grade plutonium.[4]

The two conditions appeared simple enough, but in fact they would become serious bones of contention. For whatever reason—because it was actually seeking to assemble a nuclear arsenal, because it was waiting to wring further concessions out of the United States, because internal power struggles prevented a clear policy line, or because it believed it was being mistreated by the United States—North Korea refused to budge. Little progress took place in July or August, and plans for a third round of high-level talks in late summer fell through.

During the first few days of September, IAEA officials traveled to Pyongyang for talks with North Korean leaders. The agency continued to insist on special inspections, and North Korea continued to reject them. Nothing was achieved at the talks other than to have the North reiterate its charges of "partiality" on the part of the IAEA.[5] When IAEA Director General Hans Blix proposed a second round of talks with the North in October, North Korea simply ignored the request.[6] Shortly thereafter, Washington formally postponed the third round of U.S.–DPRK talks.[7]

A Manufactured Crisis

As the fall of 1993 progressed, U.S. and South Korean officials and commentators began speaking more and more frequently about the need for sanctions, the worrisome aspects of various North Korean military moves, and the risks of war on the peninsula. This remarkable series of statements looked to some even then, and certainly appears so in retrospect, as an almost entirely self-generated crisis. At the time, however, the risk of war appeared to be real and growing.

The first hints of this urgency began in late September, with reports in the Japanese media about a North Korean military buildup along the Demilitarized Zone (DMZ) in Korea.[8] U.S. Secretary of Defense Les Aspin told the Japanese Defense Minister in late September that the nuclear issue was unlikely to be solved by negotiation, and would probably have to be referred to the UN Security Council for sanctions.[9] Other U.S. officials echoed this pessimistic line.

By October, a specific concern began to exacerbate the sense of urgency about Korea: the supposedly imminent loss of "continuity" of the IAEA inspection process in the North. With no IAEA inspectors having been allowed access to North Korean nuclear facilities for several months, agency officials reported that the film and batteries in the cameras used by the IAEA to record activities at the sites were about to run out. If North Korea were allowed a substantial period of unobserved activity at the nuclear facilities, it could conceivably reprocess more plutonium or otherwise take actions that would render any previous conclusions by the IAEA moot.

Concern over the loss of continuity was so great that, at the beginning of October, South Korean Foreign Minister Han Sung Joo, long a voice of moderation in the crisis, said pessimistically that economic sanctions could now wait "at least one or two weeks"[10]—not much of a window for action, and in fact a timetable that would quickly be abandoned. On October 1, the IAEA, citing concerns about the continuity of the inspection process, passed a resolution demanding that the North accept new inspections immediately.[11] Predictably, the North denounced it.[12]

Even as its standoff with the IAEA continued, North Korea did take steps to meet the other U.S. condition for direct talks: beginning a dialogue with the South about the exchange of presidential envoys. In early October, the two Koreas began discussing a low-level contact, a preparatory meeting for the subsequent exchange of envoys.[13] Meanwhile, North Korea settled on a strategy for showing progress with the IAEA: it would offer to allow IAEA technicians to change the film and batteries in their cameras at Yongbyon, thus maintaining the IAEA's definition of continuity of inspections, while refusing full inspections or to be classified as an NPT member with the corresponding obligations.[14] And all the while the North pressed its case for direct talks with the United States, contending repeatedly that "the nuclear issue on the Korean Peninsula can be settled only between the DPRK and the United States."[15]

The IAEA, however, rejected the North Korean offer outright. Agency spokesman David Kyd said in Vienna that the agency would not accept anything less than full inspections, presumably including the disputed special inspections of the two nuclear waste sites.[16] In so doing, the agency began a dangerous game of chicken with the North: in refusing to replace film and batteries, the IAEA was creating the possibility of a loss of continuity—which the United States had promised would lead to sanctions. The agency believed full inspections were critical, and did not want to set a precedent in which the country being inspected was able to set the terms of the inspections. The IAEA's hope was that the North would blink first. It is difficult to engage in brinkmanship without any leverage, however, and increasingly throughout the fall several IAEA member-states were forced to remind the agency of the political realities of the situation.[17]

With the IAEA's tough demands, the nuclear issue in Korea headed for another crisis. On October 13, the South Korean press reported government officials' claims that continuity was on the verge of collapse.[18] On October 20, the *New York Times* editorialized that "A diplomatic solution to the dispute is still possible, but time is running short. . . . [T]he U.S. and others are prepared to seek economic sanctions."[19] And on the 22nd, the Seoul daily *Chosun Ilbo* pointed out that "the deadline for resolving the issue—the end of October—is just around the corner."[20]

THE NORTH KOREAN ECONOMY

North Korea's economic problems, long a source of concern for Pyongyang, appeared to be reaching crisis proportions in 1993. By the end of the year, North Korean officials would make unprecedented admissions of their economic difficulties, and key players in the Pyongyang government would reportedly be demoted or reassigned for their association with the previous seven-year economic plan. Even without the imposition of economic sanctions, therefore, many observers contended that North Korea had a powerful motive to find a solution to the nuclear issue and thereby allow outside economic aid and investment.

But the real scope of the North's economic hardship was unclear, especially the degree to which it affected the leadership and its domestic allies, including, presumably, the military. No solid proof emerged to support Western reports of widespread food shortages, although anecdotal evidence to that effect seemed strong. If officials in Pyongyang believed that they could weather substantial hardship, especially among urban workers, and remain in power, and if they looked forward to better performance in coming years, North Korea's economic problems may not have created the urgent need for a nuclear deal that some in the West assumed.

Still, North Korea's basic economic predicament was stark enough. South Korea's Trade, Industry and Energy Ministry alleged in October 1993 that the North's GNP was collapsing, having declined to $21.1 billion in 1992, a nearly $2 billion drop from the year before—a drastic 7.6 percent contraction, the worst economic performance on record in the North's history.[21] (By contrast, Fidelity Investment company's vast Magellan mutual fund contained some $33 billion in investments in 1994—half again as large as North Korea's entire economic output.) According to Seoul's National Unification Board, rice production in the North reached a three-year low of 4.26 million tons in 1992, down from 4.81 million tons in 1990—this against a demand of nearly 7 million tons.[22] When Russia began insisting on hard currency for its oil deliveries in 1990, shipments to the North dropped from a million tons a year to 45,000 tons; during the same period, deliveries from China slipped by a third, from 1.6 million tons a year to one million tons.[23] Defectors came south with stories of mass food shortages, of diets based on corn or rice with only irregular deliveries of meat and fish, of actual starvation.

Amid an economic crisis of such proportions, the North Korean government and its people resorted to unusual and desperate measures. Pyongyang reportedly became a sort of geopolitical used-car dealer, buying used automobiles from Japan and smuggling them across the border into China in exchange for hard currency; according to South Korean officials, used cars accounted for 20 percent of the North's imports from Japan in the first seven months of 1993.[24] Korean residents of Japan who visited relatives in the North in 1993 returned with stories of factory workers, unable to find sufficient food, wandering the countryside to barter soap, toothpaste, and pots and pans for rice or corn. North Korean factories allegedly granted the workers several days off for such trips in order to keep their workforce healthy.[25]

One result of these dire economic circumstances was a deepening of North Korea's already substantial economic dependence on China. North Korea's trade with China represented almost a quarter of its total in the first half of 1993, with its primary imports from China being grain and crude oil.[26] Without China's help in both areas, hunger in the North would have become far more widespread, and dozens of additional factories would have had to be closed for lack of energy.

Another lifeline for Pyongyang was the stream of financial contributions from Korean residents of Japan. *New York Times* reporter David Sanger described the process: "Twice a month, under the watchful eye of the Japanese undercover police, Koreans in Japan loyal to the Communist government of 81-year-old Kim Il Sung transport huge suitcases and plastic sacks stuffed with millions of yen to a ferry that makes the short run to North Korea from the northern port city of Nigata." Sanger estimated the scope of the assistance as $600 million per year, raised in Korean-run *pachinko* game parlors in Japan and through the proceeds of Japan–North Korea trade. Some Korean residents of Japan gave their money willingly, but others described their gifts as a form of extortion—payments to keep family members safe from the North Korean government.[27]

Despite the expanded Chinese trade and continuing supplies of yen from Japan, by December 1993, the worsening economic situation in the North may have affected the political situation there. North Korean Deputy Prime Minister Kim Tal Hyon, who also held the title of Chief of State Planning and was generally known as the guru of North Korean economic planning, was removed from his posts in the government and reassigned as director of a clothing factory. Many observers interpreted this as Kim's paying the price for the North's poor economic performance, although this connection was based more on speculation than evidence.[28]

North Korea's economic stocktaking continued in an unprecedentedly public manner on December 9. That day, the Korean Central News Agency broadcast a blunt admission from the government: the economy, Pyongyang admitted, was in the midst of "grim trials" and faced a "grave situation." The statement referred to the need for a "period of adjustment" and suggested that the North would henceforth place greater emphasis on agriculture, light industry, and foreign trade[29]—quite a reversal for a nation that once prided itself on hosting most of the heavy industrial factories on the Korean Peninsula.

Yet at least one report denied the notion that North Korea stood on the verge of collapse. The November 11 issue of the Seoul-based *SISA Journal* reported that a number of economic experts believed that the North had reached the low ebb of its economic decline, and future years might see a rebound. The *Journal* cited a British Korea-watcher, Dr. Tony Michel, as claiming that the worst was over and that growing trade with Russia and China would improve the North's food and industrial situations. North Korea was reported to be buying Russian oil at prices far below the world market value and seeking out Western partners to develop oil fields in the North.[30]

Like most developments in North Korea, therefore, the true scale of its looming economic disaster remained a mystery. It was probably fair to assume that, with a contracting economy and at least the risk of serious malnutrition among large segments of its population, Pyongyang had a real interest in expanding economic contacts with the outside world. Just how urgent that interest was, however, and how much influence it exercised on the nuclear issue, was impossible to know.

Nor did North Korean economic statistics provide any definitive answers to the question of whether or not economic sanctions would succeed in forcing the North to allow inspections. Certainly, the North Korean economy was in decline, and may have been in, or on the verge of, a true crisis. Certainly, the North relied heavily on imports for two key commodities: food, to make up domestic shortfalls; and fuel, in the form of oil and natural gas, for its industries and military.

But no one could answer two key questions about sanctions. First, would China cooperate? If it did not, it could supply the North with all the raw materials and food it required. And second, even if all relevant nations agreed to sanctions, what would their effect be? Would the North submissively back down, do nothing and watch its economy crumble, or lash out and start a war?

Opinions on these two points differed. By early 1994, however, something of a consensus had developed on both, and it was not an encouraging one. China might well refuse to cooperate, most observers inside and outside the U.S. and South Korean governments believed. Yet almost regardless of what Beijing did, North Korea's paranoia, pride, and unpredictability meant that sanctions would probably not have the desired effect. Taken together, these facts may have given North Korea an indication—whether true or not—that the persistent U.S. reference to sanctions was little more than a bluff. U.S. officials thus had yet another reason to stop short of a confrontation in Korea.

U.S.–DPRK TALKS: A NEW VENUE

In late October 1993, a series of new, mid-level U.S.–DPRK talks began in New York. Led, on the U.S. side, by State Department Korea desk officer C. Kenneth Quinones and other State personnel, and on the North Korean side by UN diplomat Ho Jong, the talks were aimed at clarifying the two sides' positions and airing new ideas.[31] At the initial meeting, North Korea reportedly rejected both routine and special inspections, and asked for something less; the U.S. side made clear that progress on the nuclear issue could lead to a suspension of Team Spirit.[32] Again the two sides were working from tightly crafted scripts, but U.S. officials involved still said the direct, face-to-face dialogue proved helpful.[33] On October 26, South Korean Minister of Unification Han Wan Sang declared openly that, if the North addressed the issues of IAEA inspections and North-South dialogue, "We will affirmatively consider suspending next year's Team Spirit military exercise"[34]—although Foreign Minister Han Sung Joo was quick to say that no decision had yet been reached on the issue.[35] South Korea meanwhile continued its low-level talks with the North to plan an exchange of envoys.[36]

However, at the same time, press reports in the United States continued to raise the specter of an imminent crisis. On October 24, an article in the *Washington Post* by Lally Weymouth brought extraordinary urgency to the issue. The IAEA was on the verge of declaring the continuity of inspections broken, Weymouth contended, which would very likely lead to international economic sanctions. Meanwhile, U.S. officials were reported to be mulling over alleged promises by Kim Il Sung to reunify the peninsula—by force, if necessary—by 1995. And Weymouth related growing concerns in the U.S. Defense Department of unusual North Korean military activity at the DMZ, including a reinforcement of the North's already front-loaded units.[37]

Perhaps to head off these growing concerns, in the final days of October North Korea restated its offer to allow the IAEA to change film and batteries in its cameras.[38] But the IAEA continued to refuse, demanding all or nothing.

The first decisive moment of the nuclear crisis in the fall of 1993 occurred on November 1. On that day, IAEA Director General Hans Blix provided a report to the UN General Assembly on the status of the North's nuclear program. To the great relief of U.S. officials, Blix fell short of declaring the continuity of inspections to be broken—as he may at one point have been planning to do. While no U.S. official had directly discouraged Blix from declaring the continuity of inspections broken, Assistant Secretary Gallucci and others did make clear the difficulty of the U.S. position and the potential consequences of an unambiguous statement in that direction. Blix may also have appreciated the limits to his power, and the fact that unfulfilled threats by the agency would further erode its credibility. U.S. officials believed that Blix was hesitant to make any irreversible decisions himself; he expected the United States to do so.[39]

Blix did, however, make clear that North Korea had refused routine inspections and widened its opposition to the NPT as a whole and that continuity was on the verge of being lost. He admitted that he had rejected the North's offer of film and battery replacement, because "it is not for the inspected country to pick and choose among the safeguards it has accepted."[40] Blix therefore continued his delicate high-wire act, attempting to preserve the credibility and legitimacy of the IAEA and the principles it was bound to uphold without provoking the North and sparking a major confrontation. And while, as argued earlier, the IAEA had for some time taken a rather theological view of the sanctity of NPT obligations, Blix gradually displayed a clear and growing recognition of the need for a compromise solution and some degree of flexibility in the agency's approach. Eventually he would come to balance the agency's various concerns in a manner that nicely complemented U.S. and allied diplomacy.

The General Assembly responded to Blix's report with a 140-to-one vote urging North Korea "to cooperate immediately" with the IAEA.[41] North Korea condemned the vote; China was notable in its abstention.

In Seoul, the drumbeat of war continued. On November 2, South Korean Defense Minister Kwon Yong Han expressed concern at a press conference about the North's nuclear program, and referred to the possibility of military action to stop it. In response, the North the next day suspended the series of meetings dealing with presidential envoys, citing Kwon's remarks as an unfriendly gesture.[42]

During the annual Security Consultative Meeting (SCM) in Seoul, November 3 to 5, U.S. and South Korean officials agreed to postpone the final decision about the future of the Team Spirit military exercise. At the meeting, U.S. Secretary of Defense Les Aspin reiterated the U.S. commitment "to a nuclear-free Korean Peninsula," but said that "the ball is now in North Korea's court. The world awaits."[43] He again reminded North Korea that a continued refusal to cooperate would lead to negative repercussions.[44] And he indicated that, according to U.S. intelligence, North Korea did not appear to be making major progress on its nuclear weapons program, such as acquiring additional plutonium, while the delay continued.[45]

Also at this time, however, U.S. and South Korean officials began to say explicitly that an IAEA declaration that continuity of inspections was broken would lead inexorably to a call for economic sanctions in the UN. The director for American affairs of South Korea's Foreign Ministry, Chang Chae Young, said that "The most important variable right now is Blix's judgment on when safeguards are broken. Seoul and Washington believe this judgment *is entirely up to the IAEA*"[46] (emphasis added). Although Japanese and Korean officials were reportedly urging Washington to hold off on sanctions for as long as possible, both admitted that the loss of continuity would trigger the process.[47]

Time was growing short. Avoidance of the loss of continuity was portrayed as requiring visits by IAEA inspectors in "the next week or two."[48] On November 5, South Korean President Kim Young Sam argued that dialogue could not go on forever; "I think perhaps it is about time," the South Korean president warned, "that we should consider the possibility of setting a deadline."[49]

As the possibility of sanctions drew close, so, for some, did the risk of war. North Korea had long argued that economic sanctions were a form of conflict and continued its militaristic bluster. "It is our position to respond to dialogue with dialogue," Pyongyang radio said on November 5, "and war with war."[50] On November 6, U.S. officials again confirmed that North Korea appeared to be reinforcing its units at the border; an official on Aspin's plane, returning from Korea, told reporters that "I think that we may be entering a kind of 'danger zone' here."[51]

On November 7, President Clinton, speaking somewhat informally on NBC's "Meet the Press," stated U.S. policy in Korea in an extraordinarily unequivocal fashion: "North Korea cannot be allowed to develop a nuclear bomb," Clinton insisted. "We have to be very firm about it." When asked about the logical conclusion of his remarks—that the United States would feel justified in taking military action, if it proved necessary, to stop the North Korean program—Clinton demurred, saying "I don't think I should discuss any specific options today."[52] That same day, the London *Sunday Times* reported that Washington was indeed developing contingency plans to launch military strikes on Yongbyon.[53]

North Korea's response was comically straightforward. President Clinton, a North Korean Foreign Ministry spokesman said, is "seriously getting on our nerves."[54]

On November 9, the Paris newspaper *Liberation* reported an interview with Yi Sang U, a foreign policy adviser to South Korean President Kim Young Sam. Yi was not sanguine about the stability of the peninsula. When asked about the risk of war in Korea, he said, "today it is 50 percent. And it will remain quite strong for another two years."[55]

Beginning that same day, however, a series of positive developments began to create some hope for a solution to the standoff. Also on November 9, U.S. and North Korean officials held another unofficial meeting in New York.

Nothing in particular was decided, but the meeting was viewed as evidence of North Korea's desire to keep diplomacy alive.[56] The following day, Kim Young Sam and his top national security aides met and decided that, despite the growing press fixation on a risk of war, they had no evidence or North Korean provocations and there was no sign of imminent hostilities.[57]

Most significantly, Kang Sok Ju, a North Korean first vice foreign minister and head of the delegation to the high-level U.S.–DPRK talks, issued a statement on November 11 that sources in the South and the United States widely interpreted as a renewed offer of a deal on the nuclear issue. After the usual angry rhetoric, Kang again hinted at the sort of inspections the North was willing to accept. "[O]ne must surely differentiate ensuring the continuity of the safeguards from completely implementing the safeguards agreement," Kang said. Implementing safeguards "is an issue that must be discussed and resolved in future DPRK-U.S. talks by linking this to the issue of the United States's abandoning the policies of resorting to nuclear threats and stifling the DPRK." Kang went on to say that the North had proposed to the United States "a package solution of the nuclear problem." If the "third round of DPRK-U.S. talks are held and an agreement is reached on a formula for a package solution," then the problem could be resolved. "Now the matter depends on how the United States responds to our proposal for a package solution, renouncing its hostile policy of stifling the DPRK."[58] Pyongyang thus appeared to be almost pleading for the sort of detailed, explicit proposal the United States had so far been unwilling to make.

South Korean officials offered a muted reaction to Kang's proposal; Foreign Minister Han, for example, said that "it is not yet the stage to consider the package deal insisted [on] by North Korea."[59] The Clinton administration had been pursuing the notion of a comprehensive solution since the beginning of the New York talks in October,[60] and now the idea apparently received additional attention in the government, particularly the State Department. Within days, State was reported to be in a bureaucratic debate with the Defense Department and the Joint Chiefs of Staff over whether to "accept" the North's "offer." An interagency meeting was reportedly held on November 15 to discuss the issue.[61]

It was obvious from the press reports of the time that North Korea was not offering inspections of the two suspect waste sites, at least not at first. Some U.S. officials portrayed the potential accord as a two-phase process (though others object to the term "phase" and prefer to describe the process as a seamless one; either way, it was clear that some sequence of events would be involved). In the first phase, Seoul and Washington would suspend the Team Spirit military exercise for 1994, and North Korea would allow any inspections of its Yongbyon facilities, provided that they were inspections designed to preserve the continuity of the IAEA safeguards regime. Then, in the second phase, North Korean suspension of its withdrawal from the NPT, a permanent schedule of routine inspections, and the principle of special inspections (including the two waste sites) would be secured through a "package deal" involving such elements as U.S. and Japanese diplomatic recognition of the North and economic investment in the North by South Korean, Japanese, or U.S. businesses.[62]

Top U.S. national security officials endorsed the basic elements of this approach at the November 15 meeting. The desire for a bold new strategy resulted partly from the recognition that the existing, low-level talks had "failed." In the words of one U.S. official quoted at the time, "We could have had 27 more rounds [of talks] and it wouldn't help."[63] Again, the idea for a stronger proposal did not emerge from Kang's statement; thinking on a new approach had been underway for some time. But Kang's plea combined with earlier indications—for example, the suggestion at the Geneva talks that North Korea might give a good deal to get light-water reactors—to add new impetus to the effort to assemble a more comprehensive proposal. Washington was slowly edging, bit by bit, toward the Defense Department's bold option.

THE ARGUMENT IN THE PRESS

With the growing tensions of the fall and the deepening U.S.–North Korean dialogue came a spate of op-eds and essays offering advice to the U.S. and South Korean administrations.

A number of the articles chastised the Clinton and Kim governments for displaying such a light touch with the North. South Korean papers were especially concerned about reports of an ongoing U.S.-North Korean dialogue in New York. Thus on October 22, the Washington correspondent of Seoul's moderate daily *Chosun Ilbo* argued that "The United States is asked to abandon its current attitude, which seems somewhat irresolute and inconsistent, and show a firm and decisive attitude." Meanwhile South Korea looked like "a third party in the negotiations, detached in the air, as the United States fail[s] to hold a firm position in the negotiations."[64]

On October 28, the *Dong-A Ilbo* agreed, suggesting that Washington was being too dovish. "We should realize that the target of our negotiations is none other than the North Korean regime," the paper editorialized, arguing that the North had a long history of "reaching an agreement it has no intention of abiding by." The paper's editors "would like to question whether the [South Korean] government is not . . . mistaking North Korea for an ally who will abide by the terms of an agreement."[65]

Some U.S. commentators were equally critical in their prescriptions. Charles Krauthammer argued on November 5 that "The administration's response to North Korea's nuclear drive has not been distinguished. It has been all carrot and no stick." Krauthammer concluded with a brutal injunction.

> Enough talk. The time has come for action. And the president had better prepare the American people for it. . . . The president's task is clear. Lead. Stop talking to the North Koreans—it is time for an economic blockade—and start talking to the American people.[66]

Three days later, former Bush administration defense official Zalmay Khalilzad argued in the *New York Times* that the time had come "to impose a deadline on the North Koreans": allow inspections by December 1 or face sanctions. To get Chinese support, Khalilzad was willing to "make cooperation on the North Korean nuclear program the litmus test of our relations."[67]

On November 12, the Forum for International Policy, the think tank set up by Brent Scowcroft and other former Bush administration officials, issued a paper calling for military exercises in and around Korea, economic sanctions, and the preparations for a blockade. On the 13th, the *Economist* wrote that "at some point the talking has to stop," and went as far as to say that, "faced with a chilling choice of risks . . . America would in the end be right to strike first."[68]

Not everyone urged dramatic action, however. As noted earlier, many observers doubted that economic sanctions would work. On November 3, the London *Financial Times* argued in an editorial entitled "Handle with Care" that "a sanctions resolution would almost certainly fall to a Chinese veto in the Security Council. And in any case, tightening the international noose on what is already a pariah state would be at least as likely to result in greater instability as to bring Pyongyang's paranoid leaders to their senses." The essay concluded that "the U.S., Japan and other interested parties would be right to continue with their strategy of attempting to negotiate with Pyongyang, rather than piling on more direct forms of pressure."[69]

Many of those who had long urged a soft line toward Pyongyang opposed sanctions, but so did many observers with hard-line credentials. Congressman Dave McCurdy (D-OK), a conservative Democrat and longtime advocate of a strong defense, argued in the *New York Times* on November 8 that "UN-mandated economic sanctions offer little hope of success" and, in any case, might push North Korea "to the brink of economic collapse, . . . which is precisely what South Korea and Japan want to avoid." Meanwhile, sanctions "would probably incite North Korea to hasten its nuclear work," which would then accelerate calls in the United States for military action. The United States, McCurdy concluded, "is in no shape to play nuclear brinkmanship with

North Korea. We need to push this looming crisis to an amicable conclusion and move on."[70]

Donald Gregg, the Bush administration's ambassador to Korea, similarly praised the Clinton administration for handling the issue "sensibly," and wrote that,

> Above all, I am relieved to note that President Clinton and his staff are resisting the media's calls for what might be called "compensatory toughness" in Korea. Some of the media are saying that since U.S. moderation has not worked out well in Somalia, Bosnia or Haiti, we need to take a stand in Korea to prove our strength and toughness. Such a maneuver would be extremely dangerous. The stakes involved in Korea dwarf Somalia, Bosnia and Haiti combined. . . . It bodes well that the Clinton administration is taking a patient and moderate course towards this vital national security issue.[71]

William Clark, Bush's Assistant Secretary of State for East Asian and Pacific Affairs, went so far as to wonder, "What would happen if North Korea had the bomb?" Most nuclear proliferation had been "essentially defensive," he argued, and while North Korea had "done some nasty and stupid things," it is "not irrational." The fact that North Korea might have a bomb, Clark concluded, "should be kept in the proper context."[72]

Despite the balanced and, if anything, cautious tone of these essays, officials of the Clinton administration—especially at the Department of State and the National Security Council—complained of rough treatment.[73] Interviews with these policymakers during and after the crisis suggest that they perceived the attacks from the right as stronger and more consistent than an objective review would suggest they were, and they may have tended to group all criticism together rather than distinguishing the different messages they were receiving. These misperceptions—if that explanation is accurate—served to limit the administration's freedom of action by encouraging top officials to believe that bold, innovative proposals would be perceived as weakness. Specifically, the role of outside critics appears to have been to undermine the chances that the Defense Department's decisive option would be attempted.

Some of this may be attributable to the personalities within the Clinton administration. A great deal of officials' sensitivity can probably be chalked up to a general defensiveness caused by months of sustained and bitter criticism of the administration's overall foreign policy. And some of the blame must be shared by the majority of the opinion writers (this author included) who generally believed the administration was on the right track, but simply wasn't going far enough. By simply disparaging the administration's cautious and legalistic approach without praising in strong enough terms its dedication to a negotiated solution and its handling of various North Korean provocations, outside experts helped deprive the administration of the confidence to take bold steps rather than providing it with such confidence. Still, any administration must take ultimate responsibility for overcoming media opinion, or winning it over, by implementing a sound foreign policy; and the lack of such a policy in Korea would continue to be evident through the middle of 1994.

U.S.–ROK DISAGREEMENTS

As the U.S.–DPRK diplomacy broadened, South Korean officials became increasingly uncomfortable with their position as distant observers. The trend of toughness in Seoul's approach to the North that had begun in 1993 gained strength. Kim Young Sam seemed increasingly to believe that he could not be perceived as standing on the sidelines, watching a U.S.-run policy. His domestic political standing depended upon his being seen at the center of decision making toward the North. In the coming months, he would take steps to ensure that such a perception existed.

In the days after Kang Sok Ju's offer of a package deal, South Korean officials took pains to deny that the Americans had made any decisions, or to insist that, if they had, Seoul had agreed.[74] Various South Korean newspapers carried editorials warning about the risks of being abandoned by the United States,[75] and some officials in Seoul attempted to inject additional toughness into the equation. On November 17, Foreign Minister Han declared the "deadline" on the nuclear issue to be just a few months away, and another Foreign Ministry official was quoted the following day as saying that "Reports by some U.S. media that the U.S. Government is examining the possibility of . . . setting the deadline to resolve North Korea's nuclear issue for February of next year, [are] not true at all." In fact, the official said, the deadline was sooner than that.[76]

Han, of course, had also said at the beginning of October that perhaps "one or two weeks" remained before sanctions would have to be imposed. U.S. and South Korean references to deadlines had begun to ring hollow.

Nonetheless, Seoul's increasingly tougher line was even more in evidence at the Asia-Pacific Economic Cooperation (APEC) summit in Seattle, Washington, on November 19 and during a subsequent visit to Washington by President Kim Young Sam. Although Presidents Kim and Clinton held a press conference at the end of Kim's visit, it was clear from their answers to questions that the two sides were stumbling in their attempt to answer the North's proposal of a package solution. Officials in Seoul—after having urged caution on the Americans and, in fact, having long advocated a solution much like the one Kang had proposed on November 11—were suddenly skittish about engaging the North. They urged their U.S. counterparts to downplay a package deal and remain firmly committed to inspections and North-South dialogue.[77] Later reports indicated that Kim Young Sam, in a heated two-and-a-half-hour meeting with Clinton, had personally squelched the new initiative; he wanted to avoid the impression at home that Washington was in charge of Northern policy.[78]

In fact, these reports were somewhat exaggerated.[79] Kim had not vetoed the more specific package deal worked out by Washington. Instead he signed off on it, and the offer—virtually unchanged—was laid on the table with the North at the first opportunity, which, because of a number of delays, turned out to be the following July.[80] South Korea did not bar the United States from adding unprecedented detail and explicitness to its offer to the North. What Kim did do, however, was angrily accuse the United States of insufficient consultation and involvement of the South in diplomacy. He demanded, and President Clinton agreed to, a continuation—and strengthening—of the U.S.–ROK demand that North Korea enter into North-South talks before it gained a third round of high-level meetings with the United States.

U.S. officials, who had worked out the substance of the package deal in advance and in detail with South Korean Foreign Minister Han, were shocked by Kim's outburst. When he returned to South Korea, Kim made a number of statements indicating that he had proved to the Americans who was truly in charge of diplomacy toward the North. But his demand—a stronger precondition of South-North talks—would prove to be an empty one: in less than a year, Seoul would abandon it.

On the final day of Kim's visit to Washington, South Korean officials again expressed opposition to having key inter-Korean matters decided in a U.S.–DPRK forum. Foreign Minister Han said about a package deal that "We haven't reached the stage where we can talk about such a deal, much less what should be included in such a deal."[81] Han concluded bluntly: "There is no package deal. North Korea's obligations to nuclear inspection cannot become a subject of negotiation"[82]—striking language from someone who had for months been urging the need for precisely such an approach. Kim Young Sam even objected to calling the new policy a *comprehensive* solution as the Americans requested, a term Clinton had himself used several days before.[83] President Kim reportedly feared that the word resembled too closely the North Korean proposal; instead the South Koreans preferred to refer to the new offer as a "broad and thorough approach."[84]

What accounted for this South Korean change of heart? Partly it represented a simple loss of patience with North Korea's repeated delays. Diplomacy had been given a try, and those inclined to be skeptical of the North in any case—and some say Kim Young Sam should be included in this group—were ready to pronounce it a failure. There was also something of a contrarian approach to the South's new toughness, which it represented as a response to the softer U.S. line and the discussions in Washington about accepting North Korea's idea of a package deal. As U.S. officials were later to complain, it seemed that whenever Washington got tough, Seoul became concerned and urged a softer line; when U.S. officials talked of compromise, South Korean leaders worried about a collapse of will and demanded a firm stance against the North. Finally, and perhaps most decisively, Kim Young Sam was first and foremost a domestic politician with little experience in foreign affairs. As such, he kept a close eye on how his policy toward the North was faring at the polls. Perceptions of weakness or subservience to Washington led to a get-tough approach, which, while politically appealing, may have had little to do with the objective situation at the time.

This new South Korean adamance was also a product of the fact that, in late 1993, political disputes within the South Korean government had reached a dramatic and confusing climax. In general terms it represented a victory for the hard-liners. One signal of the increasingly tough line was the December dismissal of Han Wan Sang, the leftist Unification Minister, and his replacement with a diplomat known for his tough anti-North stance, Yi Yong Tok, who quickly began talking of the need to confront North Korea about the issue of human rights.[85] Seoul's Agency for National Security Planning and its head, Kim Deok, were said to be playing a more important role in policy toward the North, and even Foreign Minister Han toughened his stance somewhat.

Despite the obvious signs of discord, in the days after the Kim-Clinton meeting, U.S. officials continued to emphasize that a new policy of some form had been adopted, and that North Korea could obtain more benefits than ever by cooperating. Unable to spell out any specific initiatives, however, their statements fell flat. The South Koreans, for example, appeared to refuse to publicly commit themselves to a suspension of Team Spirit, which was widely viewed to be a major element of the proposed U.S. offer. The result was an announcement that, as one news report said at the time, "seemed to fall well short of the detailed 'new approach' President Clinton had promised to lay out today."[86] Another report described the shift in policy as "subtle" and noted that "many of the details remain to be worked out and would, in any case, not be announced unless North Korea acts first"[87]—something Kang had explicitly ruled out in his November 11 statement. Again, these statements were simply not accurate; behind closed doors, the United States and South Korea *had* essentially agreed to respond to Kang's request. But partly because of South

Korean concerns, neither Washington nor Seoul wished to broadcast this fact at the time.

Thus when Assistant Secretary of State Winston Lord claimed during a CNN interview that the United States was ready for a broader dialogue with North Korea, the interviewer objected that the strategy seemed the same as always. "It's the same approach in a sense," Lord admitted when pressed. "Namely, we have the same objectives we've had since this crisis began several months ago. . . ."[88]

The back-and-forth U.S. diplomacy did little to quiet fears in Seoul, and its maddening incrementalism did even less to put North Korea on the spot. In fact, it is important not to overestimate the degree of U.S.–ROK strife. Consultation between the two sides remained intense throughout the whole period of diplomacy. The vast majority of that dialogue was friendly and cooperative. And U.S. officials recognized the political pressures on Kim Young Sam and his government—for whom the nuclear issue was not simply one foreign policy issue among many, but an emotional bombshell that dominated all public discussions of foreign affairs. Nonetheless, partly as a result of Seoul's sudden unwillingness to offer carrots to the North, the promised "comprehensive approach" had not emerged. Major South Korean newspapers portrayed the policy as "inconsistent" and "in disarray."[89] The United States was not sure exactly what standard of certainty it was trying to obtain, and its approach to the North remained incremental. North Korea's skill in manipulating such a gradual process would soon become apparent again.

THE UNITED STATES AND NORTH KOREA APPROACH A DEAL

That the "new" South Korean–U.S. policy toward the North was neither new nor especially dramatic, at least in its public manifestations, was soon reflected in the fact that many U.S. officials simply did not expect it to work. As early as December 1, despite the supposed "comprehensive" new approach, U.S. Defense Department officials were reportedly anticipating the failure of diplomacy and the imposition of economic sanctions on North Korea, and considering ways to bolster the U.S. forces in the South.[90] On December 3, the *Washington Post* outlined the results of a new assessment by U.S. intelligence agencies: the analysis forecast "that the Clinton administration's efforts to get North Korea's approval for inspections of its most sensitive nuclear-related facilities will fail."[91]

The implications of such a failure were ominous. On November 29, *Newsweek* reported that two highly classified Pentagon computer simulations conducted in 1991 showed North Korea winning a war on the peninsula too quickly for U.S. reinforcements to arrive to stop them. One Pentagon source was quoted as claiming that the simulations showed "the South's defenses collapsing so fast the hair stood up on the backs of our necks as we watched. On the first run, we thought the computer must have made a mistake. But we ran the model again and again, with the same result each time: collapse."[92] Confronted with early rumors of this report at their November 23 press conference, both President Clinton and President Kim stated their faith in the ability of U.S. and South Korean forces to defend the peninsula.[93]

The issue of the continuity of IAEA inspections garnered new attention on December 2. On that day Hans Blix told the agency's Board of Governors that the IAEA could no longer "provide any meaningful assurance" that North Korea was not making additional plutonium. Blix was essentially saying that continuity had been broken, but declined to be more explicit in deference to U.S., Japanese, and South Korean requests that the IAEA not force their hand on sanctions. Continuity, said to be in imminent danger at the beginning of October, was now portrayed by Blix and U.S. officials as being able to limp along for another month or so, until the end of the year.[94]

At the same time, President Clinton attempted to tone down the war rhetoric flying over Korea. "There is no cause for any great alarm on the part of the American people or the North Koreans for that matter," he said in one interview;[95] "I'm doing what I can now to defuse the crisis and give the North Koreans a way to join the community of nations," he said in another.[96] Clinton's comments may have been calculated to set a friendlier tone for the resumption of U.S.–DPRK talks in New York, because on December 3, the two sides were back at the table, with the U.S. side now led by a slightly more senior U.S. official—Deputy Assistant Secretary of State for East Asian and Pacific Affairs Thomas Hubbard. The talks were not "high-level," however, and represented only a step along the road to the long-awaited third round of senior meetings.

North Korea's position had not changed. North Korean officials again offered inspections—but nothing approaching special inspections, indeed far less robust than even routine IAEA visits. In exchange for resolving the issue of additional inspections, the North wanted a cancellation of Team Spirit and a U.S. agreement to engage in a comprehensive dialogue, including discussion of the possibility of outside economic benefits. This strategy played itself out through the month of December and into January 1994,[97] and over time, signs emerged that the two sides were close to an agreement. "The fact that the United States and North Korea are meeting frequently," said one South Korean official, "hints that there is no great difference of opinion between the two sides."[98]

On December 11, U.S. Secretary of Defense Aspin—in one of his final statements on the North Korean issue before his resignation—again addressed the issue of the U.S. definition of success. According to Aspin, it had not changed since President Clinton's November 7 statement. Appearing on "Meet the Press," Aspin agreed with the characterization of Clinton's November declaration as an "ultimatum" to the North. *Washington Post* correspondent Bob Woodward pressed further: what Clinton had said, Woodward argued, "like George Bush in the Iraqi invasion of Kuwait," was that "this will not stand. We will not let them get the bomb." Aspin replied: "We will not let the North Koreans become a nuclear power, yes." "Nuclear weapons in the hands of North Korea," Aspin continued, "is [*sic*] not acceptable."[99]

U.S. diplomacy was complicated on December 26 by an unwelcome Christmas present from the CIA: a formal intelligence opinion, leaked to the press and blasted across the headlines of the *New York Times* that day, that North Korea had "probably" assembled at least one nuclear bomb. In going beyond the formal conclusions of earlier intelligence reports, the CIA was offering President Clinton a worst-case scenario. Reports that documented the CIA analysis as "proving" the North had a bomb seriously overstated the case. Nonetheless, the CIA report served as a sobering reminder that even the IAEA inspections under discussion in New York would do little to stop the North from fashioning the plutonium it had already acquired into one or more bombs.[100]

Nonetheless, on January 3, U.S. officials announced a breakthrough: the North had agreed to inspections of all seven nuclear sites to allow the IAEA to maintain continuity, and would presently begin talking with the agency to work out an inspection schedule. In response, the United States and South Korea had promised to forgo Team Spirit in 1994. There was much happiness surrounding the agreement, with South Korean officials talking of a new era in North-South relations and Japanese leaders proposing the resumption of normalization talks with Pyongyang.[101]

Yet this reaction resulted more from the near desperation of the regional actors to be rid of the nuclear issue than from a close reading of the accord. For North Korea had hardly agreed to anything at all. It still refused to declare itself permanently back in the NPT. It refused to recognize the principle of special inspections. It refused, even, to admit that the stopgap inspections to which it had agreed would inaugurate a new period of regularly-conducted routine inspections. Pyongyang had agreed, it turned out, to a single inspection or a very narrow set of them designed only to maintain the continuity of the IAEA's knowledge, and nothing more. The United States had essentially accepted North Korea's long-standing offer to preserve the continuity of inspections—precisely the same deal that had been summarily rejected by the IAEA from March through December of the previous year.

Critics of the Clinton administration were quick to recognize this fact. Charles Krauthammer fulminated in *The Washington Post* that he had fully expected the administration to back down, but that "even I was stunned by the extent of the capitulation in the deal the State Department has just made with North Korea. The place to properly sign an agreement of this kind is on the deck of the battleship Missouri. It is unconditional surrender." As a result of the agreement, Krauthammer lamented, the NPT was "dead," the IAEA would be "corrupted beyond redemption," and U.S. credibility would sink to "a new low." He concluded by calling the accord "shameful."[102] One Republican U.S. senator accused the administration of having undermined the IAEA, and claimed that Hans Blix was secretly appalled at the provisions of the new agreement.[103]

Of course, these arguments assumed the wisdom of the original IAEA decision to reject the North's offer of a single inspection to preserve continuity. In fact, such a deal may have made sense, depending on the U.S. goals in the nonproliferation endeavor; and therefore the January agreement would have made sense as well. The problem was that none of the assumptions of U.S. policy were clear, and other critics noted that the meandering U.S. policy was partly a product of the lack of a clear definition of success and the refusal of the administration to adopt any form of decisive strategy—whether hard-line or soft. Perhaps most fundamentally, the new administration had not really defined, for itself or the world, the real stakes in Korea; it had not decided whether this was an issue worth a crisis, or a flare-up with its allies, or, ultimately, war. As a result, U.S. officials had little idea of how tough their mandate allowed them to be. Deprived of a clear line to draw, they drew numerous fuzzy ones, and as North Korea crossed each in turn, the credibility of U.S. policy was shattered.

A substantial and powerful consensus had therefore evolved by the fall of 1993, among those experts outside the government who followed Korea closely. The United States had not yet acted decisively, this consensus held; it had not fully tested North Korea's intentions with a clear offer of incentives for cooperation, and it was allowing low-level bureaucratic inertia to stall the bilateral talks. Yet at the same time, this view admitted that North Korea might simply be unwilling to trade away its nuclear weapons program for any price. Thus the consensus proposal: formulate a broad-based, compelling package deal of economic, political, and military incentives; send a high-level emissary to Pyongyang to commune directly with Kim Il Sung on the issue; and ask for cooperation. If the mission failed, they would consider the negotiations route to have been exhausted and move to impose tough economic sanctions. As William Taylor of Washington's Center for Strategic and International Studies put it on November 19, "Before resorting to economic sanctions, we must make one more attempt at a negotiated solution. . . . Let's stop playing games and put our cards on the table."[104]

This, of course, was something akin to the long-standing Defense Department option. And though some officials elsewhere in the administration continued to oppose it—referring to it as the "Rudolf Hess option" after Adolf Hitler's right-hand man who flew to England in 1940 attempting to arrange a truce—the administration had already moved in the direction of the proposal with its fall 1993 decision to make a more detailed and compelling offer to the North. But the administration still opposed the idea of a direct envoy to Kim Il Sung, and, as Aspin's December comments indicated, it had not made a clear decision to settle on a more flexible definition of success.

Such vagueness about the definition of success may have contributed to an immediate series of disagreements after the January accord about the kind of inspections to which the North had in fact agreed. After weeks of exchanging offers and demands, on January 21 the IAEA and North Korea outlined the basic type of inspection to be conducted: a one-time visit that would be "neither a regular inspection nor a full-fledged inspection," according to the agency's spokesman. But the agency refused to dispatch its inspectors until it had some agreement from the North about the scope of the inspection—whether it would be allowed to see all declared nuclear facilities at Yongbyon. Hans Blix promised to reject any "meaningless" inspections.[105] Within a few days, it became clear that North Korea was once again intent on delay.[106] South Korean officials speculated that the North might be stalling because of some internal political dispute "or because it wants to squeeze more concessions from the United States," as one news report concluded.[107] North Korea claimed that the IAEA was seeking inspections functionally equivalent to a regular inspection; and the United States stood off to the side, promising both sides they would get what they wanted.[108] The North castigated the United States for continuing to seek routine and special inspections when, in bilateral dialogue, U.S. officials had reportedly agreed to press only for an inspection aimed at preserving continuity.[109]

The IAEA was scheduled to hold its annual Board of Governors meeting on February 21 and 22. It was widely anticipated that, if the nuclear issue was not resolved by then, the board would finally refer the matter to the UN Security Council for sanctions. U.S. and South Korean officials began warning Pyongyang of this possibility toward the end of January, as talks on the North's supposed "agreement" to inspections appeared to break down. Rumors began circulating that China believed North Korea had been given every opportunity to cooperate, and no longer felt it could block sanctions[110]—although Chinese officials in early February did refuse to participate in a proposed Security Council warning that sanctions were imminent.[111] In the United States, members of Congress began endorsing a tougher approach to North Korea as well.[112]

North Korea replied to this growing pressure by promising to meet a "hard line with [a] hard line" and calling the United States a "bluffing paper tiger."[113] On February 9, a top DPRK diplomat in Beijing said that the North was "prepared for war" if the United States moved to impose sanctions;[114] three days later, North Korea declared that it would consider the imposition of sanctions a "declaration of war." South Korean papers once again began talking of a brewing "crisis" over the nuclear issue,[115] and by the 14th South Korean officials were portraying their planned efforts in advance of the IAEA Board meeting as a "last-ditch drive" to resolve the issue short of a major confrontation.[116] Meanwhile, planning for Team Spirit 1994 was well underway and, in early February, Seoul's Defense Ministry announced that the exercise was set to begin on March 22.[117] Time was running out, and the nuclear crisis headed for perhaps its most tense moments yet.

AN AGREEMENT IS REACHED—AGAIN

After a substantial amount of last-minute maneuvering and discussion between North Korea and both the United States and the IAEA,[118] on February 15 North Korea notified the IAEA that it would accept the single inspection, or a brief set of inspections, required to continue the continuity of the existing safeguards.[119] The nuclear accord was soon followed by the announcement that North and South Korea would return to their direct dialogue, the other major condition the United States had imposed on the North. Knowledgeable observers predicted that the third round of U.S.–DPRK talks would begin soon.

And yet, statements from North Korea continued to establish the potential for misunderstanding. In numerous public pronouncements, Pyongyang insisted that the inspections related only to continuity of safeguards—in late February, for example, it declared that it had only agreed to a process "thoroughly restricted to inspections for ensuring the continuity of safeguards."[120] On February 12, explaining the previous week's discord, an official North Korean statement claimed that Pyongyang had objected to the IAEA's attempt to conduct "an unjust inspection tantamount to a comprehensive inspection, contrary to the points of agreement between the DPRK and the U.S." As a result, U.S. officials had promised that "the inspection by the IAEA should be purely one for the continuity of safeguards."[121]

Finally, on February 25, U.S. and North Korean negotiators settled their differences in a detailed, four-part agreement unprecedented in the U.S.–DPRK dialogue for its explicitness.[122] Again, the agreement referred explicitly to "inspections for assuring the continuity of safeguards." The South Korean government quickly "welcomed" this agreement and moved to propose North-South talks on March 2. Washington and Seoul had agreed on a carefully choreographed sequence of events that would take place in March to cement the deal.[123]

The renewed North-South talks began on a hopeful note. Southern envoy Song Yong Tae greeted his Northern colleagues, shook hands, and reminded them that their dialogue had been suspended last October when the winter began to set in. "As we are meeting you here today, we feel like we are waking up from a long hibernation," Song told his counterparts from the North. "I hope that the inter-Korean relations will also wake up from a long winter sleep and [that] spring arrives in Panmunjom." The chief North Korean delegate to the talks, Pak Yong Su, replied that "we wasted a whole season since we met each other last fall when grains were ripe for harvest." Pak urged the group to "clear up the problems for the exchange of special envoys within today."[124]

Once the talks began, however, they did not go well. Even after the friendly opening exchange, North Korean delegate Pak could not keep from chiding his counterpart about his large briefcase. "I only brought a small envelope containing a draft agreement because I am intent on reaching an agreement today," Pak said. "But I see that you brought a big briefcase and obviously have a lot to say about this and that." Song tried to preserve an amicable atmosphere, laughing and saying he had brought the big case to take home presents since it was Pak's turn to offer them.

The first meeting ended without progress—and without Pak's hoped-for agreement on an exchange of envoys. Perhaps hoping to quit the dialogue at Panmunjom as quickly as possible, and very possibly having never intended to treat the talks seriously once there, North Korea began pointing to the requirement of North-South discussion as a roadblock to resolving the nuclear issue. The United States was "endangering" the U.S.–DPRK nuclear talks by establishing North-South dialogue as a precondition for them, the North claimed.[125]

By March 8, moreover, the first hints began to emerge that the IAEA inspections were not proceeding smoothly. South Korean officials revealed that IAEA inspectors had reportedly been denied the ability to conduct some of their tests. The North, it appeared, was keeping the IAEA from performing any tasks not directly related to maintaining continuity of safeguards; it was allowing the inspectors only to change film and batteries in the agency's cameras, check seals on reactor components, and the like.[126] North Korean officials refused to allow the inspectors to carry out two specific measures agreed to on February 15: entering and examining the reprocessing facility and conducting broad sweeps for radiation throughout the Yongbyon facility. Both were deemed by the IAEA to be critical to determining whether additional plutonium had passed through the site since the last inspection.

North Korea also attempted to play a bargaining game even during the IAEA inspections.[127] While the inspections were underway, even as the inspectors exchanged urgent messages with IAEA headquarters in Vienna, officials in Pyongyang reportedly sent word to Washington that they would allow the full range of the IAEA's demands—but only if South Korea would agree to certain concessions in the North-South talks. When the United States and South Korea refused, North Korea barred the two important IAEA procedures. It would soon storm out of the North-South talks as well.

FINALLY, A DEFINITION OF SUCCESS?

Reports in early 1994 suggested that the Clinton administration might finally have reached a clear decision about what degree of success it would seek in negotiations with the North. Yet it was never publicly declared, and almost as soon as the decision was broadcast, it was disavowed by some administration officials. By the middle of the year, it was once again unclear what the United States was after.

U.S. officials, the reports said, had decided to bite the bullet and focus on North Korea's future nuclear research. If it could get an agreement that would ensure that the North would be unable to obtain any additional plutonium, the administration would defer—but not abandon—demands that the North allow challenge inspections to determine what it had done in the past. This strategy would have locked the North's nuclear program in place with a package of incentives, with the intention of rolling it back at a later date.

The first hints of such an approach came in the suggestion by a number of observers in the fall of 1993 to pursue a policy of "no blame" for past nuclear work. North Korean officials may have feared allowing inspections because their past nuclear research would be exposed. Congressman Dave McCurdy suggested in an editorial on November 8 that "North Korean leaders resist inspections for fear of being caught in their lies. We should tell them that, like South Africa, if they came clean, they would face no new sanctions."[128] Center for Strategic and International Studies scholar William Taylor argued on November 11 that Washington should "State that if IAEA inspections reveal that the North has been deceptive about its nuclear weapons program, the United States will not seek retribution, only termination of the program."[129]

From a policy of "no blame," it was a short leap to one of no demands for proof—that is, that North Korea's prior nuclear work would not only go unpunished, but also, for the time being, undiscovered. By early 1994, news reports were suggesting that the Clinton administration had indeed made the decision to defer—but not abandon—measures to address the one or two bombs' worth of plutonium North Korea might have acquired and focus on shutting down the reactor and reprocessing facility in the future. Thus by January 5, administration officials were being quoted to the effect that President Clinton had "misspoken" in his uncompromising statement of the previous November, that the true focus of U.S. attention was the North's future nuclear work.[130] Columnist Michael Kramer wrote in *Time* on February 28 that South Korea, China, Japan, and the United States had learned to live with the ambiguous threat of one or two bombs, and would continue to do so if the North addressed worries about the future. "As soon as the bombs' existence is confirmed unambiguously, you have to do something about it," he quoted one State Department official as arguing. "Better to let what is be and move on to cap it at the present low-level threat."[131]

Kramer's essay still carried the tone of an argument, urging the Clinton administration to adopt the approach some of its officials favored. By early March, other reports depicted the strategy as a done deal. On March 10, Jim Hoagland wrote in the *Washington Post* of the administration's "containment" policy in Korea: "The Clinton administration is prepared to live with the strong probability that North Korea has built, or can quickly build, a single nuclear bomb. The plutonium North Korea has already diverted from its reactors is so much spilt milk. The administration will not publicly admit that it is resigned to Pyongyang's keeping a proto-bomb for the foreseeable future, but that is the basis of existing policy." The line was drawn at "an extension of Pyongyang's nuclear capability"—additional bombs beyond those already acquired. Hoagland basically approved of the policy because, he argued, the alternative was war.[132]

At roughly the same time, Secretary of Defense William Perry publicly validated the new approach. "Our policy right along" in Korea, he told reporters, "has been oriented to try to keep North Korea from getting a significant nuclear-weapon capability." Perry's claim was directly at odds with President Clinton's pledge of the previous November and with former Secretary of Defense Aspin's December claims, but Perry said of the single-bomb risk that "We don't know anything we can do about that. What we can do something about, though, is stopping them from building beyond that."[133]

Predictably, this new policy was not free from controversy. Critics focused primarily on the risk of setting a bad precedent in the nonproliferation arena:

If one or two bombs were acceptable for North Korea, would they not be for Iran and Iraq also? And would not those regimes accelerate their nuclear programs as a result? And even a single bomb in the North, some argued, might eventually impel South Korea and Japan to reconsider the nuclear option. Henry Kissinger delivered a blunt verdict in July 1994 when he wrote that "no compromise is possible between a nuclear and a nonnuclear North Korea. A freeze of the North's activities leaving it in possession of the existing weapons and the growing plutonium-producing capability would pose a mounting threat. A rollback is needed." Kissinger called for an "unambiguous" U.S. message to this effect.[134]

In fact, the change in U.S. policy was not as explicit as some suggested. There was no single, clear decision to shift course.[135] Rather, the administration's policy simply evolved into an emphasis on certain priorities before others. Capping the North's nuclear weapons program was priority number one in everyone's mind. The importance of forestalling future work was never at issue; what was at issue was the degree to which demands for special inspections and other means of determining the North's past nuclear work served to undermine U.S. and allied efforts to cap the program and prevent its expansion. It never became official U.S. policy to leave questions about the past fully out of a nuclear agreement, although that option was discussed within the administration. Rather, the Clinton administration decided to acquire a commitment to special inspections up front, but not to demand that they take place immediately.

In bureaucratic terms, this conclusion represented the position of some in the State Department who had sought a middle ground on the issue. Some in the Defense Department, more concerned about North Korea's actual capabilities than the sanctity of its NPT obligations, were prepared virtually to abandon the hope of special inspections in exchange for a firm end to the future of the weapons program. Some in the Arms Control and Disarmament Agency represented the opposite viewpoint, urging a more absolutist interpretation of the NPT to uphold the credibility of the IAEA. State, under Robert Gallucci, took a middle ground: special inspections were important and must be retained, but not necessarily on the timetable demanded by a rigorous reading of the North's NPT obligations. It was this compromise position that established the framework for the 1994 U.S.–DPRK nuclear accord.[136]

A substantial change of U.S. policy therefore took place in 1994 in at least one respect. Whereas before some officials and the agencies or departments they represented were unwilling to defer investigations about the past at all, now a strong consensus existed that answering all questions immediately was too much to ask. Armed with this new perspective, the United States moved toward new talks with North Korea—and a new crisis as well.

And the stakes, it was becoming increasingly clear, were very high. In October 1993, as one U.S. deadline was collapsing into another, Pak Young Kil, a young North Korean chemical plant worker, slipped quietly into the Yalu River and swam across to China.[137] Arrested in July 1993 for "obstruction of police work," Pak had been badly beaten and sent to a hospital. But he escaped in August and made his daring swim two months later. He found a ship and sailed to the South Korean port of Ulsan, where he turned himself in and began telling some very worrisome stories.

The North Korean people were desperate, Pak told officials in the South. Food shortages were endemic, and the people clung to Kim Il Sung's uncertain promise of an economic boom attendant to unification, which he promised would happen in 1995. North Koreans believed that South Korea possessed a thousand nuclear weapons, and so were actually relieved to hear rumors that Pyongyang might have one as well.

But most worrisome were Pak's claims about the true level of resignation of the North Korean people. Because the economic situation was so bad, and because they saw unification as the only hope for relief, many North Koreans "want a war," Pak said. "Just one word from Kim Il Sung and that would be it. We do know that war would be a disaster. But with or without war, we don't think the situation would be any different."

North Korea, for all its bluster and diplomatic maneuvering, was crumbling and cornered. It had very little to lose. And its people, one young defector seemed to be convinced, almost welcomed the idea of a war.

■ 8 ■

THE DRAMA CONCLUDES, 1994

ike Selig Harrison, whose visit with Kim Il Sung in June 1994 was
described in chapter 1, Bill Taylor was one of the few Americans who
had traveled repeatedly to the Hermit Kingdom.[1] Taylor, a slim, dapper
West Point graduate and former U.S. Army Colonel, was tough and direct but
also immensely warm to his friends, among whom he counted many Koreans
in both the South and the North. By 1994, working for peace and reunification in Korea had become something of a calling for him, and in April of that
year his calling would take him to Pyongyang yet again.

Taylor had hoped for some time to convince the North Koreans to allow a
major visit by Western television stations. Such outside contact, he thought,
could only help allay misunderstandings. Western officials would believe or
not believe the North Koreans as they chose, but at least the risk of misper-
ception would be reduced. By the spring of 1994, Taylor had spoken with representatives of the American Cable News Network (CNN) and Japan's NHK
television station. Both wanted to get into the North, and Taylor set about using
his substantial contacts in North Korea to help.

North Korean officials were skeptical. Several years earlier, the last time
they had allowed foreign news crews to film there, the U.S. network CBS had
done a scathing exposé of their collapsing bureaucracy. Pyongyang did not
want a repeat, and extracted promises from CNN and NHK to offer "objective" reports. Other than that, however, North Korean officials asked for no
editorial rights over the broadcasts, and allowed the crews to send tape out
directly from Pyongyang. It was a substantial gamble for North Korea.

Once in Pyongyang ahead of the news organizations, Taylor still had to convince the North Koreans that the media visit would be in their interests. He met with Kim Young Sun, a top Politburo official and an old friend from previous visits. After two hours of intense discussion, Kim told Taylor to wait and left the room. He returned with a smile. "I have spoken to the Dear Leader," he said in a pointed reference to Kim Jong Il. "The visit is approved."

Reflecting the poor state of their finances, North Korean officials later demanded $9,650 in cash—the cost, they claimed, to charter the Tu-134 aircraft that would fly the CNN and NHK crews in from Beijing. Usually Pyongyang is serviced by only two flights a week, one in and one out; this would be a special occasion, one of the very few separate visits allowed by Kim Il Sung's secretive regime. Taylor got on the phone with the representatives of the news organizations. Each rounded up $5,000 in cash, and together they flew into Pyongyang in mid-April.

The networks, along with a number of other journalists and visitors, conducted a free-flowing, two-and-a-half-hour interview with Kim Il Sung which was capped with a luncheon of quail-egg soup, roast turkey, and kimchi. In the discussion, Kim definitively denied that North Korea had, or would develop, nuclear weapons. "We have neither the need to make nuclear weapons nor the will and ability to do so," he told the group. At one point he irritably shot back at a question on the issue: "We will never have nuclear weapons, I promise you. Who can we use them against?"

The North Korean leader reiterated an old offer that, as this chapter will describe, would be reborn as a major initiative later in the year. If the United States would help North Korea develop light-water reactor technology, Kim suggested, the alleged reprocessing facility—the center of concern about the North Korean nuclear weapons program—"itself may not be needed." At the end of the visit, North Korean officials pronounced themselves largely pleased with the coverage they had been extended. It had been, they agreed, "objective." Just before he left, Bill Taylor asked whether North Korea might allow permanent bureaus of CNN and NHK in Pyongyang. Kim Young Sun was intrigued by the idea. "We'll consider it," he said.

A NEW CRISIS

As a result of the January and February agreements described in chapter 7, IAEA inspectors had returned to North Korea in March of 1994 to conduct more routine inspections. On March 14, the inspection team left the North and arrived in Beijing. They refused to comment on their findings, but within a few weeks a clear picture of the results of the inspection had emerged. And it was a disturbing picture indeed: North Korea had progressed with its nuclear weapons work, the inspectors found, expanding the capability of its reprocessing center and laying the groundwork for changing the fuel in its reactor. Pyongyang was "poised to go forward" with a major new phase of nuclear weapons work, in the words of one official.[2]

Within two days, the IAEA reported the "failure" of the inspection, and noted that it could not guarantee that more plutonium had not been reprocessed since the previous visit. In Washington, the Clinton administration began renewed talk of sanctions and considered reviving Team Spirit for 1994. "The general feeling," one U.S. official said, "is that the IAEA has been jerked around long enough."[3] In Seoul, President Kim Young Sam worried that events were "now heading toward a situation where international sanctions cannot but be imposed on North Korea."[4]

To a substantial degree, these reactions were as emotional as they were objective.[5] The inspection had indeed maintained the continuity of safeguards. And although the North's work to prepare for a major expansion of reprocessing was worrisome, the task facing U.S. and allied officials was to develop a strategy most likely to gain outside access to that work. In the aftermath of the inspection, North Korea issued several blistering statements arguing that it had done its part—the continuity of inspections had been preserved.[6]

On March 19, the crisis reached a new degree of hostility when North Korean delegates walked out of North-South talks and threatened that in case of war "Seoul will turn into a sea of fire."[7] The following day, Warren Christopher said North Korea could only stop Team Spirit if it allowed inspectors back in immediately—but in the same breath he nearly ruled out such a compromise, saying that "I'm afraid it's gone too far for that." When asked if he saw Team Spirit as "essentially inevitable," he said, "Yes, it's a matter of timing." The threat was a hollow one; within weeks, Washington and Seoul together announced that Team Spirit could still be headed off by North Korean cooperation,[8] and in the end the exercise would not be held.

The drumbeat of crisis, and the hint of an approaching war, grew louder in the final weeks of March. On the 21st, the IAEA Board of Governors meeting demanded compliance from North Korea. In New York, U.S. Ambassador to the United Nations Madeline Albright announced that the process of sanctions was underway: the United States, she said, was preparing the draft of a resolution threatening the North with specific measures if it did not allow the IAEA back in. The draft would begin with four sponsors—the United States, Great Britain, France, and, significantly, Russia. Soon both Koreas' militaries were on alert and the United States was discussing ways of reinforcing its military position in the South.[9] On the 27th, the North warned that U.S. military reinforcement plans could lead to war, and offered an arrogant reminder: "The United States must not forget," Pyongyang crowed, "that it was Korea where it drank the bitter cup of its first defeat."[10] And on March 30, U.S. Secretary of Defense Perry warned that the United States would seek to enforce inspections on the North—even at the risk of war.[11]

China—the critical wild card in the sanctions game—restated its opposition to a strongly worded resolution, especially one threatening further Security Council action if North Korea did not comply.[12] But on March 30, China proposed its own draft, an unusual step for Beijing, and especially so because its language did contain the threat of further action. The following day, the Security Council issued its message; it largely followed the U.S. language but emerged, as the Chinese had demanded, in the form of a "statement," somewhat less forceful than a "resolution." In it the Security Council called upon North Korea "to allow IAEA inspectors to complete the inspection activities" agreed upon by Pyongyang and the IAEA. The council "decides to remain actively seized of the matter and that further Security Council consideration will take place if necessary in order to achieve full implementation of the IAEA-DPRK safeguards agreement,"[13] the message said.

At roughly this same time, the North Korean and U.S. desire to find a way out of the crisis gained concrete form: an exchange of letters between North Korean Vice Foreign Minister Kang Sok Ju and U.S. Assistant Secretary of State Robert Gallucci. Earlier in March, Kang had sent Gallucci a letter urging a third round of U.S.–DPRK talks. Gallucci replied by restating the two U.S. conditions for such dialogue: IAEA follow-up inspections and a return to North-South dialogue. Kang offered in reply that the North would allow additional inspections if the precondition for North-South dialogue were dropped.[14]

Late in March, presumably apprised of the Kang-Gallucci correspondence, South Korean Vice Foreign Minister Hong Soon Young proposed that Seoul drop its insistence on a North-South exchange of presidential envoys. His remarks were quickly disavowed by a spokesman for Kim Young Sam,[15] but on April 15, having apparently been persuaded by the United States, South Korea dropped its demand for an envoy exchange—the very demand Kim Young Sam had so urgently made the previous November.[16] The way once again appeared to be open for yet another round of U.S.–DPRK dialogue.

Outside observers watching this process became increasingly frustrated with the maddening incrementalism of it all. Nothing was ever finally decided; no bold proposals were made; the process became bogged down in legalisms and technicalities. Events since the fall had only reinforced the consensus outside the government that decisive action was required—a package solution, clear leadership within the government, a direct mission to Pyongyang.

In March, this consensus manifested itself in a powerful report authored by many of those outside government with the most intimate and detailed knowledge of the Korean situation. Issued under the auspices of the U.S. Institute for Peace, the report proposed a rough approximation of the same bold option that had been under discussion in the administration, while cautioning against viewing the nuclear issue as "an immediate military crisis." It argued that "the significance of the North's nuclear program *in its current state* should not be exaggerated." It called for the appointment of a "senior coordinator" to manage North Korea policy within the government and serve as a high-level envoy to the North. And it laid out a "package proposal" in which specific North Korean moves were requested in exchange for specific and detailed U.S. and allied incentives.[17] The irony, of course, was that this approach had much in common with ideas within the government, including the long-standing Defense Department proposal, for a more dramatic bid to North Korea. As noted in chapter 7, the United States had assembled just such an offer the previous fall—but because of Seoul's apprehension and Pyongyang's provocations, the package deal had not been laid on the negotiating table. The three countries headed for a major confrontation with a real risk of military conflict—while the initiative that could pull them back from the brink lay gathering dust in Washington. To their credit, U.S. officials recognized this state of affairs; and when an opportunity arose to break the escalating crisis and make their bold proposal to the North, they would seize it.

FUEL RODS AND THE DRIFT TOWARD SANCTIONS

For some time, U.S. officials had made very clear that one North Korean action in particular would automatically trigger a drive for sanctions: the unsupervised refueling of the main Yongbyon reactor. The roughly eight thousand spent fuel rods in the reactor held enough plutonium for four or five bombs, and if the North kept that plutonium, its alleged nuclear arsenal would double or triple in size. During the IAEA inspection of spring 1994, inspectors had noticed preparations for a refueling, and by the end of April, North Korean officials were declaring that the reactor needed to be refueled quickly. The IAEA quickly informed the North that it would demand to have inspectors present when the refueling occurred. The agency wanted not only to observe the defueling and place the spent rods under surveillance, but also to extract samples from roughly three hundred of them to obtain a clear reading as to the reactor's past operations—and, thereby, the "smoking gun" evidence of exactly how much plutonium North Korea had so far acquired. North Korea countered by offering observation and surveillance of the rods, but no sampling. As before, Pyongyang and the IAEA argued for several weeks about the procedures that would be allowed.[18]

Several times in early May, the IAEA angrily said it would simply refuse to send inspectors at all to witness the Yongbyon refueling if those inspectors were not granted the right powers. Each time, talks with North Korea continued. On May 17, a group of inspectors arrived in the North and quickly set about completing the procedures denied them a month earlier. North Korea, therefore, made good on at least one promise, and the IAEA could now declare firmly that the continuity of inspections had been preserved. This small victory, however, was quickly overshadowed by the growing controversy over the refueling of the reactor.

In the middle of this brewing controversy, the Clinton administration actually decided to go ahead with the third round of high-level talks. This decision was reportedly reached on May 20, after the North had fulfilled its promise of allowing the IAEA to complete its procedures for maintaining continuity. Some U.S. officials hoped that, if the North could be drawn into a third round of talks, a more explicit set of U.S. offers—a form of the long-awaited "package deal"—could resolve the issue once and for all, including the refueling dispute. The administration had become anxious to put its "broad and thorough approach" on the table, and seized on the belated completion of the IAEA inspections as a reason for doing so. But the timing was unfortunate, for North Korea continued and even accelerated its defueling.

Toward the end of May, discussions between the North and the IAEA broke down. The agency sent a last appeal to the North to halt the unloading of fuel, and the UN Security Council passed a resolution urging the North to heed the request—both to no effect. Press reports indicated that the Clinton administration had made the decision to accelerate its drive for sanctions at the United Nations.[19]

By June 1, the IAEA reported that fully 60 percent of the reactor's eight thousand fuel rods had been removed, and that the defueling continued apace.[20] The following day, IAEA Director General Hans Blix sent the UN Security Council a blistering letter full of apocalyptic language. The agency had already warned the Security Council several days before, Blix reminded them, that continued defueling would mean that the IAEA's ability to "make future measurements of the discharged fuel with the degree of confidence necessary to assess the history of the reactor core had not only been seriously eroded but would already have been lost irretrievably should fuel channels important for future measurement have been discharged without identification and segregation by the agency." Without such identification, future measurements of the fuel rods would be "meaningless."[21]

This, Blix continued, was exactly what had happened. Because of continued defueling, he concluded, the IAEA's opportunity to segregate and measure the fuel rods "had been lost." As a result, "the agency's ability to ascertain, with sufficient confidence, whether nuclear material from the reactor had been diverted in the past has also been lost." Any further measurements of the fuel "would have no practical value because they would have to be based on operators' records," which could be fudged. And this situation was "irreversible."[22] The letter concluded that the IAEA could no longer perform its basic function in North Korea: to determine with good confidence the nondiversion of plutonium for weapons purposes.

Not all observers agreed with this assessment. Indeed, Blix himself used a softer formulation toward the end of the letter, indicating that the defueling had "seriously eroded" the agency's ability to verify whether plutonium had been diverted—a very different statement from the claim that this ability had been "lost." North Korea argued vehemently that it had provided a way for the IAEA to examine the fuel. Some arms control experts agreed, wondering why inspections of the fuel itself, regardless of the order of the rods, could not determine the reactor's history.[23] And U.S. officials privately conceded that the statement that plutonium verification had been "lost" was something of an exaggeration.[24]

This dispute once again raised the question of the U.S. definition of success—indeed, it placed the question at center stage. North Korea seemed intent on destroying, or at least degrading, evidence of its past nuclear behavior. But it also continued to insist that it would not reprocess the spent fuel then sitting in cooling ponds in Yongbyon and offered to allow the IAEA to inspect this fuel. Pyongyang seemed to be drawing a line of its own: it would allow measures to verify that no further plutonium diversion was occurring, but it firmly rejected inspections that might leak information about what it had done in the past. This approach accorded well with the strategy of "ambiguity" mentioned in earlier chapters: whether or not it had a workable nuclear weapons program (and the debate on this point continued throughout 1994), North Korea clearly wanted to leave some doubt in the minds of U.S. and South Korean leaders on this question. North Korea was not alone in its ambiguity—by June 1994, it was also not entirely clear how the Clinton administration intended to respond to North Korea's strategy.

A HALTING MOVE TOWARD SANCTIONS

As the trend toward sanctions continued, rhetoric on the peninsula began heating up as well. On June 5, a North Korean statement reminded the world of its position that "Sanctions mean war, and there is no mercy in war."[25] The following day, South Korean President Kim Young Sam declared that "We cannot allow even half a nuclear weapon in North Korea. I will deter North Korea without fail from having a nuclear weapon."[26]

On June 10, the IAEA responded to North Korea's lack of cooperation by instituting its own mild form of sanctions: it decided to cease its technical assistance program in the North, in place since the 1970s. In response, Pyongyang defiantly announced that it would withdraw from the IAEA and refuse to preserve the continuity of inspections. And again, the North Korean statement said: "we strongly reaffirm our position that UN 'sanctions' will be regarded immediately as a declaration of war."[27] On the 13th, South Korean intelligence chief Kim Deok suggested that years of South Korean and U.S. diplomacy had been in vain, claiming that North Korea's "ultimate aim is to develop nuclear arms and they are employing delaying tactics to earn time";[28] the following day, the South Korean government called up 6.6 million reservists for a massive mobilization drill.

In Seoul, people began flooding to stores and hoarding food and provisions in anticipation of a possible war. At the end of June, a South Korean paper, the *Chugan Chosun,* summarized the war fever that had gripped the capital. "Even until a day ago, a feeling of an impending war crisis prevailed among [South Korean] citizens," the paper explained. "Food and cooking utensils for emergency situations, such as instant noodles, ran out of stock in certain densely-populated areas." Yet the peak of the crisis would "not last more than a day"—for a new diplomatic initiative had emerged.[29]

Many observers had expected a new North Korean offer designed to defuse tensions and buy time. They did not have to wait long. North Korea may have been prodded into action by China. Some reports of the time suggest that, frustrated with North Korea's lack of cooperation, furious over its needless provocation of the IAEA, and wanting to make a gesture of support to President Clinton after he renewed China's Most-Favored Nation status on May 29, Chinese leaders intervened. Both in Beijing and at the United Nations, North Korean ambassadors were warned that China could not forever shield North Korea from world opinion—perhaps a veiled threat that China might not, after all, veto sanctions in the UN Security Council. Chinese officials urged the North to recognize that its own self-interest demanded both greater cooperation on the nuclear issue and the economic and political benefits that cooperation would bring.[30]

And in fact, the U.S. strategy in the sanctions process was more nuanced than it perhaps appeared at the time. U.S. officials were well aware that the actual imposition of sanctions would ruin, or at least severely impair, the chance for a peaceful resolution of the nuclear question. Speaking at the end of 1994, several U.S. officials indicated that, as some observers suspected at the time, Washington had had something up its sleeve that spring—a new offer, an approach to the North to create one last chance for negotiations before sanctions took effect. It is not clear if this offer would have been made before the sanctions resolution was actually put to a vote or after it was passed. The resolution contained a one-month grace period, and Washington's idea may have been to pass the resolution and then propose a new settlement during that last window before the sanctions took effect. Either way, the sanctions effort did not occur in a vacuum. It was designed to set the stage for a final diplomatic initiative—one that proved unnecessary in the wake of Jimmy Carter's visit to Pyongyang.[31]

This is not to suggest that U.S. officials expected their last-ditch offer to resolve the issue, or were unprepared for a crisis on the peninsula. They recognized the risks inherent in a political confrontation that could easily escalate into a military one. Indeed, when former President Carter phoned from Pyongyang to share the results of his discussions, he happened to catch U.S. officials responsible for the Korean issue gathered with President Clinton at the White House, discussing options for reinforcing the U.S. military presence in Northeast Asia. In the spring of 1994, the Clinton administration was deadly serious about North Korea and was determined to move toward sanctions—and it is impossible to say, whether or not Washington made one last offer, if this chain of events would have led to war. What is clear is that top U.S. officials recognized that risk at the time and were willing to run it for the sake of nonproliferation.

That they were willing to do so speaks as much to the nature of policy debates within the United States as it does to the possible effect of sanctions on North Korea. Later in 1994, several U.S. officials observed that the sanctions process was as important to the Clinton administrations's self image as it was to North Korea's calculations. Given the range of opinion within the administration, Washington may have had little choice but to get tough with the North—to try at least some degree of a confrontational approach—before it could settle on a final deal. Otherwise it might have appeared that Washington had allowed its fear of confrontation to lead it into a bad deal. It is therefore possible that the sanctions process of 1994 was necessary to obtain an agreement—not only to change North Korea's thinking, but to convince officials in Washington that the hard-line option had been exhausted.

In any case, this growing trend toward sanctions apparently had an effect. Even as the IAEA was cutting off the North and the South was calling up its reserves, Carnegie Endowment Scholar Selig Harrison was making his fourth trip to North Korea—and receiving a renewed offer from Kim Il Sung. Harrison was aware of Kim's statement to Bill Taylor and the foreign news delegation that April about the North's willingness to shut down its reprocessing facility in exchange for help in building a light-water reactor. He decided to see whether the offer was real, and whether it still stood; and so he asked Kim Il Sung about it directly. The result was the exchange described at the beginning of chapter 1: North Korea would "freeze" its nuclear weapons program, Harrison reported, in exchange for diplomatic recognition and a binding commitment to provide long-term credits for the purchase of light-water nuclear reactors. North Korean officials also mentioned an end to the economic embargo and a U.S. guarantee not to use nuclear weapons first, although it was not clear how these fitted into the deal.[32] The full meaning of a "freeze" was left undefined, but more than one North Korean official explicitly said it meant a complete dismantling of the Yongbyon reprocessing facility.

When former U.S. President Jimmy Carter traveled to North Korea in the middle of June, he heard roughly the same offer. Carter's trip was something of a surprise—he had asked several times before to go to North Korea during the Bush and Clinton administrations, but was turned down each time. This time, Carter called to express his concern at the turn of events in Korea just before Clinton left for the military ceremonies at Normandy. Clinton offered to provide him with a full briefing, and Robert Gallucci visited Carter's home on the afternoon of June 5.

Carter was reportedly interested in going to the North because he was frustrated at what he perceived to be a needless drift toward sanctions and war in U.S. policy. He was also encouraged in his thinking by U.S. Ambassador to South Korea James T. Laney, the former president of Emory University in Atlanta and an old friend. Laney, who himself had been urging a nonconfrontational line toward the North, reportedly saw the Carter trip as a way to open an unofficial dialogue with the North and avert a major crisis.[33]

After the Gallucci briefing, Carter remained unsatisfied with the level of U.S.–North Korean communication. On June 6, Pyongyang reiterated its standing invitation for Carter to visit. He called Vice President Al Gore and informed him of his desire to accept. After speaking with President Clinton and other top administration foreign policy advisers, Gore called on the morning of June 7 to report that Carter's visit had been approved. After another series of official and unofficial briefings, Carter left Atlanta on Sunday, June 12 for his trip to Pyongyang.

Virtually as soon as Carter arrived, Pyongyang deftly punctured the atmosphere of tension: it would allow the IAEA inspectors to remain in place and continue their work for the time being, Kim Il Sung said, thus preserving inspection continuity. The IAEA welcomed the move.[34] Nonetheless, U.S. officials insisted that consultations on sanctions at the UN would continue.

Soon, however, Carter made a series of announcements that undermined the tough-line approach. He repeated the essence of the offer Harrison had brought back several days earlier, that the North would freeze its nuclear weapons program in exchange for a package of benefits. He criticized the Clinton approach, saying that "In my opinion, the pursuit of sanctions is counterproductive in this particular and unique society. . . . The declaration of sanctions would be considered as an insult to their country. . . . This is something, in my opinion, that would be impossible for them to accept."[35] Carter said that the crisis was over. He also—in a confusing claim that led red-faced officials in Washington into quick denials—said, "I would like to inform you" that the Clinton administration had "stopped the sanctions activity in the United Nations," which was not, at the time, actually true.[36]

When Carter and his companions returned to the border between the two Koreas, in the words of Ambassador Laney, Carter's "eyes welled up with tears . . . in part because of what they were bringing back with them."[37] And Carter did arrive in Seoul with a stunning offer: in spite of the nasty tone of North-South relations and the harsh condemnations of Seoul in the North Korean press, Kim Il Sung wanted a summit with Kim Young Sam as soon as possible. Perhaps tempted by the opportunity to be the first South Korean leader to hold a summit with the North, Kim Young Sam soon accepted.

FOLLOWING UP ON THE CARTER VISIT

Carter's visit sparked strong, and contradictory, reactions in the Clinton administration. In one decisive step, he had done what the administration had refused to do for a year and a half—conducted a high-level visit directly to Pyongyang to see what could be worked out. Yet even as he had done so, he had also directed pointed barbs at Clinton policies. Hard-line columnist Charles Krauthammer summed up the cynics' view of Carter's achievements: "The sanctions Clinton belatedly and tepidly began to press for are now, and possibly forever, dead. The coalition the United States was trying to put together is in disarray. Carter's visit . . . destroyed what little was left of Clinton's Korea policy."[38]

In fact, this view was shared by a number of furious officials within the administration. Carter appeared to be stealing their thunder, taking over diplomacy from a sitting president. Yet in retrospect, one stark fact helps endorse Carter's mission: given the trend toward sanctions then underway, it is impossible to know whether the ensuing crisis could have been resolved short of war.

History teems with examples of national leaders twisting themselves into circumstances from which an escape short of conflict seems impossible. The United States and the two Koreas seemed to be entering such a period in the spring of 1994. And while Washington had a plan to extricate itself, no one knows if it would have worked—or if in the face of North Korean provocations, U.S. officials would even have been able to make their last-ditch proposal.

In concrete terms, Carter's visit produced two solid diplomatic breakthroughs worth pursuing. If North Korea would indeed "freeze" its nuclear weapons program, the nuclear issue could perhaps be resolved without a full-scale crisis. And if the North-South summit occurred, the foundation could be laid for broader inter-Korean cooperation. With the benefit of hindsight, and the evidence of the nuclear agreement reached within months of Carter's trip, it seems that Jimmy Carter did his nation a great service in June of 1994: he prevented a drift toward war without destroying the possibility for an equitable settlement.

Once again, spokespeople for the evolving consensus view outside the government took the opportunity to press their case. Robert Manning of the Progressive Policy Institute wrote on June 19 that the end game was at hand, but that "after 16 months of diplomatic cat-and-mouse, we still don't know if any deal is possible. Washington has yet to present North Korea with a clear and precise incentive package. . . ." For diplomacy to work, Manning argued, "the highest-ranking administration officials must deal directly with top leadership in Pyongyang. Returning to the bureaucratic routine of assistant-secretary-level talks will mean a return to petty haggling and game playing." Manning again called for a high-level envoy to Pyongyang to lay out a package deal, and if that failed, for a decisive move toward sanctions and preparations for war.[39]

The following day, conservative columnist Robert Novak endorsed the same approach. He quoted right-wing scholars in the United States who recommended a package deal, albeit with more stick than carrot. But he also cited dovish Selig Harrison and Jimmy Carter. Novak recognized that the thrust of all their ideas was the same: a bold initiative; an end to the "incremental proposals to the North that have resulted in an impasse"; and a willingness to get tough if the offer failed. "If North Korea will agree to destroy its nuclear arms capability," Novak concluded, "advice from such odd bedfellows as Jimmy Carter and [former Reagan NSC Adviser Richard] Allen" to seek the route of a package solution "should be considered."[40]

The Clinton administration, of course, had done much of this. It had settled on an ambitious package of incentives to offer the North the previous November, and its proposal of a third round of U.S.–North Korean talks in the midst of the defueling crisis was designed to get this package on the table.

Publicly, however, its policy appeared to meander in the days after the Carter visit. Clinton held a White House seminar with about a dozen outside experts on Asia, but it produced no consensus. President Clinton sat in the meeting for only about thirty minutes; skeptics found the whole scene—an administration appealing to think tank pundits for a policy—to be laughable. Meanwhile, administration officials hesitated to follow up Carter's visit with rapid communications to the North; they said, one report claimed, that discussions were underway about whether to follow up "by opening a new high-level channel of contacts with North Korea, us[ing] an existing lower-level channel, or simply writ[ing] a letter."[41] The joke in one Defense Department office was that Washington was so desperate to convey a message of disapproval that it would soon be sending a secretary to lead the talks with the North.

Finally, on June 21, a letter was dispatched under the signature of Ambassador-at-Large Robert Gallucci to his counterpart in North Korea asking for an official confirmation of the proposal made to Carter. The letter offered high-level talks in exchange for a true freeze of North Korea's nuclear weapons program; the true freeze would mean no extraction of plutonium from the cooling fuel rods, no new fuel added to the reactor, and continued observation by the IAEA inspectors. Even at this late date, U.S. officials continued to pursue sanctions at the UN.[42]

The following day, North Korea replied, and the Clinton administration finally announced that it was suspending its drive for sanctions. It said North Korea had agreed to talk in theory about full inspections, which was interpreted to be a code-phrase for agreement to discuss its past behavior.[43] Soon U.S. officials announced that a third round of high-level U.S.–North Korean talks would be held on July 8. The new round of talks would be led by Ambassador Gallucci and Kang Sok Ju, the same people who had conducted the last round. It was expected to move forward over a period of weeks, with smaller agreements at the beginning establishing "confidence" for later rounds.[44]

THE DEATH OF KIM IL SUNG

Now the Clinton administration would finally have an opportunity to test the ideas of those within and outside the government who had called for a more decisive approach to the negotiations. The talks would provide a venue at which U.S. officials could put on the table the long-awaited "broad and thorough approach"—a proposal that reportedly included the immediate opening of a U.S. "interests section" (a quasi-embassy) in Pyongyang; the promise of full diplomatic relations at a later time; a pledge of nonaggression; and economic assistance in building a light-water reactor.[45] At the first meeting, U.S.

officials thought their Korean counterparts were surprised and pleased with the new explicitness of the offer.

But that very day, in a strange twist of fate, the nuclear issue was thrown into a new, confusing, and dangerous stage. For also on July 8, eighty-two-year-old Kim Il Sung, North Korea's absolute ruler and Great Leader for almost forty years, died of apparent heart failure.[46] All the tentative agreements between Washington and Pyongyang and all the apparent goodwill that had been established in the previous months seemed to be suspended. Some in Washington feared that the basis for an agreement would have to be laid once again from the ground up.

A great deal of the concern, of course, focused on the personality of the elder Kim's probable successor—his son, Kim Jong Il. A debate had long swirled around the younger Kim: was he a pragmatic reformer, allied with young technocrats trained in Eastern Europe and dedicated to opening the North to outside investment? Or was he an unpredictable, violent, tyrannical leader who would not hesitate to risk war on the peninsula and who would see nothing stop his country's quest for nuclear weapons? Upon Kim Il Sung's death, this debate began again.

Reports quickly emerged to bolster both sides of the argument. Diplomats who had been stationed in Pyongyang told of a reported occasion in the late 1980s in which Kim Jong Il, racing through the capitol's streets, ran down a group of pedestrians—and hardly even slowed down. Shadowy rumors in Beijing held that the younger Kim had ordered ten disloyal army officers to be doused with oil and burned to death in front of more than one thousand of North Korea's elite.[47] On the other hand, Kim was thought to be an ally of the economic reformers. He had reportedly ordered that the labels and brand names on imports from South Korea be left on the products—an important concession, some said.[48]

International business experts noted that the younger Kim was the world's biggest customer for Hennessy premium cognacs. For a time he bought Very Special Old Pale, which sold for $40 a bottle in Seoul. Recently, however, he had apparently switched to Paradis, which fetched the cool sum of $630 a bottle in the South. The younger Kim reportedly purchased one thousand bottles of the expensive liquor a year. South Korean analysts familiar with Korean cultural norms surmised that he handed them out to friends and confidants to gain influence.[49]

A movie director once kidnapped by Kim to help him make films testified that the younger North Korean leader was well aware of events in the outside world—he reportedly had several televisions in his office, showing Japanese, South Korean, and international news programs.[50] Anthony Mitchell, a business consultant who helps companies set up deals with North Korea, insisted that the North's special economic zones had been created by Kim Jong Il.[51] Kang Myong To, a North Korean defector and son of the North Korean prime minister, concluded that, "In a nutshell, [Kim Jong Il] is quick-tempered. . . . He is capricious, so capricious that his good mood today abruptly changes into bad tomorrow. . . . He is very tearful."[52]

No one could be sure, of course, which of these portraits was correct. And there was the confusing possibility that, to some degree, all of them were.

To the extent that events provided any evidence in the days after Kim's death, they seemed to point to a positive trend. On July 11, a senior North Korean official in Germany said his country would be prepared to re-enter nuclear talks with the United States after Kim's funeral, scheduled for July 17.[53] Moderates in the North Korean hierarchy, including their nuclear negotiator, played prominent roles in the funeral, suggesting that those in authority would be the ones with a demonstrated willingness to seek better relations with the outside world.

Very quickly after Kim's death, an interesting contrast developed between U.S. and South Korean policy. The trend of toughness in Seoul's approach to the North had now reached a new apex. While President Clinton and other U.S. officials offered condolences to the North on the death of Kim—a courageous and quite proper act designed to set the stage for successful talks[54]—Kim Young Sam and his administration began a new round of bitter attacks on the North. Seoul refused to extend condolences to the North, forbade any South Korean citizens from doing so, and barred condolence visits to Pyongyang.[55] Seoul also began rounding up student radicals and labor militants, using an excuse dating from the days of military regimes: the National Security Law, which gives the South Korean government broad powers of arrest.

North Korea's reaction was immediate and predictable, denouncing Kim and blaming him for inciting a "war atmosphere."[56] In one especially harsh statement, the North said that "the Kim Young Sam group is a group of human rubbish, a group of traitors unparalleled in the world, who have ceased to be human beings."[57] At the end of July, South Korea fired back in traditional fashion: it trooped out a North Korean defector it had been holding since the previous May, a young man who claimed to be the son-in-law of North Korea's prime minister and who insisted that the North possessed five atomic bombs—which Washington quickly labeled impossible.[58] U.S. officials took the unusual step of publicly suggesting that South Korea was not behaving in a constructive manner with such actions.[59]

By the end of July 1994, the nuclear crisis was moving into a new phase. Washington and Pyongyang were set for a new round of talks, but it was not clear what the North Korean position would be when they got there. The two Koreas were at each other's throats again, making the possibility of a summit perhaps more remote than ever. And above all these developments hung one major threat: the fuel rods at Yongbyon, cooling peacefully in ponds outside the reactor. North Korean officials had already said that, "for technical reasons," the rods could not remain in place much longer than the middle of August. The United States had said that an unsupervised reprocessing would lead immediately to sanctions. And it was not clear if there would be time for a deal to be cut at the new talks before the reprocessing began.

On August 12, U.S. and North Korean negotiators meeting in Geneva announced yet another agreement on principles and objectives. Building on the July meeting, and beginning to spell out in more detail the elements of the long-awaited package deal, the agreement involved a few basic commitments by each side.[60] The "Agreed Statement" between the two sides laid out the mutual commitments:

> The DPRK is prepared to replace its graphite-moderated reactors and related facilities with light water reactor (LWR) power plants, and the U.S. is prepared to make arrangements for the provision of LWRs of approximately 2,000 MW(e) [megawatt electric] to the DPRK as early as possible. . . . Upon receipt of U.S. assurances for the provision of LWRs and for arrangements for interim energy alternatives, the DPRK will freeze construction of the 50 MW(e) and 200 MW(e) reactors, forgo reprocessing, and seal the Radiochemical Laboratory, to be monitored by the IAEA.

The two sides also stated their readiness to "establish diplomatic representation in each other's capitals and reduce barriers to trade and investment, as a move toward full normalization of political and economic relations." The United States again declared a willingness to promise nuclear non-aggression against North Korea, and the North recommitted itself to the NPT and the North-South nuclear accord.[61] Taken together, this constituted an impressive set of mutual commitments—but the Agreed Statement remained more of a road map that a settlement, an agreed set of objectives rather than a final accord.

One especially thorny issue remained to be resolved: the question of the timing of special inspections. The Agreed Statement made no mention of them, and comments by North Korean and U.S. officials suggested a looming confrontation. At the close of the August meetings, Kang Sok Ju said clearly that "we . . . do not recognize the special inspections" demanded by the IAEA, while Robert Gallucci argued separately that "there is no chance that there will be a light-water reactor constructed in a country that does not accept full-scope safeguards," and in this case that requirement "includes acceptance of special inspections."[62] Even at this late moment, it was not clear how this chasm could be bridged.

U.S.–SOUTH KOREAN DISCORD

Seoul's official reaction to the August 12 agreement was telling. It admitted that the Agreed Statement was a step in the right direction. But it appeared to downplay the significance of an accord reached between the United States and the North alone, with South Korean officials nervously watching and waiting outside the negotiation room in Geneva. And President Kim Young Sam quickly announced that South Korea wanted to supply the light-water reactors to the North, despite the North's stated preference for a deal with anyone *but* the South.[63]

South Korea's concern over, and desire to be involved in, events affecting its own security is easily understood. By the middle of 1994, however, South Korean policy on the nuclear issue had endured so many shifts, revisions, and reversals that many in Washington believed that Seoul was no longer playing a constructive role in the process.[64]

Of course, it would be too simplistic to refer to a single "South Korean" position at the time. Reports from Seoul suggested a substantial amount of discord within the South Korean government on the issue. The defector press conference on July 27, for example, was reportedly arranged and held by the Agency for National Security Planning (ANSP), which was said to desire an end to U.S.–North Korean negotiations that left the South behind. Officials at the National Unification Board and the Foreign Ministry were reportedly furious at the act.[65]

One lengthy analysis of South Korean policy toward the North from an influential Seoul journal outlined its shortcomings.[66] Some South Korean experts said that "the government has no policy toward North Korea," the report claimed. One researcher for a government institute went so far as to say that South Korea's Northern policy was "the culmination of amateurism." These observers drew their conclusions in part from a zigzag series of statements from Kim Young Sam. In February 1993, for example, Kim said that he was ready to meet with Kim Il Sung at any time; in June he lamented that "I cannot shake hands with a counterpart who has nuclear weapons"; and in February 1994 again said he would meet with Kim Il Sung. Seoul's policy toward the North Korean nuclear issue was shot through with these same inconsistencies—at one moment favoring sanctions, the next opposing them; one moment encouraging the United States into dialogue with the North, the next restraining it.

In part, this and other reports suggested, this lack of clear direction was the result of "the lack of a central control" over Seoul's policy. Various elements within the South Korean government contended with each other over North Korea policy, and Seoul's policy veered one way or another depending on which ministry was ascendant. Once again, National Security Adviser Chung Chong Wook and ANSP Director Kim Deok were portrayed as the hard liners, with Minister of Foreign Affairs Han Sung Joo, a prominent moderate, and the Unification Ministry, known as "the standard bearer of the moderate line," both playing in the first half of 1994 "a key role in preventing [Seoul's North Korea policy] Coordination Council's meetings from adopting hard-line measures toward North Korea."[67]

Some also accused the Kim Young Sam government of playing politics with the North Korean issue. As early as the fall of 1993, Kim Young Sam himself, stung by criticism that he was allowing Washington to run the show in talks with the North, moved to reassert his influence with the United States—without a clear notion of a policy to promote. The result was a spirited confrontation with President Clinton at their Washington summit.

By the middle of 1994, these dynamics combined to produce serious tensions in the U.S.–ROK relationship. In September 1994, Ambassador Robert Gallucci publicly called Seoul to task for its crackdown on dissidents, and there were reports that private messages were exchanged to the same effect.[68] Shortly thereafter, Foreign Minister Han set off on a hastily-scheduled visit to Washington to express South Korea's concerns that the United States was becoming too deeply involved with North Korea. Even as Han's trip was about to begin, Unification Minister Yi noted that "quite a few" people in South Korea believed that the U.S. position on the North was too ambiguous. "The problems of the Korean Peninsula should be solved by South and North Korea themselves," Yi added. "If someone ignores this principle, then the North Korean nuclear problem cannot be solved at all."[69]

Yi's comments reflected the growing fear in Seoul that the expansion of U.S. diplomatic ties with the North would allow Pyongyang to rival Seoul as a partner of the United States. And many South Koreans saw in the North's long-standing request for a peace treaty to replace the armistice agreement on the peninsula a thinly-veiled attempt to force U.S. troops out of Korea. One former South Korean cabinet member wrote that "there is a growing consensus among . . . analysts in South Korea that North Korea is pursuing a Vietnamese-style unification strategy"; and the former official reminded his readers that, "After the U.S. signed a peace treaty and withdrew its soldiers from Vietnam in 1973, it took only two years and three months until Vietnam was taken over by the communists."[70]

In early October 1994, President Kim Young Sam himself gave interviews to a series of U.S. and South Korean newspapers and television networks in which he blasted U.S. policy toward the North. He called the Clinton team amateurish, inexperienced in Korea, and too ready to capitulate on key issues. "If the United States wants to settle with a half-baked compromise and the media wants to describe it as a good agreement, they can," he told the *New York Times*. "But I think it would bring more danger and peril." He insisted that Washington should not rush into an agreement; it should refuse further concessions, he said, because "Time is on our side. There is no reason why we have to hasten ourselves. It is North Korea that is restless." Kim even portrayed the South as ready to weather a military crisis: while "We don't want war," he said, "nevertheless, the North Koreans must realize war doesn't mean the end of history, not for us anyway. But it does for their system." At the same time, Unification Minister Yi criticized Gallucci for dealing with the issue from a nonproliferation standpoint rather than one focused on the Korean Peninsula; and the spokesman for Seoul's ruling Liberal Democratic Party impugned U.S. motives, saying that South Korea had "a sense that the U.S. administration is hastening to achieve a diplomatic success" in time for the November elections in the United States.[71]

Seoul was treading dangerous ground. U.S. officials had for years patiently listened to their concerns, but their patience was running out. Washington was especially furious at the predictable pattern of Seoul's inconsistency: when the U.S. turned tough, South Korea urged caution; when the U.S. backed off, Seoul talked tough. A number of U.S. officials interviewed at the time spoke matter-of-factly of the growing perception that Seoul, having proven itself to be fickle and unreliable, had simply to be left to one side while Washington pressed ahead with the talks. For several weeks, officials in Seoul were playing directly into the North's hands—and risking a severe rupture with a valued ally.

DRIVING TOWARD A DEAL

As 1994 moved into fall, tensions on the Korean Peninsula grew, and the hope sparked by the August agreement began to dim. North-South relations continued the descent into bitterness begun the previous spring. South Korean officials kept up their drumbeat of intelligence leaks and other attacks designed to disparage the North's motives. The North replied with vicious attacks referring to Kim Young Sam as an "economic prostitute" and his government as a "fascist dictatorship."[72]

As this inter-Korean haggling went on, U.S.–DPRK talks entered a crucial phase. The next few weeks would decide whether the progress achieved in

August would lead to a more formal accord—or be abandoned in a new drive for sanctions.

Early signs were not promising, because it soon appeared that North Korea was backing away from the commitments it had made on August 12. On September 10, U.S. delegations traveled both to Berlin, where the talks focused on the light-water reactor issue, and to Pyongyang, where officials discussed the technical aspects of establishing a U.S. interests section in the North. In Berlin, U.S. officials stressed the importance of South Korea's providing the North with light-water reactors; North Korean officials continued to oppose that plan, and the Berlin talks approached a deadlock.[73] In Tokyo on September 14, Ambassador Gallucci emphasized that "the only viable—technically viable, financially viable, politically viable—construct for a light-water reactor project is one where South Korea plays a central role," but admitted that North Korea was rejecting such an approach.[74]

On September 23, high-level U.S. and North Korean negotiators returned to the table in Berlin for another session of talks.[75] After several days it became clear that North Korea's shift of position was more than temporary. North Korean negotiators refused to accept South Korean light-water reactors. They said they would only halt construction of their graphite reactors when the United States actually *delivered* the replacements, not when it merely committed to them, as the North had promised in August. Meanwhile the North continued to demand billions of dollars in compensation for closing down its graphite-based reactors. It refused to agree to a U.S. request to transfer the eight thousand fuel rods removed from the main Yongbyon reactor to another country. And Kang Sok Ju flirted with brinkmanship again by saying the North was considering refueling that reactor—a move U.S. officials had promised would end all talks.[76] On the 29th, U.S. and North Korean officials suspended the dialogue and returned to their capitals for further instructions.

Various theories emerged to explain North Korea's sudden backtracking and intransigence.[77] Some U.S. officials said Pyongyang was simply marking time until Kim Jong Il was fully initiated as leader, which might happen by mid-October. Others pointed to the possibility of a split within the North Korean leadership, with a hard-line military faction emerging that refused to surrender the nuclear weapons program. Still others saw the North Korean belligerence as simply trolling for a better deal. As usual, however, analysis of potential North Korean motives relied largely on guesswork.

Washington decided to respond by waiting the North Koreans out, at least for a time. The North had started to employ better procedures to store and treat the cooling reactor rods at Yongbyon, and IAEA estimates were that they could safely remain in place for several months at least, and perhaps much longer if the water quality of the cooling ponds was improved.[78] And Chinese Foreign Minister Qian Qichen, in Washington to discuss trade and technology issues, suggested to Secretary of State Christopher that the latest North Korean stubbornness was a negotiating tactic.[79] When Gallucci returned to Washington for instructions in early October, he was told simply to wait and leave the same offer on the table—the offer Washington thought Pyongyang had accepted in August. After this brief delay, Kang and Gallucci returned to the bargaining table at the North Korean lakeside mission in Geneva on October 5.[80]

A DEAL IS STRUCK

Finally, after even more back-and-forth and North Korean threats,[81] the two sides reached a major agreement on October 16. This accord—which was termed the "Agreed Framework" and which built upon the Agreed Statement of August—would represent, if it held up, the most comprehensive resolution of the nuclear issue yet discussed in official terms. The text itself refers to the accord as an "overall resolution of the nuclear issue on the Korean Peninsula."[82]

Robert Gallucci announced the agreement on October 17. "Personally, I think it is a very good agreement," Gallucci said. "Broadly, it is an acceptable and very positive agreement." Gallucci argued that it would address concerns "about the problems of the past, present and future" of the North Korean program.[83]

The specific elements of the Agreed Framework comprised several phases.[84] In the first phase, which would last until just after the turn of the century, North Korea would freeze activity at its existing reactor and at the reprocessing site within one month of signing the framework and promise not to construct any new graphite reactors or reprocessing facilities. It would also place the eight thousand fuel rods at Yongbyon in special cans for long-term storage and resume high-level talks with the South. And the North agreed to permit regular nuclear inspections as provided by the terms of the Nonproliferation Treaty, inspections that would be performed by the IAEA under a special mandate Washington promised to work out with the United Nations—an arrangement that recognized some degree of special status for the North under the NPT.

In exchange, the United States offered an immediate promise not to use nuclear weapons against the North and to begin removing barriers to political and economic contacts between the two countries within three months. In the most tangible sense, this shift would be symbolized by the opening of interests sections—national offices with a status somewhat lower than embassies. Beyond this one move, however, it was not immediately clear how the administration attempted to achieve broader trade and political contacts.

Most important, the United States promised to arrange for the international financing and supply of two modern light-water reactor (LWR) systems at an estimated cost of $4 billion—according to the framework, by "a target date of 2003." South Korea had reportedly agreed to pay for more than $2 billion of the cost, with Japan chipping in with over a billion more; the remainder, U.S. officials suggested, would come from a consortium of countries perhaps including the United States, Germany, and Russia. But the "nuclear-sensitive materials" components of the reactors—presumably their cores and perhaps some sophisticated technology—would not be delivered until after the North had allowed the special inspections. The agreement stipulated that Washington would deliver within six months a contract for the construction of the first light-water reactor. U.S. officials contemplated a one-thousand-megawatt LWR design already used in the South—which meant that the two new reactors would produce nearly ten times the energy of the North's three planned graphite reactors combined.[85]

Finally, Washington promised to make up Pyongyang's energy shortfall in the interim by arranging for shipments of oil to the North. These shipments would begin within three months with a shipment of fifty thousand metric tons in the first year, and grow at the end of the second year to a total of half a million metric tons annually. This amount was chosen as a replacement for the roughly two hundred and fifty-five megawatts of electricity the North was surrendering in its three graphite reactors. U.S. officials estimated the cost of the larger shipment at something under $100 million. The United States indicated that it would begin paying for the first three months of oil deliveries, but hoped soon to recruit an international group of countries, led by South Korea and Japan, to bear the cost.[86] In response to Pentagon concerns that the fuel could be used to help keep North Korea's army running, the supplies were to be heavy oil, capable of use in home heating or power plants but not, if not further refined, as gasoline or in other military applications.

In the second phase, which might last roughly from the year 2000 until 2003, the United States and its allies would bring the first LWR near completion. North Korea would respond by allowing the long-awaited IAEA special inspections of its two nuclear waste sites. As the framework put it,

> When a significant portion of the LWR project is completed, but before delivery of key nuclear components, the DPRK will come into full compliance with its safeguards agreement with the IAEA . . . including taking all steps that may be deemed necessary by the IAEA . . . with regard to verifying the accuracy and completeness of the DPRK's initial report on all nuclear material in the DPRK.[87]

North Korean officials continued to insist, even as the deal was being signed, that special inspections would never be necessary, that they would be able to satisfy the IAEA's concerns short of such intrusive inspections. Nonetheless, the framework committed Pyongyang to allowing the special inspections requested by the IAEA.

At the same time, Pyongyang would begin the shipment of its spent fuel rods to another country. That shipment was to begin when the first components of the LWR arrived in the North, and finish when the first LWR was complete—a process expected to take up to three years. The United States would then allow the shipment of "sensitive components" that would allow the LWR actually to begin operations. Moreover, the United States had pledged to go at some point beyond the interests sections to full diplomatic relations, with the opening of embassies, although it was not clear when exactly this would take place.

In the third and final phase, coming some time after the year 2003, the U.S. and allied consortium would complete work on the second LWR. The dismantlement of the thirty-megawatt Yongbyon reactor and the other two graphite reactors under construction, as well as the reprocessing facility, would begin when the first LWR was complete, and proceed so as to conclude with the completion of the second LWR.

Representatives from the United States, North Korea, and other participating nations soon began to form the four working groups that would implement the Agreed Framework. These groups dealt with the issues of the spent fuel, alternative energy sources, the liaison offices, and the light-water reactors. Furthermore, the concerned nations banded together to form the Korean Energy Development Organization, a central group to oversee the terms of the framework.

Until the very last minute, Deputy Secretary of Defense John Deutch had reportedly raised at least two specific complaints over the proposed deal and declined to endorse it. His objections centered on two points: the North's ability to keep the spent fuel rods for up to a decade; and the lack of adequate controls on North Korean access to the small, but nonetheless potentially worrisome, amounts of plutonium that would be produced, even by the LWRs. Deutch's objections were discussed at length at a White House meeting on October 18th, and he reportedly received enough assurances to write the president endorsing the deal just hours before it was announced.[88]

Publicly, South Korea, pleased that the North had again agreed to inter-Korean talks, hailed the Agreed Framework. Foreign Minister Han Sung Joo said "We have succeeded in halting North Korea's nuclear program."[89] Polls taken in the South showed the public about equally split on whether the agreement was a good thing—but over 60 percent of South Koreans believed the North would not live up to its part of the bargain.[90]

Privately, however, many officials in Seoul—including President Kim Young Sam—admitted to being unhappy with the framework, which they felt did not go far enough. The normally restrained, pro-government *Korea Herald* gave public voice to these fears, blaring that "The so-called breakthrough . . . came as a glaring case of giving much and taking little," and compared the agreement to the Munich Pact of 1968.[91] The chairman of an opposition party in the parliament, Chairman Lee Ki Taek of the Democratic Party, went so far as to declare that the Agreed Framework accord proved Washington's unreliability and that, henceforth, South Korea's foreign policy "should shift from a cooperative diplomacy to a self-reliant diplomacy."[92] The Korean-language *Chosun Ilbo* concurred, noting that the agreement symbolized a U.S. shift "from the ROK to the Korean Peninsula as a whole"; that it proved the United States, China, Russia, and Japan were conspiring to prevent unification; and that, as a result, "we should break from the single-track diplomacy of depending only upon the United States."[93]

Cartoons appearing in Seoul's daily papers reflected these stinging criticisms. Some showed delighted North Koreans leaving Geneva with bagfuls of cash as Uncle Sam looked on, grinning stupidly. Another depicted Foreign Minister Han sitting in his office crying, waiting to be sacked; still another showed Kim Young Sam sprawled on the ground munching a radish, while Kim Jong Il perched on a mountain savoring the revered ginseng root. An especially pointed cartoon portrayed a smiling President Clinton carrying a commitment to nuclear inspections, flanked by a weeping South Korean official clutching a bill for $3 billion.[94]

Yet Seoul's schizophrenic approach to the North continued to manifest itself. At the same time South Korean officials were blasting Washington for going easy on the North, they were talking of a plan to increase North-South trade dramatically in the agreement's wake. The government quickly announced that, in view of the Agreed Framework, nonpolitical exchanges between North and South—academic, cultural, and religious meetings—would henceforth be allowed. Various ministries as well as Seoul's Economic Planning Board began talking about the possibilities for near-term economic cooperation, and the Daewoo Corporation announced an investment in the North's Nampo free trade zone. The opposition Democratic Party recommended that the two Koreas establish official liaison offices for the new era of "inter-Korean reconciliation and cooperation" created by the framework.[95]

The IAEA's reaction was as tepid as Seoul's. Director General Hans Blix declared of the Agreed Framework that "We welcome it" and said "we are better off" than before, even with the delays involved. But even Blix admitted publicly that "it would have been better" if the special inspections had been pushed up, and in fact said the agreement was only defensible "when we think of what the alternatives might be."[96] Other IAEA officials were more blunt, worrying especially about the agreement's provision allowing the North to hold the spent fuel rods indefinitely. One IAEA official told the *New York Times* that "This means that we are living with a country that flouted the NPT and will remain in non-compliance for years. We wanted to get the fuel out of that country, and out of the country fast. . . . It is not a good precedent to set if we have to demand a special inspection in Iran or Iraq or someplace else in the world."[97]

ASSESSING THE DEAL

In the end, therefore, one overwhelming question confronted U.S. officials and observers of the North Korean situation in October 1994: just how good was the bargain Washington and Pyongyang had struck? After more than four years of intense negotiations spanning two U.S. administrations and two regimes in the North, had the two sides produced a deal that would meet their fundamental security interests and stand the test of time?

In broad terms, the October 1994 U.S.–North Korean agreement clearly meets the criteria enunciated in chapter 1, and those that will be discussed in the two concluding chapters. The deal implicitly recognizes that nonproliferation is a gradual process; especially in the toughest cases, it will frequently defy short-term solution. Therefore, the agreement is based on a definition of success that allows some degree of ambiguity in the short term as the price for a long-term commitment to complete disarmament. And it admits that a proliferant will need a compelling package of benefits to surrender its nuclear option.

The risk of a dangerous precedent, highlighted by critics of the accord, was clear enough. As the *Washington Post*'s R. Jeffrey Smith wrote on October 20, top Iranian officials had already complained to the IAEA Board of Governors that September "that the country has received little reward for its complete cooperation with the agency's inspection requests, and hinted that its leaders may decide to withdraw from the NPT regime if more benefits are not forthcoming."[98] One can imagine Ukraine seeking to renegotiate its own "package deal" in light of the Korean experience as well.

It is of course easy enough to choose one or two elements of the agreement that one would like to see altered. Perhaps most serious is the status of the North's spent fuel, its three graphite reactors (one operational and two under construction) and its reprocessing center. Under the terms of the agreement,

Pyongyang is not required to give up the spent fuel for roughly eight years; and it is not required to tear down the four nuclear facilities until the end of the third phase. At any moment during that period, if the North grows unhappy with any element of the deal—or indeed, becomes uncomfortable with anything at all—it can simply threaten to restart its reactor, unseal its reprocessing center, and get back into the nuclear weapons business. "The agreement," Arnold Kanter recognized in retrospect, "is premised on the assumption that North Korea is prepared to forgo its nuclear option." If, on the other hand, it only seeks delay, "then one cannot rule out the possibility that as it begins to face implementation of the hard decisions, it might 'take the money and run.'"[99] In short, the agreement leaves North Korea with a great deal of leverage.

But it is a primary argument of this work that such a result was inevitable as long as both sides pursued a negotiated solution. North Korea would not have signed any accord that did not allow it some means of escape if the United States did not come through with its end of the bargain. This is common sense. Moreover, it is easy to imagine a bureaucratic reason for the North's insistence on these elements of the deal: pragmatists in the North who favored the deal could have used them as powerful arguments with hardliners. This does not permanently commit us to one course, they could have pointed out; if the United States or South Korea proves unreliable, we will not have permanently forfeited anything.

Under the terms of the agreement, moreover, Washington and its partners retain a good deal of leverage. They can stop oil deliveries at any point, thus depriving the North of badly needed fuel. Some observers suggested that the LWRs require nuclear materials as fuel that the North Koreans cannot make themselves; Pyongyang will therefore depend on outside goodwill to keep them running. And once economic contacts get underway between the North and the South, Japan, and perhaps even the United States, their withdrawal would be a source of pain to the North as well. In short, Kim Jong Il has presumably tied a fair amount of his credibility—and his nation's economic hopes—to the contacts that will result from the Agreed Framework. To abandon them would not be a decision without cost for the North, especially once the contacts become entrenched—and tens of thousands of North Koreans come to depend on South Korean investments.

The simple fact is that, *if* the deal is implemented, it will represent as near to a complete resolution of the nuclear issue as could be imagined in the real world. To argue otherwise presumes a flexibility in North Korean policy and a U.S. and allied willingness to risk conflict that simply did not exist at the time. And even if the Agreed Framework were to fall apart, as Jessica Mathews has recognized, "we will [only] be back where we were [in the] spring [of 1994], having lost nothing but diplomatic effort and the cost of some oil in an attempt to avoid nuclear conflict."[100]

One criticism of the nuclear deal was certainly misplaced: the notion, as the *Wall Street Journal* put it in an especially misinformed editorial, that the "money being shoveled in" by the deal would "only prolong the [North Korean] regime's death throes," and that what would be remembered was that "the world started pouring money into the Kim regime just as it should have been allowed to crash."[101] Such criticism assumes, of course, that it *is* U.S. policy to seek the collapse of the North Korean regime, which has not been the case in either Democratic or Republican administrations. Indeed, by 1994 a strong consensus had emerged in both Washington and Seoul that it would be preferable to achieve some sort of a softer landing through investments in the North, a political opening to Pyongyang, and other steps. South Korea, shocked by the financial and social costs of German unification and knowing a Korean version would be even more wrenching, became especially wedded to a go-slow approach—which made Kim Young Sam's criticism of the nuclear deal, that it would "prop up the North," somewhat mystif ing. As previous chapters argued, the United States, South Korea, and Japan have had good reasons to adopt a policy of engagement toward the North. An agreement that (temporarily, at least) removes the nuclear issue from the table and allows that engagement to proceed should be seen as a victory for larger U.S. Korea policy, not a defeat. This indeed was part of the motivation for the deal in the first place.

Another expression of concern possessed more merit: the fact that, as Arnold Kanter wrote at the time, "The ultimate success or failure of the agreement is largely in the hands of others."[102] U.S. administrations may have as much to fear from South Korean delays, hesitations, and political maneuvering as from North Korean intransigence. Theoretically, for example, if a new government in Seoul were to repudiate the accord and refuse to fulfil the LWR contract, the talks might be back to square one. Managing the alliance relationships involved in the years ahead will be a major challenge for U.S. leadership in Northeast Asia.

Chapters 9 and 10 will subject the final U.S.–North Korean nuclear deal to closer scrutiny. Suffice it to say here that, given the basic arguments of this book—about the degree of U.S. interests involved in nonproliferation, the nature of the nonproliferation enterprise, the constraints and needs imposed by North Korea's strategic situation, and the lack of real alternatives to a negotiated solution, the October agreement was not only about the best that could have been achieved. It was, so long as both sides adhered to the negotiated route, nearly inevitable.

The long-term success of the deal, however, is by no means guaranteed. The agreement calls for the sort of nuanced, patient engagement of the North that the United States and its allies have seldom been capable of conducting. Already, one major step toward a resolution of the nuclear issue has fallen victim to failed implementation: the process underway in 1992, when North Korea accepted inspections only to see U.S.–South Korean diplomacy collapse during the second half of the year. What the Agreed Framework will mean for the future is not completely clear, but this much is certain: if the United States stamps the Korean nuclear issue "solved" and turns to other crises, the agreement will collapse. Only by a continuous and energetic follow-up process of engagement and reconciliation with North Korea can the United States and its allies make this deal stick.

■ 9 ■

NONPROLIFERATION:
LESSONS OF THE KOREAN CASE

As a test case for U.S. nonproliferation policy, North Korea was in many ways unparalleled. The North was and remains an isolated, unrepentant socialist regime that distrusts the West (and in particular the United States) and that, according to some observers, harbors expansionist motives. A nonproliferation strategy able to persuade Pyongyang to abandon its nuclear program would offer a reasonable chance of doing so with other, less sinister nations.

This chapter attempts to draw out some of the early lessons of the U.S. and South Korean effort to open Pyongyang's nuclear facilities to outside inspection and, more ambitiously, to end the threat of proliferation on the Korean Peninsula. What have we learned about the importance and conduct of nonproliferation? To what degree are these lessons transferable to other cases?

This chapter's basic purpose is to answer three of the four fundamental questions about the North Korean nuclear case posed in chapter 1—questions regarding the North's motives, the nature of multilateralism, and the relevance of criteria for success. (Chapter 10 will lay out the possible elements of an overall strategy for nonproliferation.) In the process it will draw in other related lessons of the Korean case. One of its chief conclusions is that U.S. nonproliferation efforts have often suffered from vague and ill-defined criteria for success. As the October 1994 U.S.–North Korean agreement again demonstrates, bringing a complete end to a nuclear program may not be possible, and the United States will need a better idea of what its more limited, short-term goals will be in those cases where proliferation proves a complex and difficult nut to crack. Yet much current thinking on nonproliferation, both inside and outside the government, continues to rely on questionable assumptions—assumptions about the unique importance of nonproliferation in the post–Cold War era and about the feasibility of absolutist, legalistic definitions of success in the nonproliferation field. As the following analysis suggests, the lessons of the Korean case help to explode a number of myths in nonproliferation policy.

MOTIVES FOR PROLIFERATION

One major lesson has to do with North Korea's possible motives for seeking nuclear weapons and by extension the reasons why other nations might choose a similar path. North Korea's nuclear program came to serve a variety of military, political, and economic purposes. It became a ubiquitous tool of diplomacy and a flexible support system for the North's overriding goal of regime preservation. As such, it would not be abandoned easily, and it was entirely possible that the North would demand to keep some sliver of the nuclear program under any circumstances as insurance against the risks of succession and the chance of renewed isolation. The October 1994 nuclear agreement supports the argument that the North has been allowed to preserve much of its nuclear infrastructure for another decade.

The North Korean case also suggests that nuclear motives can evolve over time. A nuclear program that may have begun life as a simple response to a security threat eventually became much more, and Pyongyang's thinking on the program may have changed dramatically. Chapter 2 portrayed the early North Korean nuclear program as largely a response to a security challenge—dealing with U.S. and, potentially, South Korean nuclear threats without being able to count on the consistent support of either China or the Soviet Union. Over time, however, the North's motives seem to have expanded. Beginning in the late 1980s, officials in Pyongyang learned how useful an ambiguous nuclear capability could be in getting the attention of the world community, wringing security concessions out of Seoul and Washington and acquiring pledges of economic assistance and expanded diplomatic relations.

Such thinking on the part of proliferants demands a subtle and far-reaching diplomatic campaign if nonproliferation is to succeed. In 1970, North Korea might have agreed to dismantle its nuclear program in exchange for security-related concessions such as the withdrawal of U.S. tactical nuclear weapons from the South, an end to South Korea's nuclear ambitions, and a U.S. pledge of nuclear nonaggression. By the early 1990s, the United States and South

Korea offered all of those things and barely made a dent in Pyongyang's apparent determination to preserve some residue of its nuclear program.

This points, in the first instance, to the maddening complexity of the North Korean nuclear issue, a problem discussed at length in chapter 1. But it also suggests a lesson for future nonproliferation efforts. If a state is perceived to be beginning a nuclear program in response to an immediate security threat, it may be far cheaper to address that threat rapidly and decisively. Once a nuclear program becomes established, it will act as a magnet for new justifications and motives. Over time, the program will grow enmeshed with issues of regional security, domestic politics (within both the proliferant and its neighbors), economic trade and aid, diplomatic relations, arms control, and a host of other areas. Once that happens, no strategy of nonproliferation, regardless of how sophisticated or subtle, may be able to eliminate or even slow the nuclear program. This is not to say that it would be easy to stop a nuclear program early on—a regime will usually have powerful reasons for initiating a program in the first place. But those reasons might well be simpler and more readily addressed at first than after several decades. A corollary of this lesson once again emphasizes the need for flexible definitions of success in nonproliferation: realistic criteria for success, tied to each specific case, will vary depending on how long the nuclear program has been running and how firmly it has become entrenched in the proliferant's political, economic, and military plans.

In summary, then, although appreciation of a proliferant's motives must reside at the heart of any nonproliferation campaign, those motives will be neither easy to determine nor easy to address. And in some cases, they will simply rule out the common criterion of success as understood by U.S. nonproliferation specialists: the immediate, complete, and total end to all nuclear research. Most U.S. and allied officials now recognize that a motivational approach to nonproliferation is the only strategy with any hope of success. But what is not yet as widely understood is that motivational strategies, if the United States is honest in implementing them and abiding by their implications, sometimes demand more limited goals for nonproliferation, at least in the short term.

NONPROLIFERATION AS A MULTILATERAL ENTERPRISE

Once a proliferant's motives are identified, the United States will turn to the practical business of assembling a nonproliferation strategy. And the overwhelming impression one gets from observing the international diplomacy aimed at the North, and especially from speaking with the U.S. and South Korean officials who conducted policy, is the dominance of multilateral approaches to nonproliferation (and, by extension, to virtually all foreign policy challenges) in the post–Cold War era. The United States shrank from considering a tougher unilateral policy, both because such a choice was hardly feasible—China could easily defeat the effect of economic sanctions, and the American public did not appear ready for the expense of a protracted crisis or war—and because, insofar as bluster never seemed to work with North Korea, confrontation did not seem desirable to U.S. officials any more than to their counterparts in Beijing or Seoul. One is hard pressed to think of a case of proliferation, or indeed a major international crisis of any sort, where the importance of multilateralism will not be apparent.

Multilateralism Ascendant: The 1993 Crisis

These conclusions ring especially true in light of the 1993 crisis in which North Korea threatened to withdraw from the NPT on March 12. In this case, as noted in chapter 6, China held all the cards. It is fruitless to ask, as some have done, whether multilateralism "worked," or whether the United States "should have" listened to the Chinese. The plain fact is that, in these events as in many others, Washington had little choice. A confrontational stance would have alienated Beijing and undermined the credibility of any subsequent U.S. threats or statements. China's role and influence strictly circumscribed the bounds of realistic policy options for the United States in this crisis. In the process, new constraints were established on U.S. and allied freedom of action, if they do indeed hope to work the problems in a multilateral framework. But it also created new opportunities for achieving a unanimity of effort and a coherence and effectiveness of policy not possible during the bipolar days of the Cold War.

As a corollary to the lesson of imposed multilateralism, another conclusion emerges from the crisis of March 1993 and the North Korean nuclear diplomacy as a whole: the international institutions at the forefront of the nonproliferation campaign, the International Atomic Energy Agency backed by the UN Security Council, have developed into occasionally effective means of pursuing national interests through supranational means. The North Korean example suggests that global agencies can indeed become strong, independent actors. At several points, it was difficult to tell whether the IAEA or policymakers in Seoul and Washington were dictating the tempo and agenda of the crisis. Obviously, the U.S. and allied representatives on the IAEA's board approved its actions, but the fact remains that often the toughest and most confrontational stances that emerged during the various crises of 1993 and 1994 came directly from the agency.

Nonproliferation hawks will immediately applaud the revitalization of the IAEA, and in the long run it is surely a good thing. In the short run, however, national leaders may be stuck with some uncomfortable questions: Are international agencies equipped to conduct their own diplomacy? To whom are they answerable? During the NPT crises of 1993 and 1994, IAEA Director General Hans Blix possessed a good deal of independent power. The United States had to ask Blix not to declare the continuity of safeguards broken in November and December 1993. In late 1993, in fact, Hans Blix appeared to hold the question of sanctions in his own hands. It was lucky for the United States that he finessed the issue with skill; a less experienced diplomat, or a stubborn nonproliferation hawk, might have helped spark a major crisis by issuing more inflammatory public statements.

No final answer can be given to the question of whether the new multilateralism will be effective and workable. It will offer new opportunities to learn from others and assemble a more nuanced diplomatic campaign, incorporating ideas and approaches that U.S. officials might not develop on their own. International institutions can also play an important role in providing cover for neutralist nations like Japan, which throughout the crisis relied on the UN to coalesce world opinion.[1] In other instances, however, this strict new international approach to issues could prevent the United States from seeking its own interests, allow regional troublemakers to get off without sanction or even rebuke, and perhaps impede necessary diplomacy through the intervention of unresponsive and misguided international bureaucrats.

Multilateralism, this crisis suggests, can work for either good or ill. The task for the United States, now and in the future, is to monitor this evolving phenomenon, to learn how to mold it and use it to benefit U.S. interests, and to learn from its experiences. For just as the bipolar military standoff was the essential geopolitical architecture of the Cold War, so diplomatic multilateralism seems to be taking shape as the blueprint for the post–Cold War era.

The U.S. Role

A related conclusion to be drawn from this crisis about the conduct of multilateralism, and a somewhat paradoxical one given what has been said previously, is that the United States remains the only nation capable of galvanizing an effective international diplomatic campaign. To be sure, world action of some sort would have taken place in March 1993 even if the United States had done nothing. South Korea would have urged the IAEA to act, and the agency may have done just what it eventually did—refer the issue to the UN Security Council.[2] China might still have lobbied the North to forgo the idea of a nuclear arsenal.

Yet apart from the United States, no other nation in the world today is capable of leading a consistent, comprehensive nonproliferation effort. Washington's combination of economic and military power and political influence, along with its close involvement in many regions threatened by proliferation, make it an unmatched—and indispensable—nonproliferation agent. And yet this role creates risks of its own; Washington could be tempted to dominate responses to proliferation, forcing its views on its partners in nonproliferation efforts. The Korean case clearly illustrates these facts and risks. Washington served as policy coordinator, dispenser of carrots, and source of threats, and its commanding role created some controversy in Seoul.

At the broadest level, Washington worked to rationalize its own approach with those of two key regional actors, South Korea and Japan. Tokyo had strong incentives to oppose North Korean proliferation in any case, but it might have chosen various means of doing so—including outright accommodation—had it not been drawn into a coherent international strategy by Washington. Tensions between Seoul and Tokyo, and Japan's idiosyncratic motives vis-à-vis the division of the Korean Peninsula and the survival of the North, might have allowed North Korean officials to play their two neighbors off each other had it not been for U.S. influence.

The United States was also the only nation capable of offering the key security-related incentives to encourage North Korea to abandon its nuclear weapons program. As the source of many of the military, including nuclear, threats that may have inspired the North Korean program in the first place, the United States could not avoid a major role in any nonproliferation effort. A withdrawal of U.S. tactical nuclear weapons was a precondition for North Korean acceptance of IAEA inspections, and the postponement of Team Spirit helped further reduce tensions and convinced Pyongyang of U.S. and South Korean good intentions. It was thus no accident that the October 1994 agreement emerged from an intense period of U.S.–North Korean negotiations in which, perhaps more than any other time in the bilateral dialogue, Washington took the lead and pressed hard for a deal. And it is hardly surprising that the agreement is laced with phrases clearly establishing the United States as its executor.

Although it was not an issue for North Korea, moreover, if positive security assurances are required to stem proliferation, the United States remains the only nation in the West capable of extending them. For South Korea, Germany, and Japan, strong U.S. security commitments remain a major reason for these countries' continued refusal to build their own nuclear arsenal. It is conceivable that other major countries may be added to that list in coming years. And, in most cases, no nation other than the United States is in a position to back them up with credible military promises.

No major case of possible proliferation therefore exists in which the United States will be able to take a backseat role. In the Middle East, U.S. leadership in the Persian Gulf War and its continuing efforts to oust Saddam Hussein make it the undisputed leader of the campaign to root out Iraq's remaining nuclear laboratories. Long-standing U.S. security commitments to and close relations with Israel, and the U.S. cosponsorship of the ongoing Middle East peace talks, mean that any efforts to address the Israeli nuclear force must begin in Washington. Because of its influence over China, its military partnership with Pakistan, and its own unintended role in posing a marginal threat to India, the United States must be a leader in nonproliferation efforts on the Indian subcontinent as well—as was again demonstrated in the laudable, if ill-fated, U.S. nonproliferation initiative for South Asia of spring 1994.

Besides its regional connections, the United States will also be the chief actor in nonproliferation because of its influence on broader arms control questions. It is often forgotten that the United States and the former Soviet Union made commitments in Article VI of the Nonproliferation Treaty to reduce their own nuclear forces and infrastructures. Their failure to do so, and indeed the NPT's very principle of dividing the world into nuclear haves and have-nots, is the source of fundamental opposition to the treaty from such nations as China and India. With the Cold War excuse for lack of progress gone, and with the NPT up for renewal in 1995, member and nonmember states alike will be watching U.S.–Russian arms control carefully for signs of a sincere desire to fulfil treaty obligations. Chapter 10 offers a number of proposals along this line.

There are risks as well as obligations in America's leading role on nonproliferation. In any given case, the U.S. view of the ends or means of a diplomatic effort can bring it into conflict with allies or important regional powers. In the Korean case, U.S. officials continually butted heads with their Chinese counterparts, who urged a more conciliatory line toward the North. Some U.S. analysts urged Washington to make North Korea the litmus test of Sino-American relations. Had this dangerous advice been followed, the United States might have sacrificed its relationship with the world's most important emerging power because of a dispute over tactics.

Nor did the United States and South Korea always see eye to eye. As chapters 4 through 8 made clear, during both the Roh-Bush and Kim-Clinton years, U.S. and South Korean officials differed on strategy toward the North. In fact, each nation experienced a sort of policy roller-coaster, veering from hard-line to soft and back again. In the process, disagreements became endemic. By the fall of 1994, even South Korean President Kim Young Sam was speaking publicly about the need for Seoul to gain more independence from the United States.

In any given case, therefore, the United States and an ally might disagree on nonproliferation policy. If the disagreement became severe enough, the ally might openly abandon the U.S. policy. But the Korean case also points to another danger: If the United States *insists* on its own approach—as it did, on a number of issues (the most prominent being South Korea's abandonment of the reprocessing option) in Korea—it can create resentment and provide ammunition to nationalists looking for examples of U.S. hegemonism. This is exactly what has happened in Korea, where the politically helpful decline of the U.S. military profile in the South, symbolized and given substance by Washington's shift from a "leading" to a "supporting" role on the peninsula, has been broken by U.S. assertiveness on the nuclear issue. South Korean nationalists in the legislature, in think tanks and universities, and even in the government have attacked what they perceive as the United States's domineering attitude on nonproliferation. As U.S. officials will hasten to contend, these perceptions are not necessarily accurate. But they exist nonetheless.

There is a chance, albeit small, that an overly myopic and assertive nonproliferation policy could replace anti-Communism as the fundamental example of U.S. geopolitical hegemony in the 1990s. The issue is ripe for such a characterization. Nations such as India and Brazil have long accused the NPT of a fundamental unfairness, and U.S. friends and allies are even now beginning to chafe under the pressure of U.S. demands for export controls, sanctions against proliferants, and other adherence to the framework of nonproliferation. Architects of U.S. nonproliferation policy must keep this risk in mind.

This analysis suggests two basic lessons. First, continued U.S. internationalism, engagement abroad, and leadership in arms control is vital to forestall proliferation of weapons of mass destruction. Without active U.S. involvement—and, more than that, U.S. *leadership*—efforts to constrain proliferation will fragment and collapse. This general conclusion holds true for all the major nonproliferation challenges today, whether in Korea, Ukraine, South Asia, the Middle East, or elsewhere. But second, U.S. efforts must be combined with and responsive to those of other countries. A hegemonic nonproliferation strategy will fail, and no nonproliferation policy can work if it is at odds with the interests of those very countries it is designed to protect.

The Role of Intelligence

The Korean example also emphasizes the critical importance of accurate and timely intelligence to nonproliferation, and more broadly to the future of U.S. leadership in multilateral efforts. Successful examples of multilateral diplomatic or military action are built on the framework of good intelligence. This was overwhelmingly true in the Korean example as well.

U.S. intelligence lay at the root of the international diplomatic campaign aimed at North Korea. It was U.S. intelligence satellites, in 1984 and again in

1989, which uncovered troubling evidence of North Korean nuclear weapons research. This evidence played a critical role in marshalling a world consensus on the issue. The role of intelligence was especially evident in 1992 and early 1993, when the United States, overcoming objections from some in the CIA, shared key satellite photos with members of the IAEA—information that provided the impetus for the agency's demand for special inspections.

The Korean case clearly demonstrates that, as Michele Flournoy has argued, "Proliferation will put a premium on detailed and accurate intelligence assessments of the intentions, capabilities, perceptions, and behavior of new nuclear nations," or of those nations on the brink of going nuclear.[3] This same lesson can be extended to include almost any major diplomatic effort that will require a multilateral approach: reliable and timely intelligence has been critical in gaining world acceptance and support for U.S. actions in such cases as the interventions in Grenada and Panama and the Persian Gulf War. Intelligence is an area of unique U.S. advantage and leverage.

One aspect of the proliferation intelligence challenge merits attention. It is the central importance of the one piece of information that is hardest to obtain: knowledge of the specific time when a nation assembles its first nuclear device. While clear evidence can be found that a nation is far from the threshold of weaponization or has well surpassed it, Robert Blackwill and Ashton Carter write, "The threshold itself . . . at which a program becomes a small arsenal of one or two bombs, is characterized by subtle and easily hidden parameters— exactly how many kilograms of fissile material have been acquired, whether its experts have full confidence in the design, whether a workable device has actually been assembled, and what delivery system (possibly makeshift or covert) has been selected." Yet "it is precisely at the threshold," they conclude, if it could be determined, "that many of the policy measures" required to deal with proliferation "would most effectively apply." It is at that moment that proliferants "make critical decisions about whether and how to breach the threshold, and it is then that U.S. policy can best influence those decisions." This creates the dilemma, as Blackwill and Carter recognize, that "the point of highest leverage coincides with the time when intelligence uncertainty is likely to be greatest."[4]

In fact, I have argued earlier that the point of greatest leverage may in fact occur well before the threshold of weaponization. If a nation is on the verge of a nuclear weapons capability after years of work and expense, it is likely to see more value in pressing ahead, at least to a primitive nuclear capability, than stalling just at the moment of success. Nonetheless, Blackwill and Carter's point is an important one: the most important information about proliferation is also the hardest to come by—some clear estimate of the junction between research and production.

This difficulty is clearly evident in the Korean case. No firm intelligence has emerged on whether the North has crossed the threshold; U.S. intelligence agencies have engaged in guesswork, resolving the dilemma by simply offering the worst-case possibility—two assembled North Korean bombs—to decisionmakers. This inability to define that threshold in the Korean case has inhibited decisive policies. Because they cannot be exactly sure how close the North is to a bomb, U.S. officials have little sense of how much time they possess to resolve the issue, and have never had sufficient evidence to press for a confrontational stance. The Clinton administration could more easily defend the October 1994 agreement, for example, if it could offer compelling evidence that the North did not, in fact, yet have enough plutonium for a bomb.

This fact carries several implications. It again points to the need for very early attention to nascent nuclear programs. Because the moment of weaponization can never be carefully defined, it is far better to deal with a program long before a proliferant reaches that threshold. It suggests that the United States could do a better job of trying to penetrate nuclear research programs; information from operatives inside those programs may be the only reliable warning that the threshold is approaching.

And finally, the inevitability of imperfect intelligence supports the argument of this volume for flexible, as opposed to absolutist, ends and means in nonproliferation policy. Urgent and uncompromising demands for intrusive inspection regimes cannot be based on vague evidence of exactly how close to the threshold a proliferant may be. Nations such as China, which have reasons to be wary of a tough approach in any case, will not respond to the plaintive fear that the North *might* have enough plutonium for a bomb, and that it *might* have assembled a workable weapon.

Nonproliferation in the Context of U.S. Foreign Policy

The fact that U.S. allies, friends, and adversaries will have differing perspectives on proliferation, and the inevitable shortcomings of intelligence, suggest that it must be something less than an absolute enterprise. So, in fact, does a review of U.S. national interests. As noted in chapter 1, some observers and government officials have begun to characterize the issue as an overriding one, something that must take precedence over many other U.S. foreign policy priorities. This line of thinking began in the 1970s and has reached fruition in the impressive array of bureaus and specialists devoted to nonproliferation in the Clinton administration. One result is an overemphasis on nonproliferation to the exclusion of other foreign policy goals, a pattern that has become evident to some extent in U.S. policy toward Korea, Pakistan, Ukraine, and other nations.

And yet, a closer look reveals that nonproliferation, like human rights and other broad goals, is not an absolute at all, but merely one more U.S. interest to be balanced against others. As Roger K. Smith has argued, "The problem with elevating non-proliferation to a policy goal outside the traditional framework of foreign policy is that it is susceptible to either overemphasis or underemphasis. . . . Consequently, the leitmotif of non-proliferation analysis since the late 1970s has been the call for integration, or more accurately reintegration, of non-proliferation and foreign policy in such a way that the interests of the nation and of the [nonproliferation] regime are served."[5] The Rockefeller Foundation's Thomas Graham agrees that the field of nonproliferation "is becoming filled with many 'born again' nonproliferants." In fact, Graham contends that identifying "proliferation [as] our chief national security threat can lead to very *bad* policy if one assumes that the scope of the problem is larger than it is."[6]

The Korean case, for example, argues strongly that nonproliferation is only one of a panoply of U.S. interests that must be taken into account. The United States certainly wanted North Korea to abandon its nuclear program, but it also wanted a wide range of other things. Some in the U.S. government desired more normal relations with North Korea to reduce the North's isolation and set the stage for a more peaceful unification of the peninsula. The United States coveted good relations with China, and had reason to husband some of its limited leverage with Beijing for other issues, such as human rights and trade. The United States wanted to preserve warm ties with South Korea and Japan. Perhaps most of all, the United States hoped to avoid a war, and the substantial cost—in lives and resources—that it would entail.

Most of these interests clashed in some way with the goal of nonproliferation. Indeed, as chapter 3 suggested, virtually every major stake the United States has in East Asia conflicts with the practical results of a strong nonproliferation policy.

A similar collision course can be seen in other areas. For a time, the United States obsessively pursued nonproliferation goals in Ukraine when perhaps it should have been considering Ukraine in a broader strategic context. (The Clinton administration, however, has made substantial and welcome revisions in U.S. Ukraine policy, attempting to replace "pressure" on the nuclear issue with a broader geostrategic "partnership.") The United States continues to sanction Pakistan, a significant nation in the Islamic world with a strategic position in South Asia, for its nuclear work even though those sanctions have proven ineffective. Israel provides an interesting example of a contrary case, a U.S. ally whose nuclear work has been largely ignored by official Washington because of its role in U.S. foreign policy.

This is not to suggest that nonproliferation is unimportant to the United States. Clearly, it ought to be one major priority in foreign policy. The following chapter lays out a strategy for nonproliferation predicated on the notion that reducing the spread of weapons of mass destruction will be an important element of world peace in the turbulent times to come. Nonetheless, as much as the United States wants to avoid a world bristling with nuclear arms, U.S. officials must pursue this goal with the clear awareness that it is only one among a number of major priorities. If Washington does otherwise, it will not only threaten other important U.S. national interests, it will also undermine that very nonproliferation policy by provoking a strong worldwide and domestic reaction against it.

If this analysis is correct, then as long as both sides adhered to the diplomatic route, something like the October 1994 accord was simply inevitable. The agreement and the way in which it was achieved represent incremental solutions to an incremental problem. The goal of nonproliferation in Korea was important for the United States, even critical. But it was not absolute; it did not take precedence over competing interests such as peace and stability on the peninsula, peaceful and gradual reunification, or amicable relations with China. A policy that achieved nonproliferation only at the expense of these other interests could hardly be called a success. Recognizing these facts, U.S. officials had to find the best solution possible for a non-absolute interest—and the Agreed Framework of October 1994 represents just such a solution.

BUREAUCRATIC POLITICS IN WASHINGTON AND SEOUL

The management of diplomacy toward North Korea, in the governments of both the United States and South Korea, provides a textbook example of the nature and ramifications of bureaucratic politics. In both countries, various ministries and agencies debated the proper way to deal with North Korea. In both countries, the players in the debate were largely the same: the ministries or departments of defense, intelligence agencies, ministries of foreign affairs, arms-control or unification-related agencies (the Arms Control and Disarmament Agency in Washington, the National Unification Board in Seoul) and the national security adviser's office.

Previous chapters have outlined the nature of the policy debates between these various agencies. The tableau of positions of individual departments or agencies, and of particular offices within them, was highly complex and changed over time. No simple model of bureaucratic behavior could possibly capture this intricate variety of ideas and positions, which often produced surprising results.

In Washington, for example, the Department of Defense, generally defined as a "hawk" on major foreign policy issues given its military perspective, was interested in avoiding war on the peninsula and therefore was willing to defer or even write off special inspections in order to obtain a nuclear settlement. Defense found a hostile response to this idea from the Arms Control and Disarmament Agency, commonly thought of as a doveish, pro–arms control agency; ACDA's concern for the sanctity of the NPT regime led it to demand, for a time, an uncompromising stance on the question of special inspections. In the post–Cold War era, now that individual departments and agencies have broken free of their well-worn positions on national security issues, such novel bureaucratic debates will be common.

A larger bureaucratic issue also emerged: the organization of policy toward North Korea in the U.S. government. This organization underwent an interesting metamorphosis during the Clinton administration. Responsibility for the issue made its way from foreign policy regional departments to new, functional offices that dealt with proliferation as a single, inclusive issue. This change could hold important implications for the future of U.S. nonproliferation policy.

During the nuclear diplomacy of 1990 to 1992, responsibility for U.S. Korea policy resided firmly in the hands of the regional offices of the various executive departments and agencies. At the State Department, the office of East Asian and Pacific Affairs, headed initially (and then again in 1992) by William Clark, then Richard Solomon, and finally (after Clark's interim return) Clinton appointee Winston Lord, coordinated U.S. strategy toward the North. In the Department of Defense, James Lilley, Assistant Secretary for International Security Programs, whose department did Defense's Asia work, headed the effort. And at the National Security Council, the top staffer devoted to the North Korean nuclear issue was Douglas Paal, Senior Director of the NSC for Asia.

During late 1992 and 1993, however, this situation began to change, and trends already underway during the Bush administration were brought to fruition. The Clinton administration had defined nonproliferation (or "counter-proliferation") as one of its primary foreign policy challenges. To act on this decision, the administration began creating offices devoted entirely to the proliferation issue, and centralizing policy for all proliferation issues within those offices.

Thus, at the State Department, the East Asia bureau slowly gave way to the office of Political-Military Affairs under Assistant Secretary of State Robert Gallucci. At Defense, Assistant Secretary Ashton Carter was given responsibility for nuclear issues, with nonproliferation at the top of the list. And at the NSC, a small office of nonproliferation first created under the Bush administration was expanded, and its head given a title equivalent to all other NSC staff issue directors—senior director. These shifts reflected the belief that proliferation was a discipline unto itself, that proliferation challenges were best dealt with as a set rather than broken down as regional issues.

The wisdom of this approach remains to be seen. The regional offices were doing a creditable job with Korea policy through 1992, and were unusually well-equipped to understand both the unique nature of the North Korean regime and the particular security threats it faced. Those who specialize in nonproliferation as a discipline, and whose institutional credibility and future ride on the issue, may also be more inclined to take a more theological approach to enforcement than would regional specialists. Whether or not a more absolutist approach would be desirable is, of course, a matter for debate.

But in fact, a sharp distinction on North Korea policy between regional and functional offices was not always evident, and discussions with proliferation experts indicate that they can be just as sensitive to the need for a moderate approach as can regionalists. Gallucci managed to shepherd U.S. policy toward the October 1994 settlement, which signified an abandonment of the narrow, legalistic stance on nonproliferation characteristic of some offices dedicated to that discipline. Moreover, in some cases the appointment of a specific individual is all to the good insofar as it represents a dedicated effort to resolve an individual case of proliferation on its own merits. The work of Gallucci, and of Strobe Talbott on Ukraine, certainly fall into this category, and both led to more decisive policy-making by the U.S. government and important agreements to help resolve the proliferation challenges.

But whichever model one prefers, whatever type of ministry or office is best suited to handle nonproliferation policy, the Korean case provides additional evidence for one undeniable conclusion: nonproliferation issues remain subject to a bureaucratic free-for-all that can inhibit successful policymaking. In any given case, one or another office may preside over a nonproliferation initiative. First it may be Deputy Secretary Strobe Talbott in Ukraine; then Robert Gallucci may be assigned to Korea; then the South Asia desk at State may push an India-Pakistan initiative with no high-level player in charge.

Taken together, these problems suggest the need for a reexamination of the way nonproliferation policy is organized within the U.S. government. This work has not examined the issue closely enough to offer a detailed proposal for such change. Suffice it to say that any institutional reform should take account of two considerations: the need to keep regional policy firmly in the hands of regional bureaus, where the experts on particular countries reside, and the need for decisive leadership within the government. This perhaps suggests an arrangement in which all offices of "nonproliferation" are abolished save one: a senior director at the National Security Council, answerable to the national security adviser, who coordinates policy among the regional offices of the various departments. The individual in this office should be very senior; he or she will have to be the spokesperson for nonproliferation in a way other senior directors at the NSC will not.

When a nonproliferation challenge arose—in North Korea, for example, or Ukraine—this individual would work with the Asian or European departments at the departments of State, Defense, Commerce, and so on, as well as the intelligence agencies and arms control specialists at Defense and ACDA, to formulate policy. (In a sense, the position would provide a ready-made policymaker to do the casework accomplished by people like Talbott and Gallucci.) It would not have to be a consensus policy; in the end, the National Security Adviser would have the authority to recommend a particular course of action to the president. This approach would establish a clear center of responsibility whose primary advice comes from the regional specialists who understand the target country best.

A DEFINITION OF SUCCESS IN NONPROLIFERATION

Once the target of nonproliferation has been identified and the government organized for the proliferation challenge, the United States (and often its friends and allies) must work out a definition of success for the effort, a set of goals and desires, both minimal and maximal, that will be sought in diplomacy. The question of what is a useful *definition of success* was raised in chapter 1, and the Korean case points toward some tentative answers.

In efforts to halt the spread of weapons of mass destruction, the world community must decide what its goals are. In the Korean case, those goals, at the outset, were defined in a rather absolute fashion: the IAEA and UN sought a reasonably iron-clad guarantee that North Korea possessed no ability to assemble a nuclear device. Hence the February 1993 IAEA demand, despite numerous inspections and a guarantee that the North could not siphon any more plutonium off from its nuclear reactor because of IAEA safeguards, for challenge inspections to see two small sites with clues to possible past transgressions. Hence President Clinton's open-ended statement in the winter of 1993 that North Korea "cannot be allowed" to possess nuclear weapons.

The basic decision about what constitutes success, of course, will depend on the nature of the proliferant. Stephen Meyer has distinguished among three types of nations that may seek nuclear weapons: hard-, middle-, and soft-core proliferants. Soft-core nations are "uninterested" in nuclear weapons; middle-core countries may have some nuclear ambitions, but can usually be persuaded to abandon them without too much difficulty.[7] For these countries, the U.S. definition of success can be relatively absolute in the short term. The United States can aim at the complete and clear abandonment of any nuclear weapons research as the goal of nonproliferation efforts.

Hard-core proliferants, on the other hand, "already have made decisions to become nuclear weapons powers. The intensity of their motivational profiles is such that, no matter how many technology barriers are thrown up in their paths, they will continue to pursue a nuclear weapons capability."[8] Here is where the United States will find difficulty in enunciating specific, short-term goals of nonproliferation. Hard-core proliferants may simply refuse to abandon some level of nuclear research. This is the problem the world has confronted with North Korea that, as suggested in chapter 2, has seemed to want both an ongoing nuclear program and engagement with the outside world.

Ironically, though, those nations concerned with the North's program, and particularly South Korea, have also wanted two arguably inconsistent things. Seoul, and to a lesser degree Washington and Tokyo, has wanted not only to resolve the nuclear issue but also to have a form of engagement with the North. Growing economic and political contacts with North Korea would help reduce tensions on the peninsula, lower the eventual cost of unification, and perhaps encourage a stable transition of power in the North. No outside power, and least of all South Korea, wanted to see a total collapse of the North. As outlined in chapter 3, U.S. and South Korean interests argued for a growing level of engagement with the North.

But the outside world was also urgently interested in a second goal—an end to the North's nuclear research. By late 1992, the overriding question in U.S. and South Korean diplomacy toward the North was whether these goals could be reconciled with an effective response to the North Korean nuclear program. And this question quickly devolved into one of goals: could the United States define its nonproliferation interests in such a way as to render them compatible with North Korea's fundamental interests and thus allow engagement to proceed? It all came back to the simple but extraordinarily difficult judgment about what defined success; and it is not clear that, even today, a straightforward decision has been made.

Ambiguous Proliferation

Perhaps the overriding question related to a definition of success is whether nonproliferation demands, to the greatest degree possible, undermining the ability of nations such as Pakistan, India, and North Korea to pursue a "strategy of ambiguity." John J. Schulz has pointed out that an increasing number of states use nuclear "deterrence by bluff" rather than constructing an actual nuclear arsenal. This type of deterrence is "practiced by the 'maybe states'—those that may be nuclear powers, or may not. The most essential point is that the status of their nuclear capacity is unclear." Nations such as India, Pakistan, and Israel can do research on nuclear weapons and closely approach a nuclear capability without actually confirming one—baring its teeth, in a manner of speaking. And "if planners in other states are persuaded that the teeth are real, sharp, and effective—and will be used in the face of sufficient provocation—then deterrence has worked."[9] Avner Cohen and Benjamin Frankel prefer the term *opaque* nuclear proliferation, in which the acquisition of nuclear weapons is no longer seen as "an either/or issue." They list a number of the central aspects of opaque proliferation, including the lack of nuclear tests or direct nuclear threats, denial of possession, the absence of military doctrine or open nuclear deployments, the lack of open debate in the proliferant, and the organizational insulation of the nuclear program.[10]

North Korea may not have advanced far enough to implement a credible policy of ambiguity. There are still serious questions about whether it has the capability to assemble a workable bomb. These doubts do not linger over the Indian, Israeli, or Pakistani programs, which are assumed to have weaponized bombs either produced or ready for assembly. But if the IAEA process does not put a firm clamp on the North Korean program—if reports of secret, underground plutonium reprocessing facilities continue, if the North is witnessed testing its Nodong missiles with unusual payloads, if North Korean officials continue to approach Western companies for nuclear-related technologies—then eventually a consensus could emerge that the North may have a minuscule nuclear arsenal at the ready.[11]

IAEA inspections in Korea have been designed precisely to prevent such an outcome. And yet, there is no question that the IAEA inspections turned up worrisome facts. North Korea appears to have lied about the number and scale of its plutonium reprocessing, as many skeptics suggested that it would. It was possible, the fine-tuned IAEA techniques indicated, that the North had siphoned off enough plutonium for a few bombs.

Was this situation to be defined as a success or failure? Quite obviously, the IAEA and other states did not recognize it as a success, for the agency quickly demanded special inspections to begin finding the missing plutonium. The definition of success, by this action, would appear to brook no compromise: either every bit of plutonium in a given nuclear program is accounted for, every site inspected and every doubt answered, or the inspection regime must be viewed as a failure.

But one lesson of the North Korean crisis is that, in some cases and for some countries, perfection may be too high a standard for nonproliferation regimes, *at least at first.* Chapter 10 will argue that, in many cases of proliferation, no palatable hard-line option will exist, whether comprising military strikes or economic sanctions. If that is true, then it follows that the best solution produced by diplomacy is the best result possible. That is, the nonproliferation game must be played gradually, in fits and starts, with more progress coming all the time; going for complete success from the outset with a series of ultimatums or demands may be counterproductive.

This line of thought leads to the conclusion that some degree of ambiguity about nuclear weapons might be acceptable, indeed unavoidable, as a way station on the road to complete disarmament for a handful of hard-core proliferants. William Epstein argued as long ago as 1977 that, for countries with intense security considerations, "it may be necessary to work out or allow for some special status or category in which they would not be strictly neutral or non-neutral."[12] Agreements that recognize this fact, grant the existence of ambiguity, and work to keep the situation from getting any worse can in fact be a very positive tool in the worldwide campaign for nonproliferation. At the core of such agreements is a trade—leaving aside the immediate demand for the location of every bit of previously acquired fissile material in exchange for a full and complete accounting of all other aspects of a given nuclear program, including, crucially, a firm and verifiable cap on any future production of fissile materials.

To take this approach in Korea would be to essentially defer, *for the short term,* concerns about the relatively small amounts of plutonium—perhaps one or two bombs' worth—that Pyongyang may have secreted away. In exchange, the world would demand full access to the North's facilities to make sure that its potential nuclear stockpile could never grow any bigger. And through diplomatic and economic contacts, confidence-building measures, and eventually conventional arms control, South Korea, the United States, and Japan would work at creating an atmosphere on the peninsula so North Korea would never see a reason to use the bombs it may or may not have—and so that the North could eventually agree to answer all remaining questions about its nuclear research. It cannot be stressed strongly enough that a complete reversal of a proliferant's nuclear ambitions should always be the *eventual* goal of every nonproliferation effort, but that long-term goal will not always be appropriate as an immediate demand for hard-core proliferants. All of this, of course, is very much evident in the October 1994 Agreed Framework, which represents a good example of the strategy proposed here.

Former Japanese Foreign Minister Saburo Okita argued for a similar approach in 1992. "Since nuclear weapons have no military relevance on the peninsula," Okita proposed, "the best way to deal with their political or psychological use might simply be to ignore them; rushing about trying to cope with the fact that the North may have such weapons only raises their profile and political and psychological utility."[13] On this view, perhaps the best response the West could have made to the North Korean threat to build nuclear weapons was that given by former Soviet Foreign Minister Eduard Shevardnadze: and what will you do with them?

One upshot of this analysis is that the U.S. and IAEA demand for special inspections should not have been made in the form and at the time that it was. North Korea had made its position very clear in early 1993: the demand for such inspections would lead it to repudiate its IAEA obligations. Obviously, the practice of nonproliferation cannot allow the proliferant to set all the rules of the game. But it must recognize the reality that, because of the specific factors involved in each case and the limits to U.S. and allied power, in many cases the proliferant will in fact set some of those rules. India has done so for decades, as has Israel. In this case, existing IAEA inspections had already placed a firm cap on the North's nuclear program; the larger risks in that program were embodied, not in the plutonium then missing, but in the potential for future plutonium production. To insist on immediate inspections aimed at the nuclear program's past, at the expense of an inspection regime to control its future, was to put the cart before the horse.

This line of thought points to the following definition of success, sketched out quite nicely by former Congressman Stephen Solarz, who explains with characteristic frankness and clarity:

> [T]he future of the North Korean program should concern us more than its past. Our stubbornness should not be misplaced. It would make little sense to let Pyongyang assemble a stockpile of nuclear weapons simply because it refuses to surrender the one or two weapons it already may possess; and in such circumstances it would be better to reach an understanding with Pyongyang in which it is permitted to keep the fissile material it already has in exchange for precluding it from accumulating any more. A single North Korean bomb will not threaten global stability. Many North Korean bombs will.[14]

Once that short-term goal had been achieved—and the following section outlines the requirements for accomplishing it—U.S. and allied attention could have shifted to creating the conditions in which the North would be willing to surrender its rudimentary weapons, or the nuclear material that might be used to make them. In fact, as argued in chapters 7 and 8, the Clinton administration appeared for a time to have settled on just such a definition of success[15]—the October 1994 agreement largely follows this approach.

Such an approach, it is hoped, would deal with the risk of expanded proliferation—the proliferant selling its weapons to one or more other nations, thus doubling or tripling the proliferation risk—by leaving the proliferant little to sell. With only two or three weapons, a new proliferant would presumably be loath to sell one or more of them; its nuclear deterrent would be too minimal to allow such a step. Of course, there will be exceptions to this rule—and North Korea, strapped as it is for hard currency, might be one of them. Additional measures are therefore necessary to deal with this threat: careful monitoring of the proliferant's weapons program and perhaps an easing of the economic embargo on the North to reduce its craving for hard currency.

There are obviously complications and risks to such an approach, as there are in all cases of ambiguity. A violent transition of power in North Korea—a risk brought to the forefront by the July 1994 death of Kim Il Sung—could place those one or two nuclear weapons into unstable hands. Even a tiny arsenal could raise concerns in Japan and slowly erode the prevailing anti-nuclear sentiment elsewhere in Northeast Asia. Upon unification, the question of what to do with the former North Korea's little cache of bombs would spark heated debates within Korea. And it is not clear how ambiguous proliferation would affect regional stability or be kept under control; as Cohen and Frankel note, "The two central concepts of the nuclear age—deterrence and arms control—were predicated on nuclear weapons being readily observable." The rational decisions integral to deterrence theory, "difficult to make under any circumstances, are even more so under opacity."[16] Incompetent leaders, John J. Schulz concludes, might "handle the delicate process of maintaining ambiguity so poorly as to cause neighbors to panic and decide to develop new, full-blown arsenals."[17]

But the choice—in Korea as in many other cases, from Ukraine to Israel to India—remains. Down one road lies an ultimatum, a demand for perfect confidence and complete disarmament; its way stations in some cases will be confrontation, an end to IAEA inspections and other forms of international control, a fractured international community, sanctions, and possibly war. The other road holds a more accommodating approach, lessened tensions, expanded international monitoring of nuclear industries and weapons, and the hope of eventual disarmament; its price is the admission of a greater near- to medium-term risk that the proliferant might be able to hide a small amount of nuclear material.

As argued earlier and in chapter 1, nonproliferation is not an absolute U.S. national interest. Therefore, definitions of success in nonproliferation—at least the definitions that apply to the short term—cannot be absolute either. If the choice is between accepting the possibility of one or two bombs' worth of missing plutonium in North Korea and going to war, one must presume that the United States would not, at least intentionally, make the latter choice. Like human rights, peaceful resolution of disputes, and humanitarianism, nonproliferation is a broad norm that can only be achieved gradually.

Overreacting to ambiguous proliferation may also play directly into the proliferant's hands by exaggerating the importance—and the influence—of its nuclear research. In the North Korean case, once the United States, South Korea, and Japan had made the issue such a high priority, and once it became clear that they were not prepared to take or risk military action, the North held all the cards. This view is supported by the alleged comments of North Korean officials to the Chinese in 1991, as cited in chapter 4: the more the outside world feared the North's nuclear research, the North Koreans reportedly claimed, the better reason Pyongyang had for doing it.

And the simple fact is that, as controversial as this strategy might appear to some, it has long been and remains the policy that the United States always resorts to in cases of hard-core proliferation. The United States accepted ambiguous proliferation in India, Pakistan, and especially Israel for many years. When the Soviet invasion of Afghanistan threatened regional stability, the United States quickly put aside its emphasis on proliferation in favor of a close partnership with Pakistan in aiding the Afghan resistance. That this approach had become U.S. policy in South Asia, for example, was demonstrated conclusively by the Clinton administration's 1994 proliferation initiative: it proposed not to roll back the Indian and Pakistani programs, but merely to freeze them in place.

The October 1994 nuclear agreement confirms and supports this argument. The question at issue is not the purity of nonproliferation itself, but the degree to which U.S. national interests are served by a given result. In some cases, such as a militant, expansionist regime that one might expect to use nuclear weapons against the United States in short order, complete success would be a requirement. But such cases seldom occur. In the Soviet and Chinese cases, the first examples of nuclear proliferation, U.S. leaders decided that depriving bitter ideological foes of nuclear weapons was not worth a preventive war. Israel's possession of a nuclear arsenal is hardly a source of direct concern at all; India and Pakistan pose no threat to the United States, and hence their nuclear work has not, in the end, been the deciding factor in the relationship. North Korea obviously is a much greater worry, and no U.S. administration could tolerate an unbridled North Korean nuclear factory. But if the price for preventing that outcome and for avoiding war at the same time is a small degree of temporary ambiguity, that may be a price worth paying.

Yet if that is the case, some will object, the danger of absolutist nonproliferation policies may seem, on closer examination, to be nothing more than a theoretical straw man. Washington struck a deal in October 1994, and did not insist on perfection at the risk of war. What, one might ask, is the problem? If Washington does not go to war over the issue in practice, why worry about absolutist rhetoric?

The tangled history of the preceding seven chapters suggests two primary risks inherent in the mismatch between rhetoric and practice in U.S. nonproliferation policy. Either the rhetoric will not be followed by action, in which case U.S. credibility and the strength of the nonproliferation regime will be badly damaged; or U.S. officials will feel obliged to adopt policies that take the rhetoric seriously, thereby undermining their own national interests and perhaps, in coming on too strong, dealing the nonproliferation regime a death blow through overweening strength rather than a trembling weakness. Either way, U.S. national interests will not be served. The political scientist Inis Claude has recognized that "skepticism about the meaningfulness of commitments is cumulative: casual commitment leads . . . to the inability to take commitments seriously, which destroys their value as devices for warning and for reassuring." Already "the multistate system is severely handicapped by the unavailability of international guarantees worthy of the name. . . . The world can ill afford to have international engagements taken lightly. States would do well to restrict their commitments to those that they seriously intend to uphold."[18]

The solution is a broad-based approach, a new vision of nuclear weapons policy and proliferation that makes progress but that offers enough of a compromise so that even many hard-core proliferants will see advantages in joining it. Chapter 10 lays out such a vision.

Other Cases: Broad Criteria for Success

In most cases of hard-core proliferants, therefore, some level of ambiguity will persist. So the question becomes, how much ambiguity should the United States tolerate? Where does it draw the line? What criteria can it use for establishing definitions of success that are achievable and that meet our national interests?

There is no single answer to this question, just as there is no single strategy for nonproliferation. A few brief answers were given earlier for the major proliferation problems faced by the United States today. In broad terms, the United States and its allies must look at the *elements of risk* or danger posed to other countries in a given nuclear program and decide which elements they can live with. If those elements match a parallel list made by the proliferant, noting those parts of its nuclear program it believes it must maintain for its national security, then the basis exists for an agreement. A brief list of such elements might include the following:

(1) *Nuclear materiel.* The basic plutonium or uranium that forms the core of the nuclear weapon.

(2) *Weaponization.* Nuclear materiel fashioned into usable bombs. As suggested earlier, verifying the transition from (1) to (2) will be one of the most difficult nonproliferation challenges in the years ahead. But if the proliferant knows that the world community will *allow* it temporarily to have a certain level of nuclear research and to obtain a small amount of nuclear materiel, it might be willing to grant the sort of outside access that would make such verification possible.

(3) *Delivery systems.* The importance of such systems for the issue of nuclear and biological proliferation has not been fully appreciated. If North Korea had no medium-range missile program, its nuclear ambitions would be of somewhat less concern to other regional actors, especially Japan. A proliferant may be willing to forgo work in this area in order to avoid sanctions for other aspects of its nuclear work.

(4) *Soundness of command and control.* The international community may wish to augment this, not by providing technical systems as has been suggested (which presumes some level of open weaponization, a higher degree of proliferation than will be tolerated in most cases), but in the form of international supervision (but not control) of nuclear materials.[19]

(5) *Proliferant's regional ambitions and/or terrorist impulses.* This is a critical variable. Nations such as Iraq, with pretensions to regional hegemony and immediate potential uses for a nuclear arsenal (in Iraq's case, against Israel) must be viewed with more concern than those nations lacking such aggressive plans (such as Israel and India). Similarly, if a nation has a penchant for state-sponsored terrorism, its acquisition of weapons of mass destruction will be more threatening than nations that do not use such tactics.

(6) *Proliferant's willingness to sell and/or give away its bomb.* If one nation's acquisition of nuclear weapons is expected to lead to a rapid chain of proliferation, particularly among dangerous countries or terrorist groups, then the dangers of proliferation in that case are much higher.

A definition of success might take its cue from this list. It suggests that, even once a proliferant has acquired nuclear material, if the other risks can be avoided, then the immediate military risk of the nuclear weapons can be reduced. One standard might, *at a minimum,* aim to address all the elements of risk apart from the first: it would allow the accumulation, in some cases, of nuclear material, but seek to prevent weaponization and the marriage of weapons of mass destruction to long-range delivery means; keep the nuclear material under international inspection; deprive regional hegemonies and terrorists of all nuclear capability; and forestall the sale of nuclear material or know-how once acquired.

Joseph Nye has laid out a similar list of near-term proliferation goals for ambiguous cases. The first and central goal in Nye's formula is "slowing vertical proliferation"—that is, capping any new arsenals at a low level, both numerical and technological. Second, the United States would seek to prevent deployment of the weapons in operational form; the criteria proposed earlier would go further and attempt to gain agreement to a ban on the most dangerous forms of delivery systems—ballistic or cruise missiles. Third, Nye proposes that U.S. and allied governments establish a principle of "no use" of the weapons; chapter 10 will propose achieving this through a policy of no nuclear use against nonweapons states. Fourth, the United States would insist that the proliferant not transfer any weapons or know-how to other states or to terrorist groups or other nonstate actors. This goal is tied up with the first, because a state with a very small number of primitive weapons is less likely to desire or to be able to sell them to other aspiring proliferants. Finally, in the longer term, the United States would seek to reverse the nuclear program and end most concerns about past activities, as has now occurred in South Africa.[20]

This list must appear daunting, especially in the wake of nearly a decade of challenging diplomacy aimed at securing a single element of it. But it is a realistic and comprehensive approach to the threat posed by North Korea's nuclear work, and much of it was achieved—at least temporarily—in October 1994. The following chapter lays out a more comprehensive strategy for achieving these goals.

■ 10 ■

A STRATEGY FOR NONPROLIFERATION

In recent years, academics, government officials, and think tank pundits have lavished enormous amounts of new attention on the theory and practice of nonproliferation. During that same time, major crises in Korea, Ukraine, and elsewhere have placed the proliferation issue squarely at center stage in U.S. foreign policy. And now the Secretary of Defense, the Joint Chiefs of Staff, and, it appears, the American people have all identified proliferation as the chief threat facing the United States in the post–Cold War world.

One would have thought, given all this attention, that the U.S. government would by now have developed a clear policy or strategy for nonproliferation. Yet as preceding chapters have hopefully made clear, no such strategy yet exists.[1] Vague laundry lists of "carrots and sticks" substitute for carefully designed policy. U.S. officials confronting the North Korean nuclear program have been, by and large, flying by the seat of their pants from a policy standpoint. And no comprehensive statement of nonproliferation policy—a broad set of nuclear arms control initiatives combined with a specific strategy for addressing problem countries—seems to be in the works.

This chapter attempts to lay out such a strategy. It begins with a cautionary note, a reminder of the point made earlier that every nonproliferation effort will be unique, and that only broad and general guidelines will be appropriate in a generic nonproliferation policy. Yet much more can be said at that broad level, in terms of both nuclear weapons policy and diplomatic campaigns aimed at individual nations, than is being said today by the U.S. government, and the balance of the chapter attempts to do so. Most of the remarks offered later are directed at nuclear nonproliferation, but the approaches and strategies they recommend could be applied with equal relevance to cases of chemical or biological weapons proliferation as well.

NONPROLIFERATION AS A DIVERSE ENTERPRISE

Developing such a broad strategy is especially difficult because there can be almost no such thing as "nonproliferation policy" per se. Any strategy to avoid proliferation must be specifically tailored to individual countries and situations. All nonproliferation campaigns will consist of a combination of diplomatic, economic, and military measures, but it is only in this rudimentary form that policymakers should expect nonproliferation efforts to be replicated from one case to the next.

A glance at the key proliferation challenges facing the United States demonstrates beyond doubt that each case is almost entirely unique. One cannot discuss the Israeli nuclear program intelligently without a detailed knowledge of the Middle East military balance, the implications of the Persian Gulf War, Israel's internal political situation, U.S.–Israeli relations, and even the minutiae of the land-for-peace dispute. A valuable examination of India's nuclear program cannot ignore New Delhi's strategic goals, the nature and scope of its disputes with Pakistan, the threat posed by China, or the domestic importance of the program to India's politicians.

Policy choices for the United States will also differ drastically from country to country. In the case of Israel, the United States enjoys considerable leverage and has at its disposal a wide range of political, economic, and military levers to pull. Washington enjoys no such influence over India. As the U.S. role varies from case to case, so will—or should—the policy recommendations for U.S. officials.

The Korean case strongly supports the argument that nonproliferation is a specific, not a general, enterprise. Even in broad terms, the initiatives undertaken by Washington and Seoul—withdrawal of U.S. tactical nuclear weapons, suspension of local military exercises, the promise of economic aid and trade—might be entirely irrelevant in another context, such as the Middle East. And as a result of its specific historic involvement in Korean affairs, the United States was in an enviable position to offer such carrots (and occasionally to make military or economic threats). In this case, proliferation was closely tied to a host of major issues on the Korean Peninsula and in the region, from Korean unification to Japan's view of nuclear weapons.

If generic nonproliferation strategies can be ineffective, they can also be dangerous—a risk evident in the Korean case. Overall U.S. policy toward the

North became a hostage of the means by which global nonproliferation strategies tend to be conducted, and in bureaucratic terms, that policy became the
literal hostage of nonproliferation directorates within the U.S. government.
This is not to say that, in this case, U.S. and allied policy should necessarily
have been any different; that Washington and its allies could have simply written off the North Korean bomb and pressed on with engagement; or that those
responsible for U.S. nonproliferation policy are ignorant of the unique aspects
of Korean politics. But there is a case to be made that an unconventional U.S.
approach to the North, based more on Korean politics and the U.S. interest in
engagement, might have stood a better long-term chance of causing the North
to lose interest in its nuclear program. As long as a demand-and-sanction-
oriented U.S. nonproliferation strategy dominates the U.S. agenda with problem states, however, such iconoclastic approaches will be ruled out.

In this context, one overwhelming lesson of the Korean case is that, for any
nonproliferation strategy to work, it must take account of the personal and
political nature of the target government and its leadership. North Korean society and government have a number of very distinct features not found in all
other proliferants.

One of the best short summaries of North Korean political culture has been
produced by Dr. Stephen Linton of Columbia University.[2] The son of U.S. mis-
sionaries in Korea, fluent in Korean, and having traveled often to Pyongyang,
Linton offers three "general principles" for dealing with the North. First,
"develop personal relationships." Problem-solving must await the building of
personal ties, Linton writes, and requests for actions taken in friendship have
more authority than proposals of a "deal." Nor will references to international
agreements or principles of law suffice: "in traditional Korean society," Linton
notes, "personality stands behind law."

Second, Linton urges U.S. officials to "avoid threats to national existence and
social cohesion." As a regime desperately clinging to power, the North Korean
government will view with suspicion any policy options that seem to attempt
to hasten its end. This fact makes the North especially suspicious of world organizations like the United Nations. And third, although issues of "face" may be
overstated, Linton argues that "North Koreans become extremely sensitive if
they perceive what they interpret to be an attempt to humiliate them publicly."
Formal, public meetings accomplish little, as do public condemnations.

As the preceding chapters have made clear, for a time the U.S. strategy
toward North Korea represented almost the inverse of Linton's approach.
Washington withheld personal contacts until substantive issues could be
resolved; it threatened the existence of North Korea and declared an official
U.S. position that the North Korean regime was doomed; it used multilateral

institutions to pressure the North; and it repeatedly, almost gratuitously, condemned and condescended to North Korea in its public statements. Later, when U.S. officials adopted a course more consistent with the strategy proposed by Steve Linton—beginning in earnest in the fall of 1993, and continuing through October 1994—their policy had more success.

Similar analyses must be conducted for any nation at which the United States intends to direct a nonproliferation campaign. This is not to devalue the important work that has been done by those who have studied the nonproliferation problem broadly for decades. The best writers on proliferation have always combined general analysis with a knowledge of the facts of individual cases, and tailored their recommendations to those facts. My point is simply this: to the extent that anything profound can be said or done in the effort to restrain proliferation, it will be based overwhelmingly on the details of the specific case, and depend only to a minor degree on broad insights about nonproliferation as an international enterprise. And this conclusion suggests again that, to the greatest extent possible, nonproliferation should not be considered to be a discipline of its own, but should be tied closely to regional expertise.

THE FAILURE OF TECHNICAL SOLUTIONS

Once the organization and goals for nonproliferation policy have been laid out, the actual implementation of a nonproliferation policy can begin. U.S. officials must then look to the tactics and approaches they will use to pursue such diplomacy. The Korean case offers a number of conclusions on this score as well.

As noted in chapter 1, a common dichotomy in the nonproliferation literature is between the technical and motivational schools of thought.[3] Those emphasizing technical motives for proliferation have argued that the spread of nuclear weapons will follow the spread of nuclear know-how. Once a country acquires the technical and industrial capability to manufacture nuclear bombs, technical theorists suppose, it will almost inevitably begin building them. Motivational theorists are more subtle: the mere capability to proliferate, they argue, is an insufficient rationale given the potential costs and drawbacks. To understand the drive for proliferation, motivational school thinkers contend, one has to focus on the particular motives of the individual nations.

History and the Korean experience have decisively borne out the motivational school. Those borderline proliferants that face immediate security threats—Israel, India, and Pakistan—have been the least repentant in recent years. Those countries pursuing a "prestige" motive in the absence of a direct threat, on the other hand (Brazil, Argentina, and South Africa, among others), have largely backed off from their bomb programs, a shift also attributable to the advent of civilian or reformist rule. While there are a few troublemakers whose primary motive may have been acquiring nuclear weapons to support offensive actions (Iraq, Iran, and Libya), these states also face security threats of their own. Answering a proliferant's concern about its own security will usually constitute an important element of nonproliferation efforts—for symbolic as well as legitimate reasons.

These conclusions parallel the findings of Stephen Meyer. In his 1984 quantitative analysis of nonproliferation, he found little evidence that technical capabilities, in the absence of strong political-military motives, caused proliferation.[4] Rather, he found that the kind of rationales outlined earlier and in previous chapters constituted the real basis of proliferation and that addressing these rationales, rather than attempting to deny the capability to proliferate, constituted the only effective means of countering the spread of nuclear weapons. Thus an increased focus on the demand side, rather than the supply side, of proliferation seems warranted.

Moreover, the Korean example also suggests that, when motives are present, technical controls will not prevent nations from acquiring nuclear capabilities. In North Korea's case, Pyongyang was lucky enough to have large domestic supplies of uranium and an operable nuclear reactor. Its nuclear program was almost fully indigenous. And nations such as Iran and Iraq may have fewer domestic resources, but possess the riches to acquire high technology reprocessing and raw nuclear materials.

None of this is to suggest that the United States and its allies should discard export controls on those technologies useful in developing a nuclear program. On the contrary, such controls can play an important role in supporting a motivational approach. If a proliferant finds that it cannot complete a nuclear program because it lacks access to some crucial technology, its motives will be affected, and it may be much more likely to bargain that nuclear program away. And in those cases where a motivational approach fails, export controls will offer the only means of restraining a proliferant's nuclear program. A relaxation of controls on dual-use equipment relevant to nuclear weapons as well as civilian scientific research would be a grave error, and this analysis in no way supports such a step.

THE DANGERS OF CONFRONTATION

Of those general conclusions we can deduce from the Korean case, one stands out as especially important. This is the fact that a confrontational approach to nonproliferation will often collide with larger U.S. interests.

Sparking a crisis on the Korean Peninsula would have been directly inimical to each of the major U.S. national interests involved in the issue. Chapter 3 laid out the stakes for the United States: avoiding war; encouraging democracy in South Korea; promoting a peaceful transition in the North; pursuing expanded trade in and improved economic competitiveness with Asia; finding a stable regional role for Japan; and promoting reform in China and regional multi-lateralism. For obvious reasons, a confrontational approach to North Korea would risk undermining each of these interests. It would raise tensions in Korea, place the major regional powers at odds, and threaten peace, stability, and democracy on the peninsula.

Economic Sanctions: A False Hope?

There was little chance that a tougher approach would have worked, even if it had been more appealing. Hawks talked of economic sanctions, but North Korea has a long history of rejecting international opinion when it is phrased as a demand and accompanied by sanctions or the threat of them. Nor could economic sanctions be effective without the participation of China, South Korea, Russia, and Japan, each of which had expressed some degree of unease with a confrontational approach to the North and a reluctance to take any steps that might spark a rapid collapse of the North Korean system. And if economic sanctions did succeed in bringing the North to its knees, they would also have created a highly dangerous and unpredictable situation in which the danger of war, or the unstable and violent collapse of the North, were real possibilities.

Indeed, punitive strategies have rarely been effective on countries well-advanced in their work on the bomb. Lewis Dunn pointed out in 1982 that if "the threat of sanctions does not suffice to deter a country from initiating nuclear weapons activities, it is most unlikely that their actual imposition will force the target country to halt or reverse those activities. Indeed, over the past decade, recourse to sanctions has consistently failed to coerce countries to change their policies."[5] The North Korean example bears out this argument, and one can see a similar pattern in other cases. In Pakistan, the Pressler Amendment has not slowed Islamabad's nuclear work, and if anything, by undermining its conventional forces, has bolstered its nuclear motives. In Ukraine, a generally positive trend of events was at times disrupted by Russian belligerence and the cancellation of Russian deliveries of oil and natural gas.

U.S. officials also face something of a dilemma regarding sanctions and nonproliferation policy. In those cases where proliferation is held to be most dangerous—in countries such as North Korea, Iran, and Iraq—the proliferants tend to be rogue states already somewhat or largely isolated from the world economy and hence not vulnerable to sanctions. Those past and current proliferants that are more a part of the world community, such as India, Brazil, and South Africa, tend also to be more responsible and of less concern; directing sanctions against them is therefore at once less possible and less necessary. In neither case are economic or political sanctions a terribly viable option.

The Korean case also points up the danger, from the standpoint of the credibility of global nonproliferation efforts, of seeking sanctions through the UN Security Council. If the U.S. government attempts to impose sanctions, and another permanent member vetoes them (or perhaps even if it abstains and then undermines the sanctions through aid to the proliferant), the worst possible precedent will have been set. The proliferant might come to believe it is off the hook, that the outside world's threat of sanctions has been nullified, and that it is free to bargain from a position of greater strength. In the Korean case, of course, China threatened to play this role. To the extent that any member of the Security Council opposes sanctions as China has in this case, pursuing them is playing a dangerous game of bluff. If the proliferant calls the bluff and wins, it could end up stronger than before.

Here again we see the importance of moving energetically to address the proliferant's security concerns: doing so will establish a stronger case for sanctions if they prove necessary. Even by late 1994, after three years of offering vague incentives and engaging in a diffident dialogue with the North, the United States still could not claim that it had fully tested the diplomatic route. China, and to a lesser extent Japan and South Korea, urged further efforts. Unless the proliferant's motives are thoroughly tested—something that can only be accomplished with legitimate offers to address its security concerns and national interests—U.S. officials will not honestly be able to claim that every option short of sanctions has been exhausted.

But even if the United States manages to get sanctions applied, their ultimate result might well be a military crisis. In the Korean case, such sanctions would almost certainly fail to stop the North's nuclear program. In fact they would be more likely to accelerate it; and when evidence of this newly accelerated nuclear weapons program emerged, the United States and its allies would be forced to look more seriously at military options for halting the work underway at Yongbyon and elsewhere.[6] Thus when Charles Krauthammer argues that the United States "never threatened war as an alternative to agreement. It threatened economic sanctions to squeeze North Korea into complying now, not someday, with its nuclear-treaty obligations,"[7] he is really constructing a mirage—a mirage that war was not a U.S. option (which, as we shall see, it clearly was); a mirage that economic sanctions would somehow cause the militant, pride-conscious North Korean regime simply to give in; a mirage that economic sanctions can work "now" as opposed to "someday"— against all the evidence from Haiti, Iraq, Serbia, and elsewhere.

The Korean case does suggest that the de facto sanction of existing trade restrictions on a country can play a role in altering a proliferant's motives. In the case of North Korea, as with such nations as Iraq and Iran, the United States and many of its allies already have economic sanctions in place, either directly (in the form of the UN resolutions aimed at Iraq, or the U.S. trade laws barring certain trade with Iran or North Korea) or indirectly (the fact that nations like North Korea and Iran remain largely isolated from the world economic system). Such preexisting economic isolation can provide a powerful incentive for a nation to pursue accommodation on its nuclear program in exchange for expanded economic contacts with the outside world. Because such economic isolation does not demand new sanctions, using it as leverage does not risk the sort of confrontation and backlash characteristic of an effort to punish a proliferant in the midst of a diplomatic campaign.

In the Korean case, the United States and its allies could have deepened this isolation with quiet moves neither described nor admitted to be sanctions, but whose effect would nonetheless be to punish the North. The most important of these possible quiet moves would have been to modulate the financial lifeline from Korean residents of Japan, estimated at several hundred million dollars annually. Tokyo probably could not entirely have halted the money supply, but it probably could have thinned it out somewhat. Meanwhile, South Korea could have constrained indirect inter-Korean trade, which continued, albeit at low levels, right through the early 1990s. The goal would have been to put additional pressure on the North without the confrontational—and very possibly unsuccessful—effort of getting a formal sanctions resolution through the UN Security Council.

Moreover, it must be admitted that North Korea appears to have been interested in avoiding condemnation and sanctions as voted by the Security Council. Were such sanctions to be applied, they could easily prove counterproductive, as suggested earlier. But a proliferant will have as much, and often more, reason to fear a confrontation as will the United States. It may also wish to avoid the embarrassment of having made a concession *after* sanctions have been applied, and thus appear to have buckled under pressure. In short, the *threat* of economic and political sanctions can help create an environment in which a proliferant sees accommodation as a useful route.

But this conclusion must be quickly tempered with a number of qualifications. Threatening sanctions can just as easily undermine diplomacy as support it. North Korea's reaction to provocative steps by the United States and

South Korea—such as the decision to hold Team Spirit in 1993—suggests that it would be likely to lash out in some way if threats of sanctions were ever applied. Once sanctions are in place, they might actually cause a proliferant to dig in its heels, seek out friends to help it muddle through, and accelerate work on its nuclear program. Moreover, a strategy of sanctions and confrontation will only work if the United States and its allies have the political stomach to see the strategy through to its conclusion—which was clearly not the case for the United States as it dealt with North Korea in 1993 and 1994.

The threat of sanctions is an especially weak tool because a cunning proliferant can easily defuse it. Repeatedly during the early 1990s, and most especially in June 1993 and February and April 1994, North Korea averted the imposition of sanctions with last-minute concessions that represented only a part of what the world community was seeking. But the moves were sufficient to prolong discussion and fracture the consensus behind sanctions, especially in Beijing and Moscow. This strategy of last-minute, marginal concessions will be especially effective at a time when the United States is not prepared for the violent consequences of brinkmanship. In the post–Cold War era, and given the limited (but very important) national interests at stake in the issue of proliferation, one could argue that the United States will always be in such a position.[8]

In other words, the threat of sanctions can help influence the proliferant's motives, but it will never provide the basis for a complete resolution of the issue, because the proliferant will often be able to stymie the drive for sanctions with a partial concession. Something more is required—a comprehensive strategy for nonproliferation.

The Military Option

The Korean experience also indicates that military action will seldom provide a feasible response to proliferation. Even if the proliferant is completely isolated and a worldwide consensus on military action is achieved—two highly questionable assumptions—the only type of military action which would truly guarantee that a weapons program has been halted would be the conquest and occupation of the proliferant. Such a radical step would simply be too costly to be effective.[9]

In the Korean case, for example, during several especially worrisome periods when officials and academics in the United States, Japan, and South Korea feared that North Korea was stalling for time on accepting inspections of its nuclear facilities, more and more observers began pointing to the military option as a last-ditch means of stopping the North Korean bomb. Academics and former public officials referred to the possibility of military strikes against North Korea's nuclear facilities as a viable option. Opinion leaders as diverse as the *Washington Post* and the *National Review* editorialized that a military option existed and should be used if all other means, including further economic sanctions, failed.[10] Secretary of Defense William Perry later claimed that, from the official standpoint of the Clinton administration, "We did not want to rule out the possibility of a preemptive strike [against North Korea]. . . . We did not rule out that option."[11]

On closer examination, however, it became clear that the military option was not feasible at all. Such an attack might have led directly to a second Korean war; the North may have struck the South immediately. North Korean military officials have told Western visitors as much, as have North Korean defectors. In the case of a South Korean or U.S. attack, "the whole Korean Peninsula would be reduced to ashes," says Ko Yong Hwan, a former North Korean diplomat. "I'm afraid that such actions would only prompt Kim Jong Il to start a war with the South."[12] In any case, regardless of North Korean intentions, it might well have been impossible to control a conflict once it had begun.

Unlike the Persian Gulf War, moreover, Washington and Seoul might have had to fight this war—and pay the attendant human, economic, and political costs—alone. North Korea had not engaged in any overt aggression, and in fact the United States possessed little hard evidence that Pyongyang's nuclear program was close to fruition. Washington would have been hard-pressed to assemble any sort of coalition for military operations against the North, and such attacks might actually have produced angry complaints from allies and nonaligned nations alike.[13] The United Nations could easily have become a forum for condemning the United States rather than North Korea, a reversal of the Gulf War experience. And if this happened, it would have made an all-out North Korean attack even more likely: seeing the United States and South Korea isolated in the world community and perhaps even in lack of domestic public support, North Korean military leaders might have decided that they faced a last, best chance to drive south against reasonable odds.

It is of course possible that, fearing an end to its regime like that which almost occurred in 1951, North Korea would decline to start a full-scale war. Given its severe energy problems, the North may not have possessed enough fuel for large-scale military movements in 1993 to 1994, and its forces must surrender their substantial defensive advantage if they rise up out of their granite redoubts and move south along open roads. But even short of a major offensive, Pyongyang would have a number of military options in response to "surgical" strikes against its nuclear facilities. With some 70 percent of its military forces stationed close to the DMZ, North Korea could simply choose to annihilate Seoul with vast amounts of artillery and rocket fire and a few dozen suicide air strikes. It could launch missile or air attacks against South Korea's nuclear reactors, spattering radiation across Korea and all of Asia. It could begin a campaign of terrorism against South Korea and its allies, or attempt to sink South Korean and U.S. civilian shipping with its small fleet of submarines. It could send some of its reportedly 100,000-strong special forces units to wreak havoc in the South. And if it actually did possess a nuclear bomb by the time outside military action occurred, U.S. and South Korean leaders would be foolish to count on North Korean restraint with its ultimate weapon.

The risks of military strikes look even more daunting when one recognizes the overwhelming probability that the strikes simply could not work. Without having inspection teams on the ground, the United States and its allies would not know where the right targets were. Even if the U.S. military knew what to hit, the North Koreans made their shelters by digging deep into hard rock, thus making them impervious to most precision weapons.[14] One U.S. Defense Intelligence Agency publication went so far as to admit that North Korean underground bunkers are "virtually invulnerable to allied air attack."[15] Moreover, the target of potential air strikes, the North's alleged illegal cache of plutonium, was small enough to fit inside a football, and U.S. officials had no idea whatsoever where it might be. It would have been quite embarrassing to launch an air strike—or even, as some suggested, a nuclear attack—on Yongbyon only to find out that the plutonium was hundreds of miles away at the time. Advocates of a military option appeared to seek some form of fool-proof guarantee against a North Korean bomb; but as the Iraqi experience suggests, the only way to be completely confident that the North had ended work on nuclear weapons would be to conquer and occupy most of the country.

When *would* military action be appropriate in the context of nonprolifera-tion? If the strikes were launched against a state with a relatively weak mili-tary, with no means at its disposal for a devastating and immediate retaliation, with no major regional or international allies, and with a nuclear (or biolog-ical or chemical) weapons program that is somewhat isolated, out in the open, and at a stage where taking out production facilities could still provide a rea-sonable guarantee of success, they could achieve a meaningful purpose. Israel's attack on Iraq in 1981 may have met most of these conditions. In the future, further punitive raids against Iraq's damaged nuclear infrastructure, or strikes against Libya's chemical or nuclear weapons programs, might do so as well. Even in these cases, however, the decision to take military action is by no means an obvious one. Some contend that the real effect of Israel's 1981 attack was to drive Iraq's program underground and to diversify it along a number of paths, thus making it more dangerous and more difficult to verify in the long run. And for the bigger problem states, military action does not look

promising. Even for North Korea and Iran, it is unlikely if *any* of these conditions are applicable. As uncomfortable a conclusion as it may be, the fact
remains that preemptive military action will seldom offer a desirable or feasible means of achieving nonproliferation in the years ahead.

Nonproliferation and "Counterproliferation"

In recent years the theory and practice of nonproliferation have been joined
by a new intellectual cousin: the field of counterproliferation. The latter term,
coined by the Clinton administration, was introduced in a December 1993
speech by Secretary of Defense Les Aspin. Aspin heralded a new emphasis
in the nonproliferation field: with the Defense Counterproliferation Initiative,
Aspin said, "We are adding the task of protection to the task of prevention."
Specifically, Aspin argued that while past nonproliferation efforts had been
focused on preventing the spread of nuclear and biological weapons, the new
initiative recognized "that proliferation may still occur" and attempted to
plan accordingly.[16] Aspin argued that counterproliferation would complement, not supplant, the more traditional policy of nonproliferation:

> Our initiative complements nonproliferation in three important ways.
> It promotes consensus on the gravity of the threat, helping to maintain
> the international nonproliferation effort. It reduces the military utility
> of weapons of mass destruction, while nonproliferation keeps up the
> price, making them less attractive to the proliferant. And it reduces the
> vulnerability of the neighbors of those holding these weapons, further
> reducing the motive to acquire them in self-defense.[17]

Thus Defense was proposing to hedge against the failure of nonproliferation,
and, in so doing, to reduce the appeal of proliferation in the first place.[18] Aspin
proposed five specific elements of the Defense Counterproliferation Initiative:
creating a new military mission to deal with proliferation; purchasing weapons
better suited to destroying or negating nuclear or biological arsenals; modify-
ing warfighting policies to take account of the effects of nuclear and biological
weapons; developing intelligence on emerging nuclear or biological threats;
and cooperating with allies to combat the threat in military terms.[19]

   In May 1994, the Defense Department issued a *Report on Nonproliferation
and Counterproliferation Activities and Programs,* which spelled out the
practical implications of this new policy. The Defense Department would
reorient the Strategic Defense Initiative, renamed the Ballistic Missile
Defense Organization (BMDO), toward the most urgent nonproliferation
challenges, the regional rather than global threats posed by the ballistic missile and nuclear and biological weapons programs of regional hegemonies.

The Joint Chiefs of Staff would establish a department to coordinate military planning and strategic thinking for campaigns addressing a nuclear or biological threat; the Defense Department would refine its intelligence gathering and assessment capacities in the field of proliferation; and the Advanced Research Projects Agency would study new ways to detect and destroy weapons of mass destruction.[20]

The counterproliferation initiative therefore appeared, and appears in retrospect, to have had two distinct elements. One was defense: to provide U.S. military forces the ability to defend themselves against the delivery of weapons of mass destruction. This meant, in practical terms, creating regional missile defenses and designing military campaigns and tactics to take account of potential nuclear, chemical or biological use. As a result the Clinton administration's BMDO pursued several programs, from improved Patriot missiles to Theater High-Altitude Area Defense (THAAD) to naval missile defense systems, and attempted to work out with the Russians a mutually agreeable modification of the Anti-Ballistic Missile (ABM) Treaty to allow deployment of the programs.

The other aspect of counterproliferation, and by far the more controversial, was preemption. With the Counterproliferation Initiative, the United States made it national policy, in selected instances, to preemptively destroy the weapons of mass destruction (WMD) programs of threatening states. Neither Aspin's speech nor subsequent official DoD statements, however, proposed any specific examples of where such preemption might be feasible.

In the most basic sense, the U.S. military obviously should prepare for the day when nuclear weapons are used in anger against U.S. forces. Anything that could reduce the success or the effects of such an attack would be of interest to U.S. leaders. Specifically, planning to disperse U.S. and allied forces, develop alternatives to large and vulnerable ports and airfields, deal with nuclear fallout, and otherwise cope with the risk of nuclear attacks is certainly warranted.[21] More generally, however, the Korean case suggests that the counterproliferation effort is at best hollow—and at worst, a counterproductive windmill-tilting exercise that will undermine the very nonproliferation efforts it is supposed to complement.

For one thing, advocates of counterproliferation are wrong to assume the failure of nonproliferation. The last decade has witnessed great strides in the nonproliferation field, and the end of the Cold War has opened the door to dramatic global arms control initiatives that will deepen and broaden the nonproliferation enterprise. A number of key problem states have abandoned their nuclear programs. Today the nonproliferation agenda consists primarily of the nettlesome South Asian dispute and a handful of rogue proliferants—

North Korea, Iraq, Iran, and perhaps to a lesser degree Libya and Syria. Nonproliferation is on the verge of almost complete success, not collapse.

If any one act could destroy the nonproliferation agenda, however, it would be an insular and hostile U.S. commitment to counterproliferation as an alternative. Few dispute the long-term importance of tactical or regional missile defenses; given the increasing prominence of ballistic and cruise missiles in regional conflicts, the United States should indeed develop and deploy them. But it must recognize in doing so that missile defenses offer a leaky shield against North Korean or Iranian nuclear weapons, which could be delivered on anything from a submarine to a tramp steamer to a tree-hopping biplane— or perhaps more likely, in an innocuous-looking wooden crate marked "antiques" and shipped from Hong Kong or Istanbul to New York. And counterproliferation's other major component—developing the capability for preemptive strikes on nascent nuclear weapons programs—will create just the sort of hegemonic and unilateral impression guaranteed to make indefinite extension of the NPT a much more difficult enterprise. Especially to the degree that plans for such preemptive strikes include the use of low-yield nuclear weapons—the so-called mininukes and micronukes now in favor in some quarters of the Pentagon—they would alienate dozens of responsible developing countries and provide a new shield behind which rogue nations could hide and justify their nuclear weapons programs. It was just such a threat, after all, that led North Korea to begin developing its bomb in the first place; removing the threat was its one nonnegotiable precondition for allowing IAEA inspections. Finally, as noted in the previous section, the Korean case suggests that a proliferant can often render itself immune to such preemptive strikes by hiding the nearly undetectable fruits of its nuclear research.

One argument made by some (not all) advocates of counterproliferation deserves special condemnation: the idea that U.S. nonproliferation policy would benefit from a stronger U.S. tactical nuclear presence in various regions of the world.[22] A more counterproductive nonproliferation strategy could hardly be imagined. U.S. regional nuclear threats were the proximate or contributing cause to a number of cases of proliferation, and might well produce a similar effect if revived in the 1990s. U.S. officials can hardly make a credible case for other nations abandoning their nuclear ambitions if Washington is reviving many of its own.

The U.S. experience in Korea therefore argues that counterproliferation offers no real alternative to nonproliferation, either in a preventive or a defensive sense. It also indicates that the guiding belief of counterproliferation's defenders, that nonproliferation is bound to fail, is off the mark. Apart from its emphasis on defensive capabilities such as missile defenses, the new strategy of counterproliferation has the dubious distinction of being at once infeasible, unnecessary, and counterproductive.

A NONPROLIFERATION STRATEGY FOR THE 1990S

As suggested in the opening chapter, those who specialize in the study of the proliferation of weapons of mass destruction regularly exaggerate the importance of the problem, and this tendency has now spread to the U.S. government. In a world in which an unstable and potentially hostile nation, Russia, possesses 30,000 nuclear weapons which could annihilate the United States at a moment's notice, the proliferation of a handful of such weapons into the developing world seems hardly to compare as a threat. But the U.S. Department of Defense and Joint Chiefs of Staff have nonetheless identified nonproliferation as the chief U.S. national security priority for the 1990s.

And yet proliferation does constitute an important threat to U.S. national interests.[23] It can undermine U.S. flexibility in dealing with a host of other challenges. An Iraq armed with nuclear weapons would have posed a vastly different challenge in the Persian Gulf War, and made a U.S. response far more difficult. Widespread proliferation could cause new regional hostilities and undermine the U.S. goal and interest of a more open, peaceful world order. If specific U.S. adversaries acquired nuclear weapons, they could be emboldened to challenge U.S. interests as never before.

Moreover, merely because the nightmare scenarios of proliferation have not come true yet does not mean that they have been permanently averted. We approach a critical moment in the history of nonproliferation: the renewal conference for the Nuclear Nonproliferation Treaty, scheduled for spring 1995. If the global norms underlying the NPT collapse in the latter half of the 1990s, just as the knowledge for producing nuclear, chemical, and biological weapons has become so widespread, the consequences could be dramatic.

There is one more reason to be especially concerned about proliferation today, even while recognizing that it is not necessarily the dominant U.S. foreign and defense policy priority for the 1990s. That reason is the existence of two intersecting trends: the spread of nuclear and CBW know-how and the declining monopoly on force of the nation-state. As a number of perceptive writers have noted, nonstate actors, from terrorist organizations to business conglomerates to ethnic groups, have begun to drain more and more of the power and authority once possessed exclusively by nation-states. Some have even suggested that the future of warfare lies, not in conflicts between states, but in hundreds of twilight struggles between and among nonstate actors and the states they often seek to undermine.

The acquisition of weapons of mass destruction by such nonstate actors must rank as one of the most horrific prospects in the history of mankind. Terrorist groups and similarly motivated organizations have often conducted indiscriminate, essentially self-destructive acts of the kind that might properly be understood as "nondeterrable." And if a nonstate actor can succeed in keeping its identity secret, retaliation is impossible.

A new nonproliferation strategy might address all these potential threats. It might seek to construct a new bargain to replace the one that underlies the NPT, and keep the global prohibition against proliferation essentially intact. It might strengthen enforcement against renegade states like North Korea. And it might establish the sort of international control and monitoring of capabilities for mass destruction, and international enforcement should such monitoring fail, that offer the best, if highly imperfect, response to the threat of nonstate proliferation.

A Strategy for Nonproliferation: Global Initiatives

As Stephen Meyer has suggested, nations that are seeking or may seek nuclear weapons can be divided into three categories: the hard-core proliferants, such as North Korea and Iran, rogue regimes with little connection to the world community and aggressive regional ambitions; medium-core nations, such as India and Brazil,[24] with some motive to seek the bomb for prestige or security reasons but basically responsible and peaceful members of the world community; and soft-core proliferants, countries such as Sweden with little desire to seek nuclear weapons. Any strategy for proliferation must address each kind of proliferant in order to be effective.[25] Nonetheless, a comprehensive framework for nonproliferation could provide important support for such individual efforts. It could establish a context in which specific diplomatic campaigns were more likely to succeed, and create strong international norms supporting sanctions and other measures if nonproliferation failed.

A coherent approach to nonproliferation would begin at the level of broad U.S. nuclear and arms control policy. Those who object that such policy is irrelevant to the security considerations of proliferants miss the point. Whether the United States has 300 or 3,000 nuclear weapons may not *directly* change the security calculations of nations like India and Brazil. But it will *indirectly* affect those calculations, in at least three ways.

First, continued U.S. and Russian numerical reductions could eventually bring other nuclear powers into play as well, thus affecting the threat perceptions of proliferants. While U.S. levels may make little difference to policymakers in New Delhi, the level of China's strategic forces will matter a great deal. If that level can be capped and reduced through five-power arms talks, then India's—and perhaps also Japan's—rationale for a nuclear arsenal will be affected.

Second, further efforts to meet the requirement of Article VI of the NPT will have substantial symbolic value. Countries like India that have relied on the inequity inherent in the NPT to justify their own nuclear weapons programs will have to respond in some way to new U.S.-Russian initiatives. At a minimum, such steps will force proliferants to find new excuses for their programs. At best they may spark constructive responses, such as agreements to open up previously secret nuclear programs to inspection and place previously unseen stockpiles of fissile material under international monitoring.

Bold initiatives in nuclear arms control are also justified for a third reason, by far the most significant of all. Global initiatives on nuclear arms control can allow the United States and other concerned nations and organizations to establish universal norms that all nations must respect—norms that, when applied in practice, would provide new hope for restraining proliferation.

Take two examples that have already been proposed by the Clinton administration: a comprehensive test-ban treaty (CTBT) and a ban on the production of fissile materials for nuclear weapons. Critics charge that, in the proliferation context, these measures are useless, because the demand (by such nations as India) for a CTBT and other arms control measures is only a smokescreen used to conceal much more prosaic motives for acquiring weapons of mass destruction. But if a worldwide CTBT is completed and ratified, no new proliferant will be able to test a nuclear device (unless they could do so clandestinely, an unlikely prospect in most cases). This will reduce the confidence level in new arsenals, and hence their attractiveness.

A global ban on the production of weapons-grade fissile material would be even more effective in slowing proliferation. Such a ban might help prevent proliferants from acquiring nuclear weapons material, and could provide for specific sanctions in case they did so. Together with the Chemical and Biological Weapons Conventions, a ban on weapons-grade fissile material production would complete a set of treaties providing the United States and its allies with legal support for tough action to punish proliferants.

A number of other strategic arms control initiatives offer equally useful ways to combat proliferation. None of the proposals made here calls for the United States to sacrifice any element of national security for the sake of nonproliferation. Each policy option has advantages in its own right, and should arguably be implemented even without reference to its use in the proliferation context.[26] This respects the status of nonproliferation as one of a number of top U.S. foreign policy priorities, but not the overriding one. And in each case, one especially important trade-off must be considered: the arms control initiative must not be so bold or reckless as to endanger the confidence of U.S. allies such as South Korea, Germany, and Japan. United States security guarantees to those nations are an important safeguard against proliferation. If arms control measures increased concerns in Bonn or Tokyo and led to a reconsideration of a nuclear option in those countries, if would hardly have served the end of nonproliferation.

This process of nuclear arms control is intimately related to, and depends for its success upon, the separate track of chemical and biological arms control symbolized by the Chemical and Biological Weapons Conventions. A post-nuclear world must not become a chemically- or biologically-armed one. Continued ratification of the CWC by key states, and the development of a much stronger verification regime for the BWC, are indispensable if nuclear arms control is not merely to lead to a new competition in weapons of mass destruction.

No Use of Nuclear Weapons Against Non-Weapons States: The most fundamental decision regarding nuclear weapons does not involve their numbers, their capabilities, or their targets. It involves their roles in the foreign and defense policies of the nations that possess them. How nations plan to use nuclear weapons is second only to their existence in determining the threat they pose. The first and most important step toward a nonproliferation strategy, therefore, must be the pledge by the nuclear powers not to use their arsenals in any but the most extreme circumstances. A taboo has arisen against the use of nuclear weapons, and this taboo represents an investment of more than fifty years of non-use by the nuclear weapons states. It is a precious precedent to be preserved; once broken, it might not be repairable.

The five nuclear-weapons states should therefore join in a binding UN Security Council resolution banning the first use of nuclear weapons against any non-weapon state—that is, against any state that has joined the Nonproliferation Treaty as a non-weapons state and remained a member of the treaty in good standing. Such a treaty would reinforce an important precedent: the world community would resolve that no nation that surrenders the nuclear option shall face the threat of such weapons. Indeed there was some discussion of this idea in connection with the 1995 NPT Review Conference.

A Comprehensive Test-Ban Treaty: This important agreement has long been viewed as a fundamental signal that the worldwide competition in nuclear arms has drawn to a close. As noted earlier, if all nations ratified such an agreement, it would constitute an important bulwark against proliferation, helping to slow the development of new nuclear weapons both by the weapons states and by potential new nuclear powers. This treaty is currently under negotiation at the Conference on Disarmament, and a final version will hopefully have been developed by the time of the NPT Review Conference in the spring of 1995 or shortly thereafter—though many roadblocks remain.

A Fissile Material Cutoff: This agreement would prohibit nations from producing new weapons-grade fissile material for use in nuclear weapons projects. If properly implemented and verified, it would address both the risk of a renewed East-West arms race and the potential for proliferation. Such an agreement, by applying equally to all nations, would make the global non-proliferation regime substantially less discriminatory.

In many ways, the fissile material cutoff would serve as the core of the near-term arms control and nonproliferation agenda, around which the other initiatives would be built. Most important, the same regime would provide the means of dealing with the threshold nuclear powers, serving to cap their nuclear weapons programs. Including the threshold states in such an accord would not serve to validate their nuclear weapons programs; it would constitute the first step in rolling them back, and this intention could be made clear in the language of the accord.

This treaty remains some time away from completion. But consultations on its substance have already begun. Any fissile cutoff treaty must contain verification and monitoring provisions at least as intrusive as those provided for by IAEA Type 153 national inspection agreements. The commitment to such a treaty is already in place, and progress can be made by 1995 on a treaty that would take effect before the year 2000. Even before such a treaty has been concluded, the world community must devote added attention to the growing risk posed by civilian fissile materials. Stockpiles of plutonium are accumulating around the world. A more coherent process of control, monitoring, and disposal is required.

Numerical reductions: Additional numerical reductions beyond START II can play an important role in nonproliferation policy. While not always the most meaningful form of arms control, numerical reductions have immense symbolic value and offer clear evidence that Article VI is being respected. As suggested earlier, moreover, if reductions result in a five-power conference to freeze and subsequently reduce European and Chinese forces as well, then motives for proliferation in India, Japan, and perhaps elsewhere could be dampened.

At a minimum, such reductions should aim to cut START II arsenals again in half, to 1,000 to 1,500 weapons in U.S. and Russian arsenals, by the year 2000.[27] A promise to begin talks on such reductions shortly before START II implementation is complete, secured in place by the 1995 NPT Review Conference, would offer profound additional progress without threatening the basic U.S. extended deterrent guarantee to its allies in Europe and Northeast Asia.[28] It would also reduce U.S. and Russian arsenals to the level where further cuts would require a five-power dialogue—which should be promised, and initiated, before the end of the century.

Disarmament through Dismantlement: Although abolition is not feasible today and would only meet U.S. national interests in certain very stringent circumstances, it seems undeniable that the United States would benefit from a world without weapons of mass destruction. The dangers of proliferation, especially by nonstate actors, were discussed earlier. As the world's preeminent conventional power, the United States has reason to support initiatives that would maximize its area of advantage. Barry Blechman has argued that "A world without weapons of mass destruction . . . would be a far safer world for Americans." And further, "it may now be possible to conceive of creating both the cooperative international arrangements, and the coercive safeguards, that would make abolition of weapons of mass destruction a practical alternative."[29] Blechman proposes a U.S. declaration that it intends to seek the abolition of weapons of mass destruction "by a date certain—say 2020." To support this proposal, in addition to various continued arms control measures, Blechman suggests a UN Security Council resolution holding that possession of weapons of mass destruction in violation of agreements like the NPT "constitute a threat to international peace and security," thus making possible harsh sanctions on violators.[30]

But what form of disarmament would serve U.S. interests? Although we might wish it could be so, the knowledge to produce nuclear weapons can never be erased from the earth. Nor, given the prominence of civilian nuclear power industries and the existence of natural sources of uranium, can fissile materials be completely eliminated.

Many nations will always possess what might be described as a "virtual" nuclear arsenal: the technology and fissile material to assemble a sizable number of nuclear devices within several months' time. For most developed and a few developing states, the question is not whether they could have nuclear weapons, but how long it would take to deploy them. The key criterion becomes the cushion of time between a given stage of nuclear technology and a deployed nuclear force. In the future, then, disarmament measures might aim at creating this cushion for the nuclear weapons states and extending it for non-weapons states.

For nuclear-weapons states, creating such a cushion means banning the existence of assembled, ready-to-use nuclear weapons. Already, the United States and Russia have considerably reduced the levels of alert portions of their nuclear arsenals. The goal for the future should be a situation in which no nuclear weapon is assembled and ready for use. A realistic form of disarmament to be implemented in the next several decades would thus aim to dismantle all assembled nuclear devices, and, at a minimum, to place the resulting parts—warheads, delivery vehicles, and fissile material—under bilateral, multilateral, and/or international inspection. The weapons would be separated from the delivery systems in such a way that any attempt to marry the two could be verified. The United Nations Security Council would then declare the reconstruction of nuclear weapons to be contrary to international law except under very narrow and clearly agreed circumstances. The world community might set a tentative, flexible date for the completion of this process—perhaps the year 2020 or 2025.

Dismantlement is not equivalent to disarmament by abolition, at least as that latter concept is traditionally understood. Individual nations would retain the components of nuclear weapons, and could reassemble them within a fixed amount of time. No international body would take possession of the weapons. This distinction is intended to answer many of the most obvious criticisms of disarmament; no renegade state could obtain enormous leverage by constructing a handful of nuclear weapons—the nuclear powers would simply reassemble a few dozen of their own, and deterrent by threat of retaliation would have been reestablished. Knowing this in advance would presumably persuade the renegade state not to waste its effort. Moreover, the supposed existential value of nuclear weapons—that they deter the prospect of major war by rendering it unimaginably horrific—would remain, as any all-out war would lead to reassembly and thence to nuclear use. For this same reason, those nations that now rely on security pledges from nuclear powers as a rationale for eschewing their own arsenals could continue to do so.

At the same time, dismantlement would represent a major victory on three parallel fronts. First, it would eliminate the day-to-day risk of nuclear use, misuse, or accident. If the arrangement could be preserved through crises and even conventional wars, the risk of nuclear war would have been substantially reduced. Second, dismantlement goes directly to the heart of the "loose Russian nukes" problem. With Russian nuclear weapons dismantled and under Russian and international inspection (along with the weapons of all declared nuclear powers), the chance of unauthorized use or illegal sale or transfer of one or more weapons would decline substantially.

Third and finally, and of most direct relevance to the subject of this volume, a global regime of dismantlement would draw a clear line on nonproliferation: no proliferant would be allowed to assemble a nuclear weapon, and all states would have to allow verification procedures sufficient to demonstrate that this goal had been achieved. This would represent a significant improvement over the current situation, in which at least three and possibly four threshold states are believed to have assembled nuclear devices.

Dismantlement would thus offer a dramatic new framework for a revised NPT. It would allow nations such as India and Pakistan to be in the same status as the nuclear weapons states. They, too, could agree to non-weaponized deterrence, to place their nuclear programs under international inspection but not to give them up. Under this approach, a revised NPT for the twenty-first century might have two categories: non-weapons states, and non-*weaponized* states. India, Pakistan, and Israel would join the five declared nuclear powers in the second category. For a time—ten or more years—the declared nuclear powers could retain some core of their current deterrent force, such as a certain number of strategic missile submarines, actively deployed. But the goal would be to move to fully nonoperational forces some time early in the next century. This proposal fits well with the goals of nonproliferation outlined at the end of the previous chapter, which essentially outlined a form of non-weaponized deterrence as the near-term goal of nonproliferation policy in some cases.

Individual Cases: The Demand Side and "Package Deals"

Taken together, the preceding ideas would help answer the specific objections made by proliferants not a party to the NPT and would also create robust standards supporting a renewed worldwide commitment to nonproliferation. They could be presented as the core of a new vision of nuclear weapons in world politics, a vision compelling and realistic enough to serve as the basis of a broad nonproliferation strategy.

That dramatic appeal to nonproliferation and nuclear arms control should be sufficient, and indeed represents the best possible effort, to capture two types of states in the net of a new NPT: soft- and medium-core proliferants. The deepened pursuit of a nonnuclear world would hopefully lock the soft-core proliferants out of the nuclear business, and the initiatives on arms control and abolition would test the honesty of such medium-core NPT holdouts as India and Brazil. Meanwhile, the U.S. nuclear guarantee to Germany (and other NATO allies), Japan, and South Korea would remain intact.

It remains to describe the specific approach that would be used with hard-core proliferants (and a handful of medium-core proliferants as well). Here the overused phrase "carrots and sticks" represents an essentially accurate, but far too crude, description of what is required. The promise of benefits for non-proliferation, and the threat of punishment for proliferation, must indeed be present. But the Korean case suggests that it is the balance between the two, and the tone in which they are combined, that makes all the difference.[31]

To begin with, any specific nonproliferation effort must respect the political culture and social norms of the target country. As described earlier, the

U.S. approach to North Korea has disregarded these elements almost completely, and appears to be paying the price for that decision. Once cultural and social factors are taken into account, a general approach might be defined as assembling a series of "package deals" in the context of broader initiatives to address the demand side of the nuclear equation.

This strategy would begin by adopting a friendly, cooperative tone toward the proliferant, engaging it in diplomatic dialogue at high levels, and stating repeatedly the U.S. desire for a warm and expanded relationship. A hostile approach would probably only exacerbate the country's threat perceptions and provide it with additional excuses for delay. This in fact was the story of the Korean case, when Pyongyang skillfully used U.S. and South Korean accusations and confrontational steps (such as the holding of Team Spirit 1993) as reasons to put off inspections. The goal would be to create trust, if the proliferant's security concerns are genuine, and to deprive it of excuses for delay and prepare the way for eventual sanctions if they are not.

It is important to note that this approach would not demand that the United States or its allies give away anything critical to their security. Friendly dialogue generally costs nothing, and the early concessions should not involve things integral to U.S. or allied safety. In the Korean example, U.S. officials had already decided that a tactical nuclear withdrawal and a move to a biennial basis for Team Spirit would serve U.S. interests, and so those moves were not, in a sense, concessions at all. And this approach recognizes that in some cases, such as Iraq or Libya, a proliferant's other irresponsible behavior may rule out a strategy of engagement.

Having established the basic elements of pressure and having cultivated personal relationships with a proliferant's top officials over a period of months or years, the United States and its allies would move to the next phase of diplomacy: the explicit offer of incentives. Explaining their concerns about the proliferant's nuclear research, U.S. officials could portray these concerns as an unfortunate barrier to the kind of warm relationship that both sides clearly desire. Because the world community is asking the nation to make a special effort for peace, U.S. officials could explain, they recognize that the nation will expect and deserve recognition. And then the U.S. and/or allied side could lay out a very explicit, detailed package of benefits the proliferant would receive in exchange for full cooperation on nuclear inspections and related matters. In the Korean case, the resulting package included partial or full establishment of diplomatic relations with the United States and Japan, light-water reactors from abroad, the possibility of Japanese colonial era reparations payments, South Korean business investments in the North's special economic zones, and other considerations.[32]

Time magazine essayist Michael Kramer has laid out a very similar approach, using North Korea as an example. The interests of most regional actors, including the United States, mitigated against a confrontation, Kramer noted. So the United States backed off and accepted the definition of success proposed in chapter 9, focusing on the North's future research. He quotes a Japanese official as to the tone of strategy required:

> Drawing a line in the sand early is what you should have done in the '50s. Today you should be softer. Kim's bottom line is still his regime's survival, but victory is defined differently this time. Kim knows the way to win in the '90s is by joining the Asian economic boom . . . [The United States] should have told Kim, "You say you don't have the bomb. O.K., we believe you." Then, *quietly,* [Clinton] should have begun to deal. Now, when everything is public and so much pride is on the line on both sides, it's harder.

The United States, Kramer concludes, "Should actively engage the world's other rogue states before it's too late—no matter the know-nothings whose knee-jerk reaction to creative diplomacy is to cry appeasement."[33]

Stephen Solarz has proposed much the same strategy. A diplomatic arrangement will "require the United States and its allies to be clear about what they would be willing to give North Korea" in exchange for nuclear cooperation, Solarz writes. "A purely diplomatic strategy entails making North Korea an offer it can't refuse." Such an offer, he argues, should include diplomatic relations, a no-first-use pledge, and economic assistance. Such an offer "would be a relatively small price to pay" for an end to the nuclear problem, Solarz contends; and, as suggested earlier, "all things being equal, the establishment of diplomatic relations with North Korea is in our interest as much as it is North Korea's," given the benefits of opening the North's closed society to outside influences.[34]

The tough part, of course, involves deciding what the United States would do if the proliferant does not accept the offer; and perhaps even more important, what the United States should *say* about what it would do in that case. If, as argued earlier, sanctions are not a promising route, should U.S. officials rule them out, and thereby forfeit most of their punitive leverage? Or should they bluff and promise sanctions, knowing they will not want to fulfil the threat if the time comes to put them into place?

The proliferant must understand that there is a price for not cooperating. For the most part, however, that price can be left as one of loss—the failure to obtain the promised benefits—rather than the threat of punishment. At the same time, the idea of sanctions can be kept alive through matter-of-fact admissions that they remain, of course, a policy option, but one the United States hopes and believes will never have to be employed. U.S. officials could also employ surrogates—members of Congress, allied officials, columnists, think-tank scholars—to remind the proliferant of the risk of sanctions if it does not cooperate.

The proposed strategy thus emphasizes explicit carrots and largely implied sticks. Once overt sanctions have been levied, the hope for constructive negotiations might be lost; they would constitute an escalation by the world community. As beleaguered, isolated states with a bunker mentality, proliferants tend to be proud and sensitive. Ill-timed sanctions can be counterproductive. A more promising strategy, as used in the Korean example, is to create de facto sanctions by denying improved economic or political ties. Admittedly, the threat of sanctions must still reside somewhere in the mix; but the expansive nature of the engagement portion helps mitigate the risks of sanctions.

Such an approach seems to have worked in Ukraine, a very different situation from North Korea but nonetheless a proliferation challenge of the first order. The basis for good relations was established under the Clinton administration, when Ambassador Strobe Talbott and other top U.S. officials travelled to Kiev and talked of partnership rather than pressure. Early concessions were provided through expanded amounts of economic aid and other friendly gestures. And the deal for Ukraine's denuclearization was very explicit: some $175 million in aid (later doubled) to dismantle nuclear weapons; $350 million in direct economic assistance; the proceeds from the sale of uranium in the nuclear warheads; a tame but symbolically important U.S. security promise; and other benefits.

Offering such incentives is a win-win proposition for the United States. Obviously, any step that would threaten the security of the United States or its allies should be nonnegotiable. But the core of the incentive packages offered to proliferants—political and economic engagement—represents probably the best means of undermining the authoritarian governments of rogue nations in the long run. As argued earlier, most experts agree that broad U.S. goals in Korea recommend some expanded form of intercourse with the North; the nuclear issue has handcuffed U.S. policy. If proliferants will accept outside economic aid, investment, and political relations in exchange for slowing or abandoning nuclear programs, the United States and its allies will have won on *both* counts.

This strategy appears to have worked in Korea. In fact, the evidence of the preceding chapters seems overwhelming on one point: in the Korean case at least, nonproliferation policy appears to have been successful to the degree that the United States and South Korea adopted a strategy of engagement as opposed to confrontation. On balance, talking and offering incentives seem to have worked far better than threats.

The basic evidence for this argument comes from two periods—the spring of 1992 through the end of that year, and the fall of 1993 through October 1994. During the first period, U.S. and South Korean strategy slid from one of engagement—preemptive concessions and offers of benefits in a warm atmosphere of North-South relations—to one of punitive threats and sanctions. The success of the nonproliferation policy declined as this trend continued. The four major U.S. incentives of 1991 spelled out in chapter 4, followed by the two North-South agreements of that fall and the promise of further cooperation, led directly to North Korean agreement to IAEA inspections in April 1992. Positive North Korean reactions and concessions resulted directly, almost automatically, from U.S. and South Korean initiatives.[35]

During the second half of 1992, events reversed these outcomes. Washington and Seoul, deep into presidential elections, appeared to neglect the nuclear issue, and took no substantial steps to reward the North for its cooperation. That fall, South Korea's revelation of an alleged North Korean spy ring, and the decision to proceed with planning for Team Spirit 1993, put two more nails in the coffin of North Korean cooperation. The IAEA's demand for challenge inspections, which chapter 8 has characterized as unnecessary at that time and in that form, supplied the final nail. The result, again, was predictable: in March 1993, North Korea declared its intention to leave the NPT.

This same pattern, of cooperation leading to cooperation and threats begetting threats, was evident during the second crisis period of the nuclear diplomacy aimed at the North, from the fall of 1993 through October 1994. In the period of delay before the long-awaited U.S. package deal could be placed on the table, North Korean provocations and delays caused Washington and Seoul to threaten sanctions—and North Korea simply threatened war in response. It was only when U.S. officials finally presented their compelling offer in July 1994 that the ground was established for a nuclear deal. Indeed, the rapid speed with which the United States and North Korea reached the final agreement of October, amid the death of Kim Il Sung and the drawn-out drama attending to Kim Jong Il's succession to power, stands as nothing less than sensational.

Similar themes pervade the history of diplomacy toward the North. Obviously, North Korea's behavior is more complicated that this simple model would contend. Obviously, one must assume that a regime such as that in Pyongyang harbors motives that are not in accord with U.S. and South Korean interests. As previous chapters have suggested, North Korea's cooperation may have been dishonest from the beginning. But from the standpoint of effective policy, the record of the diplomacy toward North Korea suggests, at a minimum, that a strategy like the one outlined earlier is worth a try—and that it might work in other cases as well. And the key advantage of this strategy is that it does not rule out a tougher approach. If a package deal is refused, the process of offering it has strengthened, not weakened, the U.S. ability to implement more confrontational policies at a later date. Thus, even a failed engagement strategy would have its uses. As former Bush and Reagan administration official Robert Manning points out, "Even if such a precise and comprehensive offer were made to North Korea," it might well refuse. But "nonetheless, by proposing a grand bargain the United States and its allies would force North Korea to make a clear choice, deprive it of excuses, and seize the political high ground, firming up a political consensus (including China) for UN sanctions. Failure to make such an offer risks limited cooperation from China and others."[36] Diplomacy is worth the effort, Stephen Solarz concurs, even if the North rejects the offer (or, in the wake of the October 1994 agreement, abandons its acceptance at a later date). With the North's real intentions "unambiguously exposed, it would be easier to muster the support, at home and abroad, that will be politically necessary to take the tougher steps, involving sanctions and perhaps even force, that may be necessary to solve the problem."[37]

Nonproliferation and the New World Order

The strategy being proposed here follows closely the analysis of historian Paul Schroeder of the new world order. It is worth quoting a recent essay of his at length to place that strategy in the proper context.

Schroeder argues that the enforcement of international norms or laws, through sanctions or military force, is not really what the new world order is all about. In fact, this concept of "law enforcement" is dangerous and potentially counterproductive. It "makes international confrontations and conflicts into something like a gunfight between the sheriff and the outlaws," thus obstructing constructive solutions.[38] Psychologically, when sanctions are imposed, "the honor as well as the interests of the accused party are impinged, giving it additional incentives to resist" as well as "effective propaganda to rally domestic support against outsiders." Strategically, the approach "pulls the international community into pursuit of a vague, almost indefinable goal," about which debates inevitably arise and encourage "disunity and defections" from the coalition. Juridically, a sanctions-based approach "encourages challenges to the legitimacy of the action that an aggressor can easily exploit. Practically, it engenders disputes over meeting and sharing the costs and burdens of enforcement, and fears that enforcing the law will result in more suffering and damage than did the original alleged violation."[39]

As previous chapters have argued, the North Korean case illustrates that each of these pitfalls apply to a nonproliferation policy based on the "enforcement" of international "norms." Threatening sanctions against the North risked turning what should have been an exercise in horse-trading into a zero-sum confrontation. The threat of sanctions certainly affronted the North's dignity and provided its regime with domestic ammunition. Washington's inability to lay out a clear definition of success or to make clear the stakes involved led to debates, even with Seoul, about the true purposes of nonproliferation policy and contributed to a fracturing of the global consensus on the proper means and ends of the nonproliferation effort. In a legal sense, North Korea found a number of loopholes in the U.S. and IAEA case against it, loopholes beginning with the fundamental fact that no state is under any legal obligation to join the NPT. Finally, Washington and its allies did debate the potential costs of enforcement—and many of those allies concluded that eliminating risk about one or two bombs' worth of plutonium was not worth a major crisis or war on the peninsula.

Rather than a world order based on legal enforcement and threats of sanctions (what he calls a "compellence-deterrence" model of politics), Schroeder argues for a world order based on the principles of "association [and] exclusion." In the wake of the Cold War, most major and medium powers decided that certain kinds of behavior "had to be ruled out as incompatible with their general security and welfare," behavior like direct aggression, subversion of other governments, and mercantilism.[40] Those powers formed associations—the EC, NATO, NAFTA—that distributed various goods to countries that shared these basic values. And it was by offering or denying membership to these associations that the world community made its most powerful judgments about individual states. The concepts of pressure and coercion had taken a new form: the carrot of membership in regional and global associations, and the stick of exclusion from those groups.

Schroeder's way of phrasing the difference is as follows. Rather than saying to an opponent, "Stop what you are doing or threatening to do, and do what we tell you instead, or we will punish you as a lawbreaker," the world community would say something like: "What you are now doing or threatening to do is against our group norms; it will eventually fail and hurt you and all of us. If you continue to try it, you will be barred from our group and excluded from its benefits; if you change your policy you can remain in the group, or keep your chance of joining it and promoting your interests within it."[41] This is a close analogy of the offer to North Korea advocated in this and the previous chapter. Cooperation on nonproliferation would yield membership in the world political and economic community, along with specific benefits to ease that transition. Noncooperation would result in exclusion from that community, economic decline, and perhaps regime collapse.[42]

Of course, more immediate military responses to certain forms of aggression will still be required—as with, for example, the U.S. and UN effort to reverse Iraq's conquest of Kuwait. Forcible sanctions "are still needed," Schroeder concludes, "in cases where a particular evil or danger so clearly and directly threatens the general peace and the continued existence and operation of the whole international system that it must be averted promptly at almost any cost."[43] Again, nonproliferation through engagement must be abandoned in such cases.

This same distinction sheds light on the issue of a definition of success in nonproliferation. A North Korea with two or three large nuclear reactors pumping out enough plutonium each year for ten or twenty bombs, mounting nuclear weapons on ballistic missiles capable of reaching most of Northeast Asia, and selling a half dozen or more bombs a year to fanatical customers around the world—this sort of North Korea would clearly represent a "clear and direct threat to the continued existence and operation of the international system" as we know it. Military action to end such a threat—by destroying the reactors and reprocessing facilities that made it possible—might be justified.

But what of North Korean possession of a bomb or two in the basement, neither of which is likely to sell, and with its nuclear infrastructure placed under stringent controls? This result, the definition of success I have proposed above, seems much more amenable to Schroeder's model for dealing with less immediate threats to the peace. Such issues require "patience, steady attention to the long view, a willingness to wait for results, and the ability to adjust to changed reality and accept blurred, complex, uncertain outcomes and live with them if they are the best attainable."[44] These same attributes are the requirements of a wise nonproliferation policy, in Korea and elsewhere; and they are much in evidence in the Agreed Framework.

A DIFFICULT CHALLENGE

As these last points highlight, nonproliferation in the 1990s and beyond will be an enormously difficult challenge. In large part this is true because, as this chapter has suggested, the only road map we have for such efforts merely points us in a general direction. The lay of the land, its contours and pathways, the barriers to progress and bridges over them will only become apparent when we lay that map over a specific case. And once apparent, they will produce a geopolitical topography that is maddeningly complex.

Nonetheless, there are reasons for hope. In general terms, proliferation has not advanced as far or as fast as many observers expected, even as recently as the late 1980s. In terms of the case study examined here, the U.S., South Korean, and Japanese strategy toward North Korea has been at least a partial success story and should be recognized as such. By gaining inspections of the main Yongbyon reactor and the control thereby exerted over the future of North Korea's nuclear research, the U.S. campaign of diplomacy had basically met, by early 1992, many of the conditions of success proposed in chapter 9. That this progress was undermined by twin mistakes—allowing the diplomacy to lapse in the second half of 1992, and making an unnecessary and provocative demand for challenge inspections in early 1993—does not deny the general wisdom of the effort. United States and South Korean officials deserve warm praise for their calm and balanced handling of the nuclear crisis after March 1993 in the face of numerous North Korean provocations; their calm made the end result of this process, the Agreed Framework of October 1994, possible.

While its exact elements cannot be replicated to guarantee success elsewhere, the approach to North Korea at least demonstrates that a sophisticated nonproliferation strategy can work. The challenge now is to establish similar, tailored strategies for other cases—Israel and India, to name just two—and pursue them doggedly until progress is achieved. We know roughly where we need to go, and we know we can get there; now our task is to do so—and quickly, before the path is closed off forever.

EPILOGUE

In the last months of 1994 and the first months of 1995, North Korea quickly demonstrated that executing the Agreed Framework would not be any easier than negotiating it had been. In January and February 1995 talks with the United States, North Korean officials quickly began backtracking on commitments they had made in the October deal. Pyongyang demanded large amounts of direct economic assistance, for example, and insisted that, after all, it would never allow South Korea to construct the light-water reactors.

In one sense this attempt to renegotiate the nuclear deal should hardly be surprising. North Korea has a long history of abandoning commitments to hunt for a better deal—a strategy much in evidence immediately before the North endorsed the terms of the Agreed Framework. And ultimately, as the perceptive Park Moon Young explains, "the cold reality is that because nuclear potential is North Korea's sole source of diplomatic power, the nuclear question will not be completely solved before Korean unification. . . . It will remain a problem as long as North Korea exists."[1]

The disputes of early 1995 thus confirm the obvious fact that the U.S.–North Korean nuclear agreement has left a number of major problems to be resolved. The nuclear deal represents not so much a resolution of the nuclear issue as an invitation to resolve it over the coming years; addressing the remaining questions poses a major task for U.S. and allied diplomacy. Several specific issues stand out as especially important.

First there is the issue of culture. Any protracted negotiation between two countries whose cultures differ as widely as the United States's and North Korea's is bound to be a difficult enterprise. Americans and Koreans view a host of fundamental issues—the importance of national pride and recognition, the use of threats and bluffs in diplomacy, and the respect accorded written commitments—in a dramatically different light. Indeed, the United States's recognition that such cultural differences exist is precisely why Washington cast the nuclear deal as an Agreed Framework rather than as a treaty: U.S. officials believed that the United States would feel tightly bound by the terms of a formal treaty while Pyongyang would not.

Culturally influenced perceptions carry one ominous implication for the future of the Agreed Framework. The United States and other Western nations tend to perceive agreements as resolutions, end points, final decisions; Koreans and many other Asian nations see them as merely another step, and a somewhat flexible one at that, in the construction of individual or national bonds. If Washington and Seoul decide, therefore, that the nuclear issue is settled, they will be in for a rude shock.

These facts point to the importance of following the framework with a wide ranging and coherent strategy for engaging North Korea, an extension of the economic and political contacts proposed in chapter 10 as the basic strategy for nonproliferation.[2] However, U.S. and South Korean officials, suspicious of North Korea and wanting to hoard their remaining leverage, may wish to go slowly. Indeed, since the framework has been signed, comments from U.S. and South Korean officials suggest that the two governments intend to hold a full economic and political engagement hostage until the resolution of "other concerns"—from North Korea's ballistic missile program to human rights.[3]

But stonewalling North Korea now would be a mistake. Engagement of North Korea will not be a panacea—outside investment and political contacts do not always or easily promote political or economic change in the target country.[4] The North itself will doubtless attempt to modulate such investment to reduce its political impact.

Nonetheless, a broad consensus has arisen that engaging North Korea, much like signing the Agreed Framework itself, is the best of a number of mediocre alternatives. Many South Korean officials and analysts have long argued that drawing North Korea into the world community offered a far better means than isolation of encouraging peaceful unification on the peninsula.[5] In this particular case, isolation has not caused political change and appears to have little immediate prospect of doing so; following the somewhat comparable China model, some observers hope that opening the North to outside influence will have this effect over time.

Engagement offers the only hope of a gradual process of unification, which Seoul badly wants now that it has estimated the likely cost and disruption of a rapid, East German–style collapse of the North. Especially given the role of personal ties in doing business in Korean society, the United States and South Korea may also be more likely to resolve other issues of concern in the context of a broadening relationship with Pyongyang.

The potential instability of Kim Jong Il's nascent regime provides an additional rationale for outside investment in North Korea. Since October 1994, rumors have been flying in Seoul and Beijing about the younger Kim's ill-health. Should he fall from power after another year or two, a new contest for power will begin in Pyongyang. If a number of outside investments have begun by that time, demonstrating the potential value of engagement, the reformists who favor such an opening would have a stronger hand in the post–Kim Jong Il power struggle. If, on the other hand, South Korea and the United States continue to go slowly on investments and political relations, North Korean hard-liners will have a forceful argument against reform: We have tried to engage the world for the past five years, and what has it brought us? South Korea and the United States must move rapidly to demonstrate the benefits of cooperation.

A second issue relates to the fact that the Agreed Framework will place the U.S.–South Korean alliance under enormous strain, something that has become increasingly obvious in late 1994 and early 1995. However, a deal like the Agreed Framework, if implemented with respect for Seoul's concerns, may in fact pose the smallest threat to the alliance of any of the realistic policy options—certainly a smaller threat than preemptive military action. Nonetheless, U.S. and South Korean officials face a significant challenge in the coming months and years: together they must implement this deal in a mutually acceptable way, when their national interests are not always compatible.

Washington and Seoul each have one major tool at their disposal to reaffirm the integrity of the bilateral alliance. For the United States, this tool is the continued insistence, in the face of what are likely to be years of North Korean complaints, that South Korea must provide the light-water reactors (LWRs) called for by the framework. The deal almost fell apart in the negotiating stage over this issue, which was not resolved definitively in the text of the framework itself. Seoul's role as provider of the LWRs gives it great leverage in implementing the deal and serves to reassure South Korea that outside powers will not determine the final shape of the accord. The United States should stand firm on this issue.

South Korea has its own means of safeguarding its relationship with the United States. That is to take the framework for what it is—a historic opportunity to address long-term security threats by pursuing a real, rather than symbolic, engagement of North Korea. To the extent that Seoul actively and aggressively implements an economic, political, and cultural engagement of North Korea, it will gain more leverage over Pyongyang as well as a greater voice in the outcome of the framework.

At the same time, Washington and Seoul cannot become so wedded to the framework and the strategy of engagement it augurs that they allow North Korean provocations to go unpunished. Officials in Pyongyang may believe that the nuclear agreement has provided them with a new license for misbehavior: with Washington and Seoul desperate to preserve the accord, North Korean officials might think that U.S. and ROK leaders will hesitate to respond forcefully to North Korean provocations.

If such a belief took hold, U.S. and South Korean policy toward North Korea would become bankrupt. Washington and Seoul would have virtually no options aside from weak complaints for responding to political or military incitements from North Korea. Knowing this, Pyongyang would become emboldened to push the boundary of acceptable actions—a dangerous process of experimentation that would substantially increase the risk of crisis or war on the peninsula.

On issues of major concern, therefore, Washington and Seoul should treat North Korean threats as if the Agreed Framework did not exist. Any military provocation—a buildup of forces near the demilitarized zone (DMZ), shots fired across the DMZ, or any other comparable act—should be met on exactly the same terms as it would be in the absence of the nuclear issue. At the same time, the importance of the framework does suggest that the United States and South Korea should avoid the sort of gratuitous disparagement of North Korea over minor issues that has characterized both Washington's and Seoul's policy for many years.

It is of course wrong to assume that the framework has laid to rest all the risks involved in North Korea's nuclear program. In the broadest sense, the agreement has only deferred those risks, as North Korea will not dismantle major parts of its nuclear facilities for several years. Even if the parties involved fully enact the framework's provisions, various strands of nuclear weapons potential will remain in place.

Two complications in particular may emerge as the framework is being implemented. One relates to the special inspections of the alleged nuclear waste sites at Yongbyon. The importance of these inspections to the larger goal of rolling back the North Korean nuclear program poses an important question: What if the long-awaited inspections of the nuclear waste sites prove inconclusive? What if, through secret tunneling and removal of the waste or other means, North Korean technicians can dispose of the hoped-for "smoking gun" evidence? The framework commits North Korea to satisfying the IAEA about all aspects of its nuclear program, and so Pyongyang is theoretically required to allow inspections until that happens. In practice, however, officials in Pyongyang are likely to draw the line at the waste sites and complain that U.S. officials made no mention of subsequent IAEA procedures. Such developments would raise again the question of past versus future in U.S. and South Korean nonproliferation policy, and officials in Washington and Seoul should anticipate that risk.

Another aspect of continued nuclear risk would be a North Korean demand to keep the spent fuel from the light-water reactors. Such reactors are less of a proliferation risk than graphite-based models to begin with, and North Korea is prohibited by the framework from possessing a nuclear reprocessing facility, without which it could not separate the plutonium from the waste for weapons use. Precisely because of these reassurances, however, and despite recent commitments to U.S. officials to allow the export of spent LWR fuel, it is possible that once the LWRs are up and running, Pyongyang will change its tune and argue that it has a sovereign right to keep the spent fuel. U.S. and South Korean officials should develop policy options in the event North Korea attempts to press this issue.

Both these risks again point to the importance of a rapid move to enmesh North Korea in a web of economic and political contacts. If such engagement does not proceed, five years from now Pyongyang may have nothing to lose in a new series of nuclear provocations. But if North Korean officials know that such actions will call into question growing foreign investment, international economic aid, and expanded political relationships, they may be more hesitant to engage in them.

Finally, despite the best intentions of U.S. and South Korean leaders, the Agreed Framework itself may collapse. It might fall victim to new North Korean demands, or it could be undermined by the growing hard-line sentiment in Seoul and Washington and by South Korean and U.S. legislators who refuse to pay for the deal.

The United States and South Korea need a contingency plan in the event the framework does disintegrate. Washington and Seoul, notes Paik Jin Hyun, "must also remain prepared for the possibility of North Korean stalling tactics, or even the breakdown in the implementation phase that could lead to renewed tensions and confrontation."[6] Much of course depends on whether the impetus comes from Pyongyang, Seoul, or Washington. Either way, however, the United States and South Korea will once again face the challenge of deterring North Korea from an expansion of its nuclear program. If one or more parties repudiates the framework, calm deliberation and careful policy will be needed at a time when emotionalism and calls for military action will be commonplace. In order to avoid a devastating result, it is critical to begin thinking through an approach to the collapse of the framework immediately.

This book has argued that the Agreed Framework, while hardly perfect, represents a reasonable compromise on the nuclear issue in Korea. But this qualified victory will prove meaningless if the framework falls apart; and, as this epilogue has argued, the surest way to ensure this result would be for the United States and South Korea to stall on their planned economic and political engagement of the North. Locking North Korea in a bold embrace, while an imperfect approach and hardly one guaranteed to force political change or moderation in the North, offers a far better chance of success than tinkering with Pyongyang's isolation at the margins. U.S. and ROK policy toward the North on the nuclear issue has long suffered from the flawed assumption that economic and political opening is a "concession," something that benefits Pyongyang while hurting Washington and Seoul. In fact such an opening would benefit all sides—much as the framework agreement itself has done.[7] We can find no better evidence for this than North Korea's own hesitation to accept a full economic opening and Pyongyang's attempts to limit the scope and effect of outside investments.

The months since October 1994, however, suggest that key officials in Washington and Seoul have yet to accept this simple reality. If the two governments continue to procrastinate on engagement, they will duplicate the mistakes of 1992, and the framework could indeed dissolve. Then it would be time to write a new final chapter to this book, one that catalogues the senseless deterioration of a fairly successful nonproliferation strategy into a new round of crises, sanctions, and—perhaps—war.

The Agreed Framework has afforded the United States, South Korea, and Japan with a golden opportunity to rethink their approach to North Korea. But that opportunity may prove a fleeting one. The next year or two will tell if U.S., South Korean, and Japanese officials have seized or missed it. And the early signs are mixed.

NOTES

CHAPTER ONE

1. Details of the Harrison trip come from a mimeographed press release, "North Korea Offers to Freeze Nuclear Program," News from the Carnegie Endowment, June 16, 1994; an account cited in Foreign Broadcast Information Service—East Asia section (hereinafter FBIS-EAS), June 13, 1994, 27; and the author's interview with Harrison, July 1994.
2. Graybeal and McFate cited in *Shaping Nuclear Policy for the 1990s: A Compendium of Views* (Washington, D.C.: Report of the Defense Policy Panel, House Armed Services Committee, December 17, 1992), 280.
3. Robert Toth, "In Search of a Foreign Policy," *Foreign Service Journal*, vol. 71, no. 1 (January 1994): 33.
4. Les Aspin, Secretary of Defense, *Report on the Bottom Up Review* (Washington, D.C.: U.S. Department of Defense, October 1993), 5-12.
5. Cited in *Defense Daily*, January 27, 1994, 133.
6. John Mueller describes the process of elevating secondary concerns to primary ones in the post-Cold War era in "The Catastrophe Quota: Trouble After the Cold War," *Journal of Conflict Resolution*, vol. 38, no. 3 (September 1994), esp. 367-72. He does not include proliferation in his lists, but it may belong there.
7. Thus Ted Greenwood of Columbia terms the claim that nonproliferation is "the chief security threat" to the United States is "overly alarmist"; cited in *Shaping Nuclear Policy for the 1990s*, 284.
8. I am indebted to Mark Minton of the U.S. Embassy in Seoul, Korea, for helping me understand some of the following issues during a discussion in Seoul in October 1993.
9. Charles Krauthammer, "Capitulation in Korea," *The Washington Post*, January 7, 1994, A19.
10. In part this question is inspired by Stephen Meyer's superb study *The Dynamics of Nuclear Proliferation* (Chicago: University of Chicago Press, 1984). That volume remains, in this author's opinion, the most thoughtful and comprehensive analysis yet published of the phenomenon of proliferation. In it, Meyer distinguished between two basic models of proliferation: the technical, which held that

nations that could build the bomb would do so; and the motivational, which stressed the specific military, political, or economic motives of individual pro-liferators. As the following chapters will suggest, the Korean case sheds new light on this debate.

CHAPTER TWO

1. Roger Dingman, "Atomic Diplomacy During the Korean War," *International Security,* vol. 13, no. 3 (Winter 1988-1989): 60-86.
2. Ibid., 65-66.
3. Ibid., 76-77.
4. Alexander George and Richard Smoke, *Deterrence in American Foreign Policy, Theory and Practice* (New York: Columbia University Press, 1974), 235-38.
5. Dingman, "Atomic Diplomacy," 79-86.
6. At various points, the analysis that follows will borrow ideas and categories from Stephen Meyer's 1984 study of proliferation. In *The Dynamics of Nuclear Proliferation* (Chicago: University of Chicago Press, 1984), Meyer outlines each of the specific motives for proliferation he uncovered in his analysis of dozens of case studies. All but a few of them apply directly to the North Korean case.
7. Joseph Bermudez, "North Korea's Nuclear Programme," *Jane's Intelligence Review* (September 1991): 404-411.
8. On the degree to which DPRK-Russian relations have declined, see Pak Chae Kyun, "Friendly Relations with Russia Have Ended," translated in Foreign Broadcast Information Service—East Asia, hereinafter cited as FBIS-EAS, August 25, 1992, 21-22.
9. Leonard S. Spector with Jacqueline R. Smith, *Nuclear Ambitions* (Boulder, CO: Westview Press, 1990), 119. For an analysis of this same set of motives, see ibid., 124-25.
10. Stephen Meyer makes reference to this same motive, noting that a state that "per-ceives some likelihood of future security disputes" with a nuclear power, or fears an adversary with a latent nuclear capability, would have a reason to acquire nuclear weapons of its own. Meyer, *The Dynamics of Nuclear Proliferation,* 56-60.
11. Discussions with North Korean officials in New York, Washington, and Beijing, from 1991 to 1993; interviews with U.S. State Department officials, Washington and Seoul, October 1992 through October 1993.
12. Song Young Sun, "The Korean Nuclear Issue," *Korea and World Affairs,* vol 15, no. 3 (Fall 1991): 475; Leonard Spector and Jacqueline Smith, "North Korea: The Next Nuclear Nightmare?" *Arms Control Today,* vol. 21, no. 2 (March 1991): 10; and Andrew Mack, "North Korea and the Bomb," *Foreign Policy,* no. 83 (Summer 1991): 93-94.
13. Song, "The Korean Nuclear Issue," 477. Stephen Meyer notes the historic role of an "overwhelming conventional military threat" and the possibility of an "intolerable economic defense burden" serving as a spur to proliferation. Meyer, *Dynamics of Nuclear Proliferation,* 60-63, 65.

14. Stephen Meyer outlined this motive when he noted the impulse of pariah states to use nuclear weapons to "force the international community to sit up and take note. The pariah's acquisition of atomic weapons would make it impossible for the countries of the world, in particular the regional countries, to continue to ignore it." Ibid., 55-56.

15. Stephen Meyer makes reference to a number of related domestic motives for a nuclear program. One is domestic turmoil; national leaders, he notes, may "consider the nuclear option a way to direct domestic energies away from domestic problems." Governments might also "pursue the manufacture of nuclear weapons as a way to raise the morale of their defense establishments," Meyer continues, particularly in the wake of a major military defeat. Both may have been relevant to North Korea: the second during the 1950s and 1960s, after the disaster of the Korean War; and the first later, when the North's economic progress collapsed in the 1980s. Ibid., 63-64.

16. Spector and Smith, "North Korea: The Next Nuclear Nightmare?" 10.

17. Stephen Meyer has sketched out the motives for proliferation inherent in such a situation. "A country perceives itself to be in an inferior position within an alliance structure," Meyer hypothesizes. "In particular, the dominant power is a nuclear power. All else equal, the acquisition of atomic weapons would theoretically increase the military significance of the weaker partner—thereby enhancing its status within the alliance." Meyer, The Dynamics of Nuclear Proliferation, 58. North Korea may have viewed its relationship with both China and Russia in exactly this sense.

18. Peter Hayes, Pacific Powderkeg: American Nuclear Dilemmas in Korea (Lexington: Lexington Books, 1991), 34.

19. Dingman, "Atomic Diplomacy," 60-64.

20. See Kathleen C. Bailey, Doomsday Weapons on the Hands of Many: The Arms Control Challenge of the 1990s (Urbana: University of Illinois Press, 1991), 19; and James F. Elkin and Andrew Ritezel, "India," in Douglas J. Murray and Paul R. Viotti, eds., The Defense Policies of Nations: A Comparative Survey, Second Edition (Baltimore: Johns Hopkins University Press, 1989), 523-24.

21. Spector and Smith, "North Korea: The Next Nuclear Nightmare?" 10.

22. Hayes, Pacific Powderkeg, 34.

23. Harold C. Hinton, "Korean Security and the Sino-Soviet Relationship," Korea and World Affairs, vol. 10, no. 4 (Winter 1986): 736.

24. Hayes, Pacific Powderkeg, 35.

25. Ibid., 34-35, 47-49.

26. Cited in Ibid., 125.

27. Ibid., 126.

28. On October 4, 1974, North Korea charged that the USS Midway was carrying nuclear warheads into Pusan, and at the 355th meeting of the Military Armistice Commission on October 25, 1974, the North Koreans accused the United States of introducing nuclear bombs and warheads into South Korea. They also accused the UN Command of deploying nuclear weapons in front-line areas near the military demarcation line, and demanded that they be withdrawn. Ibid., 130.

29. Harry Gelman and Norman Levin, "The Future of Soviet-North Korean Relations" (Santa Monica, CA: The RAND Corporation, October 1984), 2.
30. North Korean defector Kim Chong Min argues that this was a key motive behind Pyongyang's nuclear program. See his comments in FBIS-EAS, November 8, 1991, 30.
31. Ahn Byung Joon, "The Soviet Union and the Korean Peninsula," *Asian Affairs,* vol. 11, no. 4 (Winter 1985): 6.
32. Suh Dae Sook, *Kim Il Sung: The North Korean Leader* (New York: Columbia University Press, 1988): 143; see also 137-45.
33. Ibid., 303.
34. Ibid., 145-57; and Ralph N. Clough, *Embattled Korea: The Rivalry for International Support* (Boulder, CO: Westview Press, 1987), 48-49.
35. Chung Chin O, *Pyongyang Between Peking and Moscow* (Mobile: University of Alabama Press, 1978), 27-67. During this period, Chung contends (p. 66), "the North Korean regime tried to avoid explicit commitment either to the Soviet Union or China," and maintained a "neutral stance."
36. Ibid., 66-107, esp. 104-107.
37. Hayes, *Pacific Powderkeg,* 125.
38. Clough, *Embattled Korea,* 247-49; and Suh, *Kim Il Sung,* 179-88.
39. Clough, *Embattled Korea,* 101-103.
40. Information in this paragraph is drawn from Clough, *Embattled Korea,* 250; Joseph Ha and Timothy Lim, "Soviet Foreign Policy Objectives in North Korea: Latitude and Limitations," *Korea Observer,* vol. 13, no. 4 (Winter 1982): 379; Ahn, "The Soviet Union and the Korean Peninsula," 7; Suh, *Kim Il Sung,* 177; and Chung, *Between Peking and Moscow,* 108-133.
41. Clough, *Embattled Korea,* 260.
42. Kim's statement is carried in FBIS/EAS, November 8, 1991, 30-32. Leonard Spector and Jacqueline Smith suggest that "Kim's decision to develop a nuclear weapon capability probably was made sometime during 1979 or 1980"; Spector and Smith, *Nuclear Ambitions,* 124. Their evidence for such a specific claim is spotty, however. Defector accounts released since their volume was written provide new evidence—if it can be believed—of a desire to manufacture nuclear weapons originating well before 1980. Other states facing a similar security dilemma, such as Israel and India, began going after the bomb in earnest in the late 1960s. Here my assumption is that North Korean leaders pursued their nuclear program from the very beginning on the assumption that it would provide them with at least the option of acquiring a nuclear arsenal.
43. So Yong Ha, "Capacity for Nuclear Weapons Development," *Hoguk,* July 1989; translated in FBIS-EAS, August 3, 1989, 24.
44. Bermudez, "North Korea's Nuclear Programme," 404-411.
45. See Song Yong Sun, "North Korea's Nuclear Capability and Safeguards Agreement," unpublished paper, Seoul, Korea, 1991, 8, 10; Spector and Smith, "North Korea: The Next Nuclear Nightmare?" 9; Bermudez, "North Korea's Nuclear Programme," 406; and Andrew Mack, "North Korea and the Bomb," 88.

46. There are reports that during this same period the North was constructing a second, highly secret underground nuclear facility in Pakchon, west of Yongbyon. Koh Young Whan, a North Korean defector, has said that Pakchon was the primary site for weapons research in the 1960s and afterward. He insists he had not even heard of Yongbyon until he defected. In October 1991, Japanese satellite expert Toshibumi Sakada claimed to have discovered evidence of a nuclear facility at Pakchon by using photos from earth observation satellites. Sakada said he found a one-kilometer-long complex of tall buildings with a heliport nestled in the rugged mountains there. "Defector on North's Hidden Nuclear Facilities," FBIS-EAS, November 7, 1991, 26; "Japanese Scholar Finds New North Korean Nuclear Facilities," *The Korea Times,* October 30, 1991, 2.

It remains unclear what exactly might be located at Pakchon. Presumably, full-scale nuclear reactors would have been detected by Western intelligence. Professor Sakada seems to suggest that the site is largely dedicated to splitting plutonium, that perhaps the North has constructed parallel plutonium reprocessing facilities there as well. See the article in the Asahi Shimbun Weekly, *Aera,* November 5, 1991, 70 (in Japanese). During IAEA Director General Hans Blix's May 1992 trip to the North, he and his staff visited Pakchon to see a uranium ore concentration site located there; see Transcript of Blix briefing, May 16, 1992, in "Background Materials on North Korea and Nuclear Nonproliferation," The Arms Control Association, Washington, D.C., June 1992, 8. Theoretically, Pakchon could also harbor a plant for making weapons-grade uranium, as it is about equally as close as Yongbyon from a major hydroelectric plant in the area. Blix's visit, however, did not uncover any especially dramatic or disturbing evidence in regard to the Pakchon area, and as of early 1993 public discussion of possible nuclear facilities there declined.

47. Mitchell Reiss, *Without the Bomb: The Politics of Nuclear Nonproliferation* (New York: Columbia University Press, 1988), 83.

48. For a detailed history of the troop reductions, see Subcommittee on International Organizations, Committee on International Relations, U.S. House of Representatives, *Investigation of Korean-American Relations,* Committee Report, October 31, 1978, 58-71.

49. L. Collins, "Korea and Taiwan: Security and the Nuclear Option," *International Energy Forum* (Tokyo), January 1984, 44-46.

50. Selig S. Harrison, "A Yen for the Bomb?" *The Washington Post,* October 31, 1993, C2.

51. Leonard Spector, *Nuclear Proliferation Today* (Cambridge: Ballinger, 1984), 341-42.

52. Mitchell Reiss, *Without the Bomb,* 82.

53. South Korea had begun construction of its first nuclear power plant in September 1970 at Kori; this reactor became commercially operational in 1978. In addition, South Korea has two small research reactors, the TRIGA Mark II (0.25 megawatt) and TRIGA Mark III (2 megawatt), and a small fuel fabrication plant. All the uranium used for producing nuclear energy was purchased from the United States and Canada. Joseph Yager, "The Republic of Korea," in Joseph Yager, ed.,

Nonproliferation and U.S. Foreign Policy (Washington, D.C.: The Brookings Institution, 1980), 49.

54. Subcommittee on International Organizations, U.S. House, *Investigation of Korean-American Relations,* 80.

55. Seoul signed an agreement with the IAEA for application of nuclear safeguards in 1968, which was updated in 1972; it became party to both the Partial Test Ban Treaty and the Nonproliferation Treaty. Under the terms of a November 1975 agreement with the IAEA, Seoul renounced access to weapons-grade plutonium and uranium. South Korea's bilateral agreement for cooperation with the United States for the peaceful uses of atomic energy also contained language prohibiting any use of American-supplied material for military purposes. Ibid., 86.

56. Kang Chang Song, a South Korean National Assembly member of the Democratic Party, quoted in a *Joong-ang Ilbo* article, cited in FBIS-EAS, October 12, 1993, 37.

57. *New York Times,* February 1, 1976, A1.

58. Janne E. Nolan, *Trappings of Power* (Washington D.C.: Brookings Institution, 1991), 51.

59. Robert Gillette, "U.S. Squelched Apparent S. Korea A-Bomb Drive," *Los Angeles Times,* November 4, 1978, A1.

60. The same day, however, Park Chun Kyu, the policy chairman of the ruling party, stated that South Korea could see no need for nuclear weapons "at present." Hayes, *Pacific Powderkeg,* 204.

61. Ibid.

62. Subcommittee on International Organizations, U.S. House, *Investigation of Korean-American Relations,* 80.

63. Even during his bid to withdraw the U.S. Second Division from the South, in order to placate the South for the departure of the Second Division, Carter proposed a package of arms transfer and military aid that further alarmed Pyongyang. Once this bid failed, the level of U.S. troops remained virtually unchanged while Seoul obtained access to new U.S. weapons and technologies. Contrary to popular belief, then, the Carter administration that began its Korea policy with human rights and troop withdrawal ended by embracing a new military strongman and sending more arms to Korea than any previous administration. See N. Levin and R. Sneider, "Korea in Postwar U.S. Security Policy," in G. Curtis and Han Sung Joo, eds., *The U.S.-South Korean Alliance* (Lexington, MA: Lexington Books, 1983), 52.

64. *International Herald Tribune,* August 11, 1977, 1.

65. See Chung, *Pyongyang Between Peking and Moscow,* 145-46.

66. Joseph Bermudez, "North Korea's Nuclear Programme," 408.

67. Ibid., 408.

68. Young Sun Ha, *Nuclear Proliferation, World Order, and Korea* (Seoul: National University Press, 1983), 130.

69. Hayes, *Pacific Powderkeg,* 131.

70. Song, "The Korean Nuclear Issue," 474.

71. Ibid., 477.

72. So, "Capacity for Nuclear Weapons Development," 25.
73. Kim Hak Joon, "The Rise of Kim Chong-il: Implications for North Korea's Internal and External Policies in the 1980s," *The Journal of Northeast Asian Studies,* vol. 2, no. 2 (June 1983): 81-92.
74. Jo Yung Hwan, "Succession Politics in North Korea: Implications for Policy and Political Stability," *Asian Survey,* vol. 26, no. 10 (October 1986): 1092-1117.
75. See Tony Emerson, "The Mystery Man," *Newsweek,* April 20, 1992, 22-26.
76. On the approaching transition, see the Japanese and Korean reports cited in FBIS-EAS, April 6, 1992, 13, 18-19; Edward Neilan, "Kim's Son Seems Set to Lead N. Korea," *The Washington Times,* January 16, 1992, A9.
77. See Jo, "Succession Politics," 1116-17.
78. T. Bernstein and A. Nathan, "The Soviet Union, China, and Korea," in Curtis and Han, eds., *U.S.-South Korean Alliance,* 119.
79. Song, "The Korean Nuclear Issue," 475-77; and Spector and Smith, "North Korea: The Next Nuclear Nightmare?" 10.
80. Paik Jin Hyun, "Nuclear Conundrum: Analysis and Assessment of Two Koreas' Policies Regarding the Nuclear Issue," paper given at Institute of Foreign Affairs and National Security (Seoul)/Center for Strategic and International Studies (Washington) Conference, Seoul, Korea, October 13-14, 1993, 8.
81. Jessica Mathews, "Biggest Bargaining Chip," *The Washington Post,* February 20, 1994, C7.

CHAPTER THREE

1. Don Oberdorfer, "North Koreans Pursue Nuclear Arms: U.S. Team Briefs South Korea on New Satellite Intelligence," *The Washington Post,* July 29, 1989, A9. See also Oberdorfer, "U.S. Decides to Withdraw A-Weapons from S. Korea," *The Washington Post,* October 19, 1991, A1. Interviews with former senior high-ranking U.S. officials in Washington, September-November 1993, confirmed this general time frame for the emergence of urgent concern over the North Korean program and provided additional details of the U.S. intelligence briefings to South Korea and other countries.
2. Information in this section is drawn from Dietrich Schroeer, *Science, Technology, and the Nuclear Arms Race* (New York: John Wiley and Sons, 1984), 14-33; Paul Craig and John Jungerman, *Nuclear Arms Race: Technology and Society* (New York: McGraw-Hill, 1986), 171-95; and Kosta Tsipis, *Arsenal: Understanding Weapons in the Nuclear Age* (New York: Simon and Schuster, 1983), 29-43.
3. Kathleen C. Bailey, *Doomsday Weapons in the Hands of Many: The Arms Control Challenge of the '90s* (Urbana: University of Illinois Press, 1991), 9.
4. Schroeer, *Science, Technology, and the Nuclear Arms Race,* 326.
5. Bailey, *Doomsday Weapons,* 13-14.
6. Kim Taewoo et al., "North Korean Nuclear Development," *Korean Journal of Unification Affairs* (in Korean), vol. 3, no. 4 (1991): 134.

7. Leonard S. Spector with Jacqueline R. Smith, *Nuclear Ambitions* (Boulder, CO: Westview Press, 1990), 123.

8. Ibid., note 20, 346. Both of these proliferators began their quest for the bomb in the mid-1960s, just as North Korea was installing its first Soviet-supplied nuclear research reactor.

9. This information is drawn from So Yong Ha, "North's Nuclear Capability Assessed," *Hoguk,* translated in FBIS-EAS, August 3, 1989, 25. By the time the reactor was inspected by the IAEA in June 1992, a dispute had arisen as to its capacity. Western sources had long rated the power of the reactor at about thirty megawatts, presumably based on U.S. intelligence data. When Pyongyang supplied the required declaration of its nuclear sites to the IAEA, however, it listed it at only five megawatts electric power, equal to sixteen megawatts thermal. This seemingly technical issue carried important implications: the higher the reactor's power rating, the more plutonium it would have been producing during its lifetime. By arguably underestimating the reactor's power, North Korean officials might have been attempting to conceal just how much plutonium they had acquired. Or it could have been that the reactor was capable of thirty megawatts of thermal power, but was just strikingly inefficient. These questions could only be resolved through inspections of the reactor designed to measure its level of operation; such inspections would be performed by the IAEA in mid-1992.

10. The KH-11 incident is reported in numerous sources. See, for example, Song Young Sun, "The North Korean Nuclear Issue," *Korea and World Affairs,* vol. 15, no. 3 (Fall 1991): 478; and Joseph Bermudez, "North Korea's Nuclear Programme," *Jane's Intelligence Review,* September 1991, 409. These general dates have been confirmed in interviews with former senior U.S. officials.

11. This account of Soviet assistance appears in a number of articles on the North Korean program. It has been confirmed in interviews with former U.S. and Russian officials. Like the small research reactor provided in 1965, the Soviet power plants promised by Moscow ran on enriched, not natural, uranium. Inasmuch as they were the sole source for North Korea of enriched uranium, Soviet officials may have believed this transfer would actually provide them with added leverage over the North's nuclear program. If uncontrolled, each of these new reactors could produce enough plutonium for more than ten bombs every year.

12. Interviews with South Korean government officials and officials at the U.S. Embassy, Seoul, Korea, October 1992.

13. Cheon Seong W., "Verifying a Denuclearized Korean Peninsula: Current Negotiating Agenda," *Korean Journal of National Unification,* vol. 1, no. 1 (1992): 108-110.

14. Bermudez, "North Korea's Nuclear Programme," 410.

15. See, for example, the comments of Kim Chong Min in FBIS-EAS, November 8, 1991, 31.

16. Kim Taewoo, "South Korea's Nuclear Dilemmas," *Korea and World Affairs,* vol. 16, no. 2 (Summer 1992): 258-59.

17. Kim Taewoo et al., "North Korean Nuclear Development," 139. Indeed the following comments raise the question of how Bermudez is able to conclude that North Korea "apparently" has the technical capability to build an enriched uranium bomb. He does not specify which enrichment method the North might use.

18. David Albright and Mark Hibbs, "Iraq's Quest for the Nuclear Grail: What Can We Learn?" *Arms Control Today,* vol. 22, no. 6 (July-August 1992): 6.

19. At least one South Korean analyst believes the North has used the centrifuge route. "There had been mention four or five years ago," said Yi Chang Kon of the Korea Atomic Energy Research Institute in the spring of 1993, that "North Korea bought some materials related to centrifugal separation from Japan and Europe. There is also a mine in Pyongsan, Hwanghae Province, from which good quality uranium may be obtained. There are an exceptionally large number of buildings in this vicinity. For merely a mine, there is no need for such a large number of buildings. It is thus surmised that uranium reprocessing facilities may be there."

From this and other evidence, Yi concludes simply that "I still believe that North Korea has enriched uranium by centrifugal separation." Interview with Yi in *Wolgan Chosun (Chosun Monthly),* May 1993, 342-46; cited in FBIS-EAS, June 3, 1993, 17. Few other analysts have agreed, however.

20. Leonard Spector, "Threats in the Middle East," *Orbis,* vol. 36, no. 2 (Spring 1992): 182.

21. Albright and Higgs, "Iraq's Quest for the Nuclear Grail," 4-5.

22. Interview with former senior U.S. official, Washington, D.C., September 1994.

23. FBIS-EAS, November 8, 1991, 31.

24. Interviews with nuclear experts, Washington, D.C., December 1992.

25. See the *Naewoe Tongsin* article cited in FBIS-EAS, August 7, 1992, 23.

26. One author provides an interesting parallel here. In the late 1970s, when Brazil was considered a major proliferation risk, this author concluded that "Brazil . . . has large hydroelectric resources far in the interior, where there is little use for electricity; production of enriched reactor-grade U235 might be a convenient way of exploiting that resource"; Schroeer, *Science, Technology, and the Nuclear Arms Race,* 334. Substitute North Korea for Brazil and weapons grade for reactor grade, and the Taechon Hydroelectric Plant takes on a sinister cast.

27. Interviews with nuclear experts, Washington, D.C., December 1992; and South Korean and U.S. Embassy officials, Seoul, Korea, October 1992.

28. *Choson Ilbo* report cited in FBIS-EAS, September 8, 1992, 19.

29. See "North Korea Nuclear Capabilities Reported," a *Joong-ang Ilbo* report cited in FBIS-EAS, May 12, 1989, 17. This rough time frame was confirmed in interviews with former senior U.S. officials, Washington, D.C., September-October, 1993.

30. This information is drawn from Kim, "South Korea's Nuclear Dilemmas," note 8, 260-61.

31. Peter Hayes, "Moving Target—Korea's Nuclear Proliferation Potential," *The Korean Journal of International Studies,* vol. 23, no. 1 (Spring 1992): 123-24.

32. Kim, "South Korea's Nuclear Dilemmas," 257-58; and interviews.

33. Cited in R. Jeffrey Smith, "N. Korea May Consider Reducing Atom Program," *The Washington Post,* June 20, 1992, A14.
34. Song, "The Korean Nuclear Issue," 477.
35. James Hackett, "Close to Producing the Bomb?" *The Washington Times,* November 7, 1991, G4. This same figure appeared in the South Korean Defense *White Paper* for 1994; see the articles in FBIS-EAS, October 19, 1993, 24-25. This information has not, however, appeared in official U.S. testimony on the North Korean program, and some government officials have stressed that it is not based on hard evidence; interviews, Seoul, October 1993.
36. Interviews with former senior U.S. officials, Washington, D.C., September-October, 1993.
37. Kim Taewoo et al., "North Korean Nuclear Development," 135.
38. Personal communication with individuals working with Lewis, December 1992.
39. Interviews with Russian officials, Washington, D.C., December 1993-January 1994.
40. Mikhail Ryzhkov, interviewed in *Joong-ang Ilbo,* cited in FBIS EAS, September 22, 1993, 19.
41. Incident related to the author by Dr. Paul Cole, Washington, D.C., after an interview with the former East German ambassador, 1993.
42. Andrew Mack, "Nuclear Dilemmas: Korean Security in the 1990s," paper delivered at the Fifth Annual CSIS-KIDA Conference, Seoul, Korea, October 14, 1992, 21-22.
43. *Wolgan Chosun* (Chosun Monthly), May 1993, cited in FBIS-EAS, June 3, 1993, 16.
44. Ha, "North's Nuclear Capability Assessed," in FBIS-EAS, 26.
45. This information comes from interviews with former senior U.S. officials, Washington, D.C., October 1993 through September 1994.

CHAPTER FOUR

1. The basic facts come from Andrew Mack, "North Korea and the Bomb," *Foreign Policy,* no. 83 (Summer 1991): 87-104. The accuracy of the event, and Shevardnadze's reply, were confirmed in interviews with Russian officials present in the room with the Soviet and North Korean delegations, Washington, January 1994.
2. The North Korean comments were reported in FBIS-EAS, February 15, 1990, 20-21. See also Mack, "North Korea and the Bomb," 90-91.
3. This was revealed in the March 1992 issue of *Argumenty I Fakty*; cited in FBIS-Soviet, March 17, 1992, 4-5. Later that year, North Korean interest in a bomb may have been intensified by its estrangement from the Soviet Union. Moscow was courting South Korea and appeared to be on the verge of establishing diplomatic relations—a vicious blow to the North, which had steadfastly opposed any form of "two Korea" policy. In September, a North Korean announcement proclaimed that Soviet establishment of diplomatic relations with South Korea, "will leave

us no other choice but to take measures to provide . . . for ourselves some weapons for which we have so far relied on the alliance." That same month, Soviet Foreign Minister Eduard Shevardnadze reportedly met in Pyongyang with DPRK Foreign Minister Kim Young Nam, and Kim threatened to go all-out for the bomb if Moscow recognized South Korea. Mack, "North Korea and the Bomb," 89.

4. Interview with a former senior U.S. official, Washington, February 1994.

5. This potential offer was reported in first two days of the month by a Japanese business daily. See "U.S., Soviets Said to Consider Taking Nukes Out of South Korea," *The Washington Times,* May 3, 1991, 8; and Clayton Jones, "U.S., Soviets Pressure North Korea to Allow Nuclear Inspection," *The Christian Science Monitor,* May 13, 1991, 6.

6. Interviews with former U.S. officials and former senior U.S. officials, Washington, September 1993 through February 1994.

7. Interviews with former U.S. officials, Washington, September and November, 1993.

8. Jim Mann, "U.S. Weighing Deal to End A-Arms in Korea," *The Los Angeles Times,* June 9, 1991, 1. On June 11, State Department spokesman Richard Boucher said that the United States was pledged not to use nuclear weapons against North Korea or any other state party to the NPT. See Don Oberdorfer and T. R. Reid, "North Korea Issues Demand for Mutual Nuclear Inspections," *The Washington Post,* June 21, 1991, A19.

9. T. R. Reid, "N. Korea Will Discuss Nuclear Plant Inspection," *The Washington Post,* May 31, 1991, A24.

10. Song Young Sun, "The Korean Nuclear Issue," *Korea and World Affairs,* vol. 15, no. 3 (Fall 1991): 482.

11. Wolfowitz left out mention of air-delivered systems, it is reported, to test the Koreans' reaction. Don Oberdorfer, "U.S. Decides to Withdraw." On September 23, Presidents Bush and Roh met in New York, and while the issues of U.S. nuclear weapons in Korea and Bush's impending nuclear initiative were not raised, the two leaders did discuss means of continuing pressure on the North to allow nuclear inspections. Yonhap Press Agency cited in FBIS-EAS, September 24, 1991, 18.

12. "We welcome the U.S. announcement," the official statement said, and noted that, if the United States "really withdraws its nuclear weapons from South Korea, the way of our signing the nuclear safeguards agreement will be opened"; *Korea Report* (Tokyo), no. 254 (September 1991): 1-2. Other, similar statements followed. On October 2, in a United Nations speech, DPRK Premier Yon Hyng Muk said that, "if the United States really withdraws its nuclear weapons from South Korea," the way would be open for North Korea to sign an IAEA safeguards agreement; *Korea Report,* no. 255 (October 1991): 1. That same day, DPRK Foreign Minister Kim Yong Nam said the announcement was "good news" and that it was the North's "expectation" that Bush's announcement would result in the removal of all U.S. nuclear weapons from the South. "The broad channel will be open" when that occurred, Kim said, for the North to allow IAEA inspection;

Don Overdorfer, "North Korea Welcomes U.S. Nuclear Withdrawal," *The Washington Post,* October 3, 1991, A40.

13. Interviews with former U.S. officials, Washington, December 1993 and February 1994.

14. Steven Weisman, "North Korea Adds Barriers to A-Plant Inspections," *The New York Times,* October 24, 1991, A11.

15. Cheon Seong W., "Verifying a Denuclearized Korean Peninsula: Current Negotiating Agenda," *The Korean Journal of National Unification,* vol. 1, no. 1 (1992): 110-11.

16. Press reaction in Seoul to this announcement was favorable, but comments in the North were not, as Pyongyang continued to play for direct talks with the United States. A November 10 *Nodong Sinmun* commentary called Roh's announcement "the gesture of empty words by a stooge of nuclear war." It claimed Roh tried to distract attention from the real issue, the presence of U.S. nuclear weapons in the South. The following day, an official North Korean Foreign Ministry statement said "it is needless to explain that this declaration was worked out according to the scenario written by the United States. If the United States intends to truly resolve the nuclear issue in Korea, it should negotiate directly with us. It should not avoid responsibility by using its servant and proxy." Both reported on Pyongyang Central and cited in FBIS-EAS, November 12, 1991, 16-17.

17. "Seoul Renounces Nuclear Weapons," *The Korea Times,* November 9, 1991, 1. The full speech is cited in FBIS-EAS, November 8, 1991, p. 25. Officials said that the ROK had given prior notice to China and Russia of the step and requested their assistance in pressuring the North to follow suit. Yonhap cited in FBIS-EAS, November 8, 1991, 26.

18. "All U.S. Nuclear Arms Will Be Removed at Earliest Date," *The Korea Times,* November 9, 1991, 1.

19. The source said no agreement had been reached on when the withdrawal would be complete. Because they would be pulled back to CONUS, the official claimed, "there is no possibility of their redeployment on our territory after the withdrawal." He stressed, however, that U.S. ships or aircraft carrying nuclear weapons might transit South Korean waters or airspace. Cited in FBIS-EAS, November 13, 1991, 27-28.

20. Pyongyang Korean Central News Agency, cited in FBIS-EAS, September 19, 1990, 15.

21. See *Joong-ang Ilbo* report in FBIS-EAS, September 25, 1991, 19.

22. Yonhap cited in FBIS-EAS, November 15, 1991, 14.

23. *Kyonghyang Sinmun* cited in FBIS-EAS, November 18, 1991, 15.

24. Defense Minister Lee said the two sides "did not talk about forceful military actions because they might encroach upon . . . multilateral diplomatic efforts"; *The Korea Herald,* November 23, cited in FBIS-EAS, November 25, 1991, 17.

25. Yonhap, November 21 cited in FBIS-EAS, November 21, 1991, 12; *Korea Herald,* November 23, cited in FBIS-EAS, November 25, 1991, 17. The 7,000-troop first-phase reduction would go on as planned, but the 6,000 to 7,000-troop second phase was scrapped.

26. David Sanger, "Cheney, in Korea, Orders Halt to U.S. Pullout," *The New York Times,* November 22, 1991, A7.

27. Yonhap cited in FBIS-EAS, November 21, 1991, 13.

28. Cited in FBIS-EAS, November 22, 1991, 20.

29. *Dong-A Ilbo,* cited in FBIS-EAS, November 22, 1991, 19

30. This new offer had in fact first been received when Washington-based Center for Strategic and International Studies Vice President William J. Taylor returned to Seoul from a trip to Pyongyang on November 21 with a version of it. The message was delivered by Taylor to top South Korean and U.S. government officials. See the November 22 Yonhap report in FBIS-EAS, November 22, 1991, 19; the November 23 Yonhap report in FBIS-EAS, November 25, 1991, 24-25; and Kelly Smith Tunney, "Korea—Nuclear," AP Wire report, November 22, 1991.

31. DPRK UN Mission Press Release No. 30, November 26, 1991; for the original statement see FBIS-EAS, November 25, 1991, 6-7. For analysis see Don Oberdorfer, "North Korea Shifts Stance on Inspection," *The Washington Post,* November 27, 1991, A1; and James Sterngold, "North Korea to Allow Nuclear Inspections If U.S. Does," *The New York Times,* November 27, 1991, A3.

32. Yonhap cited in FBIS-EAS, November 29, 1991, 13; the same report appeared as "A-Arm Pullout Said to Begin in Korea," *The Washington Post,* November 29, 1991, A49.

33. Paul Blustein, "U.S. Nuclear Arms All Withdrawn, South Korea Says," *The Washington Post,* December 12, 1991, A6. Earlier, on December 8, according to a *Dong-A Ilbo* report of December 16, Ronald Lehman, the Director of the U.S. Arms Control and Disarmament Agency, secretly visited Seoul and told ROK officials that the United States had unofficially informed Pyongyang that all nuclear weapons were out of the South, and had proposed a trade-off: inspections of the Yongbyon nuclear facility and Sunchon airfield in the North, and the Kunsan airbase (rumored to have held U.S. tactical nuclear weapons) along with a civilian nuclear site in the South. Cited in FBIS-EAS, December 16, 1991, 24-25.

34. Both from David Sanger, "Seoul to Permit Nuclear Inspections," *The New York Times,* December 11, 1991, A5.

35. Yonhap cited in FBIS-EAS, December 3, 1991, p. 16. In a December 20 *Washington Post* op-ed, Stephen Rosenfeld outlined this strategy well some two weeks after Lee's statement. He argued that "There is no more fateful political scheme unfolding in the world than the notably bold and imaginative—and risky—strategy by which South Korea, the United States and others are trying to stop Communist North Korea from going nuclear." The strategy: the bomb's "renunciation could make it the prime vehicle of the pariah state's reinvention as an accepted neighbor and world citizen. The allies intend to take advantage of North Korea's isolation and backwardness by offering it a prospect of international acceptance and economic rescue." Rosenfeld, "Korean Gamble," *The Washington Post,* December 20, 1991, A27.

36. Interview with a former South Korean official, Washington, January 1994.

37. Interview with former senior U.S. official, Washington, September 1994.

38. Interviews with former senior U.S. officials, Washington, September and October, 1993.
39. For one text of the agreement, see FBIS-EAS, December 13, 1991, 11-13.
40. Information on the secret meetings comes from a *Joong-ang Ilbo* report of February 1, 1993, cited in FBIS-EAS, February 1, 1993, 22.
41. See "A Cautious Race to the North," *Asiaweek,* March 27, 1992, 53-55; and Mark Clifford, "The Daewoo Comrade," *Far Eastern Economic Review,* February 20, 1992, 47-48.
42. There had been some discussion of cancelling Team Spirit in 1991, but given concerns already raised that the Persian Gulf War would tempt North Korea to believe that the United States was distracted from Asia, it was decided to wait until 1992. Interviews with former U.S. officials, Washington, D.C., November 1993.
43. Yonhap report cited in FBIS-EAS, December 16, 1991, 22.
44. Interviews with former U.S. officials and senior officials in Seoul and Washington, September 1993 through February 1994.
45. Interviews with former senior U.S. officials, Washington, December 1993 and January 1994.
46. Interviews with former senior U.S. officials, Washington, September through November, 1993.
47. Speech cited in FBIS-EAS, December 18, 1991, 13-14.
48. Transcript of Boucher press briefing, December 18, 1991.
49. The demands for bilateral talks with Washington continued as well. "It has become clear to everyone that, for simultaneous inspections to occur," the statement contended, "we must negotiate with the United States as a matter of course, as this country deployed that nuclear weapons in South Korea." Cited in FBIS-EAS, December 23, 1991, 11.
50. Yonhap report cited in FBIS-EAS, December 23, 1991, 17.
51. Cheon, "Verifying a Denuclearized Korean Peninsula," 115.
52. Yonhap report in FBIS-EAS, December 26, 1991, 20. In addition to the North-South forum, Ho Jong, in Tokyo, also noted that Pyongyang's representatives were engaged in talks with the IAEA on signing an agreement; *Dong-A Ilbo* story in FBIS-EAS, December 26, 1991, 20-21.
53. "Koreans Make Gains But Remain Short of an Accord, Says Seoul," *The Washington Post,* December 27, 1991, A18.
54. Robin Bulman, "Koreas Fail to Agree on Nuclear Ban," *The Washington Post,* December 26, 1991, p. A25.
55. The text reads: "Pledging to remove the danger of a nuclear war, to create conditions and circumstances favorable to peaceful unification of our country and to further contribute toward peace and security in Asia and the world by denuclearizing the Korean peninsula, the South and the North declare as follows:
    1. The South and the North will not test, manufacture, produce, introduce, possess, store, deploy or use nuclear weapons.
    2. The South and the North will use nuclear energy solely for peaceful purposes.

3. The South and the North will not possess nuclear reprocessing and uranium enrichment facilities.

4. The South and the North, in order to verify the denuclearization of the Korean peninsula, will conduct inspections of the facilities as chosen by the other side in accordance with procedures and means to be provided by the Joint South-North Nuclear Control Committee.

5. The South and the North, in order to implement the joint declaration, will form and operate the Joint South-North Nuclear Control Committee within one month after the joint declaration takes effect.

This joint declaration will take effect from the day when the South and the North exchange documents after going through the necessary formalities for their effectuation." Cited by *Korea Times* in FBIS-EAS, January 2, 1992, 21.

56. "Two Koreas Agree on Nuclear Ban, But Not on Method of Inspections," *The New York Times,* January 1, 1992, 2.

57. See *Joong-ang Ilbo,* April 5, 1992; cited in FBIS-EAS, April 7, 1992, 13-15.

58. Terrance Kiernan, "Bush Allays Seoul Fears By Assuaging N. Korea," *Defense News,* January 13, 1992, 6; David Sanger, "Bush Warns Seoul on Pace of Pacts with North Korea," *The New York Times,* January 6, 1992, A1; and Sanger, "Bush and Seoul Leader Offer to Drop War Games," *The New York Times,* January 7, 1992, A8.

U.S. officials, including President Bush, reportedly urged a harder line. One press account said that "After several remarkable agreements intended to end four decades of war and hostility between the two Koreas, President Bush arrived here today and quietly warned the South Korean leadership against moving too fast in dealings with the Communist North before hard evidence emerges that it is ending reported efforts to produce nuclear weapons." The report called Bush's remarks an "implicit criticism" to which Roh replied by saying "we think it is important to start the process of change in the North," which was "better than backing [Kim Il Sung] into a corner." It said that critics in Seoul worried that Roh's rapid pace of contacts was politically motivated; Sanger, "Bush Warns Seoul," A1. The essential accuracy of these reports was confirmed in an interview with a former senior South Korean official, Washington, D.C., February 1994.

59. Frank J. Murray, "Nuclear Talks with North Korea Likely Soon," *The Washington Times,* January 7, 1992, A1.

60. Frank J. Murray, "Nuclear Talks Are Set With North Korea," *The Washington Times,* January 9, 1992, A3.

61. Some of the information is drawn from news reports, such as the story in *Chosun Ilbo* on January 29; cited in FBIS-EAS, January 29, 1992, 38; most of the following details come from interviews with former U.S. officials and senior officials, December 1993 and February 1994.

62. See William Clark, Jr., "What Does North Korea Ultimately Want?" *International Herald Tribune,* November 3, 1993, 23.

63. Interviews with former U.S. officials and high-ranking officials, Washington, November 1993 and February 1994.

64. Interviews with former senior U.S. officials, Washington, December 1993 and February 1994.

65. Sanger, "Bush and Seoul Leader."

66. "North Korea Praises Seoul War Games Halt," *The Washington Times,* January 9, 1992, A2.

67. That same day a Foreign Affairs Ministry spokesman made an announcement in Pyongyang, saying in part:

> Our signing of the safeguards accord at this time is a brilliant fruition of the consistent and tireless efforts of the government of our Republic for a fair implementation of the NPT in conformity with the mission and idea of the treaty and a result of the response of the United States and the South Korean authorities to our principled demand. . . . When we undergo an inspection with the signing of the safeguards accord this time, the shady background of the false row and anti-DPRK campaign of some countries . . . resorting to all intrigues to create the impression that we "are developing nuclear weapons," will be fully laid bare. We mean what we say. We do not like empty words.
>
> Report from Pyongyang Radio cited in FBIS-EAS,
> January 31, 1992, 14-16.

68. Steven R. Wesiman, "North Korea Signs Accord on Atom-Plant Inspections," *The New York Times,* January 31, 1992, 2.

69. Yonhap report cited in FBIS-EAS, February 4, 1992, 21.

70. Yonhap report cited in FBIS-EAS, February 24, 1992, 17.

71. Elaine Sciolino, "CIA Chief Says North Koreans Plan to Make Secret Atom Arms," *The New York Times,* February 26, 1992, 1.

72. Elaine Sciolino, "U.S. Agencies Split Over North Korea," *The New York Times,* March 10, 1992, A1.

73. *Korea Times* cited in FBIS-EAS, February 24, 1992, 18.

74. Japan did face a complication of its own. Tokyo planned to import vast amounts of plutonium from Europe to burn in its civilian reactors. Thus some Japanese officials believed that they could not in good conscience demand the dismantlement of a plutonium reprocessing facility in North Korea while buying plutonium from similar operations in Britain and France; "Japan, Korea and the Bomb," *The Economist Foreign Report,* November 28, 1991, 1.

75. Interviews with U.S. Embassy and Japanese Foreign Ministry officials, Tokyo, October 1992.

76. See Edward A. Olsen, "The Politics of Adversary Relations: The United States, Japan, and North Korea," *Korea Observer,* vol. 14, no. 4 (Winter 1983): 354-59; and Shin Jung Hyun, "North Korea and South Korea-Japan Relations," *Korea Observer,* vol. 16, no. 4 (Winter 1985): 380-399.

77. George O. Totten, "Japan's Policy Toward North Korea," *Korea Observer,* vol. 16, no. 2 (Summer 1985): 134-48.

78. Denny Roy, "North Korea's Relations with Japan: The Legacy of War," *Asian Survey,* vol. 28, no. 12 (December 1988): 1285-87.

79. Jin Park, "Japan-North Korea Rapprochement: Issues and Prospects," *Japan Forum,* vol. 4, no 2 (October 1992): 330-333; and interviews with U.S. and Japanese officials, Tokyo, October 1992.
80. Interviews with Japanese officials, Tokyo, October 1992.
81. For this very reason, some more nationalistic South Korean analysts give Tokyo little credit for its role on this issue; interviews with South Korean academics, Seoul, October 1992.
82. Interviews with U.S. and Japanese officials, Tokyo, October 1992.
83. Thomas L. Friedman, "China Stalls Anti-Atom Effort On Korea," *The New York Times,* November 15, 1991, A12.
84. Michael Z. Wise, "IAEA Says Agreement Near on Check of N. Korean Sites," *The Washington Post,* February 26, 1992, A32.
85. Yonhap report cited in FBIS-EAS, February 26, 1992, 15.
86. David Sanger, "North Korea Assembly Backs Atom Pact," *The New York Times,* April 10, 1992, A3.
87. Don Oberdorfer, "North Korea Describes Nuclear Reactor Program," *The Washington Post,* April 15, 1992, A32. On the same day, North Korea also released a videotape of what it claimed were nuclear power plants at Yongbyon. It was not immediately clear what, if any, new information the tapes would reveal. David Sanger, "North Korea Shows Video of Atom Site," *The New York Times,* April 16, 1992, A3.

CHAPTER FIVE

1. The agency, its budget, and operations are described in U.S. General Accounting Office, *Nuclear Nonproliferation and Safety* (Washington, D.C.: General Accounting Office, September 1993), 14-19.
2. See report in FBIS-EAS, September 24, 1991, 19.
3. *Korea Times* article, reprinted in FBIS-EAS, October 28, 1991, 30.
4. See the report in FBIS-EAS, December 4, 1991, 17.
5. See "DPRK Government Clarifies Its Stand on Signing Nuclear Safeguards Accord," Press Release No. 30, DPRK Permanent Mission to the United Nations, November 26, 1991.
6. See the *Dong-A Ilbo* article translated in FBIS-EAS, December 26, 1991, 20-21.
7. See "DPRK Ratifies IAEA Nuclear Safeguards Agreement," IAEA Press Release 92/20, April 10, 1992.
8. Interviews with U.S. and South Korean officials, Washington and Seoul, October 1992.
9. Don Oberdorfer, "North Korea Describes Nuclear Reactor Program," *The Washington Post,* April 15, 1992, A32.
10. David Sanger, "North Korea Shows Video of Atom Site," *The New York Times,* April 16, 1992, A3.
11. See the *Joong-ang Ilbo* report reprinted in FBIS-EAS on March 18, 1994, 36.
12. Paris AFP report cited in FBIS-EAS, May 5, 1992, 12.

13. See KBS radio and Yonhap news reports translated in FBIS-EAS, May 4, 1992, 8.

14. Official statement translated in FBIS-EAS, May 5, 1992, 11-12.

15. "DPRK Submits Initial Report," IAEA Press Release 92-24, May 5, 1992.

16. Facts in this section, unless cited otherwise,are drawn from Sheryl WuDunn, "North Korean Site Has A-Bomb Hints," *The New York Times,* May 16, 1992, A1; and "IAEA Director General Completes Official Visit to the DPRK," IAEA Press Release 92-25, May 15, 1992.

17. David Albright, "North Korea Drops Out," *The Bulletin of the Atomic Scientists,* May 1993, 10; and R. Jeffrey Smith, "North Korea and the Bomb: High-Tech Hide and Seek," *The Washington Post,* April 27, 1993, A11.

18. R. Jeffrey Smith, "N. Korea May Consider Reducing Atom Program," *The Washington Post,* June 20, 1992, A14.

19. Don Oberdorfer, "N. Korea is Far From A-Bomb, Video Indicates," *The Washington Post,* June 4, 1992, A18.

20. This demand was made repeatedly during the latter half of 1992. See, for example, the official statement on September 15, 1992, broadcast on the Pyongyang Central Broadcasting Network and cited in FBIS-EAS, September 15, 1992, 4-5; and the comments of Ambassador-at-Large O Chang Rim, FBIS-EAS, September 17, 1992, 26. Occasionally, North Korean officials also made reference to the U.S. nuclear "umbrella" over South Korea, apart from the presence of actual U.S. tactical nuclear weapons there; see the *Nodong Sinmun* essay cited in FBIS-EAS, August 3, 1992, 8.

21. Cited in FBIS-EAS, October 22, 1992, 21.

22. See, for example, the comments of DPRK Ambassador to Austria Pak Si Ung in FBIS-EAS, August 3, 1992, 6.

23. KBS media report cited in FBIS-EAS, July 21, 1992, 20.

24. See generally the *Korea Times* article cited in FBIS-EAS, August 10, 1992, 22.

25. Yonhap report cited in FBIS-EAS, August 10, 1992, 21.

26. Yonhap and *Chosun Ilbo* reports cited in FBIS-EAS, August 10, 1993, 23.

27. KBS news report cited in FBIS-EAS, August 31, 1992, 10.

28. Cited in FBIS-EAS, September 22, 1992, 8-9.

29. Cited in FBIS-EAS, September 15, 1992, 4-5.

30. Yonhap report cited in FBIS-EAS, September 17, 1992, 26.

31. Reaction to this accord was not unanimous. While the *Korea Herald* proclaimed the "impressive array of achievements" at the meeting, *Chosun Ilbo* worried about the "pitfalls and loopholes" in the agreement and argued that the North "has shown no sign of moving toward reconciliation." Both cited in FBIS-EAS, September 21, 1992, 15-16.

32. David E. Sanger, "North Korea's A-Bomb Plans Seem Less Perilous," *The New York Times,* September 18, 1992, A10.

33. See the reports in FBIS-EAS, September 21, 1992, 12-13 and 16-18.

34. See the reports in FBIS-EAS, September 21, 1992, 16-17.

35. Yonhap report cited in FBIS-EAS, September 21, 1992, 17-18.

36. Yonhap report cited in FBIS-EAS, September 29, 1992, 16.

37. Reports cited in FBIS-EAS, September 22, 1992, 9-10.

38. Cited in FBIS-EAS, September 29, 1992, 2; full article carried in FBIS-EAS, October 2, 1992, 8-10.

39. KBS report cited in FBIS-EAS, September 30, 1992, 17.

40. Cited in FBIS-EAS, September 28, 1992, 4-6.

41. Cited in FBIS-EAS, September 28, 1992, 6-8.

42. Interviews with serving and former South Korean officials, Seoul, December 1992 and October 1993; and interviews with former senior U.S. officials, Washington, November and December 1993.

43. See the South Korean media reports contained in FBIS-EAS, September 9, 1992, 26.

44. Yonhap report cited in FBIS-EAS, October 1, 1992, 21.

45. Yonhap reports in FBIS-EAS, October 6, 1992, 11-12.

46. *Korea Times* report in FBIS-EAS, October 8, 1992, 20; and Yonhap report, FBIS-EAS, October 13, 1992, 47. For other information on the spy ring case, see FBIS-EAS, October 14, 1992, 20-21; October 20, 29; and October 29, 35.

47. Pyongyang KCNA broadcasts from the Committee for the Peaceful Reunification of the Fatherland, FBIS-EAS, October 9, 1992, 19-21.

48. Committee for the Peaceful Reunification of the Fatherland, cited in FBIS-EAS, October 9, 1992, 21-23. See also FBIS-EAS, October 7, 1992, 22-24.

49. For this action and the North Korean response, see FBIS-EAS, October 9, 1992, 24-25.

50. Yonhap reports in FBIS-EAS, October 13, 1992, 45-46.

51. Interview with a former senior South Korean official, Washington, February 1994.

52. Interview with a former senior South Korean official, Washington, February 1994.

53. Cited in FBIS-EAS, October 5, 1992, 9; cf. 8-10.

54. See the Yonhap reports on the SCM in FBIS-EAS, October 13, 1992, 49-50.

55. This information come from interviews with former senior U.S. officials, Washington, September and October, 1993; and interviews with Korean academics and officials, Seoul, October 1993.

56. Interview with former senior U.S. official, Washington, September 1994.

57. Interviews with current and former South Korean officials, Seoul, October 1993.

58. See FBIS-EAS, October 8, 1992, 6-7.

59. Cited in FBIS-EAS, October 13, 1992, 17; cf. same day, 16-20.

60. See FBIS-EAS, October 22, 1992, 21.

61. Cited in FBIS-EAS, October 23, 1992, 21.

62. Don Oberdorfer, "North Korean A-Arms Danger is Downgraded," *The Washington Post,* November 1, 1992, A34.

63. Statement of Kong No Myong, ROK spokesman for the North-South prime ministerial talks; FBIS-EAS, November 3, 1992, 27.

64. Of course, opinions differ as to the pledge actually made by South Korea and the United States. All published accounts support the ROK and U.S. contention that a *permanent* cancellation of Team Spirit was never promised; in 1991 and early 1992, ROK and U.S. officials offered to *suspend* the exercise for one year. North

Korean officials may have taken this to be a tacit signal that, once suspended, the exercise would not recur; or they could have understood the ROK and U.S. position perfectly well and merely lied to gain additional concessions. Either way, however, South Korean and U.S. officials most certainly recognized the real and severe tension between their nonproliferation goals and a resumption of Team Spirit.

65. Yonhap and *Joong-ang Ilbo* stories cited in FBIS-EAS, November 27, 1992, 21.
66. FBIS-EAS, December 14, 1992, 22.
67. Albright, "North Korea Drops Out," 10; the timing of the two inspections comes from Smith, "North Korea and the Bomb," A11.
68. Mark Hibbs, "Isotopics Show Three North Korean Reprocessing Campaigns Since 1975," *NuclearFuel,* March 1, 1993, 8-9. See also David E. Sanger, "West Knew of North Korea Nuclear Development," *The New York Times,* March 13, 1993, 3. Samples taken from the North Korean sites were analyzed at the IAEA laboratory at Seibersdorf, Austria, and at affiliated laboratories in Europe and the United States, including McClellan Central Laboratory near Sacramento, California; Albright, "North Korea Drops Out," 10, and Smith, "North Korea and the Bomb," A11.
69. Information from Albright, "North Korea Drops Out," 10, and Smith, "North Korea and the Bomb," A11.
70. Information from Albright, "North Korea Drops Out," 10-11; and Smith, "North Korea and the Bomb," A11.
71. Smith, "North Korea and the Bomb," A11.
72. KBS news report cited in FBIS-EAS, December 1, 1992, 19; Blix request dated to December per Smith, "North Korea and the Bomb," A11.
73. On January 29, for example, the DPRK Foreign Ministry issued a detailed analysis of U.S. nuclear deployments in the South and South Korea's own nuclear weapons program. See FBIS-EAS, February 1, 1993, 10-16.
74. North Korean media report cited in FBIS-EAS, December 11, 1992, 29-30.
75. Michael Gordon, "Korea Rebuffs Nuclear Inspectors," *The New York Times,* February 1, 1993, A9.
76. Albright, "North Korea Drops Out," 9.
77. Timothy Noah, "Energy Agency Asks Special Probe of Korean Facility," *The Wall Street Journal,* February 12, 1993, A10. See also FBIS-EAS, February 10, 1993, 20; February 11, 1993, 19-20; and February 12, 1993, 15-18.
78. Cited in FBIS-EAS, February 16, 1993, 15.
79. Cited in Associated Press wire report by Alexander Higgins, February 16, 1993.
80. David Ignatius, "Russia Turns Away From North Korea," *The Wall Street Journal,* February 12, 1993, p. A10; KBS news report, cited in FBIS-EAS, February 1, 1993, p. 21.
81. Cited in FBIS-EAS, February 16, 1993, 26.
82. Yonhap and KBS reports cited in FBIS-EAS, February 16, 1993, A27; and FBIS-EAS, February 17, 1993, 39-40.
83. Higgs, "Isotopics," 8; "hot cells" information in Albright, "North Korea Drops Out," 10.

84. Statement cited in FBIS-EAS, February 22, 1993, 13-19.
85. Patrick Worsnip, "North Korean Envoy Says Nuclear Accord with IAEA in Peril," Associated Press wire report, February 22, 1993. It is interesting to speculate what these officials meant. In literal terms, they seemed to be saying that the IAEA demand would force the North to renounce its agreement *with the IAEA*—the full-scope safeguards agreement approved by the North in April 1992. This would not necessarily require the North to withdraw from the NPT as well; after all, it had joined the NPT in December 1985 and not allowed its first IAEA inspection for nearly seven years. This distinction was perhaps why Western analysts seemed stunned that the North had decided to abandon both accords and not just the one in March 1993.
86. This story is told in Smith, "North Korea and the Bomb," A1, A11. On February 24, new U.S. CIA Director R. James Woolsey testified before the U.S. Congress on, among other things, the status of the North Korean nuclear program. His comments reflected a far different approach to those of Roh Tae Woo and ACDA Director Lehman the previous year, and emphasized the imminence of the North Korean nuclear threat.
87. IAEA Press Release PR 93/6, February 25, 1993.
88. Yonhap report in FBIS-EAS, February 25, 1993, 12.
89. See the comments cited in FBIS-EAS, February 26, 1993, 7-8; and FBIS-EAS, March 1, 1993, 19-23.
90. "Order No. 0034 of the KPA Supreme Commander," Pyongyang, March 8, 1993, printed in *Pyongyang Times,* March 13, 1993, 1.
91. Cited in FBIS-EAS, February 22, 1993, 11-13.

CHAPTER SIX

1. Cited in a *Chosun Ilbo* story, FBIS-EAS, October 20, 1993, 26.
2. The existence and basic shape of the Defense Department proposal was confirmed in interviews with current and former Defense and State officials, Washington, 1994.
3. "Statement of DPRK Government Declaring Withdrawal from NPT," March 12, 1993, mimeograph copy, North Korean Mission to the United Nations, 2.
4. Ibid., 2.
5. Ibid., 3-4. On the 12th, the North Korean ambassador to China, Chu Chang Jin, explicitly claimed that the withdrawal did not signal the North's intention to proliferate. "We have neither the plan or ability to produce nuclear weapons," said Chu; "Pyongyang Envoy Says His Country Would Counter Any Sanctions," Yonhap wire report, March 12, 1993.
6. David E. Sanger, "Son of North Korean Leader May Be Succeeding to Power," *The New York Times,* March 25, 1993, A10. This view was endorsed by former CIA Director Robert Gates during a television interview in late March 1993.
7. See the comments of Yoo He Yeol of the Research Institute for Unification, cited in T. R. Reid, "North Korea's New Nuclear Deadline Nears," *The Washington Post,* March 30, 1993, A14.

8. Nicholas Eberstadt, "North Korea: Reform, Muddling Through, or Collapse?" The National Bureau of Asian Research *Analysis,* vol. 4, no. 3 (September 1993): 15.

9. See *Joong-ang Ilbo* report in FBIS-EAS, September 25, 1991, 19.

10. This latter theory is suggested by Ha Yong Son of Seoul National University in *Wolgan Chosun,* cited in FBIS-EAS, May 26, 1993, 20-21.

11. "Government Expresses Grave Concern About Pyongyang's Withdrawal from NPT," press release, Korean Overseas Information Service, March 12, 1993; and "Seoul Urges North Korea Not To Quit the Nonproliferation Pact," mimeographed statement, Korean Information Office, South Korean Embassy, Washington, D.C., March 12, 1993.

12. David E. Sanger, "South Korea Puts Troops on Alert as 'Precaution,'" *The New York Times,* March 14, 1993, A6.

13. Yonhap report cited in FBIS-EAS, March 15, 1993, 28.

14. David E. Sanger, "North Korea Hit By First Sanctions," *The New York Times,* March 16, 1993, A3.

15. Yonhap report cited in FBIS-EAS, March 16, 1993, 27.

16. See reports cited in FBIS-EAS, March 23, 1993, 14-16.

17. Associated Press wire stories by George Gedda, March 12, 1993, and Alan Elsner, March 12, 1993. The full text of the Boucher press conference can be found in the Federal News Service State Department briefing transcript, March 12, 1993.

18. See the comments of an ROK Foreign Ministry official in "Seoul Goes Into Emergency Meetings," Yonhap wire report, March 12, 1993.

19. "IAEA Begins to Take Steps Against Pyongyang's Withdrawal from the NPT," Yonhap wire story, March 12, 1993. Later, the Board of Govervors meeting was set for March 18 or 19, and the Security Council option was reaffirmed; see "IAEA to Refer DPRK Nuclear Issue to UNSC," Yonhap cited in FBIS-EAS, March 15, 1993, 16.

20. "North Korea Expels Diplomats" and "North Korea Denies Foreigners Access," Yonhap wire reports, March 12, 1993; Andrew Steele, "Communist North Korea Reneges on Nuclear Pact," Reuters wire report, March 12, 1993; and "DPRK Orders All Delegations Abroad to Return Home," *Seoul Sinmun* cited in FBIS-EAS, March 15, 1993, 27-28.

21. Nicholas D. Kristof, "A North Korean Warning," *The New York Times,* March 13, 1993, A3.

22. "On the Truth of Nuclear Inspection by IAEA in DPRK," Memorandum of the DPRK Foreign Ministry, cited in FBIS-EAS, March 15, 1993, 11-14. For other DPRK statements during this period, see FBIS-EAS, March 15, 1993, 15-27, and March 16, 10-19.

23. Interview with former Clinton administration official, Washington, September 1994.

24. See, for example, "Apocalypse Asia," *The Economist,* March 20, 1993, 20; "North Korea's Bomb Threat," *The Wall Street Journal,* March 17, 1993, A14; and the comments of Rep. John Murtha (D-PA), who said on March 17 that mil-

itary strikes might be required even if it meant the risk of wider war. "There's no question we would have to be prepared to go to war" if the United States launched strikes against the North Korean nuclear facilities, Murtha solemnly intoned, "but it's that important to me"; cited in Associated Press wire report by Barry Schweid, March 17, 1993.

25. Douglas Jehl, "U.S. Pressing Plan on Arms Pact To Force North Korea to Comply," *The New York Times,* March 13, 1993, A3.

26. "S. Korea Rules Out Economic Ties with N. Korea Over Nuclear Issue," UPI wire report, March 15, 1993.

27. One early decision that confronted South Korean and U.S. policymakers was whether to bolster the U.S. troop contingent in South Korea. Press reports indicated that Seoul had requested that Washington leave in place the roughly 19,000 U.S. troops, F-117 stealth bombers, aircraft carrier USS *Independence,* and other equipment that had been brought over for Team Spirit. See "ROK May Ask U.S. Troops to Remain," Yonhap report cited in FBIS-EAS, March 16, 1993, 26. The ROK government clarified this position by noting that, because U.S. troops were not scheduled to depart immediately upon the end of Team Spirit (on March 18) in any case, Seoul could wait to request that the troops stay; one official said Seoul would "formulate appropriate measures after assessing North Korea's behavior during this period"; "ROK Defense Ministry on Withdrawal," *Dong-A Ilbo* cited in FBIS-EAS, March 16, 1993, 30.

The exercise had already raised tensions on the peninsula, prompting Kim Jong Il's declaration of a "semi-war footing"; on March 15 DPRK Ambassador Ri Tcheul said in Geneva that "a hair-trigger situation has been created that could lead to an outbreak of war at any moment." See John Burton, "North Korea Heightens Tension with Threat of War 'At Any Time,'" *Financial Times,* March 16, 1993, 1. While no unusual military movements were detected in the North (see "No Signs of Military Movement," Yonhap report cited in FBIS-EAS, March 16, 1993, 25), the risk of war seemed palpable. After some discussion, South Korea decided not to leave the Team Spirit forces in South Korea and to withdraw them as scheduled. This decision was reportedly taken in Seoul and supported by Washington, and was designed to reduce tensions on the peninsula. It was interpreted as a conciliatory gesture toward Pyongyang.

28. Don Oberdorfer, "South Korean: U.S. Agrees to Plan to Pressure North," *The Washington Post,* March 30, 1993, A14. See also David E. Sanger, "Neighbors Differ on How to Chasten North Korea," *The New York Times,* March 31, 1993, A9.

29. Douglas Jehl, "Seoul Eases Stand on Nuclear Inspections of North," *The New York Times,* March 30, 1993, A13.

30. Alan Elsner, "U.S. Takes Mild Approach to Korean Nuclear Threat," Reuters wire report, March 16, 1993.

31. "North Korea Gets U.N. Deadline," *The New York Times,* March 19, 1993, A8.

32. Don Oberdorfer and R. Jeffrey Smith, "U.S., Asian Allies Discuss N. Korea Arms Inspections," *The Washington Post,* March 24, 1993, A6.

33. Elaine Kurtenbach, "N. Korea Says Its 'Semiwar' Is Over," *The Washington Times,* March 25, 1993, 1.

34. See "ROK Seeks PRC Influence," KBS Television report cited in FBIS-EAS, March 16, 1993, 32.
35. Interviews with former senior U.S. officials, Washington, September and October, 1993.
36. Associated Press wire report by Gene Kramer, March 27, 1993.
37. Cited in Warren Strobel, "Defiant N. Korea Tests U.S. Effort to Control Nukes," *The Washington Times,* March 30, 1993, 1.
38. Nicholas D. Kristof, "China Opposes U.N. Over North Korea," *The New York Times,* March 24, 1993, A6. On March 24, *People's Daily* quoted Qian as saying that "China opposes international sanctions against the DPRK for its decision to withdraw from the NPT." Qian argued that the NPT "does not include rules to punish those who stay away or pull out." Cited in U.S. Information Agency, *Media Reaction,* March 25, 1993, 3.
39. Associated Press wire report, March 23, 1993.
40. "China Says No Evidence N. Korea Has Nuclear Bombs," Reuters wire report, April 8, 1993; "China Insists on Dialogue, Not Pressure, on North Korea," UPI wire report, April 8, 1993.
41. In private moments, in fact, Chinese officials can be more caustic about Kim Il Sung's regime than any of their Western counterparts—a contempt bred by familiarity. Interviews in Beijing, October 1991, and March 1993.
42. Yonhap report cited in FBIS-EAS, May 17, 1993, 20.
43. Lena H. Sun and Jackson Diehl, "Arms Issue Reported Causing Rifts Between China, N. Korea," *The Washington Post,* April 28, 1993, A13; and Bill Gertz and Warren Strobel, "N. Korea Masses Troops," *The Washington Times,* April 30, 1993, 1.
44. "Ministry Denies 'Shooting Incident' At PRC Border," Pyongyang KCNA cited in FBIS-EAS, May 3, 1993, 9-10.
45. This allegation is cited in a *Chugan Chosun* report of August 19, 1993; carried in FBIS-EAS, October 14, 1993, 41.
46. The information in this paragraph is drawn from interview with former senior U.S. officials, Washington, September-October, 1993.
47. Shim Sung Won, "South Korea Steps Up Efforts to Settle Nuclear Dispute," Reuters wire report, April 4, 1993.
48. "South Korean President Wants Moderate Response to North," Reuters wire report, April 6, 1993.
49. "North Korea Calls for Direct U.S. Talks on Nuclear Inspections," UPI wire report, April 5, 1993.
50. "North Korea Not Afraid of War in Nuclear Dispute—Envoy," Reuters wire report, April 7, 1993.
51. Douglas Jehl, "U.S. Agrees to Discuss Arms Directly with North Korea," *The New York Times,* April 23, 1993, A10.
52. "IAEA Inspection Team Leaves for DPRK," Yonhap cited in FBIS-EAS, May 4, 1993, 13.
53. "U.S., DPRK Hold Talks in Beijing," Yonhap report cited in FBIS-EAS, May 6, 1993, 15.

54. Douglas Jehl, "U.S. Sees Conciliatory Atom Steps by North Korea," *The New York Times,* May 13, 1993, A11.

55. South Korea's UN Ambassador, Yu Chong Ha, described the process as "difficult" and "agonizing"; see *Dong-A Ilbo* report cited in FBIS-EAS, May 17, 1993, 22. Other information came from interviews with former high-ranking U.S. officials, Washington, September and October, 1993. See also *Chosun Ilbo* report cited in FBIS-EAS, May 5, 1993, 18-19, and Yonhap report cited in FBIS-EAS, May 7, 1993, 18-19. The outset of the process is cited by Warren Strobel, "U.S. Tries to Craft U.N. Resolution Spelling Out Demands on N. Korea," *The Washington Times,* April 23, 1993, 7.

56. See Pyongyang media articles in FBIS-EAS, May 14, 1993, 21-24.

57. Interviews with former senior U.S. officials, Washington, September and October, 1993.

58. "N. Korea Says Talks with U.S. Are Near," *The Washington Times,* May 18, 1993, 7; and Yonhap report, cited in FBIS-EAS, May 18, 1993, 11.

59. R. Jeffrey Smith, "U.S., North Korea Set High-Level Meeting on Nuclear Program," *The Washington Post,* May 25, 1993, A14.

60. Yonhap report cited in FBIS-EAS, May 20, 1993, 16.

61. Yonhap report cited in FBIS-EAS, May 25, 1993, 23.

62. See the South Korean media reports in FBIS-EAS, May 28, 1993, 14-15, 16-18.

63. David E. Sanger, "North Korea Stirs New A-Arms Fears," *The New York Times,* May 6, 1993, A7.

64. Yonhap report cited in FBIS-EAS, May 14, 1993, 35.

65. Sanger, "North Korea Stirs New A-Arms Fears."

66. Interviews with South Korean academics and government officials, Seoul, October 1993.

67. Interview carried in *Sin Tong-A* and translated in FBIS-EAS, October 19, 1993, 28.

68. Cited in FBIS-EAS, May 11, 1993, 29.

69. *Korea Herald* article cited in FBIS-EAS, June 2, 1993, 23.

70. One example was opposition Democratic Party lawmaker Kang Chang Song, who said in October 1993 that "Our country not only needs facilities for the peaceful use of nuclear energy, such as the nuclear reprocessing facilities and uranium enrichment facilities, but it should have the capability of producing nuclear weapons"; cited in FBIS-EAS, October 12, 1993, 36-37.

71. David E. Sanger, "Wary of North Korea, Seoul Debates Building Atomic Bomb," *The New York Times,* March 19, 1993, A8.

72. Cited in FBIS-EAS, October 12, 1993, 34-36; and October 26, 1993, 33.

73. *Chosun Ilbo,* cited in FBIS-EAS, October 12, 1993, 34.

74. *Joong-ang Ilbo* article cited in FBIS-EAS, June 1, 1993, 21.

75. Smith, "U.S., North Korea Set High-Level Meeting."

76. "U.S., North Korea Hold Nuclear Talks," *The Washington Post,* June 3, 1993, A26.

77. Yonhap report cited in FBIS-EAS, June 3, 1993, 7.

78. Douglas Jehl, "North Korea Isn't Convinced It Should Stay in Nuclear Pact," *The New York Times,* June 5, 1993, I3.

79. Peter James Spielmann, "U.S., North Korea Fail to Break Nuclear Deadlock, Talks To Resume," Associated Press wire report, June 10, 1993.
80. The text of the joint statement can be found in FBIS-EAS, June 14, 1993, 13.
81. Douglas Jehl, "North Korea Says It Won't Pull Out of Arms Pact Now," *The New York Times,* June 12, 1993, 1.
82. KBS radio report cited in FBIS-EAS, June 14, 1993, 22-23; and Yonhap report cited in FBIS-EAS, June 14, 1993, 23.
83. Yonhap report cited in FBIS-EAS, June 14, 1993, 24.
84. Yonhap report cited in FBIS-EAS, June 14, 1993, 23.

CHAPTER SEVEN

1. Information on the Graham trip comes from "Kim Il Sung, Up Close and Personal," *The New Yorker,* vol. LXX, no. 4 (March 14, 1994): 32-33; and from several discussions with Stephen Linton. The "one old man to another" quote is drawn from *The New Yorker.*
2. Pyongyang did this in 1991 and 1992, in response to a number of IAEA demands, and would do so again in November 1993 in response to statements of the South Korean Defense Minister that referred to the possibility of military action.
3. See FBIS EAS August 30, 1993, 20-21; and FBIS EAS, September 1, 1993, 16.
4. See "U.S.-North Korea Talks on the Nuclear Issue," statement by Robert Gallucci, in *U.S. Department of State Dispatch,* vol. 4, no. 30 (July 26, 1993): 535-36. Gallucci's statement also notes the North Korean side's commitment to implement the two U.S. conditions and begin talking to both the South and the IAEA.
5. See news reports cited in FBIS-EAS, September 7, 1993, 24-25; and Press Release No. 32, DPRK Permanent Mission to the UN, New York, September 9, 1993.
6. Blix request cited in FBIS-EAS, October 1, 1993, 29.
7. See the news reports in FBIS-EAS, September 7, 1993, 25-26; September 8, 26; September 9, 21-22; and September 16, 13.
8. See the news reports in FBIS-EAS, September 28, 1993, 24.
9. Cited in FBIS-EAS, September 29, 1993, 25-26.
10. Cited in FBIS-EAS, October 1, 1993, 18.
11. Resolution cited in FBIS-EAS, October 4, 1993, 19-21.
12. Pyongyang Radio cited in FBIS-EAS, October 5, 1993, 10-11.
13. Details of the meeting can be found in FBIS-EAS, October 4, 1993, 21-22, and October 5, 18-20. On October 5, delegates from the two sides met at Panmunjom. South Korean officials insisted that the nuclear issue be on the agenda of any meeting of envoys, while North Korea again attacked Team Spirit as well as the "international cooperating system"—an apparent reference to the worldwide criticism of the North for its nuclear program.
14. North Korean officials reportedly offered such an interim deal to U.S. Congressman Gary Ackerman, who traveled to Pyongyang from October 9 to 12; the offer is reported in FBIS-EAS, October 18, 1993, 37.

15. *Nodong Sinmun,* cited in FBIS-EAS, October 18, 1993, 25.

16. Kyd's remarks carried in FBIS-EAS, October 14, 1993, 35.

17. Interviews with officials from the U.S. Department of State, Washington, August 1994.

18. Cited in FBIS-EAS, October 13, 1993, 35.

19. "Openness or Isolation for North Korea," *The New York Times,* October 20, 1993, A22.

20. Cited in FBIS-EAS, October 22, 1993, 15.

21. Cited in FBIS-EAS, October 20, 1993, 27.

22. NUB report cited in FBIS-EAS, August 23, 1993, 25.

23. William Branigin, "Defector Says Many N. Koreans Think War Could Improve Their Lot," *The Washington Post,* July 7, 1994, A14.

24. Cited in FBIS-EAS, November 2, 1993, 23.

25. Cited in FBIS-EAS, November 15, 1993, 31.

26. National Unification Board figures cited in FBIS-EAS, October 29, 1993, 21.

27. David E. Sanger, "North Korea is Collecting Millions from Koreans Who Live in Japan," *The New York Times,* November 1, 1993, 1.

28. David E. Sanger, "North Korea Shift Stirs Speculation," *The New York Times,* December 9, 1993, 13.

29. "North Korea Acknowledges 'Grave' Economic Situation," *The Washington Post,* December 9, 1993, 36.

30. Cited in FBIS *Pacific Rim Economic Review,* December 15, 1993, 25.

31. *Chosun Ilbo* cited in FBIS-EAS, October 22, 1993, 16-17. The dialogue was kept secret, and rumors soon began to fly in Seoul about its contents. Various news reports suggested that the United States had bargained away Team Spirit, was willing to establish diplomatic relations with the North, and was on the verge of a handful of other concessions. The South Korean media expressed concerns that the United States was making unwise deals, and one newspaper demanded to know the "contents of U.S.-North Korea nuclear negotiations"; *Kyonghyong Sinmun* cited in FBIS-EAS, October 25, 1993, 29-30. Quickly, however, South Korean government officials let it be known that they were being brought up to date daily on the substance of the New York talks.

32. Tim Weiner, "U.S. in Quiet Talks with North Korea," *The New York Times,* October 27, 1993, A7; and FBIS-EAS, October 22, 1993, 15.

33. Interview with U.S. Department of State official, Washington, August 1994.

34. Cited in FBIS-EAS, October 27, 1993, 13.

35. See the reports in FBIS-EAS, October 27, 1993, 13-14.

36. KBS television cited in FBIS-EAS, October 25, 1993, 31-32; cf. also 16-17.

37. Lally Weymouth, "Peninsula of Fear," *The Washington Post,* October 24, 1993, C1, C4.

38. Tim Weiner, "Shift on Cameras by North Koreans," *The New York Times,* October 30, 1993, 3; and Yonhap and *Hanguk Ilbo* articles cited in FBIS-EAS, November 1, 1993, 26-27.

39. Interviews with officials from the Departments of Defense and State, Washington, July 1994.

40. Paul Lewis, "UN Atom Agency Says North Korea Resists Treaty," *The New York Times,* November 2, 1993, A10.
41. FBIS-EAS, November 2, 1993, 11, 15-17.
42. North Korean statement carried in FBIS-EAS, November 3, 1993, 8-9 and 19-20.
43. Cited in FBIS-EAS November 3, 1993, 16.
44. T. R. Reid, "Aspin Prods, Warns North Korea," *The Washington Post,* November 5, 1993, A29.
45. David Sanger, "U.S. Delay Urged on Korea Sanctions," *The New York Times,* November 4, 1993, A9.
46. Cited in FBIS-EAS, November 3, 1993, 17.
47. Sanger, "U.S. Delay Urged"; and Tokyo *Kyodo* cited in FBIS-EAS, November 8, 1993, 23.
48. Sanger, "U.S. Delay Urged."
49. Cited in FBIS-EAS, November 8, 1993, 30. Kim's own foreign minister, Han Sung Joo, appeared to contradict him a week later, insisting that "dialogue should be given every chance to resolve the issue . . . . So far, we have not set any arbitrary or artificial deadline"; cited in FBIS-EAS, November 12, 1993, 40.
50. Cited in FBIS-EAS, November 5, 1993, 9.
51. R. Jeffrey Smith, "North Korea Bolsters Border Force," *The Washington Post,* November 6, 1993, A19.
52. Cited in FBIS-EAS, November 8, 1993, 29.
53. Cited in a *Dong-A Ilbo* report carried in FBIS-EAS, November 9, 1993, 23.
54. Pyongyang KCNA, cited in FBIS-EAS, November 9, 1993, 11.
55. Cited in FBIS-EAS, November 9, 1993, 24.
56. Seoul media reports in FBIS-EAS, November 10, 1993, 23-24.
57. Yonhap and *Dong-A Ilbo* stories cited in FBIS-EAS, November 10, 1993, 29-30.
58. Kang statement carried on Pyongyang Broadcasting Network, cited in FBIS-EAS, November 12, 1993, 17-19.
59. Cited in FBIS-EAS, November 15, 1993, 35.
60. Interview with U.S. State Department official, Washington, August 1994.
61. R. Jeffrey Smith, "North Korea Deal Urged By State Dept.," *The Washington Post,* November 15, 1993, A15.
62. R. Jeffrey Smith, "U.S. Weighs N. Korean Incentives," *The Washington Post,* November 17, 1993, A31.
63. Smith, "U.S. Weighs," and Seoul press reports cited in FBIS-EAS, November 17, 1993, 32. See also David Sanger, "U.S. Revising North Korea Strategy," The *New York Times,* November 22, 1993, A5.
64. Cited in FBIS-EAS, October 22, 1993, 16-17.
65. Cited in FBIS-EAS, October 29, 1993, 18.
66. Charles Krauthammer, "North Korea's Coming Bomb," *The Washington Post,* November 5, 1993, A27.
67. Zalmay M. Khalilzad, "A Deadline on Diplomacy," *The New York Times,* November 8, 1993, A19.
68. "Eyeball to Eyeball with North Korea," *The Economist,* November 13, 1993, 17.
69. "Handle with Care," *The Financial Times,* November 3, 1993, 15.

70. Dave McCurdy, "North Korea and the Bomb: Sanctions Won't Work," *The New York Times,* November 8, 1993, A19.

71. Donald P. Gregg, "Letter from the Chairman," *The U.S.-Korea Review,* vol. 11, no. 6 (December 1993/January 1994): 2.

72. William Clark, Jr., "What Does North Korea Ultimately Want?" *The International Herald Tribune,* November 3, 1993, A24.

73. Interviews with officials from the Departments of State and Defense, Washington, July and August 1994.

74. See the South Korean press reports of ROK Foreign Ministry denials that the United States had made any decisions, cited in FBIS-EAS, November 18, 1993, 35-36. See also Jim Lea, "S. Korea Denies Exercise Bargain," *Pacific Stars and Stripes,* November 19, 1993, 6.

75. See the editorials cited in FBIS-EAS, November 18, 1993, 36-37.

76. Han cited in FBIS-EAS, November 18, 1993, 35; unnamed official cited in *Seoul Sinmun* article, FBIS-EAS, November 19, 1993, 14.

77. See Douglas Jehl, "U.S. May Dilute Earlier Threats to North Korea," *The New York Times,* November 23, 1993, A6, and R. Jeffrey Smith, "S. Korean Holds Line on North," *The Washington Post,* November 23, 1993, A32.

78. Robert D. Novak, "Package Deal on Korea," *The Washington Post,* June 20, 1994, A15.

79. Interviews with officials from the Departments of State and Defense, Washington, July and August, 1994.

80. If North Korea "abandons its nuclear option and honors its international commitments," President Clinton said on the 23rd, the door will be open to a wide range of issues not only with the United States, but with the rest of the world"; cited in Ronald A. Taylor, "N. Korea Offered Openness—Or Else," *Washington Times,* November 24, 1993, 1.

81. Ruth Marcus and R. Jeffrey Smith, "U.S., South Korea Shift Strategy on North," *The Washington Post,* November 24, 1993, A12.

82. Cited in FBIS-EAS, November 24, 1993, 28.

83. Clinton's November 19 statement cited in FBIS-EAS, November 23, 1993, 17.

84. Marcus and Smith, "U.S., South Korea Shift Strategy on North." More details of the Kim-Clinton meeting and press conference are contained in FBIS-EAS, November 24, 1993, 24-28. Other information was acquired from interviews with State Department officials, Washington, July and August 1994.

85. See FBIS-EAS, January 14, 1994, 18-19. Yet also at the end of 1993, Lee Dong Bok, one of South Korea's most experienced negotiators with the North, abruptly resigned, and his step was interpreted as a result of disagreements with *moderates* in the Kim government.

86. "Differ on Offer to North," *The New York Times,* November 24, 1993, A16.

87. Marcus Smith, "U.S., South Korea Shift Strategy on North."

88. Cited in FBIS-EAS, November 26, 1993, 25-26.

89. *Chosun Ilbo* and *Hanguk Ilbo,* cited in FBIS-EAS, December 30, 1993, 26-27.

90. Michael R. Gordon, "Pentagon Studies Plans to Bolster U.S.-Korea Forces," *The New York Times,* December 2, 1993, 1.

91. In the Special National Intelligence Assessment, the Defense Intelligence Agency reportedly argued that the North would refuse to allow any further inspections at all; the State Department's Bureau of Intelligence and Research contended that Pyongyang might allow the full range of inspections; and the CIA, in what was portrayed as the compromise or consensus position, suggested that the North might allow more regular inspections but would continue to stonewall on the two nuclear waste sites. R. Jeffrey Smith, "U.S. Analysts Are Pessimistic On Korean Nuclear Inspection," *The Washington Post,* December 3, 1993, A1.

92. Bill Powell and John Barry, "Public Enemy Number One," *Newsweek,* November 29, 1993, 44-45.

93. Clinton, however, was taking no chances, and shortly thereafter he asked Defense Secretary Aspin and the new Chairman of the Joint Chiefs of Staff, General John M. Shalikashvili, to review defense plans in Korea. Michael R. Gordon, "Pentagon Studies Plans."

94. David Sanger, "U.N. Agency Finds No Assurance North Korea Bars Nuclear Arms," *The New York Times,* December 3, 1993, A8; and Smith, "U.S. Analysts Are Pessimistic," A35.

95. Cited in Smith, "U.S. Analysts Are Pessimistic," A35.

96. Cited in Sanger, "U.N. Agency Finds No Assurance."

97. Additional details of the talks can be found in FBIS-EAS, December 13, 1993, 26-27, and December 21, 1993, 25-27.

98. Cited in *Hungang Ilbo* story, FBIS-EAS, December 27, 1993, 27.

99. Aspin cited in Marc Dean Millot, "Facing the Emerging Reality of Regional Nuclear Adversaries," *The Washington Quarterly,* vol. 17, no. 3 (Summer 1994): 47.

100. Details are found in FBIS-EAS, December 27, 1993, 30.

101. See R. Jeffrey Smith, "North Korea Agrees to Nuclear Inspection," *The Washington Post,* January 4, 1994, A10; Steven Greenhouse, "U.S. Says Deal with North Korea on Atomic Site Inspections is Near," *The New York Times,* January 4, 1994, A3; and the reports in FBIS-EAS, January 5, 1994, 15-16; January 6, 8-9; and January 10, 25-26.

102. Charles Krauthammer, "Capitulation in Korea," *The Washington Post,* January 7, 1994, A19. South Korean papers were also lukewarm in their response to the agreement; see FBIS-EAS, January 10, 1994, 26-29. Another report discussing critical views of administration policy is John J. Fialka, "Check of North Korean Nuclear Sites Won't Provide Comfort Clinton Wants," *The Wall Street Journal,* January 31, 1994, 14.

103. The senator was Larry Pressler, a Republican from South Dakota; see "Senate Hearings Urged on Clinton's Korea Policy," Reuters news report, January 7, 1994.

104. William J. Taylor, "Heading Off a Korea Showdown," *The Washington Post,* November 19, 1993, A29.

105. FBIS-EAS, January 24, 1994, 36-39.

106. FBIS-EAS, January 25, 1994, 38. See also the KBS-1 report cited in FBIS-EAS, January 26, 1994, 24-25.

107. Yonhap report in FBIS-EAS, January 26, 1994, 25.

108. On January 19, the example, the IAEA presented a reply to North Korean officials that "clearly expressed its intention to conduct overall inspections—not only replacement of surveillance devices, but also extraction of nuclear materials" (FBIS-EAS, January 19, 1994, 23). Yet on January 22, agency spokesman David Kyd stressed that "The IAEA is not demanding overall inspection of North Korea"; FBIS-EAS, January 24, 1994, 36-37.

109. For an example, see the North Korean statement in FBIS-EAS, February 7, 1994, 16. See also FBIS-EAS, February 14, 1994, 25, in which a DPRK statement claims that in bilateral talks "the U.S. side made clear that the inspection by the IAEA should be one purely for the continuity of safeguards," a point on which the secretariat of the IAEA had agreed.

110. KBS-1 radio report cited in FBIS-EAS, February 7, 1994, 39-40.

111. Julia Preston, "China Breaks Ranks on N. Korean Nuclear Plants," *The Washington Post,* February 10, 1994, A24.

112. In early February, the Senate approved the annual State Department authorization bill; attached was an amendment authored by Sen. Charles Robb (D-VA) urging the President to reintroduce tactical nuclear weapons into Korea if the North continued to stall. In the House, Congressman Ben Gilman (R-NY) introduced a resolution urging the North to cooperate and, failing that, "approv[ing] and encourag[ing] the use by the President of any means necessary and appropriate, including the use of diplomacy, economic sanctions, a blockade, and military force," to demand the North's compliance. H. J. Resolution 292, introduced November 15, 1993.

113. FBIS-EAS, February 7, 1994, 17-18.

114. Cited in FBIS-EAS, February 9, 1994, 15-16.

115. FBIS-EAS, February 9, 1994, 27-28.

116. Moon Ihlwan, "South Korea Sees Glimmer of Hope in N. Korea Nuke Row," Reuters wire service report, February 14, 1994.

117. FBIS-EAS, February 8, 1994, 24-25.

118. See the accounts in FBIS-EAS, February 15, 1994, 42-48.

119. See R. Jeffrey Smith, "North Korea Agrees to Inspections," *The Washington Post,* February 16, 1994, A1; David E. Sanger, "North Koreans Agree to Survey of Atomic Sites," *The New York Times,* February 16, 1994, A1; and the various accounts in FBIS-EAS, February 16, 1994, 22-30, and February 18, 20-24.

120. Cited in FBIS-EAS, February 22, 1994, 18-19.

121. Statement cited in FBIS-EAS, February 14, 1994, 25; cf. also 26-27. A similar commentary emerged on February 21; see FBIS-EAS, February 22, 1994, 18-19.

122. The "letter of agreement" read as follows:

> With the purpose of continuing their joint efforts to resolve the nuclear issue through dialogue according to the principle of the 11 June DPRK-U.S. joint statement, the DPRK and the United States of America held a number of rounds of contact in New York.
>
> As a result of such consultations, the DPRK and the United States of America agreed to take the following four measures on 1 March 1994:

1. The United States of America will announce its decision to consent to South Korea's discontinuation of the Team Spirit-94 military exercise.

2. Inspections for assuring the continuity of safeguards will begin according to the agreement between the IAEA and the DPRK on February 15 1994 and finish by the time on which the IAEA and DPRK agreed.

3. Working-level contact for the North-South exchange of special envoys will resume in Panmunjom.

4. The DPRK and the United States of America will announce that the third round of DPRK-U.S. talks will start on March 21 in Geneva.

These four simultaneous measures are necessary for implementing this letter of agreement.

The letter was read in a North Korean broadcast cited in FBIS-EAS, February 28, 1994, 18.

123. Interview with U.S. State Department official, Washington, August 1994.

124. Cited in FBIS-EAS, March 3, 1994, 21.

125. FBIS-EAS, March 4, 1994, 21-22.

126. FBIS-EAS, March 8, 1994, 28; and March 9, 1994, 31-32. On March 10, concerns arose that some of the seals had been broken, but the IAEA quickly downplayed the report; FBIS-EAS, March 10, 1994, 23-24.

127. Interviews with two U.S. officials and one former U.S. official, Washington, March and April, 1994.

128. Dave McCurdy, "North Korea and the Bomb: Sanctions Won't Work."

129. William J. Taylor, "Heading Off a Korea Showdown."

130. Both quotes are cited by Henry Kissinger in "No Compromise, But a Rollback," *The Washington Post,* July 6, 1994, A19.

131. Michael Kramer, "Playing Nuclear Poker," *Time,* February 28, 1994, 45.

132. Jim Hoagland, "Containing North Korea," *The Washington Post,* March 10, 1994, A21.

133. Mark Thompson, "Well, Maybe a Nuke or Two," *Time,* April 11, 1994, 58. In a major address on the subject in May, Perry continued to make this distinction. While he rejected the idea that the United States "could accept such a [North Korean nuclear] program and seek to deter North Korea from actual use of its nuclear arsenal," he added a parenthetical comment that the United States could not deter "an *unchecked* nuclear capacity" [emphasis mine]. Cited in *The U.S.-Korea Review,* vol. 2, no. 8 (April-May 1994): 5.

134. Kissinger, "No Compromise."

135. Interviews with officials from the Departments of State and Defense and the National Security Council, Washington, July and August 1994.

136. Interviews with U.S. officials, Washington, D.C., November 1994.

137. Pak's story is told in William Branigin, "Defector Says Many N. Koreans Think War Could Improve Their Lot," *The Washington Post,* July 7, 1994, A14.

CHAPTER EIGHT

1. The information about Taylor's trip comes from several interviews with Bill Taylor, Washington, May through July 1994. The quotes from the interviews with Kim Il Sung are drawn from stories in *The Washington Times*, April 19, 1994, A1, A16-17.

2. R. Jeffrey Smith, "N. Korea Adds Arms Capacity," *The Washington Post*, April 2, 1994, A1.

3. R. Jeffrey Smith, "Inspection of North Korea's Nuclear Facilities is Halted," *The Washington Post*, March 16, 1994, A24; and Smith, "Raising Stakes in Korea Standoff, U.S. Weighs Reviving Major Military Exercise," *The Washington Post*, March 17, 1994, A37.

4. FBIS-EAS, March 18, 1994, 32.

5. Interview with two U.S. government officials, Washington, March and April, 1994.

6. In a March 18 statement, for example, Pyongyang claimed that it had refused three "unfair" procedures: extracting samples from facilities that had been sealed by the IAEA, conducting widespread measurements throughout Yongbyon; and examining the reactor's cooling system. The North Korean statement claimed that the IAEA had sent three telexes from Vienna demanding that these procedures be allowed or the agency would turn the matter over to the UN Security Council. See FBIS-EAS, March 18, 1994, 12-13; FBIS-EAS, March 23, 1994, 9-10; and FBIS-EAS, March 25, 1994, 11-13.

7. FBIS-EAS, March 21, 1994, 14-24, 39-47.

8. Federal News Service Transcript, "CNN's Late Edition," March 20, 1994, carried in Reuter Transcript Report wire. See also Stephen Barr and Lena H. Sun, "China's Cooperation on N. Korea Seen," *The Washington Post*, March 21, 1994, A12.

9. Korean newspapers revealed the so-called "Operations Plan 5027" of the U.S.–ROK Combined Forces Command, which called for using a North Korean attack as an opportunity to reunify the peninsula. FBIS-EAS, March 25, 1994, 20-21.

10. Cited in FBIS-EAS, March 28, 1994, 24.

11. R. Jeffrey Smith, "Perry Sharply Warns North Korea," *The Washington Post*, March 31, 1994, A1.

12. Ann Devroy and Daniel Williams, "China Resists U.S. Resolution on North Korea," *The Washington Post*, March 30, 1994, A20. An issue arose of whether the UN Security Council message would be a resolution or a "statement." The former was considered the more serious form of diplomatic demarche, although it did not require complete unanimity from Security Council members; some could abstain, as China was fully expected to do. A statement carried less weight but represented a fully unanimous position of all Security Council members. In the end, U.S. officials settled for a statement—but a strongly worded one.

13. Text of statement carried by Reuters wire service, March 31, 1994.

14. Reports cited in FBIS-EAS, March 31, 1994, 23; and FBIS-EAS, April 5, 1994, 41.

15. R. Jeffrey Smith, "U.S. Tough Talk Rattles Nerves in Asia," *The Washington Post,* April 5, 1994, A14; FBIS-EAS, April 4, 1994, 22-26; and FBIS-EAS, April 6, 1994, 29-31.

16. FBIS-EAS, April 15, 1994, 37-39.

17. North Korea Working Group, U.S. Institute of Peace, "Special Report—North Korea's Nuclear Program: Challenge and Opportunity for American Policy" (Washington, D.C.: U.S. Institute of Peace, N.D.), 11, 19-22.

18. R. Jeffrey Smith, "North Korea Refuses Demand to Inspect Reactor Fuel," *The Washington Post,* April 28, 1994, 1; Joan Biskupic and R. Jeffrey Smith, "North Korea Keeps Nuclear Inspectors at Bay," *The Washington Post,* May 1, 1994, A36; and FBIS-EAS, April 22, 1994, 20, and April 28, 1994, 23-24.

19. R. Jeffrey Smith, "U.S. Plans to Seek North Korea Sanctions," *The Washington Post,* June 1, 1994, A22.

20. Cited in FBIS-EAS, June 2, 1994, 31.

21. "Letter dated 2 June 1994 from the Director General of the International Atomic Energy Agency addressed to the Secretary-General," the United Nations, Document S/1994/656.

22. Ibid.

23. See Barbara Opall, "U.S. Arms Control Group Backs N. Korea Claim," *Defense News,* June 6-12, 1994, 8.

24. Interviews with U.S. State and Defense Department officials, Washington, June and August 1994.

25. "North Korea Reiterates That Sanctions Mean War," Reuters wire service report, June 5, 1994.

26. Cited in FBIS-EAS, June 7, 1994, 18.

27. North Korean announcement cited in FBIS-EAS, June 13, 1994, 13-14; see also David E. Sanger, "North Korea Quits Atom Agency in Wider Rift with U.S. and U.N.," *The New York Times,* June 14, 1994, 1.

28. Cited in FBIS-EAS, June 13, 1994, 26.

29. Cited in FBIS-EAS, June 16, 1994, 44.

30. Jim Mann, "China Helped Bring About N. Korea's Change of Heart," *The Los Angeles Times,* June 29, 1994, 1.

31. Interviews with U.S. officials, Washington, November 1994.

32. See FBIS-EAS, June 13, 1994, 27; and "North Korea Offers to Freeze Nuclear Program," News from the Carnegie Endowment, mimeographed copy, June 16, 1994.

33. Steve Glain, "U.S. Envoy to Seoul Aims to Meet Needs of Security Without Provoking the North," *The Wall Street Journal,* August 9, 1994, 8; and Charles Ornstein, "From Academic Frying Pan Into Diplomatic Fire," *The Chronicle of Higher Education,* August 3, 1994, A5.

34. FBIS-EAS, June 17, 1994, 21-26.

35. T. R. Reid, "Leaders of 2 Koreas Seek First Summit," *The Washington Post,* June 19, 1994, A28.

36. R. Jeffrey Smith and Bradley Graham, "Carter Faulted by White House on North Korea," *The Washington Post,* June 18, 1994, A1.

37. Ornstein, "From Academic Frying Pan Into Diplomatic Fire," A5.

38. Charles Krauthammer, "'Peace in Our Time,'" *The Washington Post*, June 24, 1994, A27.

39. Robert A. Manning, "The Defining Crisis," *The Los Angeles Times*, June 19, 1994, A25.

40. Robert D. Novak, "Package Deal on Korea," *The Washington Post*, June 20, 1994, A15.

41. R. Jeffrey Smith and Ann Devroy, "U.S. Debates Shift on North Korea," *The Washington Post*, June 21, 1994, A12.

42. Ann Devroy and T. R. Reid, "U.S. Awaits Word on North Korea's Intentions," *The Washington Post*, June 22, 1994, A15.

43. Ruth Marcus and R. Jeffrey Smith, "North Korea Confirms Freeze," *The Washington Post*, June 23, 1994, A1.

44. R. Jeffrey Smith, "Officials Forsee Step-By-Step U.S. Strategy at Talks with North Korea," *The Washington Post*, June 30, 1994, 13. Once again, Robert Manning hit the Administration with a plea for more decisive action. On July 7, he issued a brief but important paper laying out the elements of a package deal. Kim Il Sung's behavior during the Carter visit, Manning wrote, "strongly suggests that a political solution can be reached only through direct negotiations with the North's top leadership." Meanwhile, "the lapse back into bureaucratic routine" mandated by the administration "is likely to produce only incremental progress." Manning proposed sending a highly respected former government official, such as General Colin Powell or former Defense official Richard Armitage, as a presidential envoy to Kim, and laying out a compelling package. Manning, "Clinton and the Korea Question: A Strategy for the Endgame," Progressive Policy Institute *Policy Briefing*, July 7, 1994, 1, 7.

45. R. Jeffrey Smith, "The Man Who Would Tame N. Korea," *The Washington Post*, July 8, 1994, 17; and interviews with officials from the Departments of State and Defense, Washington, July and August 1994.

46. The official North Korean announcement and other various statements about the death can be found in FBIS-EAS, July 11, 1994, 16-33.

47. These stories are included in "Death of Kim May Be Beginning of End for North Korea's Communist Regime," *The Wall Street Journal*, July 11, 1994, 1, 3.

48. See the Seoul media report in FBIS-EAS, July 14, 1994, 24.

49. Steve Glain, "What Kind of Man Drinks Hennessy? Excellent Question," *The Wall Street Journal*, August 5, 1994, A1.

50. Japanese television interview cited in FBIS-EAS, July 15, 1994, 28.

51. "Kim Jong Il's Inheritance," *The Economist*, July 16, 1994, 19.

52. *Chosun Ilbo* story carried in FBIS-EAS, July 28, 1994, 59.

53. "North Korea Offers Talks on Arms," *The New York Times*, July 11, 1994, A3.

54. Senator Robert Dole criticized Clinton for this act, saying the president, in extending condolences had apparently forgotten that Kim was responsible for the Korean War; "Dole Criticizes Clinton for Offering 'Condolences' to North Korea," *The New York Times*, July 11, 1994, A3. Dole apparently believed that displaying anger over a forty-year-old war was more important than resolving the

most dangerous crisis in the post–Cold War era. His comment also reflected total ignorance of Korean society, in which such condolences are a critical element of trust-building. See Stephen W. Linton, "When the Headman Dies," *The New York Times,* July 11, 1994, A33.

55. See FBIS-EAS, July 14, 1994, 27.

56. "Pyongyang Denounces S. Korean President," *The Washington Post,* July 18, 1994, 11; North Korean media report in FBIS-EAS, July 18, 1994, 17.

57. North Korean statement carried by FBIS-EAS, July 18, 1994, 20.

58. Lee Keumhyun, "N. Korea Has 5 Nuclear Warheads, No Delivery System, Defector Says," *The Washington Post,* July 28, 1994, A25; James Sterngold, "Defector Says North Korea Has 5 A-Bombs and May Make More," *The New York Times,* July 28, 1994, A7; and South Korean reports in FBIS-EAS, July 27, 1994, 57-58.

59. Robert Gallucci said that the emphasis on the defector's story had not added "clarity [or] warmth to the dialogue" with the North; see "U.S. Faults S. Korea Rhetoric," Reuters wire service report, August 2, 1994. The *New York Times* also castigated Seoul, editorializing that "South Korea has been waging a fierce campaign against student radicals and labor militants with methods that have no legitimate place in a democratic society." These actions, the *Times* rightly concluded, posed "a far graver threat to democracy than any subversive scheme hatched in Pyongyang." "South Korea's Self-Inflicted Wound," *The New York Times,* August 9, 1994, A22.

60. See R. Jeffrey Smith, "N. Korea, U.S. Pledge Closer Ties," *The Washington Post,* August 13, 1994, A1; Smith, "Korean Diplomat Predicts New Era in U.S. Relations," *The Washington Post,* August 14, 1994, A27; and Alan Riding, "U.S. and N. Korea Agree on a Move to Diplomatic Ties," *The New York Times,* August 13, 1994, A1.

61. The Agreed Statement is cited in *Arms Control Today,* vol. 24, no. 7 (September 1994): 23.

62. Cited in Jon B. Wolfsthal, "U.S., North Korea Sign Accord on 'Resolution' of Nuclear Crisis," *Arms Control Today,* vol. 24, no. 7 (September 1994): 31.

63. Andrew Pollack, "Seoul is Offering Nuclear Plants to North Korea," *The New York Times,* August 15, 1994, 1. For specific examples of South Korean official reaction, see the reports in FBIS-EAS, August 22, 1994, 44-46; and FBIS-EAS, August 23, 1994, 35-36. The North Korean policy of desiring a Russian reactor is reported in FBIS-EAS, August 8, 1994, 47.

64. In one example, the *New York Times* editorialized in late 1994 that South Korea's hard liners' "shrill opposition to accommodation could complicate Washington's efforts to make a deal with Pyongyang." See "Seoul's Show-Stoppers," *The New York Times,* September 23, 1994, A34.

65. Kim Chae Il, "Disharmony in Government's DPRK Policy Studies," Seoul *SISA Journal,* cited in FBIS-EAS, August 9, 1994, 40; and facsimile interviews with academics and researchers in Seoul, August and September 1994.

66. The source is Kim, "Disharmony in Government's DPRK Policy," 40-43.

67. Kim, "Disharmony in Government's DPRK Policy," 41-42.

68. See the *Hangyore Sinmun* story carried in FBIS-EAS, September 1, 1994, 30-31.

69. Cited in a Yonhap report, FBIS-EAS, September 7, 1994, 50.

70. This quote, and general information on the South's growing concerns, can be found in T. R. Reid, "U.S.-North Korea Ties Worry Seoul," *The Washington Post,* September 6, 1994, A12.

71. See James Sterngold, "South Korea President Lashes Out at U.S.," *The New York Times,* October 8, 1994, A3; Choe Sang Hun, "Ruling Party Criticizes U.S. Lack of Toughness Toward North," AP Wire Service report, October 11, 1994; and Robert Evans, "What's the Rush? Kim Asks the U.S.," *The Washington Times,* October 12, 1994, 13.

72. Various North Korea print and broadcast reports carried in FBIS-EAS, September 6, 1994, 35-40.

73. Talks are cited in South Korean press reports carried in FBIS-EAS, September 12, 1994, 40-41; and September 13, 48.

74. T. R. Reid, "Dispute Could Hurt U.S.-N. Korea Talks," *The Washington Post,* September 15, 1994, A28. Instead, North Korea proposed a novel idea: North Korea should be allowed to pick who made the light-water reactors, and the United States should have the responsibility of recruiting South Korea, Japan, and other nations to help pay for them. Gallucci said that offer was "ludicrous on the face of it. . . . I don't take it seriously"; quoted in Choe Sang Hun, "U.S. Rejects North Korea's Demand to Choose Type of Reactors," Associated Press Wire Service report, September 16, 1994. North Korean officials had also reportedly demanded $2 billion in compensation for ending their own nuclear program; R. Jeffrey Smith, "North Korea Demands Puzzle U.S. Negotiators," *The Washington Post,* September 23, 1994, 32.

75. On the verge of the new high-level talks, the commander of the U.S. Pacific Fleet, Admiral Ronald Zlatoper, said that a U.S. carrier battle group had been deployed in the Sea of Japan to show toughness in talks with the North. North Korea vigorously condemned the statement, which the U.S. government quickly denied, amid indications Washington was furious at Zlatoper for his exaggeration of U.S. policy. See "U.S. Warships Sail Off North Korea," *The Washington Times,* September 23, 1994, 13.

76. R. Jeffrey Smith, "U.S.-N. Korea Nuclear Talks at Stalemate as Pyongyang Takes Hard-Line Stance," *The Washington Post,* September 28, 1994, A25. See also J. F. O. McAllister, "Back to Square One," *Time,* October 10, 1994, 51; Louise Lief, "No Cheers for Diplomacy," *U.S. News and World Report,* October 10, 1994, 36; and the Seoul news reports in FBIS-EAS, September 26, 1994, 51-59.

77. R. Jeffrey Smith, "U.S.-N. Korea Talks Snag on Pyongyang Demands," *The Washington Post,* September 30, 1994, A36.

78. McAllister, "Back to Square One," 51.

79. R. Jeffrey Smith and Ann Devroy, "U.S. to Hold Its Course In North Korea Dealings," *The Washington Post,* October 5, 1994, A6.

80. Elizabeth Olson, "Negotiators Restart High-Level Talks on Nuclear Issues," Associated Press Wire Service report, October 5, 1994.

81. See the reports in FBIS-EAS, October 13, 1994, 41-42. In particular, South Korean officials revealed publicly a reported U.S. agreement to postpone the special inspections until the LWRs were 75 percent complete—a period of perhaps five years. Officials in Seoul found this proposal shocking, but it turned out to be very close to the provisions of the final agreement. For details see Carolyn Henson, "U.S.-North Korea Nuclear Talks Stall," Associated Press Wire Service report, October 15, 1994.

82. "Agreed Framework Between the United States of America and the Democratic People's Republic of Korea," mimeograph, 1.

83. Alan Riding, "U.S. and North Korea Agree to Build on Nuclear Accord," *The New York Times,* October 18, 1994, A1.

84. Details of the agreement are drawn from the text of the Agreed Framework, mimeograph copy, October 21, 1994, 1-4; The White House, Office of the Press Secretary, "Statement By The President" and "Press Briefing By Ambassador Robert Gallucci," October 18, 1994; U.S. Department of State, Office of the Spokesman, "Remarks by Secretary of State Warren Christopher and Director General of the IAEA Hans Blix," October 19, 1994; David E. Sanger, "Clinton Approves A Plan to Give Aid to North Koreans," *The New York Times,* October 19, 1994, A1, A14; Arnold Kanter, "The North Korean Nuclear Agreement," Forum for International Policy Issue Brief, Washington, D.C., October 1994; R. Jeffrey Smith, "Clinton Approves Pact With North Korea," *The Washington Post,* October 19, 1994, A1; Robert Burns, "Accord is First Step, But Experts Say Dangers Remain," Associated Press Wire Service report, October 19, 1994; Jim Mann, "U.S. Deal With N. Korea Averts Riskier Alternatives," *The Los Angeles Times,* October 20, 1994, 1; and William Drozdiak, "N. Korea, U.S. Sign Broad Pact," *The Washington Post,* October 22, 1994, A1, A25. The description of the phases can be found in Michael R. Gordon, "U.S.-North Korea Accord Has a 10-Year Timetable," *The New York Times,* October 21, 1994, A8.

85. North Korea, of course, had originally refused even to consider LWRs provided by South Korea. And indeed, when South Korean officials first put this request to Washington, U.S. negotiators rebuffed them, knowing the complications involved. Diligent efforts by the U.S. negotiating team, however, produced no alternatives; and North Korea, presented with this result, agreed to have South Korean teams build the reactors. Interviews with U.S. State Department officials, Washington, October and November, 1994.

86. Yonhap report cited in FBIS-EAS, October 20, 1994, 34.

87. Agreed Framework, 4.

88. This episode is described in Smith, "Clinton Approves Pact with North Korea."

89. General facts about the deal, and Han Sung Joo quote, are drawn from R. Jeffrey Smith, "N. Korea, U.S. Reach Nuclear Pact," *The Washington Post,* October 18, 1994, A1, A28.

90. *Chosun Ilbo* cited in FBIS-EAS, October 20, 1994, 36.

91. Cited in Michael Breen, "U.S. Officials Reassure S. Korea," *The Washington Times,* October 20, 1994, 13. For more detail on Seoul's official reaction and the general mood in South Korea, see the press reports in FBIS-EAS, October 18,

1994, 51-62, and Selig S. Harrison, "Beware the Hawks in Seoul," *The New York Times,* October 21, 1994, A31.

92. Cited in Associated Press Wire Service report, "Opposition: South Korea Should Become Less Dependent on U.S.," October 20, 1994.

93. Cited in FBIS-EAS, October 20, 1994, 44.

94. The cartoons are described in Thomas Wagner, "Editorial Cartoons Show Humiliation, Anger at Nuclear Accord," Associated Press Wire Service report, October 22, 1994.

95. Cited in FBIS-EAS, October 21, 1994, 38-41.

96. Blix quotes drawn from Robert Burns, "U.N. Agency Praises U.S.-North Korean Nuclear Deal," Associated Press Wire Service report, October 20, 1994; and Ben Barber, "N. Korea Nuke Pact Defended," *The Washington Times,* October 20, 1994, 1.

97. Cited in Sanger, "Clinton Approves A Plan," A14.

98. R. Jeffrey Smith, "N. Korea Accord: A Troubling Precedent?" *The Washington Post,* October 20, 1994, A32.

99. Kanter, "The North Korean Nuclear Agreement," 4.

100. Jessica Mathews, "A Sound Beginning With North Korea," *The Washington Post,* October 21, 1994, A25. For other defenses of the deal, see "The Content of the Korea Accord," *The Washington Post,* October 21, 1994, A24, and Michael Kramer, "A Tough, Smart Deal," *Time,* October 31, 1994, 34.

101. "New Deal for Pyongyang," *The Wall Street Journal,* October 21, 1994, 14. Similarly nonproliferation hawk Gary Milhollin argued that "We're about to rescue North Korea from its poverty, but they don't give up very much"; cited in Ben Barber, "Nuclear Pact Debated on Eve of Its Signing," *The Washington Times,* October 21, 1994, 1.

102. Kanter, "The North Korean Nuclear Agreement," 5.

CHAPTER NINE

1. "Tokyo Favors UN Involvement in DPRK Issue," Tokyo *Kyodo* report cited in FBIS-EAS, March 16, 1993, 3.

2. Of course, without the U.S. leadership in the Persian Gulf War, the world might never have uncovered Iraq's secret weapons program—and the IAEA might never have overcome its smug incompetence and become an organization with teeth. Without Desert Storm, it is possible that in March 1993 the IAEA would have done nothing; or, more probably, that it never would have requested challenge inspections in North Korea in the first place.

3. Michele A. Flournoy, "Implications for U.S. Military Strategy," in Robert D. Blackwill and Albert Carnesale, eds., *New Nuclear Nations: Consequences for U.S. Policy* (New York: Council on Foreign Relations Press, 1993), 157.

4. Robert Blackwill and Ashton Carter, "The Role of Intelligence," in Blackwill and Carnesale, eds., *New Nuclear Nations,* 233.

5. Roger K. Smith, "Opaque Proliferation and the Fate of the Non-Proliferation Regime," in Benjamin Frankel, ed., *Opaque Nuclear Proliferation: Methodological and Policy Implications* (London: Frank Cass, 1991), 106-107.

6. Thomas W. Graham, comments cited in *Shaping Nuclear Policy for the 1990s: A Compendium of Views* (Washington, D.C.: Defense Policy Panel of the House Armed Services Committee, U.S. Congress, December 17, 1992), 274-75.

7. Stephen Meyer, *The Dynamics of Nuclear Proliferation* (Chicago: University of Chicago Press, 1984), 62.

8. Ibid., 160.

9. John J. Schulz, "Bluff and Uncertainty: Deterrence and the 'Maybe States,'" *SAIS Review*, vol. 7, no. 2 (Summer-Fall 1987): 184-85.

10. Avner Cohen and Benjamin Frankel, "Opaque Nuclear Proliferation," in Frankel, ed., *Opaque Nuclear Proliferation*, 18, 21-22.

11. Australian analyst Peter Hayes argues that this is exactly the strategy adopted by the North, which "has maximized ambiguity as to its ultimate intentions to increase its leverage in a range of bargaining fora with the South and the international community." See Hayes, "Moving Target—Korea's Nuclear Proliferation Potential," *The Korean Journal of International Studies*, vol. 23, no. 1 (Spring 1992): 118-19.

12. William Epstein, "Why States Go—and Don't Go—Nuclear," *Annals* of the American Academy of Political and Social Sciences, vol. 430 (March 1977): 24-25.

13. Okita cited in Amos A. Jordan, "Coping with the North Korea Nuclear Weapons Problem" (Honolulu: Pacific Forum CSIS, Policy Report Series, November 1993), 8.

14. Stephen J. Solarz, "Next of Kim," *The New Republic*, August 8, 1994, 27.

15. William C. Martel and William T. Pendley would go even further; see *Nuclear Coexistence: Rethinking U.S. Policy to Promote Stability in an Era of Proliferation* (Maxwell Air Force Base, AL: Air War College Studies in National Security No. 1, April 1994), esp. 133-178. Martel and Pendley argue for a new look at proliferation on the assumption that proliferation is neither good nor bad per se; rather, the stabilizing cases must be distinguished from the destabilizing, and U.S. policy adjusted accordingly. I would not go so far; chapter ten will argue that devaluing nuclear weapons can only be done across the board, not in an inconsistent manner. Moreover, in practice distinguishing good from bad proliferation may be much more difficult than a brief review of individual cases suggests.

16. Cohen and Frankel, "Opaque Nuclear Proliferation," 17, 33.

17. Shulz, "Bluff and Uncertainty," 194.

18. Inis L. Claude, Jr., "Casual Commitment in International Relations," *Political Science Quarterly*, vol. 96, no. 3 (Fall 1981): 379.

19. See Steven E. Miller, "Assistance to Newly Proliferating Nations," in Blackwill and Carnesale, eds., *New Nuclear Nations*, 97-131.

20. See Joseph S. Nye, Jr., "Diplomatic Measures," in Blackwill and Carnesale, eds., *New Nuclear Nations*, 81-84.

CHAPTER TEN

1. For further proof of this point, see the U.S. statement of national security strategy, *A National Security Strategy of Engagement and Enlargement* (Washington, D.C.: The White House, July 1994), 11-12.

2. The following quotes and points are drawn from Stephen W. Linton, "Approach and Style in Negotiating with the DPRK," mimeographed copy, January 1994.

3. See Stephen Meyer, *The Dynamics of Nuclear Proliferation* (Chicago: University of Chicago Press, 1984).

4. Ibid., 88-90.

5. Lewis A. Dunn, *Controlling the Bomb: Nuclear Proliferation in the 1980s* (New Haven: Yale University Press, 1982), 112.

6. For an argument that such options should be considered in nonproliferation policies, see William R. Van Cleave, "Swift Military Action Can Prevent Proliferation," in Charles R. Cozic, ed., *Nuclear Proliferation: Contending Viewpoints* (San Diego, CA: Greenhaven Press, 1992), 204-210.

7. Charles Krauthammer, "Romancing the Thugs," *Time,* November 7, 1994, 90.

8. In retrospect, it is amazing that Saddam Hussein chose not to employ this kind of strategy, perhaps withdrawing from all but a small corner of Kuwait and two strategic islands in the Persian Gulf, in the fall of 1990. Most policy analysts in Washington certainly believed he would do so, and predicted that the step would succeed in fracturing the international consensus in favor of military action.

9. For a detailed discussion of this point, see Kim Taewoo, "South Korea's Nuclear Dilemmas," *Korea and World Affairs,* vol. 16, no. 2 (Summer 1992): 267-71. Kim adds the argument that, regardless of the scenario assumed, there is no way to avoid contaminating large portions of the Korean Peninsula with radioactive waste with any attack on the North's facilities.

10. For a more detailed examination of the military option, see Philip Zelikow, "Offensive Military Options," in Robert D. Blackwill and Albert Carnesale, eds., *New Nuclear Nations: Consequences for U.S. Policy* (New York: Council on Foreign Relations Press, 1993), 162-195.

11. "Conversations With William Perry," *Aerospace America,* October 1994, 11.

12. Cited in FBIS-EAS, November 7, 1991, 26.

13. On the difficulty of assembling a coalition even in the Gulf, see Andrew Fenton Cooper, Richard A. Higgott, and Kim Richard Nossal, "Bound to Follow? Leadership and Followership in the Gulf Conflict," *Political Science Quarterly,* vol. 106, no. 3 (1991): 391-410.

14. See Ko's claims in FBIS-EAS, November 7, 1991, 26.

15. Defense Intelligence Agency, "North Korea: The Foundations for Military Strength," cited in Marc Dean Millot, "Facing the Emerging Reality of Regional Nuclear Adversaries," *The Washington Quarterly,* vol. 17, no. 3 (Summer 1994): 41-71.

16. "Remarks by Honorable Les Aspin, Secretary of Defense, National Academy of Sciences Committee on International Security and Arms Control, December 7, 1993," Defense Department text of speech, 4.

17. Aspin, "Remarks to the National Academy of Sciences," 6.
18. A December 1993 National Security Council memorandum attempted to spell out the differences between these two strategies. It defined nonproliferation as "the use of the full range of political, economic and military tools to prevent proliferation, reverse it diplomatically or protect our interests against an opponent armed with weapons of mass destruction or missiles, should that prove necessary. Nonproliferation tools include: intelligence analysis, global nonproliferation norms and agreements, diplomacy, export controls, security assurances, defenses, and the application of military force." Cited in Zachary Davis and Mitchell Reiss, "U.S. Counterproliferation Doctrine: Issues for Congress," Congressional Research Service Report 94-734 ENR, September 21, 1994, 8. Counterproliferation, on the other hand, consisted of "the activities of the Department of Defense" in combatting proliferation, including "diplomacy, arms control, export controls, and intelligence collection and analysis," with special emphasis on protecting U.S. forces should they "confront an adversary armed with weapons of mass destruction or missiles"; Ibid., 8. The latter definition actually appears somewhat broad, compared to what Aspin originally outlined. There he had talked clearly about the need, not to prevent proliferation, but to deal with its military consequences.
19. Aspin, "Remarks to the National Academy of Sciences," 4-6.
20. Report cited and discussed in Davis and Reiss, "U.S. Counterproliferation Doctrine," 9.
21. Some of these initiatives are described in Millot, "Facing the Emerging Reality of Regional Nuclear Adversaries," 60-65.
22. One especially foolish discourse on this subject argued that U.S. tactical nuclear use in Korea would grant "extraordinary leverage over small states now possessed of nuclear arms" and, in the long run, "probably save tens of millions or perhaps hundreds of millions of lives that otherwise might fall victim to atomic wars in the Third World"; Mark Helprin, "My Brilliant Korea," *The Wall Street Journal,* July 25, 1994, 14. How surprising, by this logic, that U.S. conventional dominance after World War II did not stop conventional wars in the Third World. How surprising that the Japanese people did not welcome the fireballs above Hiroshima and Nagasaki for their deterrent effect. The obvious problem, of course, is that the United States does not know where in North Korea the supposed nuclear bombs are; short of flattening every inch of the country with atomic weapons, even nuclear first use would not rule out a retaliation. And then, far from saving "a city or two in the developed nations," as Helprin goes on to argue, U.S. first use would guarantee their destruction. And elsewhere in the world it would merely convince more countries to go nuclear as quickly as possible to stave off American nuclear peacemaking.
23. See, for example, Lewis A. Dunn, "New Nuclear Threats to U.S. Security," in Blackwill and Carnesale, eds., *New Nuclear Nations,* 38-44.
24. Some might place India and Pakistan into the hard-core category. There must be some way, however, of distinguishing their programs from those of dangerous states like North Korea. Therefore, even though the motives and momentum of

their nuclear programs may be just as powerful, I have chosen to place them in a separate category for the purposes of this analysis.

25. As one commentator has argued, "Probable proliferators fall into distinct categories which give the United States very different policy options depending on the country. . . . [E]fforts to develop universalistic nonproliferation policies reflect an idea which in my opinion was abandoned by some of the most thoughtful specialists in the field a decade ago"; Thomas W. Graham, cited in *Shaping Nuclear Policy for the 1990s*, 275.

26. This case is made in the Nuclear Strategy Study Group, Center for Strategic and International Studies, *Toward a Nuclear Peace: The Future of Nuclear Weapons in U.S. Foreign and Defense Policy* (Washington, D.C.: CSIS, June 1993), and Michael J. Mazarr, "Minimum Deterrence and the United States," in Peter Gizewski, ed., *Minimum Nuclear Deterrence In A New World Order* (Toronto: Canadian Centre for Global Security, March 1994), 15-35. Many analysts now agree that, in the words of McGeorge Bundy, William Crowe, and Sidney Drell, "As matters now stand, every vital interest of the United States, with the exception of deterring nuclear attack, can be met by prudent conventional readiness"; McGeorge Bundy, William J. Crowe, Jr., and Sidney D. Drell, *Reducing Nuclear Danger: The Road Away From the Brink* (New York: Council on Foreign Relations, 1993), 81. This fact provides the United States with enormous leverage in making further arms control proposals, and a powerful reason for doing so.

27. This number is endorsed by the Committee on International Security and Arms Control, National Academy of Sciences, *The Future of the U.S.-Soviet Nuclear Relationship* (Washington, D.C.: NAS Press, 1991), 30; Bundy, Crowe, and Drell, *Reducing Nuclear Danger*, 98-100; and the Nuclear Strategy Study Group, Center for Strategic and International Studies, *Toward a Nuclear Peace*, 19. My own calculations suggest that between 300 and 600 warheads would be sufficient, but this may be too radical a proposal in the near term; see Michael J. Mazarr, "Military Targets for a Minimum Deterrent," *The Journal of Strategic Studies*, vol. 15, no. 2 (June 1992): 147-171.

28. Numerous interviews with Japanese, South Korean, and German officials during 1992 and 1993 produced almost no negative reaction to the idea of simultaneous, verifiable reductions in U.S. and Russian forces to 1,000 warheads on each side. Officials in all three countries expressed confidence that the U.S. security guarantee could remain in place with arsenals of such size.

29. Barry Blechman, cited in *Shaping Nuclear Policy for the 1990s*, 77-80.

30. Barry Blechman, cited in *Shaping Nuclear Policy for the 1990s*, 77-80. Robert Manning has similarly proposed a U.S. commitment to disarmament by a date certain, perhaps 2045, if certain conditions were met; Manning, *Back to the Future*, 29.

31. These conclusions again mirror the findings of Stephen Meyer's 1984 study on proliferation. Discarding the technical school of proliferation, Meyer contends that "proliferation decisions are reversible when motivational profiles change to produce lower nuclear propensities." The most effective nonproliferation strategies, Meyer concludes, "will be those that are most 'in tune' with the process of nuclear pro-

liferation and, correspondingly, that can devise and implement narrowly tailored corrective measures—that is, tailored to the prospective proliferant's individual motivational situation"; Meyer, *The Dynamics of Nuclear Proliferation,* 165-66.

32. See Robert Manning, "Offer North Korea a Package Deal to Drop Its Nuclear Program," *The Los Angeles Times,* February 20, 1994, A25.

33. Michael Kramer, "Playing Nuclear Poker," *Time,* February 28, 1994, 45.

34. Stephen J. Solarz, "Next of Kim," *The New Republic,* August 8, 1994, 25-26.

35. This same argument is made by the U.S. Institute of Peace North Korea Working Group in "North Korea's Nuclear Program," 14.

36. Manning, *Back to the Future,* 45.

37. Solarz, "Next of Kim," 26.

38. Paul W. Schroeder, "The New World Order: A Historical Perspective," *The Washington Quarterly,* vol. 17, no. 2 (Spring 1994): 29.

39. Ibid., 29.

40. Ibid., 30.

41. Ibid., 33.

42. Indeed, Schroeder mentions North Korea as an example of a case where "the best hopes for change and means to promote it are those of association-benefits/exclusion-denial"; Ibid., 35.

43. Ibid., 39.

44. Ibid., 41.

EPILOGUE

1. Moon Young Park, "'Lure' North Korea," *Foreign Policy,* no. 97 (Winter 1994-1995): 104.

2. This argument is made persuasively in Park, "'Lure' North Korea."

3. For a good recent survey of South Korea's on-again-off-again strategy of engagement toward the North, see Paik Jin Hyun, "The Geneva Framework Agreement and South Korea's Strategy of Engagement," *Korea and World Affairs,* vol. 18, no. 4 (Winter 1994): 629-641.

4. Nicholas Eberstadt, "Inter-Korean Economic Cooperation: Rapprochement Through Trade?" *Korea and World Affairs,* vol. 18, no. 4 (Winter 1994): 642-661. Ronald Lehman similarly argues that "subsidies to dictatorships legitimize their existence and lengthen their tenure"—Lehman, "Some Considerations on Resolving the North Korean Nuclear Question," *The Korean Journal of Defense Analysis,* vol. 6, no. 2 (Winter 1994): 30.

5. See, for example, the prototypical South Korean argument on this score applied to the nuclear agreement—Kim Dae Jung, "The Impact of the U.S.-North Korean Agreement on Korean Unification," *The Korean Journal of Defense Analysis,* vol. 6, no. 2 (Winter 1994): 85-100.

6. Paik, "The Geneva Framework Agreement," 632.

7. This case is made in Koh Byung Chul, "Confrontation and Cooperation on the Korean Peninsula: The Politics of Nuclear Nonproliferation," *The Korean Journal of Defense Analysis,* vol. 6, no. 2 (Winter 1994): esp. 75-83.

INDEX